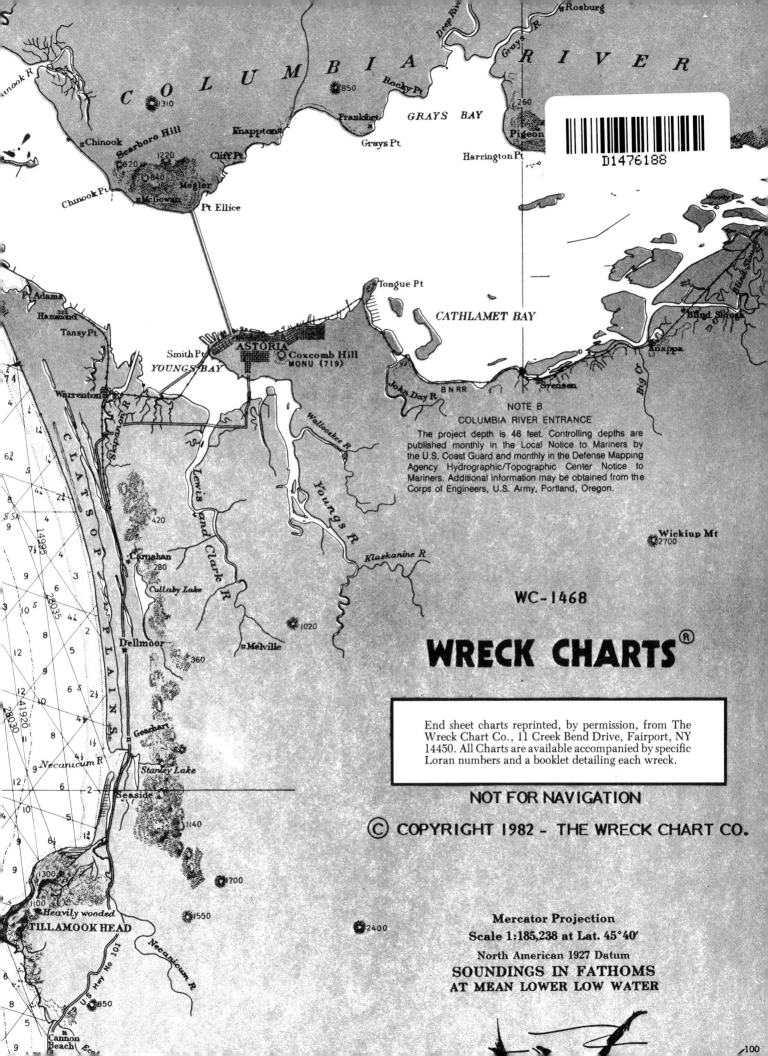

COLUMBIA RIVER

Rosburg

GRAYS BAY

Deep R.

Grays R.

850 Rocky Pt

260 Pigeon

Frankfort

Knappton

Grays Pt

Harrington Pt

Blind Slough

Chinook R.

310

Scarboro Hill

Chinook

820 1220

1840

Cliff Pt

Megler

McGowan

Pt Ellice

Chinook Pt

CATHLAMET BAY

Tongue Pt

Blind Slough

Knappa

Pt Adams

Hammond

Tansy Pt

Smith Pt

ASTORIA

Coxcomb Hill
MONU (719)

John Day R

B N RR

Svensen

Big Cr

74

Warrenton

YOUNGS BAY

Skipanon R.

Walluuskee R.

Youngs R.

NOTE B
COLUMBIA RIVER ENTRANCE

The project depth is 48 feet. Controlling depths are published monthly in the Local Notice to Mariners by the U.S. Coast Guard and monthly in the Defense Mapping Agency Hydrographic/Topographic Center Notice to Mariners. Additional information may be obtained from the Corps of Engineers, U.S. Army, Portland, Oregon.

Lewis and Clark R.

Klaskanine R.

Wickiup Mt
2700

Carnahan
280

Cullaby Lake

1020

Melville

WC-1468

WRECK CHARTS®

Dellmoor
360

CLATSOP PLAINS

Gearhart

Necanicum R.

Stanley Lake

Seaside

1140

NOT FOR NAVIGATION

1300

700

1100

Heavily wooded

TILLAMOOK HEAD

1550

2400

Mercator Projection
Scale 1:185,238 at Lat. 45°40'
North American 1927 Datum
SOUNDINGS IN FATHOMS
AT MEAN LOWER LOW WATER

Necanicum R.

US Hwy No 101

850

Cannon Beach

100

Oregon Shipwrecks

Dwarfed by the mighty Mimi, *an onlooker may have become a victim of her capsizing, as did many of her crew in the rigging.* (Wayne Jensen, Jr. collection)

Oregon Shipwrecks

by
Don Marshall

Binford & Mort Publishing
Portland, Oregon

OREGON SHIPWRECKS

Printed in the United State of America
Library of Congress Catalog Card Number: 84-71477
ISBN: 0-8323-0430-1
First Edition 1984

DEDICATED

to

VICTORIA NICHOLS and the many who died on the Columbia Bar

and to

HENRY NICHOLS, one of the few who survived.

Preface

English philosopher Jeremy Bentham (1748-1832) wrote in his *Rationale of Punishment*, "...the worse possible use that could be made of a man was to hang him; worse still is to make a common sailor of him." Yet, these "common sailors" dipped the first hesitant oars of civilization into the vast sea-like wilderness of the great Northwest.

Brooks and Davis discovered from their research of the 1870's that some sixty or more junks touched upon western America's shore either by accident or design and no doubt the Oriental common sailor contributed to the enrichment of the northwest aborigine blood lines. Spain, via her fleet of galleons, left her mark on the coast...Oregon's Beeswax ship and the resultant offspring of a common seaman survivor continues to intrigue historians and scholars alike.

From the borders of New Spain to the frozen lands at the top of the world, the common seaman of Bentham's time, the men who should have been hung, braved the fury of the elements day-in and day-out to follow Lewis and Clark, MacKenzie, Cook and Vancouver. The general public classed the lowly seaman as only a beast of burden, preferring to ignore that this beast of burden could think...and think he did, and work, and bleed and die. At the first recorded seaman's burial in the Pacific Northwest, the Hawaiian *Kanikau*, the lament for the dead, and one of the world's most beautiful chants, was recited at the graveside of an unknown mariner as his shipmates tenderly laid him to rest in the pristine forest of Cape Disappointment.

Jeremy Bentham never realized that through the efforts of John Little, a common sailor, historians learned of the last moments of two of Bentham's countrymen, Donald McTavish and Alexander Henry; McTavish's tombstone is one of Astoria's oldest and most precious relics. Peter Corney, a common sailor, left to posterity the necessary clues to track the Pacific Northwest's most enigmatic female, Miss Jane Barnes.

The common sailor fought fierce Rogues at Battle Rock and founded the town of Port Orford; the common sailor braved the sniping of the Bannocks during the Indian Wars and, rightly or wrongly, drove his laboring steamboat against raging currents to rescue terrorized settlers living in isolated farms and settlements.

Travel by water through the great Northwest became necessary in spite of the dangers. The great Episcopal missionary Lemuel Wells described a journey he undertook in 1870: "First a railroad to Roseburg then 45 miles by stage to Umpqua; from there, transferred to a rowboat and carried downstream to Gardiner and then by steamboat 10 miles to the ocean, where transported by surf wagon along the smooth, hard beach-sand 20 miles to Coos Bay for a sailboat crossing to Empire City. From there, polled a small boat another 8 miles to Coquille and then on to Myrtle Point by handcar along 3 miles of narrow-gauge railroad. Thence to Port Orford by hired horse and the final leg of the journey to Gold Beach aboard a mule."

The lack of adequate ships checked commercial development of the Northwest until 1850. Washington's and Oregon's fertile soil lay waiting while stale eastern produce glutted San Francisco markets. The *Caroline* was the first steamer to off-load fresh produce from Northwest farms onto San Francisco's wharfs. The *Goldhunter* and *Columbia* quickly followed suit and soon, established trade routes and the exchange of goods nominated Portland as a viable port of commerce.

James W. Troup, a common sailor, opened the great Northwest wheat country to commercial trade and that breadbasket continues to feed the world many times over. After repeated requests from farmers in the great Columbia Plain, Troup proposed to his employers, Oregon Steam Navigation Company, that they haul the wheat to market, but the company reasoned it a useless effort and refused. Undaunted, Troup approached J. C. Ainsworth, a company partner, and secured his permission. This common seaman's foresight gave birth to the magnificent Grain Fleet. These ships soon swarmed the waters of the Columbia; six carried out a total of 4,379 tons of wheat in 1870, but by 1874, 75 vessels transported 70,530 tons and by 1878, 151 ships' masts and yards blotted the sun from Portland's waterfront as their wheat cargo of 144,383 tons delivered food to the hungry mouths of the world. It seemed as though the exodus would never cease via these great grain ships but, all too soon, steam replaced the wind and acres of white sails disappeared from the river scene. As the great Grain Fleet passed with little notice into the shadows of time, it left in its wake an established, bustling Port of Portland.

The common sailor, as he landed along the great northwestern coast, contributed to the pioneer Oregonian who displayed humor in the face of tragedy, who pitted himself against Nature's devastating tempests, who turned adversity into adventure and who became that rugged individual to lash out with fierce pride against all who dared transgress against the sanctity of the Northwest Territory.

The world asked what right did this bastard country have in the over-all scheme of things? It claimed no parentage and lay surrounded by hostile Spanish California to the south, the jagged and impenetrable Rockies to the east, the frozen tundra northward and a leaping, shouting, athletic sea to the west. Even early cartographers blotted out the area with sea serpents and static information to hide the unknown, unexplored regions; one map shows the country as a large, water-filled hole in the ground.

The territory, never able to claim a descendancy from Russia, Spain, England or the United States, became a combination of all of these through the common bond of the sea and the common sailor who sailed her. In spite of her mysterious, lusty parentage, Oregon claims 429 miles of the finest beachcombing on the Pacific coast. Each day, the white surf rushes in with a new prize from an ancient tragedy and buries it in a sandy grave to await discovery by casual strollers who, should they pause and listen very carefully, might hear the voices of those who went on before...the men, women and children as they perished aboard a ship devoured by an unexpected, lurking wave. Even the long-departed "common sailor" can be heard upon the cry of the wind and can be seen in the epoch of a dissolving wisp of foam.

Acknowledgments

Thanks to all those who offered encouragement, time and suggestions throughout this manuscript:

Mr. Michael Naab, Director of what I consider the west coast's finest museum, the Columbia River Maritime Museum, located in Astoria, Oregon; Larry Gilmore, Curator, and Richard Fencsak, Program Director.

Gloria and Doug Onyon and staff of the Clatsop County Historical Museum who so cheerfully gave of their extra time to assist in my research.

Patricia Stone, Director of Lincoln County Historical Society.

Hazel Standeven and Victor West, Curator and Maritime Historian of Coos-Curry Museum.

George Abdill, Director of the Douglas County Museum, and Patricia Miller of the Chetco Valley Historical Society Museum.

Wayne Jensen, Jr., Director of the Tillamook County Pioneer Museum whose packed and tiny quarters offered a wealth of information.

Gordon Manning, Librarian of the Oregon Historical Society, and E. W. Giesecke, research expert on the great Northwest.

Holway R. Jones, Head Social Science Librarian at the University of Oregon.

Webb Terwilliger, State Marine Board at Salem and E. Nolan, Lane County Archivist.

Roger Tetlow, who devotes his life to Astoria's history.

Gale Visavatanaphongse and Sue Scully, who so accurately assemble Fort Stevens' history for the Oregon State Parks. They continually brought messages into the field where I, under the able direction of Archeologist Brian Harrison and wife, Marg, of Clatsop Community College, excavated historical sites; invariably, just when something good was coming to light, I would be called away to leave all the hard work to them.

D. R. Sutton, General Manager of the Tillamook County Creamery Assoc., who generously donated his time to my quest for information on the *Morning Star of Tillamook*.

Bruce Berney, Library Director, and staff of Astor Library…one of the finer small libraries in Oregon.

Mike Weiner, of Wreck Charts Inc. of New York, with whom I spent many hours comparing notes and gaining information from his remarkable collection of wreck locations.

J. W. "Bud" Forrester, Editor of the *Daily Astorian* and President of the Columbia River Maritime Museum Board of Directors, and his crew of able reporters: James Holman, Bill Wagner, Ben Silverman and Chris Genna. They so patiently endured all my probing.

Then I must mention Dave Roscoe, Jr. (Rear Admiral, USN, ret.) and Mr. Whitcomb Crichton, both of whom have interests in all things marine. Bruce B. McCloskey of the famous McCloskey steamboaters helped with many memories, and last but not least, Sam Foster of Seaside, Oregon…photographer and friend.

All these marvelous people have answered my questions with alacrity and accuracy. If I have overlooked anyone, and undoubtedly I have, please accept my apologies and remember…people do make mistakes, after all, nobody's human.

Astoria
May 1982

Contents

Chapter One
    California-Oregon border to Blacklock Point   1

Chapter Two
    Blacklock Point to Tenmile Creek 29

Chapter Three
    Umpqua River to Salmon River 55

Chapter Four
    Cascade Head to Nehalem River 77

Chapter Five
    Cape Falcon to Cape Disappointment 101

Chapter Six
    Cape Disappointment to Tongue Point 147

Chapter Seven
    Missing at Sea and Unknowns 168

Chapter Eight
    Columbia River, Tributaries, Idaho, Montana 191

Appendix A
    Passengers and Crew of the *Brother Jonathan* 222

Appendix B
    Crew of the *Alaskan* 224

Appendix C
    Passengers and Crew of the *Gazelle* 225

Appendix D
    Passengers and Crew of the *General Warren* 226

Bibliography 227

Index 229

Shipwreck lists are of ships 50 tons or more except where an exceptional story exists; dates include from the earliest recorded (possibly 1705) to 1955.

California – Oregon Border to Blacklock Point

BROTHER JONATHAN, OREGON MYSTERY?

Grossly maligned as an old and tender vessel, the Brother Jonathan *was in reality a well built luxurious liner offering the finest in passenger accommodations.* (National Maritime Museum, San Francisco)

I, S. J. De Wolf, Master of the Steamship Brother Jonathan of San Francisco

do solemnly *Swear* that I will support, protect and defend the Constitution and Government of the United States against all enemies, whether domestic or foreign, and that I will bear true faith, allegiance, and loyalty to the same, any ordinance, resolution, or law of any State convention or legislature to the contrary notwithstanding; and, further, that I do this with a full determination, pledge and purpose, without any mental reservation or evasion whatsoever; and, further, that I will well and faithfully perform the duties which may be required of me by law. So help me God.

S. J. De Wolf

SUBSCRIBED and sworn to before me, this *8th* day of *December* A. D. 1864.

W. W. Parker Dy Coler,

Oath to the Union signed by Captain Samuel J. DeWolf of the ill-fated Brother Jonathan.
(Clatsop County Historical Museum)

"Mother, I can't seem to get this youngster to stop his crying. Whyn't you see what you can do with him?" called Grandpa Charles Place as he carried his sobbing, tear-drenched three-year-old grandson into the well-furnished ranch-house and deposited the hysterical babe into the waiting arms of his loving grandmother.

"There, there, Master Charles Brooks," cooed the older lady, "why don't you tell your granny what it is that's frightening you so. After all, Grandpas don't know what it is that makes little ones cry, do they?"

Her gentle chiding distracted little Charles' hysterics only long enough for him to sob out, "Ma an' Aunt Mary went down in water in ship...." Turning his head after delivering this chilling message of doom, the little tad buried his face in Grandma's blouse and resumed his fit of convulsive sobbing.

The day was Sunday, July 30, 1865. The time... approximately 2:15 in the afternoon.

"Lordy, Grandpa, where do you suppose he got that notion?" puzzled Mrs. Place. "He didn't know of his mother's trip. I didn't tell him... did you?"

"No, Ma, but the way he's carrying on, I feel something's awful wrong. I'm going into town right now and see what I can find out."

Late that night, the wealthy Napa Valley rancher returned home. A kerosene lamp in the window signaled that his anxious wife had not yet retired. Little Charles Brooks, exhausted, lay fast asleep.

"What is it, Pa? What's happened?"

"The *Brother Jonathan* has gone down. It came over the wire."

"Oh, dear God, no!"[1]

At the exact moment little Charles broke into his pitiful lament earlier that day, nearly three hundred miles away, off the Oregon-California border, the steamer *Brother Jonathan*, taking in great gulps of water, slid, bounced and careened down the side of a submerged rock pinnacle in a slow-motion dance-of-death to rest forever on the bottom. Within her bosom, numerous bug-eyed, gaping-mouthed passengers and crew clawed in silence through the cold, green water for precious air that would never be theirs. Among the doomed was little Charles' mother and his Aunt Mary.

The *Brother Jonathan* logged a colorful and varied history. The steamer, built in New York for the Long Island Sound trade, saw service on the New York-Panama route and was then sold to Vanderbilt who ordered her to the Pacific. Captain C. H. Baldwin,[2] Chief Engineer Hiram Sanford, First Assistant L. V. Hogeboom, Second Assistant Dan Saltus, Purser C. A. Low and First Officer George Hutchinson delivered the *Brother Jonathan* around the Horn to San Francisco.

Her next owner, J. T. Wright, re-christened the steamer the *Commodore*. While sailing under his flag, she ran into trouble in 1858 and nearly sank with 350 passengers. She underwent reconditioning in 1859.

California Steam Navigation Company bought the vessel in 1861 and immediately assigned Captain A. M. Burns to supervise her second reconditioning by seventy-five of San Francisco's finest shipwrights. The work began at the Pacific Street wharf with the stripping away of all upper-works and furnishings. The ship was then moved to Hathaways wharf for her machinery overhaul. Old boilers went by the board, replaced with a new Martin tubular six furnace unit. Her original engines underwent a thorough overhauling. At the graving dock, shipwrights stripped off the sheeting and pronounced her timbers sound.

The editor of the *Alta California* reported on May 4, 1861:

She looks for all the world like the skeleton of some antediluvian megatherium[3] or mastadon raked out from ruins of an extinct creation, for however much like a singed cat she may look now, she will come out gay as a pink[4] about mid-summer.

---

[1] Actual conversation, at this late date, can only be surmised, but the event, as described, appeared in an article on Aug. 7th, 1865 edition of the *Oregon Statesman*.

[2] He later became an Admiral in the United States Navy.

[3] An extinct giant ground sloth.

[4] A delicate flower *Dianthus* or *D. plumarius*, also a small sailing vessel.

She now sported a new copper bottom reinforced by a new false keel and two bilge keels; her sound diagonal braces needed no repair. Douglas fir, the strongest wood available on the west coast, was used for her new spars. Colorful redwood paneled the staterooms; family suites and double berths fashioned her main deck cabins. An enlarged dining salon measured 120 feet in length. Reduced from three decks to two, she registered 900 tons.

True to the *Alta California*'s prediction, the *Brother Jonathan* emerged seven months and $100,000 later "gay as a pink." Although not a fast ship, she maintained a steady pace that assured her immediate success as a plush, pure-bred coastal workhorse between San Francisco, Portland, Seattle and Victoria. Occasionally, she docked at lesser, in-between ports.

On a San Francisco morning, July 28, 1865, a gay group of travelers from all walks of life, the great and the lowly, boarded the *Brother Jonathan*. Brigadier-General George T. Wright, West Point graduate, hero of the Florida Indian Wars and the war with Mexico, a career military man, solicitously cupped his wife's elbow as they stepped aboard the luxury steamer. The couple turned and waved a final farewell. Friends below, wishing the General every success with his new command of the Washington-Oregon Military District, shouted "Bon voyage."

Rose Keenan, notorious from San Francisco to Victoria as a madam well versed in profligacy, a woman eternally condemned by moralistic citizens and hailed as a saint by rough and tumble carnal-minded denizens of the water front and possibly by some city fathers, too, herded her seven soiled doves toward their staterooms. Possibly she envisioned her journey and that of her "girls" as a mission of mercy in bringing comfort and relief to the woman-starved male population of the far north.

Honorable A. C. Henry, a most important figure in the nation's capital and Surveyor of all the Washington Territories, stepped aboard the *Brother Jonathan*, still in mourning over the recent loss of his close personal friend, President Abraham Lincoln.

The ticket agent turned to a fresh page of his passenger list and entered the name of Victor Smith, a recent shipwreck victim of the *Golden Rule*.[5] Little did the ticket agent realize that Victor Smith, *ex*-Collector of Customs at Port Angeles, Washington Territory, was dismissed from his post in disgrace as a direct result of Surveyor Henry's accusation that he conspired to set up his own little dynasty. How soon would these mortal enemies cross paths aboard the close confines of the *Brother Jonathan*?

The ticket agent, either too bored or unable to spell odd-sounding names, hastily scrawled his entry of "two unknown Indians"; they walked down the companionway and into eternity; whither bound or why, no one will ever know.

David and Aplona Rowell scooted their four exuberant children up the gangplank and admonished them not to scatter once aboard the ship. The children, followed by their parents,[6] gathered at the rail. Their eager faces scanned the pier far below where passengers, sweating stevedores, jumbled piles of luggage and late-arriving ship's supplies created a jig-saw puzzle of bustling activity.

"Oh, Mary," worried Mrs. A. C. Brooks as she climbed the sloping gangplank to the weather deck of the *Brother Jonathan*, "maybe I should have let little Charles come with us, after all. He misses his father so much. The Captain and I promised him we'd take him on this trip to the South Pacific. I hope his father won't be upset that I left Charles behind."

Mary Place quickly admonished her older sister, "Oh, don't be such a worry-wart.

---

[5] Went to the bottom off the coast of Nicaragua. 635 passengers spent a week marooned on Roncador Reef before rescue.

[6] The close-knit little family's grave markers may still be seen in the Brother Jonathan Memorial Cemetery at Crescent City. Survivor Mary Garretson, nee Tweedale, years later could not speak of the family without a choke in her voice. "...That sweet family," she recalled, "father, mother standing on that pitching deck, their little ones clutched about them, the wind and spray lashing at their clothing, and she, that beautiful woman, gazing down at us so wistfully as we pulled away."

Mother will take good care of him and Father will see to it that he gets to ride the horses ...he'll keep him busy. Ooooh," she quickly changed the subject, "this is so exciting. This beautiful ship and all these fascinating people. What fun! Do you think the Captain will have finished loading his barque by the time we get to Vancouver?" Before her older sister could answer, Mary continued, "If the *Cambridge* [lost off Cape Flattery, twelve years later] is still loading on cargo, maybe we'd have time to do some shopping in Vancouver or Portland. I'd like to pick up a few more things before we sail for Oyhee. Oh, Sister, I'm so glad you married a ship captain and can invite me on a trip like this...you're sure he won't mind?"

The captain's lady smiled in reassurance, then gently hushed her exuberant sister as they presented their tickets to Purser John Benton.

Sam DeWolf, forty-three years old and veteran captain of the *Brother Jonathan*, began his sailing career on the Liverpool-New York run at age sixteen. At age twenty-seven he served as First Officer aboard the *Onward* and sailed with her to the Pacific coast. Soon, he became master of the brig *Fremont* and ran the coastal waters of the great northwest. He signed on with the California Steam Navigation Company at age thirty-one and became one of their most reliable men.

Elijah Mott, Chief Engineer of the *Brother Jonathan*, was born in 1828; he sailed to California aboard the *Pacific* (later lost off Cape Flattery). He immediately became the most sought-after engineer on the west coast, no doubt due to his prior experience aboard the steamer *Empire* as she plied the Hudson River.

Little is known of Fireman John Hensley other than he worked as a ranch-hand in Napa, California, but even as a lowly Fireman aboard the *Brother Jonathan*, he became a giant among men when on that tragic day he declared, "...there are others to help," and declined to save himself. He tossed a fire bucket to the rowers of the lifeboat; that bucket was the only instrument by which the boat and its occupants survived.

The diversity amongst the crew of the *Brother Jonathan* existed as it does aboard all ships. Mexicans Diaz and Gonzales, newly arrived from the south, free Negroes G. W. Hill, Jacob Yates and John Clinton, Germans, Irish, Portuguese and others were thrown together in an uncommon situation; yet all became equal by their heroic actions toward their ship and her passengers.

At noon, the great steamer swung away from San Francisco's quay in obedience to the barked commands of Captain DeWolf. "Stand by, Engine Room...let go aft spring! Port your rudder, Mr. Yates," he directed from the bridge, then turned to the con, "Starboard wheel slow ahead...port, slow reverse. You! You down there, shift that spring further astern...that's right!"

Answering her captain's barrage of orders, the huge ship shuddered as the thirty-three foot wheels bit into green harbor waters. The passenger's last farewells faded across the widening gap.

The starboard wheel's slow reverse signal flashed to Mr. Mott as he monitored his precious controls deep within the hissing bowels of the *Brother Jonathan*. The massive four-hundred horsepower low-pressure engine moved in answer to the bridge commands of "Starboard your rudder, Helmsman."

"Let go that line down there!"

"Signal Mr. Mott slow ahead."

"Port your rudder, Mr. Yates."

Passengers threw their last kisses toward shore as the *Brother Jonathan* moved into the stream on a journey from which she would never return.

Two days later, off the Oregon coast, Captain DeWolf stood on the bridge of his laboring vessel and silently debated two serious problems, the comfort of his passengers and the safety of his ship. Forty-eight hours of continuous heavy sea-swells now rendered a majority of passengers into a state of deathly seasickness. The second, and more serious problem, forced a deep frown to crease his brow as he contemplated a possible threat of capture by the Confederate raider, *Shenandoah*. *That fool pirate Captain Waddell,* he must have thought, *if he don't know the war's over, he's dangerous.*[7] *If he does know the South surrendered, then he could be twice as dangerous. In either case, he'd put quite a feather in his cap with the capture of the* Brother Jonathan *and a General, a Surveyor, the entire Army Staff and an Army payroll. Our passenger list was no secret when we left San Francisco and its hot-bed of Confederate sympathizers.*

Captain DeWolf released his knuckle-white grip on the railing, his dilemma resolved.

"Hard about she is." Quartermaster Jacob Yates responded to his captain's order.

The huge steamer rocked and reeled for a moment in the trough of a swell before answering the helm; she then steadied with the port-quarter wind. The time was about 12:45 p.m.

"Mr. Allen, kindly inform Mr. Mott we have put about for Crescent City harbor to lay up. He'll not need to worry over excessive coal use now."

"Aye, aye, Sir."

For almost an hour the sweating, rocking ship dipped first one wheel into the sea, then the other. Seldom were both wheels able to take a full and steady purchase on the ship's directed course.

"Is that Seal Rock there, through the haze, Cap'n?"

"I believe it is, Quartermaster. Take her southeast by south."

This new change of direction decreased the steamer's roll, but now forced her into a deep pitch.[8] The ship gained headway, but brought little comfort to the suffering passengers. For them, whether by pitch or by roll, their malady continued.

The *Brother Jonathan*'s churning, splash-covered wheels, now biting the sea to their fullest, obediently ground ever forward, driving the copper-covered hull toward a hidden evil awaiting just below the surface of the slate gray roiling Pacific.

At 1:50 that afternoon the doomed steamer rode to the summit of a colossal briny escarpment, then she plunged in a head-long, roller coaster descent to the base of a shallow trough where, for sixty million years, a basaltic spire patiently awaited this exact and so terribly fatal moment.

The full weight of the *Brother Jonathan* dropped onto the razor-sharp pinnacle. Mortally gutted deep within her belly, the impaled ship screamed in her final death throes.

Passengers and crew crashed violently onto the decks in jumbled heaps. Dishes, bottles, furniture and luggage flew across started planks and slammed into jammed cabin doors. Screaming passengers tumbled down companionways in gigantic disarray. Horses and camels bellowed in terror as they lost footing and crashed to the spray-covered deck.

Far below, the sweating and cursing black gang stumbled in semi-darkness over broken lanterns scattered across the iron grating. They tripped and fell as tons of coal poured from broken bunkers.

The slime-covered pinnacle, alive with seaweed and animal life, thrust its pointed head through the splintered timbers just forward of the fireboxes. As it wrenched and ripped through the bowels of the steamer, a fountain of cold, gray water erupted in a deadly garland.

A furious cadence of staccato bell signals clanged from the bridge. Brass arrows danced in a lightning arc across the dial of the engine room telegraph signaling *stop*, then *reverse*.

Engineer Mott grabbed the working bar[9] and forced it down with his full weight. At the proper moment, he forced the bar up, then again brought it down. Slowly, ponderously, the mammoth paddle wheels reversed their

---

[7] Lieutenant James I. Waddell skippered the Confederate raider *Shenandoah* between October 18, 1864 and November 6, 1865, during which time he traveled 58,000 miles, captured 38 ships and destroyed 32 of them. He captured 1,053 prisoners. His Pacific escapades came to an end when he sailed south along the northwest American coast with the intention of capturing San Francisco. Waddell, a declared pirate, stopped the British bark *Baracouta* on August 2nd for news of the war between the states. He was stunned to learn the war ended April 9, 1865.

[8] Also called pile-driving.

[9] A heavy iron bar approximately 6 feet long used to turn a floor-level shaft which, when revolved, simultaneously opens an intake

direction. The sweating engineer cracked open the main steam valve. The plunging wheel-buckets lifted tons of foaming water in a virtual Niagara through the wheel-boxes . . . all to no avail, for the *Brother Jonathan* remained pinned to the rock.

The captain ordered his ship abandoned and admonished all hands to look to the safety of the passengers. Third Officer James Patterson, rudely thrown from his bunk by the sudden shock, raced to his boat station where he commanded an immediate and orderly loading of forty passengers and crew into the Francis patent metallic lifeboat. He directed the craft lowered and released from the parent ship. The well-trained crew strained at the oars to gain headway. Moments later, a hissing, white-maned comber leaped in frothing fury to pounce upon all in its path. When next sighted the boat floated upside down; it righted almost instantly, empty.

Captain DeWolf whispered a silent prayer for those forty lost souls before turning his attention toward the loading of the starboard boat just aft the wheel box. Second Mate J. D. Campbell manned the helm; crewmen positioned themselves at the oars. Women and children scrambled aboard; amongst them were General Wright's wife and Mrs. Rose Keenan, a motherly hen clucking after her seven chicks. The lifeboat, tethered to the davits, swung away from the steamer, then dashed back with express-train speed to crash against the side of the ship, dumping its human cargo of the dead and the living into the drowning sea. Campbell fought his way through submerged debris, surfaced and grabbed one of the *Brother Jonathan*'s chain plates. Thus secured, he reached for a mass of floating clothing and held it fast. In this manner, he rescued Mrs. Wright and returned her to her General.[10]

The swirling water about the steamer was now aswarm with multi-colored patches of colorful dresses; each denoted the presence of a floating corpse or a weakly struggling victim whose faint gurgling cries for help could scarcely be heard over those of a dying ship.

GEN⁺ GEO. WRIGHT, U.S.A.

Military to the end, the General and his lady died with as much dignity as possible on the wreck of the Brother Jonathan, *July 30, 1865.*
(Marshall Collection)

The ship pivoted; each swell of the sea broached the vessel with tons of water while the basaltic spire corkscrewed deeper into the timbers of the helpless steamer.

Tremendous pressure worked against the keel. It gave way and the mast step weakened. The *Brother Jonathan* lurched; the foremast plunged like an arrow through the bottom of the ship. Its one hundred and ten foot length came to a crashing stop at midpoint when the spread of the lower yardarm collided with the deck.

---

valve on one side and an exhaust valve on the other of the huge cylinder. With a roar of steam the piston will begin to move. When it reaches the top of its stroke, the engineer reverses the direction of the bar from down to up, then down again as the walking beam reaches its limit. This "hand action" in valving is necessary to achieve a rocking motion of the paddle wheels in the desired direction. Once completed, the engineer is then at liberty to tend to other matters.

10 On deck, General George T. Wright tenderly wrapped his military cloak around his wife's shivering, wet shoulders. Together they walked to the upper deck and stood there with as much dignity as possible on the pitching vessel awaiting their inevitable end.

Engineer Mott turned on the bilge injection valve, but received no response from the pumps . . . the fire boxes were flooded with sea water and all reserve steam had long ago escaped through wrenched and cracked pipes.

Third Engineer G. W. Hill fought his way up and out of the fast-flooding engine room. Mr. Mott stood by his post, ordering others to save themselves. Hill was the last man to escape the inky-black maelstrom swiftly welling up from below; all others drowned in that mass of wreckage-filled water.

One small surfboat filled with nineteen persons, three of whom were infants, pulled away from the carnage and rowed into history. They were the last living humans on earth to witness the *Brother Jonathan*'s final agony-filled moments, except for the little boy three hundred miles away who, in his innocence and in some unexplained manner, visualized the brutal death of two of those most close to him . . . his mother and his aunt.

Comments on the *Brother Jonathan*

Over one hundred years have passed since that terrible day in 1865 and yet numerous legends continue to enhance the mystery of the *Brother Jonathan*. One of the most devastating and false tales maligned her as an unseaworthy ship. Careful study of the facts conclusively prove the *Brother Jonathan*'s sound qualities, fine accommodations and cuisine were surpassed by none.

The hue and cry of "overloading" became an accusatory charge against the captain who supposedly succumbed to a junior freight clerk's demands of overburdening the cargo capacities of the steamer with extra freight. The much-respected and able Captain De-Wolf would never have fallen prey to any amount of pressure from a junior freight clerk, nor would he have sailed without adequate safety equipment.[11] There is no doubt that Captain DeWolfe set sail from San Francisco under threat of the *Brother Jonathan*'s capture by the Confederate raider, the *Shenandoah*. Confederate sympathizer Ford Patterson assassinated the *Jonathan*'s previous captain at the Pioneer Hotel at Front and Washington Streets, Portland. The hotel's owner, H. Arrigoni and Ben Stark, ex-U.S. Senator, posted $10,000 bail for Patterson.[12]

Some claimed the *Brother Jonathan* sank due to structural damage sustained on a previous voyage in a collision on the Columbia River, July 14. Not true, for the other ship, *Jane A. Falkenburg*, continued on her way with merely a broken bowsprit and sailed another thirty-four years before abandonment at sea at the ripe old age of forty-five. The *Jonathan* sustained no damage from the minor accident.

Major disasters go hand-in-hand with tales of premonition or precognition. Army Paymaster Ellery W. Eddy, in charge of a $200,000 payroll en route to the northern garrisons, sensed some form of presentiment since he carefully balanced his private accounts, wrote his will and informed his friends he would never return. As for little Charles Brooks, well, his story has already been told.

The effect of the *Jonathan*'s wreck upon Oregon and surrounding territories was long lasting. The loss of General Wright, an experienced Indian fighter, caused concern for settlers in an area subjected to daily uprisings. Mr. Logan, respected Indian agent, carried $10,000 of Indian treaty monies. When he and the money went down with the *Jonathan*, it most certainly fed fuel to the young bucks' suspicion of "another of the white man's tricks."

James Richards of Portland's Richards & McCracken Co. left a bereaved wife and several children; other businessmen, J. S. Geddes

---

[11] The steamer was equipped with 4 Francis Patent metallic lifeboats (U.S. Steamboat regulations required only 1). The *Jonathan* also carried 2 wooden surfboats and 397 lifebelts. The only ship's boat to survive the disaster was a wooden one.

[12] Oregon's Governor John Whiteaker, a pro-slaver, refused to honor President Lincoln's call for troops. In 1862, A. C. Gibbs defeated him at the polls; Oregon immediately raised two regiments of troops to replace the regular Army now assigned to aid the Union cause, but Oregon's integrity had been tarnished and the state became classified as an "exception to the Loyalist States." This onus caused so much braggadocio amongst the rebels and worry to the Loyalists and the Federal government that the Union forced Oregon to bear the financial burden of protecting the miners, settlers and guarding the Oregon Trail, a duty that usually fell to Federal troops. The ultimate bill amounted to $1.3 million, which the State of Oregon is *still* trying to collect.

of Bosworth & Geddes, Crandell of Crandell & Towne and Mr. B. Mathewson of Providence Mining Co. (delivering one hundred tons of machinery), left devastated family and friends. The mill companies Goldsmith & Friendly, Ellsworth & Belshaw and Underwood of Springfield lost vital equipment. Sam Luckey's wife and children would be sorely missed in Eugene, as would the Jerimiah family whom they were escorting.

An estimated one hundred and seventy bodies were recovered; most drifted into Pelican Bay, north of Crescent City. Sixteen washed ashore between Gold Bluffs and Trinidad and were buried. Forty-six souls were interred in the Crescent City cemetery.

Several corpses floated as far as the Rogue and Smith Rivers; the remains of Miss Mary Berry, hotel-owner Arrigoni's niece, drifted an incredible ninety miles southward before washing onto the beach. One male victim's body was recovered seven miles at sea.

Captain Brooks and Mr. Arrigoni arrived in the captain's bark *Cambridge* to search for their loved ones, but the ship continued on to Honolulu without the captain's wife and sister-in-law who sailed the *Jonathan* in anticipation of an exciting holiday. Their bodies were never recovered.

Crescent City Coroner J. E. Eldrige's records offer a succinct insight to travelers of the world:

body #21, a mulatto woman, large hoop earings studded with pearls and rubies, a ring set with opal.

body #33, a girl, 12 years, 3'10" height, striped calico dress, white skirt pantalettes, stocking and gaiters.

body #36, a white man, 5'7", 36 years, black hair and goatee, looks like a German, heavy-made large build, false teeth, American silver watch #18-493 and a gold locket shaped like a key with black hair in it. (watch stopped 2:15)

body #24, a sailor, unknown, kerchief around neck.

body #76, a woman 18, 110 lbs, dark calico dress, white wove nubia or comforter, gold and diamond ring w/initials J. W. C.

body #45, a man, $420 in coins, $8,500 in currency.

And so it went, sad reports coming in from all along the shoreline. The identified bodies were preserved in alcohol, placed in metal boxes and the lids soldered shut. Upon relatives' request, the remains were shipped or buried. Mr. A. F. Miller, first and only Postmaster of Chetco Creek, placed an ad in several newspapers:

A man in a life preserver with a double heart gold ring "S Irwin" a comb and $10 gold piece in pocket & papers & inventory of men and women's clothing with prices as lost on board steamer Golden Rule with notation 'John B. Ferguson, SE corner of Howard and Thompson St. Philadelphia — to John Irwin'. Effects are being held by A. F. Miller of Chetco Creek and the body was buried by him.

Captain Buckley, U.S. Army, Camp Lincoln, established temporary headquarters on a lagoon mid-way between Crescent City and Smith River and another at the mouth of the Klamath; he ordered a two week patrol of the areas. His reports listed finding one woman with the following items tucked in her blouse: a common breast pin, a thimble, seven plated spoons, three ivory handle knives, a $1,000 note, 5 $20's, 7 $10's, 2 $100's, 5 $50's and one $5 note on the bank of Poughkeepsie. Mr. Mathewson was found with a $21,000 note in his pocket. One distraught family arrived a year later to have their beloved husband and father exhumed; they recovered $4,000 from his clothing.

The *Brother Jonathan*'s grave remains a mystery. Jonathan Rock, an outermost projection of the St. George chain of reefs, is a popularly accepted location, although intensive searching of the area fails to reveal a single clue to substantiate the theory. History buffs continue to argue over the steamer foundering just off Crescent City, further north or as far distant as the Rogue River.

Captain Peter Gee stated the ship went down in 33½ fathoms, 2 miles NW of Jonathan Rock at a site called Saddle Rock or just 300' north; rather precise considering he was not present at the time of the disaster.

A gentleman by the name of Stroud claimed he heard the *Jonathan*'s distress cannon while he walked 7th St. in town; and states the wreck lies no farther than ½ mile from Point St. George and Castle Island, at least two miles south of Jonathan Rock.

Captain Connor of the *Sierra Nevada* reported he passed the scene of the wreck Sunday (he had expected to meet DeWolf and his ship there to exchange papers), twenty-five miles *north* of Crescent City and that the one and only surviving lifeboat came ashore eight miles from Chetco Harbor.

Two Indian squaws briefly paused in their quest for shellfish on the beach below Camp Lincoln when they heard the firing of the ship's distress cannon; they thought it merely a practice round from the fort.

Captain Johnson places the ship ten miles above the town while one lady reported she watched the disaster just south of the Rogue River.

Mrs. Mina Bernhardt, a survivor, stated they were afraid to land below the cliffs because the Indians were above and the survivors feared an attack. They rowed past a small crop of basalt called Bird Rock and into the harbor. Ben West, owner of Ben West's Saloon, watched through his telescope with only mild interest as the lifeboat came ashore; he wondered why such a small boat was so crowded with one man dangling his feet in the water as he straddled the bow.

G. W. Hill, the surviving engineer, haunted the waterfront for many years with his telling and re-telling of the adventure. On at least one occasion he sold the location of the ship for a reputed $200. The gullible buyer, whose name is mercifully lost in the passage of time, fared no better in his 1894 search than did his predecessors.

The steam tug *Mary Ann*, dispatched from San Francisco immediately following the disaster, was the first of many treasure expeditions. She returned empty-handed except for an old anchor of the wrecked barque *Acadia* recovered from Trinidad Harbor.

The William Ireland expedition tried and failed in 1867. In 1869 the schooner *Charles Hare* appeared and spent several weeks in the vicinity while the expectant salvors spent several thousands of dollars in town on equip-

ment and supplies. The much-touted Brother Jonathan Treasure Company ended in failure in 1872 when they arrived in their new steamer *Coquille* with an over-abundance of faith in their pair of new-fangled diving bells.

The only known recovery of the ship's treasure occurred in the early thirties. A fisherman, area unknown, hauled aboard an unusual object some sixty-eight years following the disaster. He caught in his net a shattered, rusted, caved-in mass that somewhat resembled an old Francis Patent Lifeboat. After draining the water from its sprung and corroded seams and stripping away decades of marine growth, the curious and extremely lucky fisherman discovered a rotted leather valise tightly wedged under the lifeboat's crushed seat. The valise apparently belonged to a woman of means for eleven gold bars, weighing a total of twenty-two pounds, lay within its mouldy recesses. Once again the mysterious traits of the *Brother Jonathan* leap from the mists of time and labor mightily to further obscure any traces of her location.

During the thirties, the Roosevelt Administration outlawed the holding of gold by private citizens. The lucky finder of the eleven gold bars, not wishing to declare his illegally held discovery and yet, understandably not wishing to surrender his briny loot, hid his water-borne treasure until 1974, at which time American citizens were once again allowed to possess gold. The bars were sold on the open market for a considerable sum; however, in the intervening four decades, the exact location of his remarkable discovery was long forgotten.

Wreckage and much of the passenger's luggage floated ashore, indicating the ship broke up. The wheel box's huge, gilded wooden eagle was retrieved and placed on display in the San Francisco Maritime Museum. The ship's wheel, forty feet of upper deck with the bell attached, two trunks (one belonging to David Rowell and the other containing a pair of Colt pistols) floated ashore near Gold Bluff. Two bodies, that of a man named Cardiff with a $20 Confederate note in his pocket and a small boy wearing two life preservers, washed ashore at the same spot and were buried. The wheel graced Henry Saville's Saloon, Crescent City, for years before Roy Clark of Eugene purchased it. It has now found its way to the Oyster House, Portland. The *Brother Jonathan*'s bell hung on display at the old lighthouse near the entrance to Crescent City Harbor until a burglar made off with it in 1977.

Even now the location of the *Brother Jonathan* with her once glittering illuminated reflective ornaments dulled by years of shadowy sea growth, rotted crimson-cushioned settees scattered over plush carpet-covered oak floors and ghostly cargo of drowned humans defies discovery as the currents whisper in the shadows of her decayed Oregon-oak hull.

FEARFUL LOSS OF LIFE!
We venture to say that everyone on board the BROTHER JONATHAN would have been saved if they had Houston, Hasting & Co. Life Preserving Vests, and the price...places them within reach of all.

Classified ad section
Alta California
August, 1865

CAMDEN AND *LARRY DOHENY*

Captain D. M. Davidson, veteran coaster, stood on the bridge of the *Camden* as she lay fifty miles off the coast from Coos Bay and, with a practiced seaman's eye, watched the sun rise. He mentally noted that the dawn held a promise of a clear day with a light northwest wind. It felt good, this October 4, 1942, to stand on the bridge and take in the beginning of a fine new day without that chilling pressure of which ship will the enemy strike next. The latest newspaper reports reassured all of America that the Battles of the Coral Sea and Midway successfully crippled the entire Japanese fleet.

He took a long, deep breath, expanding his lungs to the fullest with salty, cold, sea-damp air. Exhaling in a steamy whoosh, he turned and leisurely strolled toward the bridge. He knew no reason to deny the engineer's request to halt the *Camden*'s power plant for an hour or two in order to work on a few minor repairs. He lifted the ship's phone and signaled the engine room. "Sure, go ahead, Chief. Take your time; all's fine topside."

The lookout aboard the Japanese submarine I 25 lowered his binoculars, rubbed his reddened eyes in disbelief, then eagerly peered through them again. There, just ahead of the sub and clearly outlined by the rising sun, a large American freighter lay dead in the water. Like a stalking crocodile, the I 25 silently slid beneath the calm surface with scarcely a ripple. Commander Meiji Tagame took over the periscope and meticulously focused its cyclops eye upon the fat target frozen in almost perfect firing position. He accurately computed the distance of 1000 meters to the motionless hated American freighter. Except for a low hum, the submarine maintained a well-disciplined tomb-like silence. Torpedoman Kenji Takezawa waited tensely. The signal flashed; instantaneously he triggered two deadly missiles toward the unsuspecting enemy.

"Torpedo!"

"What'd'ya mean, torpedo?"

"Right there; see it?" yelled the lookout, frantically pointing out the speeding monster as it hissed toward the *Camden*.

Captain Davidson watched the lethal torpedo race harmlessly past the bow of his ship and immediately ordered Seaman T. E. Goehringer from the bridge, "We're under submarine attack. Tell Sparks to start sending an S S S!"

Before Goehringer could say, "Aye, aye, Sir," the second torpedo struck home. The exploding shock knocked Captain Davidson flat and at the same time hurled Seaman Goehringer head-over-heels out of the bridgehouse, somersaulted him over the railing towards the catwalk below and conveniently deposited him, feet first, directly adjacent to the radioman's door. The starboard forepeak fuel-laden tank erupted in a volcanic blast of fire, oil and black smoke.

11

Torpedoed off the coast of Oregon by the Japanese Sub I 25, the tanker Camden, *shown here under tow, went to the bottom shortly after this photo was taken.* (*Naval Historical Center*)

Goehringer burst through the radioman's door to order the submarine attack signal, but the fast-thinking Sparks already had the wires humming with "••• ••• •••"

Three seamen quickly threw on a new type of life saving suit and leaped from the flaming deck, but once in the water, as Mate Carl Petterson recalled, "The damned things nearly drowned us.[13] We had to cut ourselves of them and climb back aboard the ship and get into a lifeboat."

Crewman Nathan A. Astaskin of Sitka, Alaska, a victim of two prior torpedoings,[14] abandoned a sinking ship for the third time and wondered just how long his luck would last.

The raging fire on the *Camden* confined itself to only one fuel tank. The flames soon subsided, but the now totally-abandoned, mortally-wounded vessel lay bow down, her seams opened by the strain of the initial explosion.

Later that day the *Rio de Janeiro*, an old fishing boat, transported Lt. Commander W. B. Brust and his navy salvage team[15] to the floundering vessel. Brust and his men discovered the ship so filled with volatile fumes that they declared her a virtual floating bomb.

The tug *Kenai* rushed to the scene and immediately took the *Camden* with her valuable cargo of 76,000 barrels of gasoline and oil into

---

[13] Charles Flick, Alhambra, Ca. and Chalmer Thompson, Perryville, Mo.

[14] He survived two sinkings in the freezing waters of the North Atlantic. The first time, he drifted 17 days in an open boat and was one of only two survivors. The second time, he was adrift for only five days. After abandoning the *Camden*, he was rescued in five hours.

[15] Lt. G. L. Gerhard, Seattle; A. J. Paetzold, San Francisco; Ens. J. R. Schultz, Meadville, Or.; Radioman W. E. Richards, Seattle; K. A. Bomstad, Spokane, Wash.; C. E. Bartle, Port Townsend; E. E. McNally, Tacoma, Wash.; L. Z. Lillybridge, Aberdeen; V. L. Israelson, Petersburg, Ark.; O. E. Johnson, Anacortes; M. D. Delancy, Soaplake, Wash.; L. S. Miller, Portland; C. Bruke, Chicago.

tow. The salvage party remained aboard the *Camden* under the most adverse of conditions. The fume-permeated ship, its boilers previously dumped by the far-sighted Captain Davidson, negated the use of any type of flame induced heat. Hot coffee and hot food became a treat only in the memories of the shivering salvage team. Each man received an issue of six blankets to ward off the bone-chilling October cold.

The *Kenai*, with the crippled vessel in tow, approached the Columbia River entrance, but the *Camden* lay too low in the water to chance the dangerous bar crossing. The two ships sailed on for Seattle.

After five days aboard the settling tanker, Commander Brust determined the additional time involved in a tow to Seattle meant doom for the old girl. With his men's safety foremost in his thoughts, he signaled an attending Coast Guard ship to stand by while they abandoned ship.

The following day, on October 10th and at about 6 a.m. a wrench may have slid off a workbench deep within the bowels of the wallowing, vacated hulk, or perhaps a straining bulkhead sheared and popped a rivet that fell with a metallic clank to the steel deck. Whatever the cause, a bright, generating spark ignited the spilled cargo and the *Camden* exploded into flames. She went to the bottom fifteen minutes later. She lies in fifty-two fathoms at 46°46′38″N, 124°31′15″W off Grays Harbor, Washington.

The day after the I 25's attack upon the Camden *the Japanese sub cruised in a southerly direction. Night fell and the sub rode the surface under the protective velvet-black blanket of a moonless sky. Tagami's alert lookouts again reported an enemy target. The sub's commander saw no reason to submerge. He could easily stalk the slow-moving tanker, keep her in sight without fear of detection and continue to re-charge the batteries until the proper moment for attack presented itself.*

The Richfield Oil Company's tanker, *Larry Doheny*, en route from San Pedro to Portland, plugged along at ten knots as she approached Cape Blanco. In strict compliance with wartime regulations, she showed no lights. The captain maintained radio silence and posted lookouts on the bow, gun platforms and bridge. For the second and final time during WW II, the 7,038 ton vessel was about to fall prey to an attacking sub.[16]

At about 8 p.m., Commander Meiji Tagami ordered two torpedoes loaded into the firing tubes and all hands prepared for a surface attack. He again meticulously calculated the target data and ordered, "Fire." All hands waited tensely, counting the seconds to the explosive blast. Their intended victim sailed serenely on, oblivious to its imminent danger. Tagami stood dumbfounded . . . how could we have missed such a perfect target?

The *Larry Doheny's* crew felt and heard a mysterious, heavy, dull thud.

The Japanese submariners, bitterly disappointed with their failure, now stalked their antagonist with a vengeance. Within the hour they re-positioned for another attack. Commander Tagami ordered only one torpedo loaded; he must save his one remaining fish for some future tempting target on the homeward journey.

Chief Torpedoman Kenji Takezawa again depressed the firing key; his muscles tensed as the model 95 torpedo with its half-ton of explosive and fifty-knot speed raced toward the target. It slammed home on the tanker's port side, just forward of the bridge. The resulting sound of a tremendous explosion sent a surge of pride flooding through every fiber of Takezawa's body.

Submariners seldom witness the aftermath of their long, toilsome labors, but in this case Commander Tagami deemed it safe enough for all one hundred of his crew to come topside for a brief view of their fiercely burning target.

The all-engulfing inferno obliterated any possibility for the *Larry Doheny* to transmit an S S S message. Exploding machine gun ammunition forced Captain Olaf Breiland to abandon the bridge immediately. Of the thirty-six crewmen aboard, one died by

---

[16] See *California Shipwrecks*, page 23.

drowning and another perished in the flames. Four men of the ten-man navy gun crew burned to death in the holocaust.

The victorious I 25 submerged at once and an elated navigator computed their homeward course.

The *Larry Doheny* drifted through the night while her crew shivered in lifeboats and watched their stout ship burn. In the morning, the *Larry Doheny* slowly went to the bottom on or near the California-Oregon border west of Gold Beach. The steamer *Coos Bay* rescued the disheartened seamen and landed them safely at Port Orford that night.

Five days later, the I 25 paused on her homeward journey only long enough to fire her last remaining torpedo and sink the Russian submarine L 16 off the Washington coast.

FRIENDSHIP

Palembang, Surabaya, Bandung, Sumatra; their very names exude the essence of tropical, balmy evenings alive with the exotic scents of the Spice Islands. Captain Charles Endicott was enjoying just such a night as this, quite unaware that crafty Malay pirates watched his every move. His bark, *Friendship*, lay tranquilly at anchor, sails furled, in the roads just off Quallah Battoo on the northwest coast of Sumatra.

Pepper, his intended cargo, promised profits as high as 700% in almost any port of Europe, England or America. He merely needed to make the proper deal here ashore.

Endicott headed for the morning market place of the Malay village. Before he could begin bargaining, a trusted native trader, Po Adam, approached the captain to complain of First Mate Knight, whom the captain had left in charge of the ship.

"He no look sharp. He no understand Malay-man," carped Po Adam, still smarting over Knight's insulting braggadocio of the previous day when he claimed that using only a handspike, he could clear the deck of a hundred of those skinny little Malays.

The trader's warning came too late for Endicott to prevent the pepper boats, loaded with armed natives intent upon taking his ship, from shoving off the beach. Second Mate Barry raced to the village to report trouble on board; he had seen crewmen jumping overboard.

Endicott later learned that Mate Knight, thinking the natives approached to unload pepper, allowed them to board. The canny Malays distributed themselves in strategic positions about the vessel; on signal, they fell upon the unsuspecting crew. The ship's steward saw two Malays stab Knight in the back and side but, before he could shout an alarm, received a deadly *kris* in his chest...the steward's life was saved only because his rib bone diverted the dagger's blade. A man named Chester fell into the forward hold, decapitated by the swift blow of a razor-sharp *kampilan*. Another seaman stood on a stage over the ship's side and met the same fate, but his companion dove into the water and swam to safety. The remainder of the crew tried a rush for the arms chest in the aft cabin but were thwarted by the Malays previously stationed in the companionway. The bewildered crew gathered their wounded and leaped to safety over the side.

Endicott gathered his shore party and raced toward his imperiled command. They fought off a guard-boat of the wily natives while en route, but upon their approach, realized they were powerless to recapture the bark. Heavily-armed Malays lined the rails. One poor wretch of a crewman clung to the top gallant yard; some ten or twelve seamen were in the water. Endicott retrieved the swimmers and returned to shore under the burning jeers and insults thrown by the pirates.

That night Endicott and his men rowed along the tropical coast to another post, that of Muchie. There they located three American ships trading for spices and solicited their support. The *James Monroe*, with both crews, sailed to Quallah Battoo and prepared to retake the *Friendship* by force, but upon their arrival, found it unnecessary. The Malays, apparently satisfied with a thorough looting of the ship's stores, abandoned ship and raced for shore.

Endicott and his remaining crew exercised great restraint bargaining for pepper the following day. They were confronted in the town market with hundreds of natives sporting articles of their personal clothing, along with the ship's tablecloth draped over the shoulders of one proudly strutting, yet innocent-acting, Malay.

The wounded, including Knight, recovered and, for the moment, swallowed their indignity over being sorely robbed. Within a year the ship and crew were avenged when the U.S. frigate *Potomac* arrived, bombarded the Malay forts and landed a force of Marines to burn the town; the Malays were given notice it would be far healthier for them to stick strictly to the business of tending their pepper farms.

The *Friendship* ran into more serious trouble in 1860 as she sailed south along the coast to San Francisco under close reef and top sails. Heavy seas unseated her rudder and swept her deck. Tons of water flooded through her torn hatch covers. Knight, now the captain of the *Friendship*, ascertained the old ship could not long survive this Oregon storm and ordered his men to abandon ship.

Four bodies, including that of Captain Knight, were found at the mouth of the Siuslaw River; another body washed ashore three miles north of the Umpqua. The old bark stranded three miles north of the Sixes River and was ground to pieces. Her battered boat, containing only a quadrant and some soggy gear, eventually drifted onto the beach at Siuslaw.

ONLY FOOLS RUSH IN

Captain William White expertly maneuvered his 100 ton schooner *W. L. Hackstaff* through San Francisco's Golden Gate on July 22, 1849, then turned his attention to checking his charts as the former east coast pilot ship's nose cut the waters for the mouth of the mighty Columbia River.

Satisfied that all went well, a broad grin broke across the Skipper's weather-creased face and triggered a warm flood of exhilaration...at long last he sailed a course for Oregon Territory and a lucrative pilotage business. The veteran river pilot naively dismissed a nagging concern about challenging the high seas of the northern Pacific Ocean. After all, the captain reasoned, if one had already chalked up an enviable piloting record on the tricky waters of Eastern rivers, then surely navigating a short trip north to the Columbia would seem a veritable vacation.

The Pacific, in a fit of pique that a newcomer so easily broached her waters, howled and raged in a three-day protest. The *Hackstaff* bucked and pitched in a heroic effort to gain ground against gale-force winds that continued to drive the vessel and its twenty-seven paying passengers completely off course. Satisfied at last that she had proved her point, the Pacific gale blew herself out. Captain White confidently took a sighting and unhesitatingly declared the Argonauts now lay along a point twelve miles south of Monterey, California. The skipper, totally ignorant of navigating the Pacific Ocean, plotted course after erratic course while the *Hackstaff*, with her trusting crew and passengers, blindly traversed through cold, green waters for the next fifteen days.

At last a much-welcomed shoreline broke the horizon and revealed a group of friendly Indians enthusiastically waving from the dunes. Captain White urged passengers and crew alike to enjoy a short respite and go ashore to mingle with the natives. Six men took up their Skipper's offer and shoved off in the ship's boat. Just as they prepared to catch the next swell to the beach, their horrified coxswain screamed orders to back off and row for their lives back to the safety of the ship; the Indians, brandishing weapons, were a welcoming war-party bristling for another coup against the hated white man.

"Nonsense," guffawed Captain White after his sweating crew scrambled aboard the *Hackstaff*, "California Indians are never warlike...they're simply children dancing with joy at the prospect of trading with us."

"Hate to argue, Captain," interrupted James M. Chapin, a part-time fur trader and veteran of the Oregon Territory, "but them there Indians're Rogues and that there welcoming committee's a scalp-hunting war-party 'cause we ain't in California. . . we're in Oregon Territory!"

"My good man, my calculations place this ship no more than 200 miles north of San Francisco and well within the California boundary," the doting captain patiently explained. "We have experienced a terrific buffeting by headwinds and will have to proceed much further along the coast before we meet your warring Rogues." With that, the captain ordered an immediate setting of sails and the schooner plowed northward.

All too soon the bungling skipper discovered the unanticipated lengthy voyage had reduced the ship's water supply to a dangerously low level. A dismayed Captain White vowed to correct the problem at first opportunity and ordered his ship into the next river. As luck would have it, he was enticed into the voracious mouth of the Rogue River. She fell captive to the swift, swirling currents which threw her onto the punishing sands of the bar. Grinding, bucking and heaving, the wounded vessel fought free of the ripping obstruction, only to be picked up again by the angry river and tossed onto the beach. She lay aground, broken and a total loss.

Passengers and crew escaped with their lives intact, but little else. Merchants William Shively and Cornelius Hills, who had unfortunately consigned their trade goods to the inept captain, lost everything. Hordes of murderous Indians swept down upon the beach and swarmed over the wreckage. While the savages concentrated upon looting the vessel, the distraught Argonauts beat a hasty retreat toward the inland wilderness.

They inched their way inland for the next seventeen days, grubbing on scanty food scratched from the hostile land. Bereft of tools and weapons, the near-starving hikers blindly followed their captain over hill and dale, hoping against hope that civilization lay just beyond the next rise.

Part-time fur-trapper Chapin recognized a hillock near the river and joyfully declared it the very same campsite he used two years prior. Merchant Charles Mulligan challenged Chapin's landmark. Discouraged and disgusted, Mulligan contended that since their illustrious captain managed to get lost at sea then Chapin most certainly couldn't do any better on land. The two men wagered a $10 gold piece over the trapper's description of the campsite and fire pit lying just over the crest. Chapin, the winner, pocketed the gold piece and the bone-weary shipwreck victims found renewed strength to continue their tedious trek to salvation.

Thankful to be walking on familiar ground at long last, Chapin led the men to Cow Creek, then to Crawfish and Myrtle Creek, where they met an immigrant train near Roberts Hill.

Captain White never again ventured into the Pacific Ocean. Content to sail the inland waters of the Willamette, he eventually became a pilot of some note.

The year following the wreck of the *Hackstaff*, Herman Winchester led a party of whites in search of the Klamath River, California. They entered the Rogue River, mistaking it for the Klamath, and discovered portions of the grounded vessel. They purchased a bit of her chain and a bobstay from the Indians.

THE SIEGE OF BATTLE ROCK

Jessie Applegate's quotations in the ensuing narrative have been simulated by the author, based upon James M. Kirkpatrick's later recall of his visit to the home of the early Oregon pioneer. All quotations of James Kirkpatrick are as he recorded them.

"William Tichenor was either incredibly stupid or incredibly greedy. Stupid 'cause he should've known those Siwash Indians, some call them Rogue River Indians, are as mean a bunch of blood-thirsty savages as ever roamed the face o' the earth. Then again, maybe he knowed that all along and, as I said, was greedy about wanting to start that town down the coast below Coos Bay. In any case, son, you're powerful lucky to get away with your scalp. Yessir, you sure are."

With that, Jessie Applegate, early pioneer of Oregon, no doubt folded the newspaper describing the death of the very man who now sat opposite him at the rough-hewn table.

"Come on, lad, dish yourself up another plate of vittles and tell me that story again about your escape from those heathen savages."

"Mmmph," young John Kirkpatrick might have grunted as he munched another large mouthful of pork and beans. "Well, you see, all of us were pretty eager after hearing Captain Tichenor's sales talk about a new town he planned to start down south as a supply station for the miners back in the gold diggings in southern Oregon. He told us that in these peaceful days of 1851 we needn't fear the least particle of danger from coastal Indians. He said that he, himself, wandered freely amongst them many times and knew them as friends. He guaranteed, if we joined him and his two partners, to give us a share in property plus bonus profits from being town-founders. As you know, Captain Tichenor owned the steamer *Sea Gull*, a screw propeller he runs between San Francisco and Portland. His partners in the venture were his boat's Purser, Mr. Hubboard, and a fellow named Butler King, Chief of the Custom House in San Francisco. The good captain also promised to supply everything we needed...blankets, grub, tools, except he didn't mention anything about guns. Naturally, I expected Tichenor to furnish us with guns, mainly 'cause I had a bit of an experience with Indians when I crossed the Rockies with Kit Carson, so the rest of the boys sort of left that end of it up to me.[17]

"The captain, just to satisfy me, I suppose, said he'd get us some arms right off. He walked into the nearest junk shop and bought three old flintlock muskets, one old rusty sword, about ten pounds of lead, and four pounds of powder. 'Now just don't you worry yourselves none, boys,' he told us. 'I admit these weapons don't look like much to you, but just having them around will scare those Indians enough and make you look mighty dangerous.'

"Well, just then a lieutenant from Fort George stepped up and said he owned a very good United States rifle he'd sell me for twenty dollars, so we go take a look at the piece. It's a good one, so I buy it and some more ammunition and powder. Our total arsenal now consists of my U.S. rifle, one six-shooter rifle of Carigan's, the three old flintlocks, a rusty sword, one thirty-eight caliber revolver, and a pair of derringers loaned to me some time ago by a friend in Portland. We also carried five pounds of rifle powder and ten of lead.

"On June 6th we stored our gear aboard the *Sea Gull* and sailed out of Astoria." The weedy young man probably gulped down another swig of scalding coffee before continuing with his narrative. "On the morning of the 9th we unloaded our supplies onto a sandy beach near a big rock that kind of stuck out in the ocean aways from shore. The few Indians we saw didn't look so all fired friendly, so I told Captain Tichenor to unload that old cannon he carried aboard the steamer. Well... mind if I have some more of that grub?"

"Help yourself, son."

"Thanks."

The speaker must have scraped the old wooden spoon around the interior of the pot until absolutely no crumb of beans or drop of juice remained for the dishwasher's rag. The youthful adventurer probably again seated himself at the wooden table before he continued. "Anyway, Captain Tichenor laughed, but then he saw we weren't fooling. He thought it over and finally let us unload and freight the cannon to shore. Now Eagan, a

---

[17] J. H. Eagan, John T. Slater, George Ridoubt, T. D. Palmer, Jose Hussey, Cyrus W. Hedden, James Carigan, and Ralph (Jake) Summers.

gunner in his younger days, returned with three or four bag-cartridges, each of which held two pounds of powder. The captain, laughing and saying he'd return in fourteen days with more supplies and men, shoved off in the *Sea Gull* for 'Frisco.

"We stood alone on the beach and took another good hard look at those Indians, then decided to set up camp on that funny-looking rock that stuck halfway out in the water. At least there the water protected us on three sides and, in the front, only a kind of narrow causeway led to the beach.

"I'll tell you, we hustled our stuff up there mighty fast. Those Indians started crowding around on the beach with more and more savages arriving all the time. We set down that old gun about halfway up the rock on a flat spot about thirty feet wide and primed it in record time. Eagan and I loaded it while

the others started building breastworks. We charged the cannon with a two-pound sack of powder. I shoved in an old shirt while one of the other boys took an ax and chopped up the bar lead. We poured in as much lead as I could hold in my two out-stretched palms, then crammed in some newspapers on top of that. Eagan pricked the sack, we primed the touch hole with fine powder, and trained the piece so's to rake the approach."

"Have a pipe, if you're amind to," the older man would have suggested.

"Thanks, sure will." Kirkpatrick no doubt gratefully reached for the offered clay pipe, stuffed it from the tobacco jar, lighted up with a hot coal, puffed contentedly, and no doubt continued, "The minute them Indians saw the *Sea Gull* weigh anchor, they commence making signs like they didn't want us around and would have our scalps if we

A shipwrecked Russian seaman led hundreds of Rogue Indian warriors against nine white men atop this rock at Port Orford. The siege of Battle Rock, a little known but exciting portion of Oregon history, lasted 14 days. The prospective settlers finally managed to escape under cover of darkness.

(Mike Marshall Collection)

stayed. I wondered just where all those friendly redskins were that Captain Tichenor knew so well.

"The next morning the savages started delivering arrows, but from a distance that didn't much concern us. Then we noticed a large canoe moving up from the direction of the Rogue River with twelve warriors in battle gear plus one great big red-shirted fellow yelling and waving his arms and raising all kinds of fuss. The war party beached the canoe . . . Red-Shirt pulled out a long knife, waved it over his head, and then with about a hundred of them beach warriors, started for us with a rush.

"I scrambled down to man the cannon and stood by with a smoldering tarred rope until they got closer. Carigan grabbed a pine board about fifteen inches wide and eight feet long. He jumped behind me and held the board in front of the two of us with both his arms around me. Later, we counted thirty-seven arrows stuck in it . . . some with their points shoved all the way through the inch and a half thick slab.

"Palmer let out a thick gurgle as an arrow pierced his neck. Ridoubt caught one right in the chest. Luckily, it stuck in his breast bone, so didn't sink in any further. Slater ran and jumped in a hole behind the tent. Just about then a bunch of yelling banshees, led by Red-Shirt, scrambled up the rock causeway. I waited 'til they was about eight feet in front of me before I touched off the prime powder with the fiery end of my rope. That cannon belched off with a fearsome roar, then tumbled over backwards.

"Well, you never seen such a mess. The execution was fearful . . . at least twelve or thirteen Indians blown up right off and a bunch others sure had daylight peeking through. What redskins we didn't knock down, jumped or fell off the rock. All except

two. One, eyeing my scalp, kept coming right at me. Carigan shot him in the shoulder, then Summers shot him in the middle . . . he still kept coming. He swiped at me with his knife, but I knocked it out of his hand. When he reached for it, I pulled out one of my derringers and shot him in the head. The ball slammed in one temple and burst out the other. Believe it or not, he turned and ran about twenty feet before falling dead amongst the others. The other Indian headed for Eagan. Eagan's musket misfired, so he smashed the redskin over the head three or four times with it, which knocked the Indian off the rock and into the ocean. You know, Eagan bent the barrel of that musket six inches!"

Kirkpatrick could have leaned back and exhaled a cloud of smoke toward the open beam ceiling before continuing. "Them Indians never saw a firearm as big as a cannon before, so naturally they thought we brung down thunder and lightning from the sky. Soon, their chief walked to within hailing distance, laid down his bow, quiver, and knife, making signs like he wanted to talk. I climbed down the rock onto the beach and met him. He was muscular, well proportioned, and tall; one of the finest specimens of manhood I ever did see. He made signs about wanting to carry off his dead brothers . . . a kind of truce, so I agreed. Some of the other warriors laid down their arms, then packed off the dead and wounded, all except for the big one in the red shirt. I tried to make them cart him off, too, but they refused. Then the chief did something we couldn't figure out. He tore off that red shirt, gave the body a good swift kick, and walked off.[18] Since the savages wanted nothing to do with him, we had to bury old Red Shirt ourselves. After that, things quieted down for a bit.

"Hussey walked over to tell me something.

---

[18] The body was that of a *Russian* seaman shipwrecked many years prior. Because of his physical prowess, he became a pseudo-leader in the tribe. The identity of his ship is impossible to determine, for few records exist regarding Russian wrecks. One possibility does exist . . . slavery was a common practice among the coastal Indians who often traded their slaves with other tribes (if the captured were fortunate enough to survive these bloody potlatches). Sometimes slaves ended up hundreds of miles from their original capture point. Occasionally an especially talented slave was allowed to better his lowly status and became a member-in-good-standing. The "red shirt" in this instance might conceivably have been the young lad from the ship *Saint Nickolas*, wrecked in 1808 in Clayoququot Sound.

Just as he put his hand on my shoulder to get my attention, a bullet sang over and almost cut his thumb off. That was too close for my taste. That was the first time in all this ruckus that the Indians fired a bullet and it really surprised us. The Indian with that gun had crawled unnoticed to within about sixty yards of us. He was so sure he hit me that he leaped up and showed himself. Now it was my turn. I had a slug and five buckshot in my rifle, so drew a bead and let fly. He lolloped about three feet high, then fell dead. Eagan ran down to retrieve the injun's gun. When he found it defective, he broke the stock and left it. He did bring back the brave's headdress, though...it was made of different colored shells and mighty handsome. That was the last savage we killed that day. We counted twenty of them dead.[19]

"By now we sure wanted out of there. If these be Captain Tichenor's *friendly* Indians, then I'd sorely hate to meet up with any that were mad at us."

Jesse Applegate must have chuckled at that as J. M. continued, "Anyhow, we made it plain to the chief that when our ship returned in thirteen days we'd leave, so he agreed to a temporary truce. We spent some mighty worried next few days, but they was as good as their word and never even came within sight of our rock.

"On the thirteenth day a bunch of braves gathered on the beach. When no ship anchored to take us off, they became mighty irate. They figured we broke our promise. The chief pepped them all up with a talk, then pulled out his knife, and led them howling savages up our rock. I ordered Jim, the best shot of all the men, to take a bead with me on the chief and fire when I did. The chief dropped with two slugs in him.

"All those blood-thirsty warriors let out a terrible groan, then carried him off over the hill and out of sight. In about an hour, another big chief showed up, started the same kind of pep talk, and danged if he don't lead them the same way...all the while they're making signs with their knives that they're going to cut our heads off. Soon as the new chief gets close, we fire. He drops dead and that stops all that nonsense for the rest of the day.

"Soon we spotted all kinds of canoes coming in and a lot of campfires blazing down on the beach. We count about five hundred Indians and only nine of us. We decided to try to fool them into thinking we're staying, that way maybe they'll hold off their attack. We busy ourselves with building more breastworks and pretending to settle in.

"When we see their spies run off to tell the new chief we're staying, we sneak off, taking only our weapons, an ax, and some rope. We headed north on the beach at a fast run. About three miles up, we ran into about thirty braves on their way down to join the others. We yelled, then charged them. They were so flabbergasted that they scattered and we didn't even have to fire one single shot. We kept on going fast, beating through the brush all night.

"The next day we came to a large, flat plain and could hardly believe our luck. At last, now we'd make good time. But when we got onto it, the plain turned out to be a soft, mushy swamp thick with roots, water to our arm pits, and black with millions of mosquitoes. We spent all night crossing it. The next morning we hit hard ground and found a wide trail made by the hundreds of Indians who were after us, but passed us during the night. We located the spot where they turned off to look for us inland.

"Finally we reached the Coquille River, but discovered three or four hundred Indians from a *different* tribe standing on the other side. They barred our crossing, so we trekked along the stream. Them savages kept opposite us all the way. We clawed to the top of a cliff and kept parallel to the river on high ground.

"After a time, we figured we left the Indians far enough downstream to chance fashioning a raft and crossing in the fog to the other side. Too late, we discovered we landed on an island and, fools that we were, had let our raft drift off.

---

[19] Actually 23.

"The fog cleared, but we found no wood for another raft. George swam across to cut a pine for the men who couldn't swim. They could hold our rifles and hang on while we pushed. Then, doggone if four Indians don't come along in a canoe. They spot George and we spot them, but as soon as they saw our guns leveled on them, they tamed right down and agreed to canoe us across.

"Well, we got safely to the other side and kept moving 'til we came to a beach. Here we found some mussels on the rocks. After starving for three nights and four days, we ate them raw. All of us ended up sick, so we chanced a fire. The cooked mussels stayed put this time.

"One of the Indians who canoed us across the river shoved his way through the brush to say he knew me from Portland and followed us from the river to tell us to hurry since a war party trailed close behind. We headed up the beach until about three that afternoon, at which time we discovered a twenty foot high white pole stuck in the sand and anchored with rocks around its base. Our tame Indian told us that marked the boundary line between the Siwash and the Coos Bay, Umpqua, and Clickatat tribes. If the Siwashes took one step past that pole, they'd be hunted down and killed by the other tribes.

"Further along we met up with some friendly Indians who fed us, then gave us some salmon, elk meat, and berries. After two more days of traveling in the direction our friendly Indians pointed out, we ran out of food. Fortunately a storm hit the area and threw a lot of fish up on the beach, which we roasted.

"Some Indians ran on ahead to alert the whites that the ones who used thunder and lightning to kill so many Indians down the coast were coming. We met a bunch of settlers at the Umpqua River and eventually got to Scottsburg.[20] I left my companions there to recuperate and, anxious to get back to Portland, I came on ahead."

"Son," the famous aging pioneer must have drawled, "I'm sure glad you made it. I just read in today's newspaper about you and the others being massacred down there. Danged if you don't come knocking at my door! Here's a blanket and you just comfy down over there in that corner. I'll see you in the morning." The veteran pioneer grabbed a kerosene lamp with his leathered fist and clumped off to the other room. He muttered half to himself, "If that don't beat all. Reminds me of when I was up on the Snake...let's see, that was back in . . . . "

John M. Kirkpatrick, whose story appears above, was born in 1825. He died in 1910 and is buried in Central Point, Oregon. William Tichenor died in 1887 and is buried at Port Orford. Eagan settled in Portland and married, while Palmer went to Salem and opened a saloon. Slater (Salter) was killed by Indians in 1866 on the Rogue River near the place where Hedden just barely escaped with his life in 1855 after a skirmish with the same Indians.

The red shirted Russian, washed out of his burial place, was discovered by Tichenor and his party on their return. Assuming it was the body of one of the original party, it was reburied and word was sent north of the massacre of the entire party. He was never identified nor was his wrecked ship ever located. The steamer *Sea Gull* wrecked on the north spit of Humboldt Bay January 25, 1852 and became a total loss.

COASTAL DESCRIPTION
California-Oregon border to Blacklock Point[21]

From the California-Oregon border for 3.8 miles to the Chetco River, the coast is composed of low rocky cliffs bordered by numerous rocks and ledges, covered and awash and backed by a low narrow tableland. Several prominent rocky knolls rise from 100 to 200 feet above this tableland. Due to numerous

---

[20] Both the towns of Scottsburg and Gardiner were established as the result of a shipwreck. See *Bostonian*.
[21] See Nautical Charts numbers 18602, 18601, and 18589.

dangers the coast should not be approached closer than 1.5 miles.

Chetco Cove, 15.5 miles north of Point St. George, affords some protection from northwest winds but is exposed in southerly weather. There are numerous visible and covered rocks fringing the shore of the cove and its approaches. The smokestack of a plywood plant in Brookings is very prominent for several miles off the entrance to Chetco River. Chetco River empties into the north side of the cove. The river is entered through a dredged channel which leads between two stone jetties to Brookings Basin, about 0.3 mile above the jetties. Brookings Basin is protected on its west side by an 1800 foot long dike. It consists of a barge turning basin and two small craft basins to the north. The entrance channel is marked by a 030° lighted range and other aids; a light and fog signal are off the outer end of the north jetty.

Berths with electricity and water are available in the lower small craft basin. Depths of about 2 feet can be carried to the highway bridge about 0.7 mile above the jetties. The bridge has a clearance of 59 feet. The mid-channel depth to the basin is 7 feet; the basin is 9 feet.

A Coast Guard station is on the east side of the river 450 yards inside the entrance. A marker radiobeacon is at the station. A lookout tower atop the building at the station is used to observe the bar during heavy weather. The Coast Guard has established a *rough bar advisory sign*, 34 feet above the water, visible from the channel looking seaward, on the north end of the Coast Guard boathouse. The sign is diamond-shaped, painted white with international orange borders and the words "Rough Bar" in black letters. The sign is equipped with two alternating flashing amber lights that are activated when the seas exceed four feet and are considered hazardous for small boats; however if the lights are not flashing this is *no guarantee* that sea conditions are favorable. Minor engine repairs can be made at the basin and a 15 ton crane there can be used by the public in emergencies.

From Chetco Cove for 4.5 miles to Cape Ferrelo the coast is composed of high broken cliffs bordered by numerous rocky islets and ledges extending in some cases up to one-half mile offshore. At Goat Island, locally called Bird Island you are 17.5 miles north of Point St. George and 500 yards offshore. There is deep water off the west and southwest faces but foul ground extends 350 yards from the southeast point. The island closely resembles Price Island off Pyramid Point.

Cape Ferrelo 20 miles north of Point St. George is the prominent headland north of St. George Reef and, though not projecting seaward to any extent, is conspicuous because of its bold rugged face. Several rocks and islets lie up to 0.5 mile directly off the cape.

From Cape Ferrelo for 9.5 miles to Crook Point the coast is very rugged and rocky with several large and prominent islets and reefs extending well offshore. In some cases these form anchorages for small vessels in northerly weather. Whalehead Island, the outer of two rocky islets 2.3 miles north of Cape Ferrelo, is 107 feet high. The inner of the two islets is 128 feet high. A rock lies awash 800 yards south of the highest point of the island. Next, 3.3 miles north of Cape Ferrelo you will see a rugged cliff from 200 to 300 feet high; the face is about one mile long and behind it rises a treeless triple-headed hill to 800 feet.

Thomas Creek, 3.7 miles north of Cape Ferrelo is crossed by 101 highway and the highest bridge in Oregon, 345 feet above the creek.

Leaning Rock is 49 feet high and lies 0.5 mile off shore and 3.5 miles north of Whalehead Island. It has a perpendicular face on its northwest side and slopes gradually southeast. Several other rocks are near it. Between Whalehead and Crook Point are two prominent grassy areas in the forest near the crest of the hills. They are about two miles apart and situated at an elevation of 2000 feet; the south one is known as Rocky Prairie.

Yellow Rock, 84 feet high, lies 4.5 miles north of Whalehead Rock and 0.5 mile offshore. The rock is yellowish in color and can be recognized from four miles offshore. Bosley Butte is 8.5 miles northeast from Cape Ferrelo and shows above the coast ridges from the west and northwest. It is flat topped with two summits separated by a slight depression; the northeast summit is rounded and somewhat larger but slightly lower than the eastern summit.

Mack Arch is a double headed rocky islet 0.8 mile offshore, 1.5 miles south of Crook Point and 8 miles NNE of Cape Ferrelo. The west head is 231 feet high and the east is a little lower; both are black almost to the tops, then white from bird poop. The arch, about 100 feet high, is under the east summit and shows prominently from the south. A rock awash lies 125 yards south of the east point. The bight east southeast of Mack Arch has been used as a temporary anchorage during moderate NW weather. The rocks and reefs break the swell. In approaching the anchorage, pass to the south of Mack Arch about midway between it and Yellow Rock. Anchor in 11 fathoms, sand bottom, with Mack Arch bearing 296° and Yellow Rock bearing 155°. No breakers have been observed, but caution should be exercised as the place has not been closely surveyed.

Mack Reef extends from Mack Arch to Crook Point and comprises many rocks, visible and sunken from awash to 133 feet high. From the south these rocks stand out conspicuously when seen against the white sand dunes north of Crook Point. Mack Arch, because of its size and height, is the most prominent.

Mack Arch Cove lies immediately east of Mack Reef and affords fair shelter in NW weather in six to seven fathoms, sandy bottom. In entering from the south, pass east of Mack Arch, giving it a berth of about 150 yards, but taking care to avoid the rock 125 yards south of its east point. Then bring the 125 foot rock, in the north part of the reef, to bear 352° and steer for it on that bearing until up to the anchorage abreast the group of rocks 0.5 mile north of Mack Arch. As in all cases, *use caution* and check your current Coast Pilot.

Crook Point is moderately low, but terminates seaward in a rocky knoll 175 feet high,

with a slight depression immediately behind it. The rocks close to the point often show up during moderately thick weather; several have very noticeable pinnacle formations.

From the vicinity of Crook Point to the mouth of the Pistol River are sand dunes which show prominently in clear weather and distinctly mark this section. In thick weather these dunes are not readily seen. From the mouth of the river to Cape Sebastian are numerous rocks and rocky islets extending 0.3 mile offshore and in some cases are 150 feet high. The Pistol River bar opens in the rainy season; *its location varies from year to year*.

Hunters Cove, a small contracted anchorage under the southeast face of Cape Sebastian, is formed partly by the cape and partly by Hunters Island in the entrance. The island is 0.2 mile in extent, rocky, flat-topped and 113 feet high. Shoal water extends from it east to the beach. The cove is used occasionally by launches and small craft. During strong NW weather the sea at the entrance is rather lumpy for small boats. With moderate SW weather a heavy sea piles up across the entrance between the cape and Hunters Island.

Cape Sebastian, 33.5 miles N of Point St. George, is conspicuous from either north or south. It is the seaward termination of a ridge transverse to the coast, and rises abruptly from seaward to a height of 694 feet, with a depression behind it and then more gradually to a height of about 2000 feet. The seaward face is precipitous and broken, and has few trees; southward the lower part is grass covered. A rock covered 1½ fathoms that seldom breaks is 0.5 mile offshore and 0.9 mile northwest of the western extremity of the cape.

From Cape Sebastian for six miles to the mouth of Rogue River, the coast is considerably broken, rugged and low near the beach, and has a few outlying rocks. The outer of three exposed rocks off the entrance to Hunter Creek, 3.7 miles north of Cape Sebastian, lies nearly 0.5 mile offshore.

Rogue River, six miles north of Cape Sebastian, is an important *sport fishing* stream.

Several float landings and a hoist for trailer-drawn craft are just above the old lumber dock on the north side of the river near the mouth. Gold Beach, on the opposite side of the river from Wedderburn, is the larger town. Several wharves and piers here are used for mooring and offloading of fish. The entrance to Rogue River is protected by stone jetties and buoys mark the approach. A light and a seasonal fog signal are on the seaward end of the NW jetty. *Caution:* the controlling depths in the Rogue River channel and basin are usually considerably less than projected depth, and are subject to continual pronounced change. Use local knowledge.

There is a Coast Guard rough bar advisory sign 20 feet above the water and visible from the entrance to the small boat harbor at Gold Beach. The sign is diamond shaped, painted white with an international orange border, with the words "Rough Bar" in black letters. The sign is equipped with two alternating quick flashing yellow lights that are activated when the seas exceed four feet in height. It is *no guarantee*, however, if the lights are *not flashing* that the sea is favorable. About 170 berths, some with electricity, gasoline, diesel fuel, water, ice, launching ramps and marine supplies are available in Gold Beach. A repair facility here specializes in aluminum hull repairs, and minor engine repairs.

The *wreck* of a fishing vessel is charted on the SE edge of the dredged channel about 210 yards W of the end of the SE jetty; the position is *doubtful*. A concrete arch bridge across the Rogue River, 0.8 mile above the mouth, has a fixed span clearance of 30 feet. An overhead power cable with a clearance of 77 feet crosses the river about 0.2 mile east of the highway bridge; the bridge is prominent when off the mouth of the river.

The north head at Rogue River entrance that reaches a height of 700 feet a mile north of the river, the marked depression in the coast range made by the river valley and the rocks of Rogue River Reef are prominent from seaward.

Rogue River Reef, extending over four miles northwest from Rogue River entrance, includes many visible and covered rocks; because of the broken bottom, vessels should stay over five miles offshore when passing this area. A 0.5 mile wide channel separates the reef from the shore; it is *not safe* to use without local knowledge. Northwest Rock, four miles NW of Rogue River entrance, is the outermost visible rock of the reef. A rock, covered 2½ fathoms, is 0.3 mile west of Northwest Rock. Needle Rock, 1.1 miles SE of Northwest Rock, is the most prominent of the rocks in the reef. The needle is on the S side.

North of Rogue River the coast trends N for 10 miles and then NW toward Cape Blanco. The mountains are high, irregular, dark and covered with chaparral. The beach is bordered by numerous rocks for five miles, then is almost clear with the exception of Orford and Blanco Reefs.

A group of covered and visible rocks, 1 mile long and 0.5 mile wide, lies 5 miles north of Rogue River and nearly 2 miles offshore; these rise abruptly from 12 fathoms. North Rock, seven feet high, is the largest and nearest to the beach. A rock, covered 1¼ fathoms, lies about 0.6 mile NW of North Rock.

The channel between Rogue River Reef and the mainland, and North Rock and the mainland, is sometimes used by coastwise freighters in clear weather. This channel *should not* be attempted by strangers.

Brushy Bald Mountain, nearly nine miles NE of Rogue River entrance and three miles inland, shows up in hazy weather as a flat rounded peak, with a gentle slope from a W and S direction.

Sisters Rocks are a group of three rocky islets 10.5 miles N of Rogue River entrance. The smaller, 0.8 mile offshore, is the outermost. There is fairly smooth water in NW weather under the lee side of the largest.

Colebrooke Butte, two miles E of Sisters Rocks, appears from the W as a cone with gentle sloping sides. The upper part usually shows against the skyline and is readily recognized. From the south it shows as a rounded peak which resembles Brushy Bald Mountain though somewhat lower. The north part of the summit is tree covered and dark green.

The slopes are timbered except for the lower part of the seaward slope, which is bare and brown.

Lookout Rock, 2.3 miles north of Sisters Rocks, is a prominent projecting cliff, with a marked depression behind it. The seaward face is steep.

Bald Mountain, 3.2 miles NE of Lookout Rock, appears from offshore as an irregular knob at the NW end of a long ridge. Rocky Peak, on the SE end of the ridge, is a sharp peak. From a SW direction, three peaks or knobs show; from a NNW direction, two peaks show almost in range. These peaks were used by early navigators as a landfall for Port Orford in coming from the north.

Prominent Humbug Mountain, 3.3 miles north of Lookout Rock and 4 miles south of Port Orford, is conical in shape, and its seaward face is rugged and steep.

Island Rock, 1.3 miles off the seaward face of Humbug Mountain, is flat on top. A needle rock is 200 yards off its NW end. These rocks are prominent when approaching Port Orford from southward. Except for 2 small rocky patches covered 6¾ and 10 fathoms, within 0.5 mile of the north end of Island Rock, there is deep water around these islands and between them and the beach.

Redfish Rocks are a group of islets covering an area of 0.5 mile square, lying 2 miles off Island Rock to the north and nearly 1 mile offshore. They are six in number and range from 10 to 140 feet in height. There are many covered rocks in this area; *use caution.*

Port Orford, 6.5 miles south of Cape Blanco and 19 miles north of Rogue River, is a cove that affords good shelter in NW weather, but is *exposed and dangerous* in southerly weather. It is easy of access and is probably the best natural NW lee north of Point Reyes.

The town of Port Orford, on the north side of the cove, is the home of the famous yellow cedar. Lumber is trucked from the town.

The Heads, forming the west point of the cove, appear from the south as a long ridge with three knobs. The inner two are slightly higher and covered with trees. Tichenor Rock lies 175 yards south of The Heads. The white lookout tower in The Heads is prominent from the south and *can be mistaken* for the Cape Blanco Light tower. The white tank on the summit shows just clear of the trees; it too can be mistaken for the Cape Blanco Light when viewed from far offshore.

Klooqueh Rock, 0.3 mile off the NW face of The Heads, is black and conical in shape. It is prominent, especially when coming from the NW inside Orford Reef. Rocky ledges are between this rock and the shore.

Anchorage may be had in about the center of Port Orford in 6 to 10 fathoms, sand bottom; however, it is reported that many anchors *have been lost* near the rocky 2½ fathom shoal 0.2 mile east of the south end of the breakwater. Aha, a clue maybe?

The cove is marked by a lighted bell buoy and a lighted buoy, 0.5 mile south and 0.8 mile ENE of Tichenor Rock, respectively. Small craft may anchor closer to The Heads where better protection is afforded against the NW winds, which sweep with considerable force through the depression at the head of the cove.

Battle Rock, in the north part of the cove close to the shore, is high, narrow and black; it is detached only at extreme high tides. Visible and covered rocks extend up to 0.5 mile from shore around the cove, but a passage with a least depth of 1 fathom is available through the center of the cove to the wharf east of Graveyard Point. A 550-foot breakwater extends SE from the point.

Depths of five to nine feet are alongside the outer east face of the wharf; depths are shoaler inshore, and a three-foot depth is about 20 yards east of the wharf. Gasoline and diesel are piped to the wharf; boats to 11½ tons, 37 feet long and 13½ feet wide are lifted to cradles on the wharf by a hoist. Marine supplies can be ordered from Coos Bay, 51 miles by highway.

From The Heads for 6.5 miles to Cape Blanco, the coast extends in a general NNW direction. North of The Heads the shore is a narrow sand ridge, rising at one point to 160 feet, covered with grass, fern, and brush, and ending abruptly nearly three miles from The

Heads at the edge of the Elk River Valley. North of this point are sand dunes extending to the mouth of Elk River, a small unimportant stream. Beyond the mouth of Elk River to Cape Blanco, the coast consists of vertical cliffs, wooded to the edge, and in some places over 150 feet high.

Orford Reef, from two to five miles offshore between The Heads and Cape Blanco, is composed of a group of irregular rocks up to 149 feet high and ledges, many of which are awash or show a break. Kelp extends from Orford Reef to within 1.3 miles of the shore. A lighted whistle buoy, 6.5 miles SW of Cape Blanco, is the guide for clearing this reef.

Fox Rock and Southeast Black Rock, 1.3 miles apart, almost 5 miles SW of Cape Blanco, are usually marked by a heavy break. Northwest Rock, 3 miles SW of Cape Blanco, is the northernmost visible rock of Orford Reef, although several rocks, covered 5 fathoms, are 1.2 miles NE of Northwest Rock.

Blanco Reef, extending 1.5 miles SW from Cape Blanco, consists of numerous rocks and ledges, some of which are marked by kelp. Black Rock, 1.2 miles SW of Cape Blanco Light, is the southernmost visible rock of Blanco Reef.

Pyramid Rock, 1 mile W of the light, is the northernmost visible rock of the reef, although a rocky patch uncovers about 3 feet 0.4 mile to the north. Rocky patches, covered ½ to 6 fathoms, extend from 0.5 mile SW of Black Rock to 0.4 mile W of Pyramid Rock. In clear weather small vessels with local knowledge sometimes use the passage inside the Orford Reef and between Orford Reef and Blanco Reef.

Cape Blanco projects about 1.5 miles from the general trend of the coast. It is a small bare tableland, terminating seaward in a cliff 203 feet high, with low land behind it. A large black rock lies close under the south side of the cape. From seaward the cape is not prominent, but from north or south, it appears like a moderately low bluff islet. Buildings at the cape are easily seen.

Cape Blanco Light, at 42°50.2'N, 124°33.8'W 100 feet above water, is shown from a 59 foot white conical tower near the flat part of the cape; a radiobeacon is close to the north of the light. The tank and lookout tower at The Heads should not be mistaken for the light tower. Numerous covered and visible rocks extend 0.5 mile or more NW from the cape.

Gull Rock, one mile N of Cape Blanco Light, is surrounded by covered rocks. Its seaward face is black and rugged, and the summit has two knobs, the higher to the south. A rocky patch, covered 3 fathoms, lies 0.5 mile W of Gull Rock.

Castle Rock, 1.5 miles NE of Cape Blanco Light and 300 yards off the mouth of the Sixes River, rises abruptly from the sea and is readily made out 10 miles to seaward. Many low rocks and islets are within 400 yards, and several rocky islets are to the W and NW.

Blacklock Point is a precipitous rocky point 2.5 miles NNE of Cape Blanco. The cliff is 157 feet high. A sharp high point, bordered by rocks, stretches out for nearly 300 yards. A narrow curved line of rocks extends 0.8 mile WSW from the point. A rock that breaks in heavy weather is one mile NW of the point. Rocky patches, covered 4 fathoms, are within 1.3 miles of the point in a W and NW direction.

SHIP DISASTERS
Oregon-California border, Chetco to Blacklock Point

(Note: Engine specifications refer to cylinder size. A compound engine would, for example, be listed as high pressure cylinder 45 ", low pressure cylinder 90 ", stroke 48 ", or 45 " × 90 " × 48 ". In some cases, large engines, like the one on the *Bristol* of 1867 out of New York, had a main cylinder bore of 110 " and a stroke of 12 feet!)

Alice H. 9/23/1950 61 tons, foundered off Port Orford.

Andrew Jackson 5/2/1954 Oil screw, 71 tons. Foundered 5 miles off coast north of Gold Beach.

Anita 1852 Bark, U.S. Transport, Captain J. H. Belcher. Used for a recruiting ship, she arrived at the Columbia River March 15, 1848 to secure men for the Army in Mexico; unsuccessful, she returned south and became a total loss on the rocks at Port Orford.

Brother Jonathan 7/30/1865 Sidewheel steamer, built by Perrine, Patterson & Stack at Williamsburg, New York. 221' × 36' with wheels 33' in diameter, driven by a vertical beam engine with a 72" diameter cylinder and an 11' stroke. Lost on rocks north of Crescent City near California-Oregon border. More than 190 souls perished. See story. Approximate position: Lat. 41°49'00", Lon. 124°19'30"; Loran C, chain 9940, W:14329.27, X:27569.96, Y:43871.82.

Bunkalation 6/1870 American schooner stranded at Cape Blanco. A total loss, $7,000.

Cottoneva 2/10/1937 Steam schooner launched as *Frank D. Stout* in 1917 at St. Helens. 190' × 43' and 1113 tons; cargo of 150,000' lumber. Charles R. Ayers of the Stelltree Line purchased the vessel only one week prior to her demise. She was at Port Orford dock when a storm fast approached; she cast loose and attempted to beat to sea, but was driven back and grounded about 200' from Battle Rock. Port Orford Coast Guardsmen, under CPO Nils Nilson, rescued the crew. Capt. E. Stahlbaun commanded the *Cottoneva*.

Cyclone 1897 Two mast schooner. Ship took six years to build and was documented while still on the stocks. Prior to her launching, she was destroyed by a forest fire.

Esther Colos 10/21/1879 Schooner. A total loss on the Rogue River bar.

Friendship 4/14/1860 Bark. Four bodies recovered; see story.

Fulton 2/12/1904 Steam screw. Ashore at Port Orford, one dead.

Harriet Rose 1/28/1876 Schooner. Ashore on The Heads, Port Orford. Cargo saved.

J. A. Chanslor 12/18/1919 Tanker, 4938 tons, built in 1910 at Newport News, Va. En route Goleta-north. Owned by Associated Oil, cargo of bulk oil. Fog and currents drove her into breakers where she broke in half near Tower Rock, Cape Blanco, in sight of lighthouse. Captain A. A. Sawyer and two crewmen survived after spending 34 hours in an open boat, which capsized when it drifted ashore. The seamen were found wandering on the beach. A portion of the ship showed above water about 400' offshore at a point about ⅛ mile north of Cape Blanco, near a number of rocks. There was little hope of recovering her 36 dead, since victims of shipwrecks in that area seldom wash ashore. Lat. 45°50'17"

Lon. 124°32'02". Loran C, chain 9940, W:13800.03, X:27695.43, Y:43913.63.

Joan of Arc 11/15/1920 Steamer, wood, built by Rolph in California in 1918. While en route Portland-San Pedro, she hit Rogue River reef; refloated, but drifted onto the beach for a total loss.

Larry Doheny 10/5/1942 Tanker, Richfield Oil Co., 7038 tons, cargo of 66,000 bbls oil. Capt. Olaf Breiland. Torpedoed at Lat. 42°20'N, Lon. 125°02'W by Japanese sub I-25. Six dead. See story.

*Melanope 12/1906 British ship, capsized off Cape Blanco, salvaged and converted into a barge, then went into breakwater at Royston, Vancouver Island. She was built in 1876 at Liverpool. Vessel was en route Eureka-Tacoma when she wrecked.

Mose 6/25/1884 Vessel and cargo of 60,000' of lumber were a total loss at Port Orford.

Northwester 1875 Schooner, valued at $8,200. A total loss on the Rogue River bar.

Ocean King 12/26/1887 American ship, en route Nanaimo-San Pedro with cargo of coal. Captain C. H. Sawyer. Totaled by fire off Cape Blanco. The 2434 ton ship, valued at $50,000, carried 3850 tons of coal worth $15,000. The schooner *Angel Dolly*, Captain Tellus, came to the rescue of all hands at sea.

Osmo 5/17/1922 3 mast schooner, 160' in length, built at Marshfield in 1904 by K. V. Kruse. In 1918, the ship was sold Mexican, but was held in port on suspicion of her intended use as a German raider. The ex-*Hugh Hogan* foundered and became a total loss off Port Orford.

Phyllis 3/09/1936 Steam schooner, 215' in length, 1,266 tons, built at Aberdeen in 1917. Ashore in fog one mile north of Humbug Mountain, 2½ miles south of Port Orford between Coal Point and Redfish Rocks. Captain Victor Jacobsen felt forced to drive her ashore after she sprang a leak in heavy seas. Her cargo was high-lined 1¼ miles from the wreck to high ground; ship was a total loss.

Rogue River 11/16/1902 Sternwheel, 80 tons, 66' in length, built at Portland in 1901. Wrecked at Boiler Rapids where her boiler is still visible. Captain Burns.

Rosalind 2/18/1890 Three mast schooner, 288 tons, built by Hall Bros. at Port Blakely in 1883. Ship became a total loss three miles north of the Rogue River.

Rustler 8/24/1919 Gas screw, 61-footer built by Kruse & Banks in 1911. Ship burned for a total loss four miles south of Fox Creek.

San Buenaventura 1/14/1910 Two mast schooner, 180 tons, built by Bendixson at Fairhaven in 1876. Abandoned with lumber cargo just off Northwest Seal Rock. The ship drifted north and may lie at Lat. 42°25'18"N, Lon. 124°25'30"W.

South Portland 10/19/1903 Steamer, brought from

---

* Refloated or partially salvaged.

the east coast by Boston & Alaska S.S. Co. in 1899. En route Portland-San Francisco under the command of part-owner Captain J. B. McIntyre, the vessel carried a wheat cargo, 14 passengers and a crew of 25. She struck Cape Blanco reef bow-on at seven knots and immediately began to fill; the first boat away contained the captain; two other boats capsized. Mate Charles Bruce remained aboard and tried to run the sinking vessel to shore. He later endeavored to protect the captain by testifying that *he* asked the captain to leave; 18 souls perished from drowning and exposure. The captain was found criminally negligent for leaving the ship. The *South Portland*'s name-board drifted north to Cape Lookout and is now on display at the Boy Scouts of America Camp Meriwether. The ship was a total loss.

Susan Olson 11/15/1942 Steam schooner, wood, 903 tons. Ex-*Willamette*, ex-*California*, built by Bendixson at Fairhaven in 1911. The crew were saved after they abandoned the old 195′ whale processor and her cargo of lumber in heavy seas off Chetco Point. The ship foundered in the vicinity of Port Orford.

T. W. Lucas 10/24/1894 Brig. Sailed en route Hoodsport-San Francisco under Captain Bose. Caught in a severe SE gale and on her beam ends. The crew was rescued by the steamer *Homer*, Captain Paton. The derelict drifted in the vicinity of Port Orford for several months before she broke up at an unknown location.

Victoria 11/28/1883 Steamer. Sailed en route Victoria-San Francisco under Captain Reichmann when she ran afoul of the Cape Blanco-Orford reef and became a total loss. She was insured for $12,000; the wreck sold for $900, the cargo for $110. Very little is known of the event.

Washcalore 5/21/1911 Oil-powered wood schooner built by Kruse & Banks at Marshfield in 1905. Capt. Peterson carried a crew of 13 aboard when the 140 footer struck Rock Island, a small, bare reef 200 to 300 feet south of the mouth of the Rogue River. The ship drifted and eventually broke in two near a place then called Hunter Point, which may be the same rocks as those located just off Hunter Creek. Captain and crew were saved.

Willapa #2 12/2/1941 Steam schooner, 1185 tons, ex-*Florence Olson*. Built at North Bend in 1917. Captain Oscar Peterson and his crew of 24 men were bound Marshfield-San Francisco when the ship ran into trouble about 20 miles south of Port Orford. Fortunately, the alert Coast Guard personnel saw the vessel's distress rockets and effected a rescue just in the nick of time before the vessel went to the bottom. The severity of the storm prevented the Coast Guard from using their bulky lifeboat to land the survivors at Port Orford. Fisherman James Combs volunteered his services to take two seamen at a time in his dory through the crashing surf; he successfully landed the drenched castaways 800 yards up the beach.

W. L. Hackstaff 8/1849 Pilot schooner. Captain William White. Ship wrecked on the Rogue River bar and looted by Indians. See story, "Only Fools Rush In."

Joan of Arc *wrecked at Port Orford.*   *(Curry County Historical Society)*

2

Blacklock Point to Tenmile Creek

THE *CAPTAIN LINCOLN* AND THE GREAT GOVERNMENT SURPLUS SALE

"Were it not for the troop who worked unceasingly at the pumps, her shorthanded crew might have met with a watery grave, and although with a lot of rough fare in the hold, in consequence of deluging waves no fires could be kept to cook it, the only sustenance and nourishment we had for many days were from the little stores of knick-knacks purchased ere leaving Benecia [sic], from our scanty soldier's pockets," so recalled Henry Baldwin, a member of the 1st Dragoons, also known as the "Mounted Rifles,"[1] under command of Lieutenant Stanton, United States Army.

Baldwin and his fellow troopers boarded the leased revenue schooner *Captain Lincoln* on a balmy December 28th, 1851. They gathered at the ship's rail and waved goodbye to their friends at the Benicia, California Army Post. The ship's captain, an experienced coastal seaman named Naghel, expertly guided the vessel into the Sacramento stream, past San Francisco and the narrow Golden Gate, then northward along the rugged coast toward their destination of Port Orford, Oregon, where the Army maintained a station to protect the settlers from continual Indian uprisings. The hard-bitten troopers aboard the *Captain Lincoln* carried orders to relieve the Army contingent of their current tour-of-duty. At the moment, the fierce Rogue Indians seemed quiet, but only a few

short months prior they initiated the bloody siege of Battle Rock. The Rogues' reputation for treachery reached far and wide...even the friendly tribes of the Coos contemptuously referred to the rebellious tribe as the "California Siwashes" and refused them passage beyond a certain bleached pole marking the tribal boundary of Coos territory.

On the second day at sea, the weather worsened. Soon the ship struggled valiantly against ever increasing odds. Her sharp bow bit chunks out of each storm-driven wave. The elements unfolded in fury. The vessel plunged onward...freezing seas cascaded over her bulwarks, poured through open hawse holes, tore off grating, smashed doors and breached her every seam.

Captain Naghel fought desperately to keep the *Captain Lincoln* afloat but knew he must soon concede the lopsided battle to the unforgiving, unrelenting Pacific Ocean. Pitch black weather erased all trace of sheltering landmarks and propelled ship, captain and crew two miles north of the dreaded Coos Bay bar, some fifty miles beyond their intended destination of Port Orford. Accepting the inevitable, the harried captain requested Lt. Stanton to alert his troopers to prepare for abandoning ship; the skipper ordered all sails unfurled, then barked out the command, "Hard alee!" in a last-ditch effort to drive his dying ship through the crashing surf and onto

---

[1] Dragoons were more heavily armed than the average army man and usually mounted.

the beach. With an uncanny instinct, he had chosen an ideal landing site of this desolate shore.[2]

"...We were carried toward the beach," wrote Phillip Brack, a trooper on watch at the time. "We seemed to strike a bar that was about two hundred yards from the shore, but the huge breakers lifted our trembling vessel over into deeper water, but she settled to the bottom and for awhile the breakers rolled over her decks."

Dragoons and crew, frozen to the bone, huddled in the cold, dead ship until the abating waves permitted five volunteers to wade ashore and anchor a salvage line. All hands turned to the vital task of salvaging precious ship's stores and cargo. A hasty survey of the landfall revealed two nearby fresh water lakes. Soon, with the aid of salvaged galley equipment, Cookie stirred a bubbling stew over a merrily blazing campfire. The men constructed tents and huts from sails and wreckage, then turned to stacking Army and ship's stores and covered the cache with salvaged tarps. The American flag, waving proudly from the newly erected broken mast of the floundered vessel, marked the official site of "Camp Castaway." Lt. Stanton ordered his men to retrieve every scrap of salvable material from the wreck, which they did so successfully that, in time, it caused an almost insurmountable problem at the Benicia Post Headquarters.[3]

No rescue ship dared breach the pounding surf to recover the carefully stored supplies at Camp Castaway; freighting the material overland southward to Port Orford proved impossible due to high cliffs and various natural obstructions; portaging the salvaged items in heavily loaded wagons northward along the beach to Umpqua was an exercise in futility. Camp Castaway and the valuable cargo lay in the heart of Indian territory...to abandon the supplies to the whim of Indian thievery was unthinkable, but to maintain a contingent of trained Dragoons at *full pay* to cavort vacation-like about the beach and surf was the height of folly.

Kerosene lamps burned far into the night at Fort Benicia as the General Staff paced the floor and nervously chewed on burnt-out cigar stubs. Official stomachs churned and growled as acids, borne of frustration, fomented and gnawed. Gentlemanly debates became lost in shouting matches; respectful silences turned to insulting confrontations; lifelong friendships fell by the wayside.

At last, a faint glimmer of hope pierced through the pall of the smoke filled room. "A Surplus Sale! Yes, sir, a real honest-to-goodness genuine As Is, Where Is, Surplus Sale!" A sure-fire way to recoup the Army's losses, pay off Captain Naghel for the loss of his ship and get these troopers back to digging ditches or slaying Indians like proper soldiers ought to be doing. "All that is needed, Gentlemen, is an Officer of the Quartermaster Corps to proceed north to handle the details."

This last statement, of course, brought on a lot of paper shuffling and averted eyes. An Officer? But Camp Castaway lay isolated in unexplored Indian country. After all, the amount of material salvaged really didn't require the presence of an Officer and besides, there was the annual Spring Ball coming up and....

All eyes turned slowly toward the end of the table where Morris Miller, Junior Officer and Assistant to the Quartermaster, sat. Noting the chain-of-command surrounding him, Miller astutely surmised his bottom-of-the-totem-pole position left him no choice but to accept the mission.

The next morning the young man bravely

---

[2] Only twice before had this particular area been visited by white men, once in 1826 by Alexander McLoed and his small band of trappers and again the following year by Jedediah Smith and his group of adventurers.

[3] 2 anchors, 7 lots of chain, 90 barrels of pork, 16 barrels of beef, 7 barrels of sugar, 1 barrel of molasses, 7 barrels of beans, 8 barrels of vinegar, 8 barrels of rice, 53 barrels of hardbread, 245 sacks flour, 7 boxes soap, 1 large iron boiler, 2 tins turpentine, 1 keg (25 lbs) black paint, 15 shovels, 3 coils hawser, 1 box and 1 keg powder, 7 parcels rope, 1 coil hemp, 2 buckets, 1 keg (100 lbs) white lead, 4 stoves and part fixtures, 1 box sheet copper, 1 side leather, thimbles, standing rigging, 2 iron boat davits, 7 boxes harness, 1 can oil, 5 barrels salt, 2 ship's compasses, 2 copper gudgeons, and 1 hawser. Later, two complete wagons, 2 wagon saddles and 12 horse collars would be added.

packed a few personal items and with grave misgivings boarded a coastal steamer headed for that vast unknown called "Oregon Territory." The first mishap in the Jr. Quartermaster's odyssey occurred when a slightly confused ship captain ran the vessel close in to shore, assured Miller his embarkation point was at hand and ordered him rowed ashore. Fortunately just before the seamen landed him, they discovered their captain's mistake. A band of hostile Indians lay in hiding behind the low-lying brush...with much cursing and splashing of oars, the straining crew managed to turn the landing boat in the swirling surf and beat a hasty retreat to the ship. The incompetent captain showered Miller with profound apologies, then headed north for Port Orford. He missed the Port, passed Cape Blanco, Coos River and Camp Castaway, sailed on beyond the Umpqua and finally managed a right turn into the Columbia River. The ship's lookout sighted St. Helens before the captain ordered the anchor dropped. Needless to say, the Junior Officer insisted upon being returned at once to Port Orford, and this time, the captain fared better on the return voyage. At last, Miller stood with feet firmly planted on the sands of Port Orford.

Here Miller enlisted the aid of several mule-skinners and commandeered the garrison's sickly grain-starved mules. The group wended slowly over tortuous terrain toward Camp Castaway. High cliffs, downed trees and dense, fog-shrouded swamps challenged their every turn. The last portion of the fifty-mile journey consisted of swimming mules and men across the Coquille and Coos Rivers.

In spite of extensive advertising, San Francisco shipping interests evinced little interest in the intended Government Surplus Sale. Word of the sale spread to small, remote settlements along the Oregon and Washington shores. Three men from Umpqua "City" trekked thirty miles south to Camp Castaway to inspect the goods, but it was soon apparent they came more out of need for company than

an interest in the sale. After chatting with the Dragoons, the Umpqua men conducted a cursory examination of the goods, but "...allowing we're all farmers we'd have a right hard time getting one of them anchors to work like a plow" declined to purchase.

A few straggling peaceful Indians wandered by, but their offer to trade roast salmon and a few mangy beaver pelts was not what the Army had in mind as a means to recoup their losses.

Assistant Quartermaster Miller soon realized the Camp Castaway Surplus Sale was a miserable failure. He retraced his steps back to Port Orford in a last ditch effort to complete a sale, but met with failure. He met with Naghel, the skipper of the ill-fated *Captain Lincoln*, and the two men joined forces for the benefit of their mutual interest...Miller, to carry out his assigned mission and Naghel, to assure his reimbursement for the loss of his ship. They contracted with the south-bound schooner *Fawn*[4] to pick up two wagons, plus tack, in San Francisco and, on the ship's return trip, to deliver the items at Winchester Bay on the Umpqua. The Jr. Officer and the land-locked skipper then proceeded to Winchester Bay to await delivery.

A week later and some seventy miles north at Umpqua "City" they tried, but failed, to interest the settlement's three occupants in the Army's beached wares. Miller and Naghel marched upriver to Gardiner, a settlement founded some months prior as the result of the wreck of the sail ship *Bostonian*. The town's two inhabitants likewise refused the sale offer. The disheartened salesmen retraced their trail to Winchester Bay, there to await the *Fawn*'s arrival.

Miller accepted delivery of the wagons and tack and immediately dispatched them south along the smooth beach to the site of the wreck. He and Naghel remained behind to find a ship, any ship, with a captain brave enough, or foolish enough, to run the gauntlet of the Coos Bay bar. Miller informed Benicia Army Headquarters of the difficulties in im-

---

[4] Lost at Cape Perpetua, 1856.

plementing this latest plan. His dispatch read, in part, "The difficulty attending the undertaking arose from the fact that no vessel had ever been into the Kowes [Coos] River, nor was it supposed that any vessel *could* enter it...." The two men reasoned that if a ship could safely cross the Coos bar, then the two wagons on their way to Camp Castaway could be utilized in transporting the salvaged goods from the campsite, across the sand spit (a distance of about a mile) to the west shore of the bay and there loaded aboard the waiting vessel.

After exhausting negotiations, they chartered the brig *Nassau* which was in the process of unloading at Gardiner on the Umpqua. Captain Naghel agreed to sail aboard the *Nassau*, act as pilot over the dangerous Coos Bar, then stay with the ship until she safely anchored opposite the campsite on the east bank of the spit. Somehow Miller and Naghel conveniently neglected to mention that Naghel, except for shipwrecking on the Coos Spit and tromping around it with the mule train, possessed no local knowledge of the bay and its dangerous bar. But be that as it may, the good captain sailed with the *Nassau* while Jr. Officer Miller raced back to Camp Castaway in an optimistic fervor. The Dragoons began moving the goods to the inner side of the spit on April 30th and completed the task by May 4th.

The *Nassau*, beating before a brisk southwest wind, triumphantly crossed the bar on May 5th. She cleared three and a half fathoms at low tide. On the 24th of May, just two months to the day that Jr. Officer Miller reluctantly accepted his assignment to conduct the Great Government Surplus Sale. He sailed into the Benicia Army Post with the supplies, the troopers, and valuable knowledge of a grand new bay.

The Army considered the episode a costly affair, but in time it proved worthwhile. Within a year the three settlers from Umpqua, Pat Flannagen, his brother James, and their friend James Breen (who originally came to Camp Castaway to inspect the goods) moved to the area. The Dragoons, Baldwin and Brack, joined the new settlement when they finished their hitches in the Army.

Local deposits of coal were discovered in 1853 by drovers of a mule train. Enchanted with the area, half of the forty mule-skinners elected to stay and settle. The brig *Nassau* played the most important role in all these events, for without her safe entry and exit over the dangerous and unknown Coos bar, establishment of one of the most vital harbors between San Francisco and the Columbia River would have been delayed for years. The *Nassau*, unfortunately, enjoyed life for only a short time following her brave exploit of Coos Bay. On July 22nd, after making a spanking return run from San Francisco, the happy ship struck on the south spit of the Umpqua and became a total loss.

Surplus sales have, apparently, been around for a number of years. The Aug. 26, 1851 issue of the *Statesman* carried the following: "Sale of war items at Washington. Muskets 50¢, Swords 47¢, 2000 cartridge boxes $40, Bayonets 786 per 100, 750 gun stocks 2½¢ ea, 75 tents $112...." Added to this announcement was the comment, "a great chance for Cuban invaders?"

OH! THAT WILD, WILD WEST

The romance and excitement of western America's early frontier life captured the hearts of eastern Americans and Europeans alike. Rough-and-tumble prospectors, stagecoach bandits, cowboys and Indians supplied fertile ground for such popular writers as Mark Twain and Bret Harte. Europeans, starved for news of relatives now migrated to the "New Land,"[5] avidly read glorified newspaper accounts of a buckskin-clad frontiersman brandishing a bowie knife in one fist and a six-shooter in the other as he single-handedly held painted savages at bay. Few Europeans questioned the authenticity of these heroic-proportioned tales.

---

[5] Not all immigrants stayed. Records reveal that from the vast amount of newcomers each year, there were many who through fear, loneliness or disappointment returned to their homeland. Over 18,000 packed up and left in 1855 alone.

The following letter, written by Louis Scholl from Fort Dalles in March of 1856 to his parents in the Bavarian Alps, convinced the old German couple that America's frontier was truly the wild, wild West. One might well imagine Herr and Frau Scholl reading to the Burgermeister and numerous friends their son's latest communique describing his less-than-simple excursion from San Francisco to Fort Dalles:

Fort Dalles, March 1856. My last lines of February [sic] will have reached you safely, they were dated from San-frco this time they come from the Columbia River in Oregon, whose banks at the present are alive with thousands of hostile savages.

"Ooooh," gasped the villagers surrounding Louis' parents.

"Ach, Papa, I told you he never should have gone."

"Hush, Mama, so everyone can hear what he has to say," chided the older man.

...from its source [Columbia River] to its mouth in the broad sea, the noise of weapons resounds. In the North to the British possessions, in the south through the Sierra Nevada to the 41st degree of latitude the howling of savages resounds with the screams of terror of ravished wives and daughters and scalped men, yes, even the infant is not spared, his brains plastered on the smoking huts of the farmers.

Louis Scholl, one of three brothers who left Germany to seek their fortunes in the United States, worked in New York for two years before setting out for Missouri. Once there, the vast wilderness stretching out toward the west beckoned and he crossed the plains for California in 1852.

He found employment with the United States Army as a map-maker and, under the supervision of Col. E. J. Steptoe, charted routes between Salt Lake City, Oregon and California. In pursuit of one of these mapping expeditions, Louis Scholl boarded the ship

Republic, which was headed north to Oregon and Fort Dalles (Vancouver) with a small army detachment and supplies.

I left San Francisco the 20th of February[6] on the steamboat Republic, an old, miserable washtub. Our trip was not one to give pleasure. The first day at sea, "old Neptune" demanded his tribute, since a sharp North wind threw everything on the ship into disarray, Groans and moans were heard everywhere, Uphill, downhill the ship rocked, we were alternately thrown from the deepest abyss to the most awesome heights. I crawled out of my cabin in order to turn over my deep sorrow to the fish. The water rushed over me on the foredeck, like a raging stream, and at times the bass voice of the 2nd Captain sounded out.

I really wished for myself that I had been pursuing a life full of activity after months-long boredom; also had a premonition from the stormy clouds, which only too soon were rattling over me. The 2nd day at sea a storm broke loose. Our washtub groaned and moaned. Sea upon sea broke over our ship and like a stream poured into our cabin. From the sweet dreams in which I found myself on the greening Plains, which I will always chose in the future (especially when drowning is so near before one's eyes), I was suddenly awakened by the running to and fro above on the foredeck, A shout rings out and in the next moment all sickness is forgotten. On hands and feet, I crawl (swim) to the steps, over which the sea water was plunging like a waterfall, I reach the foredeck, The ship is saved from the flames—the last cask of quicklime was thrown overboard.[7] We had 80 of them on board and crew and passengers competed with one another in throwing them overboard, before the heat could burst their bands and burn through the floor.

Toward evening the storm quieted, and no one suspected that still greater danger awaited us.

"Ooooh!" the wide-eyed group exhaled in unison.

"Papa, you write to that boy and tell him to come home at once!"

Papa adjusted his glasses, cleared his throat and continued with the letter. "Toward evening the storm quieted,...oh no. I just read that. I begin again. Let's see; oh yes, here."

---

[6] Actually, it was the 23rd. The night before at Gold Beach, near Port Orford, Captain John Poland and many of his men (10 remained behind to guard the camp) attended an Anniversary Ball. That night, Indians attacked the campsite and killed eight men; two of the ten guards escaped through the woods. The following day the Indians tricked Captain Poland and Indian Agent Ben Wright into visiting their village...both were killed; Poland's heart was cooked and eaten. The rest of the day saw every house on the Rogue River below the big bend (60, in all) burned and 31 persons massacred.

[7] Quicklime reacts to water in an exothermic manner and, at times, with explosive violence. This type of cargo has burned and sunk numerous ships.

The next day, it was 20 minutes after 2 o'clock the cry "Fire!" resounded for the 2nd time, and in a few minutes the middle of the ship was enveloped in thick smoke, which was growing thicker by the second. The firemen (stokers) clambered to the foredeck; however, the engines calmly continued to work, in spite of the fact that the engineer had to leave his post, The sea had pretty well become calm. Land was likewise visible some 20 miles away. We found ourselves 25 miles from Port Orford. Steering the ship steadily with the wind, it was decided to put up sails and with double speed our tub shot through the foaming flood. Women and children were, during this time, brought into the rear cabin on the foredeck, Some were ordered into the 4 boats. I myself with a young officer took the watch of one under our protection. With cocked weapons we remained quiet spectators. The entire crew was assigned, partly to the pumps, partly to carry water. The engineer, before he left the engines still had the presence of mind to start the pumps. At the beginning no one knew, where the location of the fire really was. The under-foredeck was chopped through during this time, the smoke broke through the cracks at various places and became more dense. 2000 lb. of powder, designated for this post, were in the hold under the cabin, and only by the greatest exertion was this quantity of powder, together with 50 boxes of cartridges, thrown overboard. Half suffocated, the bearer threw the last cast from the foredeck. We approached the land with a rushing rip-swell; we are only 10 miles away from terra firma. The crew, as well as the passengers, especially the stokers, behaved with exceptional calm, no yelling and running was noticeable. The location of the fire is finally discovered and the smoke decreased. The engine is working with great speed, and the thought forces itself upon me, whether the "boilers" could stand the double heat; if not, the ship will fly into atoms in a few minutes. The boilers have a thick woolen covering, which has been put on to hold the heat, and I know for sure, this will spread the fire to the foredeck, scarcely half an inch away.

At first death in the flames stared at us, then this thought cooled itself off in a wet grave, and finally there appeared before my eyes a trip in the air by the explosion of the powder or the bursting of the engine. With anxious expectation I count the revolutions of the wheels, whose velocity steadily increases, and finally takes on a furious speed. But suddenly also this premonition falls. The wheels are almost stopped. The coal-fire is about to go out. At the same time the engineer takes his post, giving the Captain the answer "I'll stay with her until the last breath." About 5 o'clock we reached the nearest land. (Rocks, islands) away from the continent, against which the breakers broke with a terrible roar, only 5 miles farther and we are in Port Orford. At the same time, the fire was contained through the joint strengths of the crew and passengers, and the ship was saved. By sundown we reached Port Orford, a small port about one-half mile square. The anchors were cast, and soon the foredeck was covered with curious people, to announce the sad news of the murder of 18 settlers with women and children in their neighborhood. The Rogue River trail scarcely 25 miles away. The place is a Govt. post; 1 company of artillery is located there under the command of 2 officers with whom I crossed the plains last year, Major Reynolds & 1st Lt. Chandler. The indians massacred everything that fell into their hands. Some of the settlers living nearest saved themselves and their families at the block-house,[8] but how many perished, can not be determined for a long time. The fire in the neighborhood lasted the whole day. (gunfire?) For 2 nights the men did not close an eye. The number is so small, 80[9] against hundreds of savages. However, on the return voyage, our ship took back 70 men of the 4th regiment to strengthen the place.[10]

At midnight in bright moonlight our ship weighed its anchors and continued its course northward. On the middle deck there were 60 mules; what these animals endured during the fire I will leave to the reader. Packed in like herrings, unable to lie down, it is incomprehensible to me that we lost none. The forage was thrown over-

---

[8] Charles Foster, under cover of darkness, arrived at Port Orford with the news that 130 men, women and children were under siege at an unfinished blockhouse at Gold Beach called Miner's Flat. Relf Bledsoe, a lieutenant and survivor of Poland's decimated group, had, with great foresight, concentrated all people and stores in the area at Miner's Flat in anticipation of a siege from which no force in the area could deliver them.

[9] Major Reynolds dare not divide his few men. The settlers numbered only 50 and demanded the Army remain to protect the families. Six men, H. C. Gerow, John O'Brien, Sylvester Long, William Thompson, Richard Gay and Felix McCue volunteered to take a whaleboat and supplies to the defenders at Gold Beach. The boat overturned in the surf in sight of the besieged settlers who watched the Indians rush forward and butcher the men in the water. Two other attempts were made to rescue the people of Gold Beach (Whaleshead). The schooner *Nelly*, owned by Captain Tichenor, failed due to adverse winds; the schooner *Gold Beach* with a volunteer company of men was thwarted by high surf.

[10] After 31 terror-filled days and nights of savage Indian attacks, the besieged settlers harkened to the far-distant, faint sound of military fifes and drums. In true wild-west fashion, 2 companies of United States troops from Fort Humboldt marched over the horizon and saved the outpost just in the nick of time.

board in the thoughtlessness, neither hay nor oats can be found for them, and with good luck we reached the Columbia River in 2 days, during which time they never saw fodder. Of the beams, which served them for feed, not one was left, the poor mules ate wood like corn.

The second day, as I mentioned, we crossed the Sand Bar, 2 times our heavily laden ship ran aground, This Bar is the most dangerous along the entire Pacific. I saw several wrecks bedded in the sand on the shore. We reached Astoria toward midday; it is a rocky place surrounded by thick fir forests. The dark green firs make the shores of the Columbia River green, thicker for about 200 miles upstream from its mouth, and always reminded of our old Father Rhine, whose water separating me from the homeland, carried me down to the wide ocean.

Real nutshells called steamboats, some scarcely 40 feet long, are the only means of keeping communication open in Northern Oregon. It has few roads, and they are very short: to keep the connection between settlement and the nearby village, is very difficult, the woods too thick and the lowland roads too muddy; foot paths, called trails, wide enough for a single pack or riding animals, which hundreds of years ago were followed by indians, cross the land in all directions.

Our steamboat landed in view of Fort Vancouver. The salute of the place with the boom of cannon had to be omitted, since all our munitions were thrown overboard. You have already, most likely, often heard the expression "fort" but you must not imagine a fortress as they are found in Europe. It is just a depot of the government with one or several companies of soldiers, no mention of fortifications. The Hudson's Bay Co. neverless erected a regular fort, formerly 2 octagonal towers diagonally flanked by the trading post which is surrounded with 15 foot high treetrunks set vertically in the earth; the towers are each equipped with 6 cannon. However, one burned down recently. In front of the dwelling of the English Governor I saw 2-36 pounders.

Our government is already in negotiations to acquire this place through purchase 500000 [*sic*] to have control of the various Indian tribes by itself, and at the same time to retain a reserve for our animals. It is the only place along the entire Columbia River, from its mouth to Walla Walla, which can found for such a purpose. Only a few houses are here however, with the expiration of the English titles, this will doubtless be the location of the largest city in Oregon. Large ships can reach here at low water level.

Permission to reprint the Louis Scholl letter was graciously given by Priscilla Knuth, Executive Editor of the *Oregon Historical Quarterly*. The letter, donated to the Oregon Historical Society by Mrs. Geraldine (H. Dean) Guie was translated from its 19th century German by Rev. Carl F. Nitz. It appeared in Vol. LXXXI, #2 of *Oregon Historical Quarterly*, Summer, 1980.

THE *SAMUEL ROBERTS*

Thousands of settlers joined the great migration to the Pacific coast in the mid-1800's. Although the majority of pioneers came by land, many adventuresome souls braved the dangerous sea routes. A fierce rage for discovery possessed the people, whether it be to develop mineral wealth, townsites or Oregon farmland. Exploration parties roamed from the Klamath River[11] to Puget Sound and from the Montana Territory to the Pacific Ocean.

Seventy-some men met in the spring of 1850 in San Francisco to formulate plans for locating the Klamath River where they intended to establish roads, town and businesses to accommodate future argonauts. Out of that meeting came the birth of the Winchester-Payne Exploration Company.[12] The well-financed group chartered the schooner *Samuel Roberts* and manned her with a four-pound carronade. After mining a fire-gutted San Francisco hardware store for over a half-ton of nails, screws, hinges and other "hard" items for cannon shot and equipping themselves with small arms, thirty-five company men set out in the well-supplied vessel in May, 1850 and pointed their ship's bow northward.

The ship's owner, Captain Lyman, assigned management of the ship to Peter Mackie, Robert Griffen and Second Mate Sam Smith, an Englishman with a bit of knowledge of the ocean. In spite of an ample amount of Doctorates sprinkled throughout

---

[11] Through an error in surveying computations, John Charles Fremont located the Klamath River in Oregon Territory.
[12] Herman Winchester and brother, Dr. Henry Payne, Dr. E. R. Fiske and Dr. J. W. Drew were the "brains" of the expedition.

the participants, navigation proved to be "by guess and by golly." The vessel plowed steadily northward, the Klamath beckoned, but the men unwittingly sailed by and eventually reached the mouth of the Rogue. When they discovered their objective now lay far to the south of them, the group opted to explore the Rogue's uncharted waters. Six men manned a boat and set out to sound the channel. It overturned; two of the six drowned. The four survivors were rescued by some two hundred or so Indians who had lined the shore and were interested only in acquiring the white men's clothing.

In the interim, the schooner managed to make it across the bar. When the crew discovered their shivering, naked comrades being ushered about in a most undignified way by wild, war-whooping savages, the crew bravely anchored the vessel with the intent of sallying forth in a rescue attempt. Unfortunately they soon found their ship swarming with local redskin inhabitants, whose intent was not to harm their white captives, but to appropriate the ship's stores. Only a minimal amount of fur trading ensued as the natives carried off load after load of goods. A company man later noted the thieves "exhibited the ingenuity of a London pickpocket." Clothing disappeared, along with the eye glass of the ship's quadrant...glass beads tucked in a shirt pocket quietly slipped out through a hole gnawed in the cloth. Indians alongside the schooner started nails with their teeth and peeled copper sheeting from the hull; one aborigine attempted to saw through the ship's anchor chain by repeatedly diving under water and working on the links with his iron knife. The explorers, alarmed lest their ship be dismantled beneath their feet, fired the carronade and dispersed the bandits. A hasty vote decreed they set sail for the north to explore the Umpqua.

The *Samuel Roberts* entered Coos Bay and rounded what is now called Winchester Bay. Shouts from shore greeted the argonauts. Jesse Applegate, Levi Scott and Joe Sloan, having come downriver on an exploring expedition of their own, had expected to meet the United States surveying schooner *Ewing*.

Total cooperation blossomed all around, for in this vast wilderness there was land enough for all and Indian reprisals seemed a thing of the past since there had been no massacres since Jedediah Smith's unfortunate encounter some years prior.

The *Samuel Roberts* bumbled upstream for about eighteen miles while the inept explorers became totally mesmerized by the stream's beautiful shoreline. A gravelly bar at the foot of a high cliff grounded the schooner in eight feet of water and, as the tide ebbed, held the ship captive. The argonauts, with little to do as they waited for high tide on a balmy August day, took advantage of the ship's ample brandy supply in the interest of safety...all aboard feared the distant danger of one or more snakes swimming from shore to ship with the intention of biting as many passengers as possible. After riotous indulgence and the advent of high tide, the *Samuel Roberts* floated free of the obstruction, which the crew christened "Brandy Bar" (a name it bears to this day).

During the following three weeks, the company selected sites for the future towns of Elkton, Winchester and Scottsburg. Their work finished, the group split up with some members returning to San Francisco and others remaining to sell lots. Those who returned to California dispatched the brig *Kate Heath* with pre-fab zinc houses, milling machinery and other necessities.

Oregon unfortunately passed a land law in September of that year that prohibited companies and non-residents from land speculation. All too soon the company partners found themselves either deeply in debt in San Francisco or stranded in the Oregon wilds.

The adventurous company made only one real discovery during their ill-fated expedition; it was the remains of another unlucky exploring schooner, the *W. L. Hackstaff*.

MURPHY'S LAW

"Don't worry Captain, I know every rock on the Oregon Coast," bragged the pseudo-pilot. At that very moment the ship bumped heavily, bounded up and over an underwater obstruction. "See, there's one of 'em now!"

CONFEDERATE CHICANERY

When news of Lincoln's re-election in 1864 was received at the city of Albany, the major portion of the population held a public celebration accentuated with the firing of numerous salutes from the mouth of an old Sandwich Island shipwreck cannon that had been mounted in the town plaza.

This so infuriated the rebel sympathizers, they organized a raiding party and that night, stole the piece, towed it to the Willamette River and tossed it in.

The relic was re-discovered by a company excavating gravel January 11, 1933.

GUSSIE TELFAIR

A dying Confederacy, brought to its knees by the Federal blockade, gave birth to the *Gertrude* in Greenock, Scotland. She came forth as a racing blockade-runner equipped with a propeller for speed and maneuverability. Her telescoping funnel, when lowered, gave her minimum silhouette upon the horizon; her two masts pivoted for the same reason. When all three devices were brought into play, they transformed the *Gertrude* into a totally different ship. She carried anthracite coal, blew off steam underwater and, in the event of a shot wound in her bowels, could switch steam from one boiler to another without loss of vital pressure. She was a deceptive child of the times, created for smuggling and dedicated to earning a king's ransom for her greedy owners who encouraged the struggling Confederates to fight on a little longer.

She sailed immediately for Bermuda waters to join her sisters at the Ports of Nassau and Saint George. Blockade runners, whether coming from England or heading to Charleston, found these harbors vital to their open dealings. Secrecy, necessary in every other port in the world when dealing in smuggled goods, was not needed here. Twenty or thirty blockade runners at a time anchored in the warm, safe waters as they awaited orders, time or tide to sneak past the Union ships lying in wait off the coast of the southern states.

Gertrude traveled in a group reminiscent of the days of swashbuckling pirates; reckless captains and mates who never in their lives earned more than $50 or $75 a month now received as much as $10,000 in gold for a trip to southern harbors with contraband cargoes. These swaggering seamen spent their days in port drinking, chasing buxom girls and laughing at President Lincoln's proclaimed blockade of the Confederate ports, which covered an incredible amount of some 3,500 miles of coastline and 187 ports.

The United States Navy sailed only one steamer on the Atlantic coast and owned only forty steamers in a ninety-ship fleet, most of which were stationed in the Pacific and Indian Oceans or were in decommission.

The rowdy seamen also laughed because President Lincoln's choice of words created a tactical blunder that destroyed the effectiveness of his proclaimed blockade.[13]

Blockade-busting combines and corporations formed overnight...Collie & Company, Fraser, Treholm & Company, the "Bee" boys. All conspired to reap huge profits by aiding the rebels. They bought and sold goods, supplied captains and crews and built ships like the *Gertrude* to carry their illicit goods past the inadequate line of decrepit, old ships the Federals anchored beneath the frowning forts of the southern ports.

Gradually, the Northern Navy grew, imperceptibly at first with a ship added here and the next day, a ship added there...slowly,

---

[13] In regards to internal conflicts and in international legal jargon, ports should be merely described as "closed." Only when at war with a foreign country is the word "blockade" acceptable. Thus, due to a poor choice of grammar, Lincoln officially recognized the Confederacy as a sovereign country and thus left Europe free to trade with a recognized nation.

the Federals lulled the South into a fatal trap. By the end of 1861, the Union owned 137 fighting vessels, 79 of them steamers. By the war's end, 600 ships enforced the blockade while the remainder of the fleet hammered away at port after port, denying the rebels any succor from outside sources.[14]

Blockade-running profits at 100% to 200% soon rose to an astronomical 2,000%. The South clamored for goods; southern belles demanded the latest in European fashions, corsages (cloth accouterments for bodices), catalogues and toothbrushes. Storekeepers demanded tools, fine wines and, of all things, coffin screws. As one merchant explained, "There is no place in the south where these are being made, and the bodies will not stay still in the coffins without them...especially when being sent any distance for interment." The Confederate government, preferring cargoes of cannon and munitions to feminine frills, eventually passed a law against importing contraband contraband.

Most of the blockade ships were low, sleek, fast sidewheelers and a few resembled ships of the British navy. On several occasions these ships boldly flew the Union Jack as they steamed past the Federals in pretense as neutral "observers" and anchored in Wilmington or Charleston harbor. Then, while under the teeth-gnashing gaze of the deceived Union officers they unloaded their goods, wined, dined and waited for the opportune moment to make good their escape.

The *Gertrude* lay just off Eleuthera Island in the Bahamas on April 16, 1863. The USS *Vanderbilt* successfully sneaked up on the sleeping blockade-runner and took her captive; just how the *Vanderbilt* accomplished this feat is lost in the mist of time, but the *Gertrude*'s illegal activities ended when she sold in prize court and became an integral part of the U.S. Navy, skippered by Acting Master Walter K. Cressy and assigned to the West Gulf Blockading Squadron under Rear Admiral Farragut. Armed with two 12-pounder rifles and six 24-pounder howitzers,

the *Gertrude* captured on the tenth day of her new role in the U.S. Navy her former sister blockade-runner *Warrior* after a nine hour chase. The *Ellen* fell prey to her prowess in January of 1864. She sailed back and forth between Galveston and Sabine Pass. In February of 1865 she gobbled up the *Eco*; in April of the same year, she pursued the famous Confederate runner *Denbigh* and, although unable to capture the culprit, she forced her to jettison over fifty bales of cotton valued at $10,000. The *Gertrude*'s elated crew recovered and shared the bounty.

The U.S. Navy decommissioned the *Gertrude* on August 11, 1865 at the Philadelphia Navy Yard; shipping magnate John Wright bought her on November 30, re-documented her as the *Gussie Telfair* and brought her to the west coast.

She wound up in the hands of Holladay & Brenahm for the Portland-Victoria route. New owners, Frank Bernard Company, gave her a work route from Portland to Coos Bay, Empire and the way-stations.

The *Gussie*'s end came as mysteriously as her capture. She sailed inside the Coos Bar, nearing Rocky Point under the command of Captain Butler. Suddenly she swerved from channel and drove hard into the bank for a total loss. The cargo and passengers were taken off with no trouble. The wreck of this exciting ship sold for a mere $550. Parts of her can still be seen at very low tide near the first jetty on the east side of Rocky Point.

NOTHING TO IT

The shortest distance between two points is not always the quickest. In days gone by, west coast seamen drove or guided their stout ships up and down the fog-shrouded waters off the far edge of the United States with a skill that seemed to be rather commonplace. Bar changes due to run-off, bottom changes from earthquakes or seaslides, rocks growing

---

[14] Historians, for the most part, have chosen to ignore the thrilling action of the blockade runners. During the conflict, the Federals captured 1,165 prizes and ran ashore, burned or sank 335 vessels for a total loss to the Confederacy of $30,000,000.

A sleek blockade runner for the Confederacy, the captured Gussie Telfair *became a model U.S. citizen prior to her loss at Coos Bay.* *(Coos County Historical Museum)*

where there had been none before (Noonday Rock, for example), fog, snow, unimpeded current and wave action galloping from the far Orient like Attilla the Hun's ravishing hordes combined forces in a conspiracy to trap the unwary seaman.

A Coast and Geodetic Survey superintendent wrote in 1918 of his admiration of west coast mariners, "The fact that disasters to passenger-carrying vessels do not occur oftener than they do is not due to accurate charts based on complete surveys, but rather to the skill and vigilance of those in command."

An old sailing master wrote sailing directions for the benefit of an eastern deepwaterman en route to Astoria for the first time:

After you leave San Francisco and are northerly, avoid Blunts Reef, it has dangerous rocks and reefs, but get within hearing distance of the Blunts Reef Lightship so as to hear the navigational signal to plot a new course... there is a change of current

in either direction that may prove dangerous, don't forget to use your compass, stars, sun or whistle buoys and lights, if you can see shore, use your eyes for land-marks, if you can't then try dead reckoning, simply calculate your speed from your last known fix and figure compass direction, strength of wind and current set then take soundings and some samples of the bottom while you hollar or sound your whistle to get an echo off the shoreline cliffs, it's simple.

Then the old duffer concluded:

...just don't hit the bar when you come in.

COASTAL DESCRIPTION
From Blacklock Point to Tenmile Creek[15]

From Cape Blanco for 112 miles to Yaquina Head the coast is almost straight and trends in a NNE direction. It differs from the

---

[15] See nautical charts numbers 18580, 18587 and 18588.

southern coast in that the mountains are lower along the coast, the high ones being inland. The shore consists of high yellow sand dunes and cliffs broken by bold rocky headlands. These headlands are of moderate height and are backed by low pine covered hills. There are few outlying dangers, the outermost being Blacklock Point, Coquille Rock and Cape Arago.

From Blacklock Point the shore continues rocky with cliffs gradually decreasing in height for 1.5 miles north, then for 11 miles the shore is a broad sandy beach backed by dunes and long narrow lakes. The tree line is at an average distance of 0.2 mile from the beach. From the end of the sand beach for 2 miles to the mouth of the Coquille River the shore again consists of rocky cliffs 40 to 80 feet in height. There are several outlying rocks up to one-half mile from shore. Covered dangers extend 1.6 miles west from Coquille Point. The land directly behind this stretch of land is flat and wooded and rises to heights of 1000 feet two and a half to three miles inland.

Coquille River is 18 miles north of Cape Blanco and is used for the barging of lumber from the two mills nearby. The larger of the mills is at Bandon, 0.8 mile above the entrance. The smaller mill is three miles above, near the highway lift bridge. Some fishing boats operate from Bandon and there is a small fishery near the city pier.

Coquille Point is 0.6 mile south of Coquille River entrance. Several rocky islets extend 0.5 mile off the point and rocks showing breakers in any swell extend 1.2 miles west and one mile northwest of the point.

Coquille Rock is 1.6 miles NW of the point, covered 28 feet and breaks in heavy weather. A long low area of shifting dunes lies north of the river entrance. The conical tower and dwelling of an abandoned lighthouse is near the inward end of the north jetty.

The entrance to Coquille River is protected by jetties, a seasonal light and fog signals on the south jetty. A marked dredged channel leads from the entrance to the lower sawmill at Bandon. In August, 1977 the depths were 7 feet to 11 feet at midchannel from the en-trance to the port dock, then 9 feet and 13 feet at midchannel to the lumbermill dock. The *channel is subject to change* and the deepest water is not always on the entrance range. Local knowledge is essential when the bar is rough. The reported depth above Bandon is about 6 feet to Coquille, 21 miles above the entrance.

The Coast Guard patrol station at Bandon is on a bluff on the south side of the channel about 0.6 mile inside the entrance. A boat patrol is maintained by the Coast Guard from May 15 to October 15. The 390-foot port district wharf on the south side of the channel entrance has been condemned for commercial use. The city pier, 175 yards east of the port wharf has reported depths of 16 feet at the face. Gasoline, diesel and water are piped to the pier. There is a small craft basin between the city pier and the port district wharf. There are about 180 berths; gasoline, diesel, a launching ramp and marine supplies are available. There is a machine shop at Bandon. A highway bridge three miles above the entrance has a lift span clearance of 28 feet down and 74 up. An overhead cable east of the bridge has a clearance of 72 feet.

Prosper, four miles above Coquille River entrance, has a small craft basin; berths are available with depths 12 to 15 feet.

North of the entrance of the Coquille River sand dunes extend for about four miles and then are succeeded by cliffs.

Fivemile Point, 6 miles north of the river entrance, is a rocky cliff 60 feet high with a cluster of rocks, 10 to 40 feet high extending more than 0.3 mile offshore.

North of Fivemile Point the coast consists of cliffs 40 to 80 feet high, which rise to heights of 100 to 250 feet 2 miles south of Cape Arago and are cut by deep gulches, named Seven Devils. Many rocks of various sizes and shapes border the beach.

South Cove, immediately under the south point of Cape Arago, is used extensively as a summer anchorage by small craft and fishing boats with local knowledge.

Cape Arago, 29 miles NNE of Cape Blanco, is an irregular jagged point projecting about a mile from the general trend of the coast. There are no high mountains immediately behind the cape, and it is conspicuous only when the mountains in the interior are obscured. The seaward face of the cape, 2.5 miles long in a northerly direction, is a narrow sparsely wooded tableland 50 feet high, with rugged and broken cliffs and outlying rocks of the same height as the cliff. Immediately off the cape are reefs extending northwest for about a mile. A small cove near the north end, inside the reefs, is sometimes used by small boats with local knowledge.

Cape Arago light shows at 43°20.5'N and 124°22.5'W; it is 100 feet above the water on a 44 foot white tower attached to a building situated on a rocky partially wooded island close inshore, 2.5 miles north of the cape. A radiobeacon and fog signal are at the station.

Baltimore Rock, 0.6 mile NW of Cape Arago Light is covered. It is a ledge, 11 feet under and usually breaks. It is the outermost rock of a ledge extending from the lighthouse island in a NW direction. A bell buoy is 450 yards N of the rock.

Coos Head, 229 feet high, 1.8 miles ENE of Cape Arago Light is on the south side of the entrance to Coos Bay. The cliffs are about 100 feet high and terminate in several small rocky points with sand beaches between them. A Coast Guard station is on the south point at the entrance 0.3 mile east of Coos Head. The buildings of the U.S. Naval facility for the oceanographic research are conspicuous on the bluffs just SW of Coos Head.

Coos Bay, 33 miles N of Cape Blanco, is used as a harbor of refuge and can be entered at any time *except in extreme weather.* Coos Bay is one of the most important harbors between San Francisco and the Columbia River, and one of the largest forest products ports in the world. Principal foreign exports are logs, woodchips, lumber and paper. Coastwise trade consists of gravel, plywood, gasoline and distillate fuel.

From the entrance, the bay extends NE for about 8 miles with widths of 0.3 to 1 mile, then bends SE for about 4 miles to the mouth of Isthmus Slough. The dredged channel through the bay is bordered by marshlands and is intersected by several sloughs.

Coos Head, Umpqua River Light and the Cape Arago Light are good guides to the entrance. The sand dunes north toward the Umpqua River are prominent. The entrance to the bay is protected by jetties. A light with a seasonal fog signal marks the north jetty. A lighted whistle buoy is 1.8 miles WNW of the entrance. The channels are marked with lighted ranges, lights, buoys and daybeacons.

Vessels should make sure of the entrance range before standing in close. There is *usually a current* sweeping either N or S just off the jetties, and this should be guarded against. The entrance ranges should be watched carefully until clear of all dangers. The south current is often encountered *during the summer.* With strong south winds during the winter the current sometimes sets *to the north.*

Approaching from *any* direction in thick weather, great *caution is essential.* The currents are variable and uncertain. Velocities of 3 to 3.5 knots have been observed offshore between Blunts Reef and Swiftsure Bank, and greater velocities have been reported. The most favorable time for crossing the bar is on the last of the flood current, and occasionally it is passable *only at this time.* Anchorage for deep-draft vessels with good holding ground, sand bottom, can be had about 1 mile NE of Coos Bay Lighted Whistle Buoy K. Anchorage for small craft can be had almost anywhere in the bay outside the dredged channels and below the railroad bridge.

Guano Rock is located on the south side of the entrance channel and is 280 yards NW of Coos Head; it uncovers only at extreme low water. A submerged section of the N entrance jetty extends about 300 yards W of the visible jetty; and a submerged section of the south entrance jetty extends about 100 yards west of the visible jetty. Because of submerged jetties, it is reported that there are breakers in these areas most of the time. *Extreme caution must be used at all times.* A submerged jetty extends 500 yards off the E shore of Coos Bay just inside the entrance, 0.8 mile NE of Coos

Head. In entering with a strong NW wind large vessels have difficulty in making the turn and may set toward the submerged jetty.

The mean range of tide at Coos Bay is 5.6 feet. The range between mean lower low water and mean higher high water is 7.3 feet. A maximum range of about 12 feet could occur. Observations near the entrance indicate a current of 2 knots. The greatest observed was a little over 3 knots. Predictions for the entrance may be obtained from your Tidal Currents Table. During runoffs on the ebb, 5 knots have been reported near Guano Rock.

Marine supplies are available at Coos Bay and above-the-waterline-repairs can be made by several machine shops on the waterfront. The largest marine railway in Coos Bay is at the mouth of Isthmus Slough and can handle vessels to 400 tons, 120 feet long and 32 feet wide with 12 foot draft. The cities of Coos Bay are served by U.S. Highway 101 and SP railroad. There is also the North Bend Municipal Airport just to the NW.

South Slough, shoal and navigable only for small craft, extends 4 miles south from its junction with Coos Bay near the entrance. A marked channel extends south from the junction for about 0.6 mile to the Charleston Boat Basin, and then for about 0.5 mile to a highway bridge. The midchannel depths are about 11 feet through the entrance to the boat basin and 7 to 10 in the basin and about 10 feet at the bridge.

Charleston Boat Basin is operated by the Port of Coos Bay; across the slough is Barview. The basin is used by commercial and sport fishermen; there are 500 berths available, served with electricity, gasoline, diesel, water, ice, etc. There is a marine railway for craft up to 70 feet long and 22 feet wide. Electronic repairs can also be had. There is a Coast Guard station on the south side of the basin.

The west shore of Coos Bay as far as the bend is formed by a sandspit covered with dunes and partly wooded. In some places the dunes are as much as 90 feet high. On the east shore and above the bend are low rolling hills with houses and several prominent buildings.

Haynes Inlet and North Slough, which join the bay through a common inlet on the north side are navigated by small boats. A causeway with a fixed bridge having an elevation clearance of 18 feet joins the State highway fixed bridge over Haynes Inlet, the latter having an elevation clearance of 32 feet. The power cable over the common entrance of the two streams has a clearance of 67 feet.

From Coos Bay for 19.5 miles to Umpqua River the coast consists of sand beaches and dunes backed by low hills. The mouth of Tenmile Creek is 13.7 miles north of Coos Head.

SHIP DISASTERS
Blacklock Point to Tenmile Creek

Acme 10/31/1924 Steam schooner, wood, 416 tons, built by John W. Dickie at Alameda in 1901. Ashore at Coquille River bar, a total loss.

Adel 2/10/1920 Gas, 35′ in length, built in 1905 by W. Holland. The passenger-freighter servicing the route between Gardiner and the Coos Bay area burned in the bay and became a total loss.

*Admiral Wainwright 1927 Steamer, steel, freighter, two-decked, two masts, 1,783 tons, 221.5′ × 40′ × 22.5′, built at Long Beach, California in 1913. Aka as *Grace Dollar*. She and her crew of 27 became stranded on the Coquille River bar.

Advent 2/18/1913 Three mast schooner, 399 tons, built at North Bend in 1901 and owned by Simpson Lumber Co. 151.5′ × 35′ × 13.6′. Captain M. Eaton attempted crossing the bar on a calm day, but the wind failed; the ship's anchors failed to hold and the currents carried her onto the spit. The ship sailed in ballast en route Santa Rosalia-Coos Bay. The Coos Bay lifesaving team rescued captain and crew while the surf pounded the ship to pieces.

Alaska 12/1869 140 ton schooner owned by Rufus Calhoun. Under Captain Godfrey, the three-year-old ship put out from Coquille with a cargo of lumber for Hawaii and ran afoul of the bar.

Alvarado 3/16/1945 Steam schooner, steel. With 1,250,000 feet of lumber, the 2,500 ton vessel broke

---

* Refloated or partially salvaged.

in two when hit by a 95 mph gale eight miles north of Coos Bay. Her crew of 31 were all saved. She lies on the rocks, 100 yards off shore.

Arago 10/20/1896 Steamer, propeller, 947 tons, built by Union Iron Works of San Francisco in 1885 for the Coos Bay coal trade. 207′ × 30′ × 16′ with a compound engine of 22 ″ × 44 ″ × 34 ″. Originally the *Emily*, she wrecked at Coos Bay bar in 1891 with the loss of one life. This time, she hit again at the same spot; Joseph A. Younker of the U.S. Life Saving Service was on duty both times and participated in rescuing both crews. The ship struck a submerged portion of the jetty and sank; 13 of 37 died. Loran C, chain 9940; W:13539.52, X:27770.23, Y:43927.78.

Baltimore 1861 Schooner. Wreck was discovered on the rocks 0.6 mile northwest of Cape Arago Light. Half of the ship lay in Lat. 43°21′03 ″N, Lon. 124°23′00 ″W. Her stern appeared at a place known as "Tunnel Point." Very little else is known of this wreck.

*Bandon date unknown Steam screw, 642 tons, 172′ in length, built by Kruse & Banks at North Bend in 1907. She wrecked six or so times and, after being laid up at Bandon, was sold Mexican and named the *Atrevedo*.

*Baroda 8/29/1901 Bark, British, built in 1891 at Dunbarton, Scotland. She was reported wrecked in 1894 also. After the 1,417 ton ship sank at Coquille, it was raised and rebuilt into a barge. She sank again and was re-raised in 1910 at Esquimalt. She may still be afloat.

Bawnmore 8/28/1895 Steamer, British. En route Nanaimo-Peru when she went ashore in the fog and wrecked 15 miles south of Bandon.

Brush 4/26/1923 Steamer. A 5,543 gross ton ship belonging to NA&W Steamship Co. She struck on the north side of the reef just off Sunset Beach near Cape Arago where she quickly settled and broke up. Lat. 43°19′00 ″, Lon. 124°30′00 ″.

Captain Lincoln 1/13/1852 Three mast schooner. Captain Naghel commanded this 300 tonner whose bones now lie in the Dunes National Recreation area near Horse Fall Beach, 1½ miles south of the parking area off the Dunebuggy trail. See story, "Captain Lincoln and the Great Government Surplus Sale."

C. A. Smith 12/16/1923 Steam schooner, wood, 1878 tons, 275′ in length, built by Kruse & Banks in 1917. Due to a shortage of engines during the war, the ship saw use as a barge until 1921, at which time she was fitted with steam turbines and twin screws. Under Capt. T. Blomberg, she carried 1,500,000 feet of lumber when she went on the North Jetty of Coos Bay Harbor. 10 of her people died, 14 were saved.

Chansey 5/1854 Little is known of this vessel except that her cargo of coal from the Nathan Boatman mine had to be wagoned 1½ miles to Coal Slough, then lightered out to the ship. Apparently this was the first commercially mined coal in the area and the first attempt to ship it across the bar. Ship and cargo were a total loss at Coos Bay.

Charles Devans 2/1870 This three mast bark registered 253 tons, 155′ × 25′ × 11′1 ″. While carrying a cargo of lumber, she bumped so heavily upon the Coos bar that she had to be towed in and was declared a total constructive loss.

Chinook 4/12/1907 785 ton lumber schooner, en route with a cargo of dynamite Coos Bay-Coquille River. The tug *Columbia* towed her out to meet another tug, but when it failed to show, the *Columbia* towed her back and, while crossing the bar, lost the tow. The *Chinook* went ashore for a total loss on the south spit.

Claremont 5/22/1915 Steam schooner of 747 tons en route San Francisco-Willapa under Captain S. Benson. She struck the extreme end of the sunken Coos Bay jetty. Although the ship and her general cargo became a total loss, the Life Saving crew broke all records with their breeches buoy rescue of 21 crew and 2 passengers at a rate of 1 person every 3½ minutes! The ship, built at Aberdeen, Washington, measured 188.4′ × 38.4′ × 12.6′. She was owned by Claremont S.S. Co. of San Francisco.

Cohansa Lost on Coos Bay bar. NFI.

Columbia 2/17/1924 Steel steam schooner owned by Crowley and under charter to McCormick S.S. Co. when she ended her days attempting to enter Coos Bay. It is said that dissension on the bridge caused the ship to plow into the north jetty and, despite all efforts of the steamer *Homer*, she became a total loss. The ship was built at Wilmington, Delaware, in 1912.

Commodore 1870 Steamer, built at Benicia in 1863. She struck Brown's Point just opposite Bandon.

*Congress 9/13/1916 Steel passenger liner, 7985 tons gross, 424′ × 55′ × 17′. Built in 1913 at a cost of $1,200,000 at Camden, New Jersey, for the Puget Sound-San Francisco run and the largest ship in the Pacific Coast S.S. Line. While just off from Crescent City, Captain N. E. Cousins was notified of a raging fire in #2 hold and immediately ordered the *Congress* to race for Coos Bay. 175 crewmen and 253 passengers banded together in fighting the stubborn fire which eventually spread from the 1231 tons of cargo and engulfed the entire ship. Fortunately no lives were lost and evacuation proceeded in good order. The ship was rebuilt as the *Nanking* and later as the *Emma Alexander*.

C. W. Wetmore 9/8/1892 A rather aptly named whale-back steel steamer resembling a cigar with a foc'sl and bridge. Built in Wisconsin in 1891, she measured 265′ × 38′ × 24′ with 3000 dead weight tonnage and 1075 net. On her first voyage she carried 100,000 bushels of wheat through lakes and locks to the sea, then across the Atlantic to Liverpool. Eventually she was brought around the Horn by Captain Joe Hastings and experienced good luck until she reached the California-Oregon border. From then on, her trip went sour. She unshipped her rudder and drifted unmanageably for several days until sighted off the Columbia by the steamer *Zambesi*, who took her into tow. The *C. W. Wetmore* broke loose coming over the bar and very nearly ended up on the rocks. She was rescued just in time and brought to Astoria, repaired and placed in the coal trade. The *Zambesi* received $50,000 for her rescue efforts. After that, the poor *Wetmore* bumbled around, running aground, crashing into wharfs or banging into other vessels and, as the joke went, hitting everything within sight or sound, Puget Sound, that is. Captain Hastings removed himself from command and the ship was taken over by Captain "Dynamite Johnny" O'Brien, who soon found his vessel ashore in the fog off Coos Bay. She remains there to this day. Her demise proved welcome news to coal-shipping agents, for the *Wetmore* was instrumental in cutting coal-carry prices to $1.35 per ton on the San Francisco route.

Cyclops Spring of 1862 Schooner, en route San Francisco-Coquille. A total loss on Coos Bay bar with the exception of two cross-cut saws and one plow.

*Cynthia Olson 6/9/1952 Lumber freighter, 3117 tons, 310', built at Flensberg, Germany in 1935. The ship, working for Oliver Olson & Co., bumped so heavily upon the Coquille River bar that she sprung her plates and 80% required replacement. The ship was rescued from total loss by the efforts of the *Salvage Chief*, one of the most famous salvage vessels in the world.

Czarina 1/12/1910 Steamer, coastal, 1045 gross tons, 216' × 30.8'. Captain Charles Dugan and a crew of 22 sailed her for the South Pacific Railway Co. when she ran into trouble on the Coos Bay bar. A heavy sea struck the vessel as she crossed, virtually demolishing her bridge. Out of control, she bumped heavily while drifting wildly. The anchor was let go and the ship was pinned down in the breakers, forestalling removal. The crew and one passenger took to the rigging where, numbed by freezing, gale-force winds, they dropped one by one into the churning surf. Only one survived.

Daisy 1907 On the ways at Fair Harbor, the ship, destined as a steam schooner, was destroyed by a forest fire. A total loss before she was ever launched.

Dawn 2/3/1887 Steam scow. Trouble came in the form of a bursting steam pipe and she drifted across the bar to sea. Signals to the *General Canby*, under command of Captain Thomas Parker, were either misinterpreted or ignored, for the scow was offered no assistance. This apparition drifted for nine days while the crew shared only one loaf of bread and a well-gnawed ham bone. Rescue finally arrived in the form of the steamer *Empire* at a point some 75 miles south of the Columbia. The men were taken aboard and the scow towed to Coos Bay, but due to being water-logged, the *Dawn* was abandoned before entering the bay.

Del Norte 1905 Steam schooner, built by M. Turner at Benicia in 1887 and owned by J. G. Wall, a survivor of the *General Warren* debacle. This 100 tonner collided with the *Sea Foam* and went to the bottom off the Coquille River.

D. M. Hall 10/3/1868 Bark. En route in ballast San Francisco-Coos Bay. She became a total loss on the spit. Two died.

*Echo Steam, sternwheel, Captain A. Ellingston. This little 66 footer went down in the Coquille, but was later raised.

Ella Laurena 12/18/1895 Three mast, 223-ton schooner, built at Portland in 1895. The ship anchored off Cape Arago and began unloading lighthouse material. The weather worsened and the crew deemed it safer to go ashore for the night, which proved fortuitous. The next morning they found the ship draped across Ramsay's Reef and a total loss.

E. L. Smith 1/1/1936 64-ton gas schooner. The small freighter was thrown upon the rocks at the Coquille River bar.

*Emily 7/17/1893 Steam schooner. Captain F. G. Lucas. Ship struck and broke rudder. One dead. See *Arago*.

Energy 1862 Brig, lost on the Coos Bay bar. The only survivor, Julius Larson, was an able-bodied seaman from Norway who found work with the Simpson Lumber mill and later became a farmer. He founded the Larson Dredging Co.

Escort 12/21/1886 Steam tug, 88' × 21' × 9', 99 tons, built by James B. Magee and J. Howlett in 1868. Magee was one of the most capable of the bar and ocean pilots on the west coast. The ship's boiler blew in the bay, just off Marshfield.

Eureka 11/30/1899 Schooner, two masts, 123 tons, built by M. Turner at Benicia in 1877. Captain A. F. Asplund. While en route San Francisco-Coquille, she went ashore just north of the river for a total loss.

Express 9/8/1891 Steamer, 62', built at Pleasant Point by H. Sengstacken. Lost by fire near Marshfield.

Fifield 2/21/1916 Steam schooner, 160', 634 tons with 500 hp and twin screws. Captain C. Bakeman. Built for Estabrook of San Francisco. The first *Fifield* was destroyed on the ways by forest fire. Kruse & Banks launched her in 1908. She became a total loss on the south spit at Coquille.

Fort Bragg 9/14/1932 Steam schooner, 705 tons, wood, built at Fairhaven in 1910 by Price. Under Captain John Samuelson, the ship piled up on the south jetty of Coos Bay bar in a heavy fog. She drifted helpless onto the sand 500' inside the jetty where, while her forlorn crew stood by, thousands of people looted the stranded ship.

General Butler 12/8/1891 Bark, en route Port Gamble-San Francisco with one million feet of lumber. The ship lay about 100 miles southwest of Cape Arago as she fought against a fierce gale. When she began breaking up, Captain Parker ordered all hands to abandon ship. Part of her hull drifted to Yaquina where it struck the jetty.

George L. Olson 6/23/1944 Steam schooner, steel, built by Stone at Oakland, 1363 tons, 950 hp, 223′ long. The ex-*Ryder Hanify* became a total loss at Coos Bay.

*Golden Bear 1937 Diesel electric freighter under Captain Louis Van Bogaert. While struggling against high seas, her superstructure, along with several pipes, worked loose. Leaking fumes from the exhaust pipe sickened the crew and they soon became incapacitated. The *Active* towed the disabled vessel to Coos Bay; she was declared a loss and turned into a barge. She now forms part of a breakwater in British Columbia.

Golden West 3/29/1936 Motor freighter, 61.2′ long and 72 tons, built at St. Helens in 1923. Owned and captained by William Crone of California Cargo Co. She was transporting general merchandise when thrown upon the rocks at the Coquille's north jetty. The crew was saved, the ship was not.

Gussie Telfair 9/25/1880 Steam propeller, built at Greenock, Scotland, as the *Gertrude*. 350 tons, 156′ × 21′ × 11′. She served as a blockade-runner during the Civil War. See story, "*Gussie Telfair.*"

Helen E. 4/1951 Motor vessel, a converted patrol boat. Grounded and burned four miles north of Coos Bay bar.

Ida D. Rogers 12/15/1869 Brig, 200 tons, built at Essex, Connecticut in 1856. Owned by N. M. Norton, she was under tow on the Coos bar when the hawser parted and she struck. The helpless wreck drifted in and became a total loss.

Ida M. 9/23/1948 Oil screw, 122 tons, built in 1943. Stranded 10 miles north of Coos Bay.

Jackson On Coos Bay bar. NFI.

*Jenny Thelin 1874 Schooner, two mast, 145 tons, built at Davenport Landing, Santa Cruz, California in 1869 by Olaf Reed. Jack London used her as his model for "The Ghost"; her captain Alex McLean gave London the idea for his "Sea Wolf." The vessel (a notorious seal poacher and smuggler of Chinese) was re-floated after grounding. Eventually she wrecked for good on the coast of Punta Maria, Mexico.

Julia H. Ray 1/26/1889 Schooner, 177 tons, built at San Francisco in 1884. Wrecked on south spit of Coos Bay.

Laura May 1874 2 mast, 127-ton schooner, built by E & H Cousins at Eureka in 1868. While en route San Francisco-Coos Bay, she became lost in the fog and totalled six miles above Coos Bay.

Marconi 3/23/1909 693 ton, four mast, schooner, built by A. M. Simpson at North Bend. En route Coos Bay-Valparaiso with a load of lumber. While under tow, the hawser parted midway across the bar. She drifted onto the south spit and broke up.

Mary Schowner about 1876 Schooner. Captain Alfred Machado and one other person survived the wreck on the Coquille Bar. NFI.

Mary E. Moore 2/23/1927 Steam schooner, steel, 1783 gross tons, 221.5′ × 40′ × 22.5′, built in 1913 at Long Beach, California as the *Grace Dollar*. She sank in heavy seas about the same spot where the *Acme* of the Moore Lumber Co. disappeared 2 years prior. Capt. Karl Rosenblad and his 26 crewmen were rescued by the motor freighter *Admiral Peary* and taken to San Francisco. The ship and her 200 tons of general cargo lie about one mile beyond the breakwater of the Coquille.

Messenger 1876 Sternwheeler, 136 tons, 91″ × 20′ × 6′ with engines 12″ × 36″. Built at Empire City, Oregon in 1872 by Captain M. Lane. Ship burned for a total loss in Coos Bay.

*Monterey 5/19/1900 Power schooner. Got into trouble on Coos bar, struck and was abandoned. She drifted to sea and was later salvaged and converted to a whaler. NFI.

Moro 12/6/1897 Gas schooner, 94′. The vessel was the first good-sized motor boat in the northwest. Built by G. C. White at Alameda in 1894, she was a total loss on the Coquille bar when en route San Francisco-Alsea.

New World Lost on Coos bar. NFI.

North Star #1 1/20/1912 Motor launch, built at North Bend in 1908 by C. A. Johnson. She capsized between Marshfield and the south inlet, killing her captain and 5 passengers. The wreck later drifted over the bar.

Novelty 9/20/1907 Four mast schooner, 168′ long, 584 tons, 39′ wide and 13′ deep, built at Coos Bay by John Kruse. The vessel went on the rocks between Coos and Umpqua.

Noyo 1868 Schooner, two mast, 195 tons, built by J. C. Cousins at San Francisco in 1861. She struck the Coos bar heavily enough to spring her planks and allow water to get into her cargo of lime. The lime ignited and the ship was beached. She burned to a total loss.

Occident 5/3/1870 Barkentine, three mast, 297 tons, 130′ × 31.5′ × 9.6′, built by Simpson in 1867 at Coos Bay. She ended her days on the Coquille bar.

*Oliver Olson 11/3/1953 Steam freighter. This 300 footer was built as the *Point Bonita* in 1918 by Albina Engine and Machine Works. Insured for $250,000, the vessel and her crew of 29, under Captain Carl Hubner, ran aground at the tip of the south jetty at Coquille. She was partially salvaged before the hull was filled with rocks and became an integral part of the jetty. Her sister ship, the *Cynthia Olson*, had grounded near the same spot the previous year, but was salvaged.

Onward 2/25/1905 Schooner, 3 mast, 134 feet, 276 tons, built in 1901 by S. Danielson at Parkersburg. En route San Francisco-Coquille, the ship attempted to cross the Coquille bar while under sail. The wind died, leaving her to drift into the spit.

Oregonian 1/16/1877 Two mast, 246 ton schooner

built by John Kruse at North Bend in 1872. An error in reckoning caused the $20,000 ship to go ashore for a total loss five miles south of the Coquille River.

Osprey 11/1/1912 Gas schooner, 58'. Under Captain Johnson, the vessel capsized on the bar, righted herself and ran direclty onto the rocks where she immediately broke up. Her cargo of salmon and five tons of gold-bearing sand bound for Coos Bay were lost with the ship. All five men aboard drowned.

Ozmo 5/17/1922 765-ton gas freighter, aka *Osmo* and *Hugh Hogan*. Some confusion exists as to the actual location of her loss, since she's been reported as totalled on Port Orford Reef and as striking the south spit of Coos Bay bar while under tow.

Parkersburg 11/18/1889 Schooner, 100', built in 1883 by S. Danielson. She missed stays trying to enter Coquille during a storm (this is unusual because a vessel usually fails to complete a tacking maneuver due to too *light* a wind). Ashore and a total loss one-quarter mile below Coquille River.

Perpetua 10/24/1876 Brig, 276.85-ton, valued at $17,000, en route Coos Bay-San Francisco. The brig foundered in a gale just outside Coos entrance and when she shipped a heavy sea, it filled the foc'sl and started her deck load of lumber. The *Perpetua* went on her beam ends. An entanglement of rigging and mainmast that had gone by the boards formed a raft which drifted until the 27th before breaking into three parts. The captain and four men clung to one piece, two crew rode the second and one man hung onto the third. The schooner *Rebecca* picked up the survivors 92 miles west-by-south of Cape Gregory. Four died in this tragic mishap.

Port of Pasco #510 12/12/1953 Barge owned by Upper Columbia Towing Co. Wrecked on the north spit jetty, cargo saved.

Quadratus 1856 Schooner wrecked and delayed the building of Simpson's sawmill until the cargo of mill machinery was salvaged from the Coos Bay bar. NFI.

Randolph 4/15/1915 Gas schooner, 60', 42 tons. Vessel struck rocks of Coquille River bar and rolled over. Three died on this Herman Bros. built, five-year-old vessel. Rescuers chopped a hole in the bottom of the beached wreck and successfully saved the trapped engineer.

Sacramento 10/15/1905 130-ton, two mast, centerboard schooner. A total loss when she stranded four miles north of Coos Bay.

Santa Clara 11/2/1915 Steam schooner, wood, 1588 tons. Originally named *John S. Kimball* and later *James Dollar*. Built at Everett for the Portland-San Francisco S.S. Co. Under Captain August Lofstedt, she struck an uncharted shoal while entering the Coos Bay bar near south entrance. Her seams opened and flooded the engines. 16 died in this wreck which totalled the ship. Her whistle was salvaged and used at the Weyerhauser Mill in North Bend.

Sinaloa 6/15/1917 Auxiliary gas schooner, 1648 tons. This Norwegian-built ship sailed under the American flag, en route San Francisco-Astoria with Captain James Sannaes in command. She ran ashore someplace in the vicinity of Blacklock Point after she struck a reef in the a.m. hours. Ship and her cargo were a total loss; crew was saved. The *Sinaloa* is variously listed as north of Cape Blanco, three-quarter mile south of Cape Blanco station and 300 feet south of Cape Blanco (it was foggy at the time of the wreck).

Sujamico 3/1/1929 Steamer, 3285 tons, built in 1920. Stranded and a total loss eight miles north of Coos Bay.

Wallacut 11/3/1918 Barge, 708 tons, built at Portland in 1898. While en route under tow Port Ludlow-San Francisco with lumber, the tug tried to cross the bar at low tide. The *Wallacut*, under Capt. Charles Emson, struck the sunken portion of the jetty.

Welcome 1/11/1907 Sternwheel steamer, 56', built in 1900 at Coquille by S. H. McAdams. She became stranded at Myrtle Point.

Western Home 11/13/1904 Schooner, 135 tons, two masts, built by Ludwig Mortenson at Maine Prairie, Sacramento, in 1874. Ashore on the north spit of the Coquille River.

Y M S #133 2/21/1943 Minesweeper, 260 tons. She became caught in a trough one-half mile from the harbor entrance; vessel rolled over and over toward shore. 13 died.

Much of the 5543-ton Brush *still graces the bottom off Simpson Reef.*　　(*Coos-Curry Museum*)

Bearing the ever popular name Columbia, *this vessel became a total loss at Coos Bay.*
(*Oregon Historical Society*)

Orderly evacuation and calm seas prevented the loss of life when the passenger liner Congress *took fire.*
(Columbia River Maritime Museum)

Unidentified steamer crossing the Coos Bay bar. *(Marshall Collection)*

Czarina, *a hard working coaster in better days.*

Disabled on the Coos bar. The life crew were unable to shoot a line against the fierce wind and could only stand helplessly by as the ship's crew took to the rigging.

Fewer now, and totally at the mercy of an unforgiving sea, half-frozen men wonder who will be the next to go.

A clean beach and a forlorn mast. Having been satiated with the lives of 24 men the sea is quieter now.

Largest piece of the steamer Czarina *to come ashore.* (Coos-Curry Museum)

A thirty-foot breaker engulfing the Fifield *at Coquille.* (Wayne Jensen, Jr. collection)

Awaiting low tide, the first of many hundreds of people gather to loot the Fort Bragg. *The helpless crew could do nothing; the ship was totally stripped.*   (Coos-Curry Museum)

Total devastation, bound for Valparaiso, the 693-ton Marconi *got only as far as the south spit of the Coos bar.*

Hard-working George L. Olson *before and after, a total loss at Coos Bay.* (*Coos-Curry Museum*)

The wreck of the Novelty *became a sort of coffee stop for the Drain-Coos Bay stage line.*

(Coos-Curry Museum)

Straight as an arrow, the Oliver Olson *impaled herself on Coquille's south jetty; partially salvaged topside, the larger portion of her hull is an integral part of the jetty today.*

(Columbia River Maritime Museum)

3

Umpqua River to Salmon River

THE *ALASKAN*, 1889

"It's no use, Captain, I'm too old. I can't make it.... I'd rather go down with my ship." Oldtimer Al Hahles, ship's steward, sealed his fate with unshakable resolve.

"Al, you've sailed by my side for years; c'mon, you can make it. It's now or never. At least, give it a try. I've got to cut 'em loose mighty quick."

A stubborn shake of the gray-haired head gave silent notice that Captain R. E. Howe's plea fell upon deaf ears. Slowly, deliberately, the skipper lifted his axe above the manila line which trailed off the taff rail....

The new sidewheeler *Alaskan*, anxious to serve her masters well in the lucrative Northwest trade, first dipped her graceful bow in the mighty Columbia's cool, green waters early in the spring of 1884. Although handsome and speedy, the 1,718-ton steamer's gluttonous appetite for mountains of precious coal ended her every trip in the red for the Oregon Railway and Navigation Company.

Captain James W. Troup, with Archie Pease as Pilot and Thomas Smith as Engineer, guided her first sailings on the Columbia; soon, hotly competitive river races with the elegant stern wheeler *Telephone* resulted whenever the two giants steamed a parallel course. The rakish *Telephone*'s reputation as the fastest steamer on the Columbia became legendary under the capable hands of veterans Captain W. H. Whitcomb and his side-kick, Chief Engineer Newton Scott. On a few memorable occasions, the deep-drafted *Alas-*

kan, skillfully guided by Captain Troup and Pilot Pease, nudged her arch rival into the river's cramped, shallow waters. The *Alaskan*'s loyal passengers cheerily waved a fond adieu to the *Telephone* wallowing far behind trying to thrash her way free of these cleverly laid traps.

On May 11, 1889, the *Alaskan* (after doing a stint in the Puget Sound area) pulled out of the Oregon Railway and Navigation dock at Astoria in ballast for an overhaul in San Francisco. Her long brass whistle challenged the mighty Columbia; she maneuvered into the stream and headed for the open sea.

At 11:30 a.m. that Saturday morning she crossed the treacherous Columbia River bar and, with a slight wind from westward, enjoyed smooth sailing on her southerly course.

Cape Foulweather light bore ENE fourteen miles at 11:00 p.m.; the barometer sat at 29.85 with passing rain showers and wind up slightly.

Sunday morning heralded a drastic weather change. The steamer labored in rough seas eighteen miles offshore at 43.5° latitude. Captain Howes ordered a trisail set forward to keep her head to the wind and sea, then rang the brass telegraph for dead slow.

The staunch *Alaskan*, never designed as an ocean-going vessel, began to feel the strains of her hard-driven racing days on the Columbia. The ever increasing winds lifted her high, then slammed down wave after punishing wave upon its wildly rocking victim. Seesawing side-to-side in rolling heaves, the ship's leeward paddle wheel lifted clear of the water to slap at the wind while its counterpart plunged deep into the frenzied water only to fight against itself. This futile cycle sustained its deadly cadence as the ship wallowed, pressing her body ever deeper into the sea.

Captain Howes fought for footing in ankle-deep water and heard his drenched slicker-clad seaman relay Second Officer Weeks' message, "...and the after house worked loose with the bolts pulled clear through the planking. We're stuffing blankets and ticking in the cracks, but he says to tell you we're still taking in tons of water!"

"Very well," the veteran skipper shouted above the wind as he tried to dodge a washtub full of water that crashed through the broken bridge window. The icy brine dripped from his bearded face, "Stand by," he ordered, "while I check with the engineer." Howes pulled the plug from the brass speaking tube marked *Engine Room* and blew into its opening. He heard metallic clanks filtering through the tube, then a muted voice, "Engine room."

"Mr. Swain, are the pumps holding up?"

"Just a moment, Captain, I'll check." A pause, then, "Seems to be doing all right, but I don't think they can handle another drop."

"Very well, Mr. Swain, thank you." Quickly replacing the cap, the captain turned and shouted above the wind's roar, "Tell Mr. Weeks to keep that water out at all costs!"

The seaman acknowledged, then lurched to the bridge door. He fought it shut against the gale's force and disappeared aft in the wet darkness.

A rending, splintering crash warned of a new peril. The heretofore stout oak and iron bulwark cap and stays, port side just forward of the wheel, gave way and began twisting back and forth in the raging seas. Then, with a sickening finality, the beleaguered cap guard plunged overboard, taking with it the upper sheer and topside strakes. Captain Howes immediately recognized this fatal open wound as a killing blow...nothing

could prevent his ship from going to the bottom now. With great reluctance the disheartened captain signaled "Prepare to abandon ship," thankful he carried no passengers.

It was now midnight; launching the life boats in a raging, refrigerated ocean presented a near impossible task. The first boat swung out, returned with the speed of a torpedo, then splintered into matchwood against the ship's iron hull. Boats 2, 3, and 4 dropped successfully and managed to stay afloat with bow lines tethered to the stern of the wallowing parent.

One by one the crew, clad in life preservers, grasped the trailing manila aft line and lowered themselves hand-over-hand into the bucking, wildly pitching boats.

A shout went up, "There, there! Look, a light, just to the north!"

A flurry of excitement took hold of the men remaining aboard the floundering vessel. They procured two rockets from the deckhouse locker and, in spite of the spray, managed to ignite them. The rockets' arching fingers stabbed skyward; in their brief splash of exploding light, the crew's hope of rescue quickly faded for the other vessel was in the same difficulties.

A shrill scream pierced the storm's roar as a crest of green sea hurled the ship's Quartermaster Shielderup into the exposed wheel well. The huge thirty-two foot paddle wheel's inexorable revolution delivered its screaming human victim to the deep, dark cavern of the well's dripping, moss-covered lair.

The drenched skipper addressed those remaining on deck, "All right, Al, you don't want to go. Swain, how about you?"

The Chief Engineer shook his head in refusal.

Turning, the captain faced the last man. "Denny, this is your only chance," he pleaded; his shoulders seemed slumped under the weight of doomed men.

"No, Captain, I'll stay."

The master of the dying vessel poised his axe, then severed his men's last link with salvation with one quick chop to free the boats before the bigger ship pulled them under.

Officer Weeks excused himself and went below, followed by the aged steward. Neither was seen again.

The ship began sinking quickly now. Howes raced to the upperworks and dived into the water as far as possible from the doomed vessel. When he surfaced, the *Alaskan* was gone.

A piece of broken flotsam supported Howes for about an hour before he spotted Engineer Swain. The two joined forces to collect more of the bobbing wreckage and formed a makeshift raft. The storm's fierceness abated, but the high seas still heaved in mountainous waves.

Dawn's light revealed three survivors, a hundred yards off, clinging to the top portion of the *Alaskan's* pilot house. Against the advice of Captain Howes, Swain tucked two pieces of wood under his armpits for support and paddled toward the forlorn group. The sea's swift currents imprisoned the weakened seaman and carried him off to eternity.

Captain Howes spent thirteen hours in the bone-chilling sea, twelve of them upon his hands and knees on a small piece of wreckage, before Captain Edward McCoy of the tug *Vigilant* rescued him.

The three men on the pilot house were rescued, as were the men in First Officer Wood's life boat. Quartermaster Shielderup was picked up alive, but died shortly afterwards. His badly mutilated body, one leg nearly severed, was consigned to the deep with appropriate services.

THE MYSTERIOUS WRECK OF 1808

Oregonian, Dec. 25, 1852

Mr. Editor, Sir,

Mr. Henry R. Schoolcraft, the well known writer on Indian language, manners and antiquities, who is now engaged under authority of the Department of the Interior in preparing a great national work on these subjects, has lately written to me making inquiries as to the existence of any mounds or earthworks in Oregon and more especially some that have been reported to exist on a river supposed to be the Deschutes or Falls River. He says, "I mentioned to you, I think, an old Oregon manuscript journal now in my possession. Mr. LaSalle, who was the author of it, was wrecked in 1809 in the ship Sea Otter on the Pacific coast about a hundred miles south of the Columbia River at False Cape. From this he crossed the continent to the head of the Red River of Louisiana with three men. He describes certain large earthworks on a river named Onalaskala east fork and the tribe who occupied the country which he calls Onalus which word I suppose denotes the Mullalas of the Willamette. Will you inquire into this matter? I am putting this discussion on a broad basis, and think it might be expedient in so partially explored a region as Oregon, to call attention to it by a few lines in an Oregon newspaper."

As a fact of considerable interest, I beg you to insert this and would ask the same favor of other papers in the territory in hopes that our mountaineers may be able to throw some light upon it. Any communications may be forwarded either direct to Mr. Schoolcraft at Washington or through

GEORGE GIBBS, Astoria

Henry Rowe Schoolcraft (1793-1864) was, without a doubt, the 19th century's earliest and most important authority of American Indian culture. In addition to being an explorer in his own right and the discoverer of Lake Itasca as the source of the mighty Mississippi, Schoolcraft spent much of his life living among the redmen whose mores he greatly admired. He authored a monumental work titled *Historical and Statistical Information Respecting the History, Conditions and Prospects of the Indian Tribes of the United States*, a six-volume project still held in high esteem by present-day anthropologists.

Mr. Schoolcraft's request to Mr. Gibbs for information regarding "certain large earthworks" situated near the Deschutes or Falls River and of Indian origin brought hoots of derision from all sides.

"Never," scoffed Peter Skene Ogden, Hudson Bay trapper and the one man most likely to be acquainted with the surrounding country. "Mounds in the Mississippi Valley, mounds in Ohio and Illinois, but Indian mounds in Oregon? Bosh!"

"Mullalas called Onalus? Absurd," thundered another writer to the *Oregon Statesman* on January 1, 1853.

Thus, the eminent historian's question went unanswered in the affirmative. Eventually, with the exception of a passing scoff later in the century by Hubert Howe Bancroft, Schoolcraft's folly faded into history.

It is unfortunate that Schoolcraft's inquiry to Mr. Gibbs of Astoria failed to impart specific details or, if it did, then Mr. Gibbs neglected to mention pertinent information regarding a rumored crossing of the continent by a party of men that occurred *after* Lewis and Clark's 1805-6 and *prior* to the 1811 settlement of Astoria. Both men, it appears, were too involved in their favorite subject of Indian lore to be lured into investigating the escapades of four shipwrecked men.

Schoolcraft verifies LaSalle's journal by a brief resume.

In a manuscript journal of adventures by V. Lavalle, a native of Philadelphia, put into my hands in Philadelphia, by James Duane, Esq., he describes a journey performed in 1809, with three men, from the Pacific, across the Rocky Mountains, till they reached the source of Red River of Louisiana. On crossing the Willamette valley and Des Chutte river, he describes, near the latter, extensive ruins of earth works. No testimony to the existence of such works can be found in modern Oregon. — H.R.S.

pg. 663 Appendix — Antiquities

With that concluding thought, Schoolcraft dismissed the entire matter. The existence of the journal has become a debatable subject among modern historians, for no trace of the manuscript was discovered among Schoolcraft's effects.

In 1927 the *Oregonian* article of 1852 drew the attention of Rev. J. Neil Barry, an avid Oregon historian. He authored a short piece titled "A valuable manuscript which may be found" for the *Washington Historical Quarterly* in 1928. His article sought further information of the four distressed sailors' continental journey.

The Rev. Barry's article piqued the curiosity of Judge Frederick W. Howay of British Columbia, who was considered the absolute authority on fur trade, shipping and early colonization of the Pacific Northwest. The Judge investigated every ship on both sides of the Atlantic that bore the name *Otter* or *Sea Otter* that may have journeyed to the west coast of America during that period of time. He discovered two *Otters*; one was an American brig owned by T. C. Amory and Obrier Keating and commanded by Samuel Hill; the other was an American ship out of Boston in 1796 and owned by Dorr & Sons, commanded by Ebenizer Dorr. He also located a *Sea Otter* of 1786 that sailed off the Oregon coast under the command of Captain Hanna. All three ships charted one or more journeys through the area in question, but none wrecked nor was he able to associate them with the name of LaSalle (Lavalle).

Judge Howay submitted an article for the *Washington Quarterly* in 1933 in which he concluded,

. . . there is an air of improbity about the whole matter. And there I leave the puzzle in the hope that some one else may be able to offer a solution.

Judge Howay's failure to shed light upon a shipwreck shrouded in mystery is not surprising, for secrecy in the fur trade of the eighteenth and nineteenth centuries was the key to a successful business venture. Investors, ship owners and captains deliberately relayed false destinations to Harbor Masters, friends or relatives before embarking upon a journey.

In 1791 Mr. Sydenham Teast of London, owner of the 101-ton *Ruby*, issued the following written orders to Captain James Bishop:

You must keep your orders, your route and instructions a profound secret, and if you are not in want of assistance have no intercourse (especially while you are making trade) with any other ships and you must not part with any of your articles of trade in barter with other ships, not even for furs.

These matter-of-fact instructions left no room for doubt; had the *Ruby* wrecked along the coast, her very existence would pose a mystery to today's historians. Fortunately, the *Ruby* survived and by a lucky turn of fate she, her orders and her captain provide us with another clue to the tale of Mr. LaSalle and the questionable wreck of the *Sea Otter*.

Captain Bishop arrived on the Oregon coast in 1791. During the course of his travels, he crossed a bar at the mouth of a river and sailed into a rather quiet bay which he named Port Sydenham[1] in honor of his employer. Bishop spent the next twelve days trading with the aborigines for their abundant stockpile of furs. He noted they were not to be trusted. He took on fresh river water and replenished the *Ruby*'s larder with fresh game. The *Ruby* successfully concluded her mission and returned to London. Captain and crew alike now held valuable trade secrets of immense worth to rival investors. Their information and services went to the highest bidder. Could one of them, armed with this secret information of landfalls along the Northwest coast, have signed aboard the mysterious *Sea Otter*?

Schoolcraft, in his letter of inquiry to Gibbs, erred in his statement, "...about a hundred miles south of the Columbia River at False Cape."

False Cape lies about 200 miles south of the Columbia, whereas the Umpqua, at 43°50′, is possibly the key to the solution; Captain Bishop reported the Umpqua at 43°40′N.

Although Judge Howay concluded his research of the *Sea Otter* with the feeling of "improbity," he relayed the following information regarding the ghostly ship as written in a Boston newspaper, the *Columbian Sentinel*, on July 25, 1810:

In a Norfolk paper under date 20th June we find an account of four men's arrival from the N.W. coast of America stating they belonged to the ship Otter from London which was lost 22nd August, 1808, 200 miles south of the Columbia river (which lies in Lat. 46 deg. 15′N). They gave no particulars of the wreck.

Once again, a tantalizing hint, the merest taste of a shipwreck that promises, if true, to lay the foundation of a tale that would add four more names to the pioneer heroes of early Oregon and of the nation.

The Judge's research supplied two important clues to the story. One, that the ship *Otter* sailed from London; the other, that the location of the wreck lay 200 miles from the Columbia and thus confirmed the area of False Cape. If the survivors were stranded in the vicinity of the Umpqua, then the trails along the river would lead to the Willamette valley, through or near the mounds, as the shipwrecked sailors made their way across the continent. These well-worn trails were first used hundreds of years ago by the redmen, later by the Hudson Bay trappers of 1824 and followed by Jedediah Smith in 1828.

Anthropologist Gibbs worked hard to clear the mystery of the *Sea Otter* and the Indian mounds. He contacted Dr. John McLaughton and numerous army officers familiar with the valley. He read General Fremont's account, but discovered no mention of Indian mounds. Gibbs wrote, "I myself have crossed from the Willamette valley to the sea 80-100 miles from here. Oddly, I saw a piece of a vessel wrecked long ago in the little bay on which we camped but I don't think it was your Frenchman's." He mentions his search carried him to the land of the Klamaths where "...the rascals did their best to shoot me on one occasion and I had to aid in the burning of some of their best towns."

"Unfortunately," concluded Judge Howay, "the correspondence [referring to Schoolcraft and Gibbs] seems to have been chiefly concerned with the existence of certain mounds mentioned in the [missing] journal."

Thus, the matter of the mysterious Mr. LaSalle and his three unknown companions, a ship's name without a ship and a dubious 2000-mile trek across the continent was summarily laid to rest for the next twenty-eight years.

It re-surfaced through the efforts of a staff writer for the *Oregonian*. Alice Bay Maloney's interests became aroused when she read an extract of a letter from a gentleman at Natchez to his friend at Norfolk that was printed in the August 16, 1810 edition of the St. Louis newspaper *Louisiana Gazette*:

---

[1] Known today as the Umpqua.

Your friend W— has overtaken me at this place, from whence we shall go in company to the Oppolusa country. As usual he is full of news, but what is most surprising he actually brings us something unusually interesting. He informs me that in descending the river, he fell in with a party of four men (or rather heroes) who after suffering shipwreck on the Northwest coast, had not only the spirit to plan, but courage to attempt; and the fortitude to persevere and succeed in one of the most daring undertakings I have ever heard of, viz— a journey across the continent from the Pacific to the Atlantic ocean, with no other provision than their guns with six pounds of powder and 20 pounds of shot. Incredible as this circumstance may appear, the short account given by Mr. Babtiste Lavall to Mr. W—. carried the strongest evidence of the facts.

Mr. Lavall was born in the city of Philadelphia, although a republican himself, yet the attachment of his father and family to the king rendered it necessary for them to remove to Canada after the close of the war, where he ever since has been engaged in the fur trade— That having fallen heir to an estate he went to England to receive it, and there embarked on a trading voyage to the North West Coast on board the schooner Sea Otter of 170 tons and commanded by John Niles— that he was part owner, as well as supercargo— and on the 22nd August 1808 the vessel, cargo and crew consisting of nine souls were all lost in a violent gale, about 200 miles south of the Columbia river; while he, together with Michael Conner, Jean Lozier and Emmanuel Silver were providentially saved by being on a hunt on an uninhabited island— That after waiting some time, in hope of meeting with some vessel, they gave up that point in despair, when he prevailed on his companions to attempt to cross over the continent by land— That after passing through an endless number of strange and savage nations amongst whom they were often detained as prisoners, and suffering every privation and hardship that it was possible to endure they happily succeeded in accomplishing their desperate undertaking.

Mrs. Maloney's discovery of this article confirms Schoolcraft's claim of documentation of this unusual journey. The article not only answers numerous questions and identifies Mr. LaSalle's three companions, it confirms the name *Sea Otter*, background information of her owner and most important of all, it provides a more exact location of the wreck.

Schoolcraft no doubt wrote his letter of inquiry while relying upon his memory of the journal's contents and used the date of 1809 as the year of the survivor's continental crossing rather than the date of the wreck.

The variations in the spelling of LaSalle and Lavalle could be a printer's error in either newspaper account or simply Schoolcraft's error of memory in his letter to Gibbs; the location of the wreck at 100 miles instead of 200 miles from the Columbia again may be attributed to the writer's memory or the printer's error. In any event, the 1810 article definitely confirms that *something* of import occurred on the Oregon coast.

What now becomes intriguing is *where* on Oregon's coast can it be said there exist any islands of a size large enough to warrant a hunting party? Certainly the isolated outcroppings of rock along the shoreline cannot be considered. There remains that nagging location of False Cape and "200 miles south of the Columbia." No islands, as such, exist, but what of the sandspits that resemble islands?

Another possibility arises: if, as a fur trading expedition, the men decided to hunt and trade, then these small rocky islets would provide ample, though less valuable, seal and sea lion skins. A more attractive enticement might be the prized sea otter, who confines itself to the kelp beds which grow in profusion around the rocky outcroppings.

Could the *Sea Otter*, after a long and tedious trip from London, be in need of provisions and fresh water? Could it be possible one of the *Sea Otter*'s crew was a veteran of the *Ruby*'s visit in 1791? This crewman, with his valuable information of landfalls along Oregon's coast, would naturally direct his captain to make for Captain Bishop's Port Sydenham, an ideal location to fill the ship's barrels with fresh river water, trade with the locals (who were not to be trusted) and dispatch a party to one of the numerous river islands to hunt game in relative safety from hostile savages, while at the same time, the *Sea Otter* would be free to move about and attend to other matters.

It is well known that the mouth of the Umpqua begins its shoaling season in late August; the *Sea Otter* wrecked on the 22nd; the river does not scour itself out until the latter part of October.[2] The four marooned seamen well knew, by the very secrecy of their mission, that rescue by a ship would come only by chance,[3] not by design. Their sole chance of survival lay in trekking eastward in hope of finding a land expedition or, as seems to be the case, reaching civilization.

Whether or not the wreckage found by Gibbs was that of the "Frenchman" remains unknown, but his trip from the valley to the sea lends credence to LaSalle's report of the trail that brought the seamen to the Willamette valley where, in spite of derisive hoots and hollers to the contrary, Indian mounds/earthworks *do exist*.

Some 400 mounds of early Indian origin were discovered in an area mostly east of the Willamette bordering Fall Creek and the Calapooya River for a distance of 45 miles between Albany and Eugene. The mounds range in size from 50' to 100' in diameter and 5' to 8' in height. Farmers in the area considered the mounds an infernal nuisance, for their ancient tree growth and proximity to stream beds and river banks rendered them difficult to plow or plant.

Mr. J. L. Hill, in 1883, performed the first recorded work on the mounds. Around the turn of the century, Dr. J. B. Horner of Oregon State College located and removed many ancient artifacts and skeletons. No other serious work was undertaken until the advent of an article titled "Excavations in the Calapuya Mounds of the Willamette Valley, Oregon," written by William S. Laughlin, 1941 edition of *American Antiquities*.

Local farmers such as C. E. Corben, Carl Arnold and Miller discovered Laughlin-inspired field parties of eager anthropology and archaeology students sifting through tons of primal earth in quest of aboriginal knowledge. The Mullalas tribe (mentioned by Schoolcraft), never a very large one and quickly decimated by disease for which they had no immunity, occupied the portion of the

valley and trail described by LaSalle. The Mullalas were ignorant of information or legends regarding the construction or purpose of the mounds; through the course of time their tribe had replaced a large and more powerful community of Calapooyan Indians. The Calapooyans, over a period of centuries, occupied the region on six separate occasions and most likely originated the earthworks.

Modern excavation unearthed arrow points, mortars, scrapers and human remains, which led to the speculation that the flat-topped mounds served as islands of refuge during the winter months when surrounded by water-covered flood plains.

Regardless, Mr. Babtiste LaSalle (Lavalle) and his castaway companions most certainly recognized Indian mounds when they saw them. When, at some unknown future date, Henry Schoolcraft's "important manuscript" is discovered, it promises a magnificent adventure throughout its musty and archaic pages.

THE ORDEAL OF THE
MINNIE E. KELTON

Built in 1894 as a Great Lakes lumber hooker with her wheel house on the foc'scle, the *Minnie E. Kelton* eventually worked her way to the west coast where, after several rebuildings, she banged around doing a so-so job as a typical coastal workhorse.

Under the guidance of Captain James McKenna, the *Minnie E. Kelton* lay just off Yaquina on May 2, 1908 en route to San Francisco with her usual load of lumber. Heavy seas pounded the laboring vessel; her heavy lumber load shifted with a grinding crunch. The resulting shock wave ignited a fire in the engine room and its billowing smoke forced the engine crew from their stations. Water poured in from the overhead, whose seams

---

[2] The brig *Bostonian* came to grief on the bar 40 years later on October 1.

[3] Records show only six ships off the Oregon coast this year: *Belle Savage*, Boston, Captain David Ockington; *Guatimizin*, Boston, Master S. Burnstead; *Amethyst*, Boston, Captain Bowers; *Pearl*, Boston, Captain John Ebbetts; *Mercury*, Boston, Captain W. H. Davis; *Derby*, Salem, Captain James Bennett. None of the ships sailed in the vicinity of the alleged wreck of the *Sea Otter*.

had been opened by the shifting cargo. The ship's pumps failed and Captain McKenna ordered the crew to abandon the low-riding, wallowing ship. Wave after monstrous wave violated the sanctity of the crew's wooden home and tore from them their only means of escape...the lifeboats.

A towering sea engulfed eleven of the men on deck, sweeping them and massed lumber into the churning water. As they grabbed for the gunnells of the floundering smaller craft, storm-tossed timbers beat them into bloody pulps. Chief Engineer C. Lund, Steward Sven Peterson, Cabin Boys R. Little and George Johnson screamed in terror as the crashing waves carried them into the stygian darkness. Twisted deck lines entangled the lifeless bodies of the oiler, fireman and five seamen while splintered, floating wreckage pounded against the doomed vessel. The desperate skipper let go the *Kelton*'s anchors and in the company of the remaining crew members sought refuge in the foc'scle.

All through the night they huddled in the numbing cold while Captain McKenna called roll in an effort to do something...anything. First and Second Mates Martin and Mortenson, Engineer Carney, Oiler Walt Hoffman, Firemen Howold and Hansen seemed in fairly good shape as did Seamen Anderson, Kaskensen and Neilson...no others survived to answer the captain's call.

The seas subsided a bit by morning and the wreck, with only her foc'scle above water, was sighted. The Yaquina life-saving crew put out and took off the shivering mariners. The tug *Washington*, under Captain Nason, towed the derelict to Astoria and grounded her at Smith's Point. The sea deposited the bodies of her victims upon the storm-carved beaches; the body of one crewman was recovered from a lifeboat.

The *Minnie E. Kelton* was re-floated and used as a rock hulk in the building of the Columbia River jetty. In 1914 the disgraced steamer found new friends to rebuild her as the 831-ton *Rochelle*. On her first trip for her new owners, the Columbia Steam Ship Company, she sailed en route from Boat Harbor, British Columbia with a cargo of coal for Portland; the *Rochelle* ran aground on Desde-

mona Sands. Captain Matthews, her pilot, claimed one of the channel lights was out.

Once again, the ship was in peril and caught fire. Captain Kildahl and his eighteen-man crew escaped with their lives, but the uninsured *Rochelle* became a total loss.

STRUAN

The following narration, written by deck-boy A. Th. Madsen, appeared in the Jubilee Edition in connection with *Haugesund Rederiforenings* of 1935:

In the year 1889 the ship-owner Erich Lindöe among others decided to buy the ship "STRUAN" at that time lying in Liverpool. The ship measured 1475 n. r. tons and was 12 years of age. She was paid by £10.000,-. As captain was appointed T. H. Skogland. Towards middle of October the crew was sent from Haugesund. "STRUAN" was docked and was sheathed with copper. The ship was contracted with a cargo of coal from Birkenhead to Iquique. She was fully loaded, 2.650 tons. The voyage started November 1889. It proved to be a hard trip with constant storm. The ship worked hard in the rough sea, at last she sprang a leak. All hands to the pumps, it was a fight for life. The course was made for a harbour of refuge. One afternoon we observed a ship flying distress signal. After a lot of trouble we succeeded in getting the crew onboard "STRUAN". There were 11 men. The ship was a Russian schooner, who sunk the moment after. This reinforcement of the crew was of very good help with the pumps. We arrived at Falmouth, and at this place the damage was repaired. We installed a windmill, and so we could continue the voyage. After many hard turns we arrived at Iquique after 212 days. Here the cargo was discharged and ballast was taken in, and then we left for Vancouver. Now we got an eye for "STRUAN" being a very good sailer. With fair wind the sailer run fast and she made up to 13 knots. After a voyage of 40 days we arrived at Port Discovery. Here we took in a timber-cargo-lumber of great scantling, bound for Adelaide. On the 23 November 1890 we started again and it proved to be a recurrence of the first part of the voyage. Storm on all hands. Generally the sailer was lying for failing stumps. At daybright the 3rd December the wind turned round, and then we could continue in the right course. The press of canvas was increased, and the ship worked hard in the heavy ocean. At eight o'clock she was free. One hour later the first-mate — Sven Höie — found that the ship worked very hardly. He went a trip down in the ventilator where the pumps were installed. He was, however, stopped at the lower deck as the water reached his knees. At once a report was sent to the captain. The hold was soon filled. The proud sailer was on the point of turning over. The yard-arm for foresail was lying in the water. The rigging was cut, and the ship was again coming to rights. At the same time the rigging went down, the helm was broken quite close to the stern frame. Our ship was driving helpless in the stormy ocean. The great logs on the deck menaced to smash everything. A bouncer[4] of about 70-80 feet rushed aft on starboard side, went in the poop through the storeroom, broke down the captains berth and went out through the stern frame something more than 10 feet. On port side aft all was broken down. The stores were ruined. The little saved was kept in the sailcot[5], the only place where we had some cover.

The board from 3/12 to 19/12 was composed of seawet biscuits of which we had enough, and some boxes of milk. We got daily one teaspoon each. We had no drinking water. The 18/12 a sailer was observed. On the 19/12 we run up a flag of distress. The third mate — Mandius Hauge — went up with it. When the flag was fixed a ratling beneath him was broken and he tumbled in the deck and was badly damaged. He had been on board only about one month. The sailer approached our ship with the order: "If we wanted to come on board their ship we had to come at once." We had only a great patched lifeboat. It was rough sea, and after 14 hours toil we succeeded in entering the other ship. We got M. Hauge over in a case.

The ship we had entered was native of St. John. It tasted good to get food and water. We thought we got rather little each time, however, it was best so. We stayed on board for one month. We were crossing in and out by the coast waiting for some one to help us on shore. At last a tug hailed us and took us on board. At full speed we went to San Francisco, and we arrived at this town on the 17th January 1891. We were taken good care of by the concul, and we got quartering in the sailors' home.

Mandius Hauge got medical treatment, and the crew was discharged. As far as I know only the captain, the first mate and M. Hauge returned home to Norway.

Every few years the remains of the Norwegian sail ship Struan *are uncovered by wave action.*
(Darrel Redberg collection)

---

[4] A large log.
[5] A small shelter for the sailmaker. It sometimes adjoins the carpenter's shack.

THE *JULIET* IN OREGON, or
A STATE OF CONFUSION

Oregon Statesman, February 17, 1852

At wreck of schr. Juliet, supposed to be about thirty miles south of Columbia River. This vessel was wrecked on the beach on the morning of the 28th day of January—all hands being saved, and since, a small portion of cargo. The writer of this, former master of the above-named schooner, wishes to be informed by whom ever this may fall in the hands of, of the nearest and best route to Columbia or Willamette rivers, and of the character of the natives, should the route be south. We have many Indians around who are annoying, but disposed peaceably. The portion of the cargo saved is valuable, and we wish not to leave it for the plunder of the Indians. In the summer season a portion of this may probably be got off the beach, but at present it is necessary for us to leave; and whoever this shall reach will confer a great favor by coming or writing with that information they may have. Write by the bearer by all means and if horses can be had they will bring them, six or seven in number, and oblige many persons. I sign for all.

J. Collins

The obviously lost Captain Collins shipwrecked almost a hundred miles south of the Columbia with the Willamette fifty miles inland to the east. He assumed he lay north of both when he wrote, "...the character of the natives, should the route be south."

In spite of his dilemma, the good and able captain remained gravely concerned over his Oregon-bound cargo.

Oregon Statesman, March 16, 1852

Sir, I notice in your paper of the second instant, a letter published over the signature of J. Collins, giving account of the wreck of the schooner, Juliet, and in your remarks you say it [the letter] was brought through the gap by an Indian to the settlement on the South Fork of the Yamhill, and from there forwarded to you by a friend...you were misinformed. The letter came to me first of all, on the South Fork of the Lukiamute, in Kings Valley, in the county of Benton. A meeting was immediately called, a letter written giving the information desired, and [having done] all in our power...we forwarded the letter received for publication. The Indian stated the vessel is wrecked a half day's travel North of the Aquinna Bay, and that he came direct from Aquinna to our valley, and that he was two and one half days in coming.

Chas. Allen, King's Valley

Mr. Allen, his heart in the right place, took all the necessary action in regards to Captain Collins' written plea; however, he also took umbrage with the *Statesman* editor's negligence in publishing proper credit to the first recipient of the shipwrecked captain's letter.

Oregon Statesman, March 16, 1852

I find in the Statesman of the second instant, the letter of Capt. Collins, giving an account of the wreck of the Juliet. That was the first news we had of her loss. It was reported here that the pilot boat will go to the relief of the men.

Yours, V.
Astoria

V. of Astoria, no doubt his heart also in the right place, took all the necessary actions to make public the planned rescue; however, he no doubt planned to thwart rival claims for salvage of the vessel and cargo. His following letter to the Editor reveals his frustration.

Oregon Statesman, March 23, 1852

We have heard nothing of the Juliet during the past week. Capt. Collins was certainly mistaken as to his whereabouts when he wrote the letter which was published in the Statesman giving an account of the wreck. She must have gone ashore in the neighbourhood of Aquinna Bay. It is said that the mail steamer will stop in at the place where she is supposed to be, if the weather will permit.

Yours, V.
Astoria

Oregon Statesman, April 6, 1852

The Juliet was wrecked on the morning of the 28th of January, and since about one quarter of her cargo has been saved in a damaged condition. The portion saved belongs equally to the different shippers by that vessel, and is at present under charge of the first officer and one seaman. There is no doubt that it may be taken off in the summer season, but with little difficulty.

Capt. J. Collins

Oregon Statesman, April 6, 1852

Capt. Collins, of the schooner Juliet, who visited Aquinna Bay during his captivity, informs us that he found there...a fine river, navigable for vessels drawing six or eight feet of water in a distance of twenty miles...but from the appearance he deemed the inlet to be a bad one. He says that the river abounds with oysters, clams, and fish of all kinds. The land around is level and highly productive. The timber has been nearly all destroyed by fire. None of the land in that vicinity is claimed yet.

Editor

Over two months elapsed before Captain Collins saw fit to visit the offices of the *Statesman*. He gave no thanks to anyone for an assist to himself, ship, crew or cargo. He enthusiastically described the bay near the wrecked *Juliet*; the *Statesman* eagerly promoted the newly-discovered area, now known as Yaquina Bay.

The wreck of the *Juliet* and subsequent events gave birth to that incredible group of mariners, the Oregon Oystermen.

A TOUGH BREED, THOSE OYSTERMEN

Ben Simpson, Indian Agent for the Siletz Reservation at Yaquina Bay, complained bitterly in a memo to his supervisor J. W. Perit Huntington that Richard Hillyer, oyster pirate and captain of the schooner *Cornelia Terry*, not only continued to violate the rights of Simpson's oyster contractors (Captains Solomon Dodge of the sloop *Fanny* and James J. Winant of the schooner *Annie G. Doyle*) but steadfastly refused to honor the rights of Simpson's Indian wards.

Captains Dodge and Winant, always forthright in their dealings with Simpson and the Siletz tribe, paid 15¢ per oyster bushel to the reservation and $1.00 per bushel to the Indian oystermen or squaws who tonged the prized *ostrea lurida* from the bottom of Yaquina Bay and still managed a respectable profit upon sale to San Francisco's gourmet restaurants at $10.00 per bushel. Captain Richard Hillyer, on the other hand, refused to pay either the reservation or the Indians for his prize catches by reason of the "free right of all citizens to take fish in American waters."

It fell to the lot of the United States Army and Corporal Royal A. Bensell to settle the dispute. The corporal, a frustrated volunteer from California who enlisted with the idea of protecting his country from the rebellious Confederacy, now envisioned a deadlocked military career as guardian to harmless Indians. Bensell, in command of seven men, departed his post on the Yamhill and headed for Oysterville (Yaquina Bay) in two leaky canoes found in the brush some miles upriver.

Bensell and his tiny expedition received a warm greeting from contractors Dodge and Winant and, following a hearty meal, the group retired for the night.

The following day, the uniformed company properly observed Washington's birthday and noted the national colors run-up by the ships in bay. Army Corporal Bensell then proceeded to the *Cornelia Terry* and, after presenting restraining orders, explained to Captain Hillyer his pending arrest should he continue to take oysters without proper authority from Agent Simpson. The gentlemanly captain greeted Corporal Bensell and his unwelcome news with aplomb, even courtesy, and fully agreed to abide by the orders shown him. Satisfied with the successful outcome of his visit, Corporal Bensell sent his men back to their campsite while he returned to the *Annie G. Doyle* to partake of a meal salt junk and duff.[6]

Fortunately, one of Hillyer's employees exposed his captain's plot to sneak into the soldiers' camp and secretly dose their food with enough laudanum[7] to render them unconscious while he loaded his ship and stood out for San Francisco.

The oyster pirate kept a close watch from his schooner; at the first crack of dawn, he noted the soldiers up and about and quite oblivious to the fact that they should have been in their bedrolls throughout the day. His plan thwarted, Hillyer took the bull by the horns and demanded Corporal Bensell produce a copy of the orders of prohibition.

---

[6] Salted, boiled beef and dessert.
[7] A pain killer, predominantly opium.

When the corporal refused, Hillyer proceeded to load his ship.

Bensell's men borrowed a skiff and quickly rowed out to the schooner, but the irate pirate warned them off, hoisted the *Union Jack* and dared the soldiers to come aboard...which they did and after placing him under arrest, unloaded his ship. Hillyer left immediately for Corvallis to file suit for $15,000 against Agent Simpson and Corporal Bensell. He telegraphed General George Wright[8] in San Francisco for relief from his arrest and cessation of the Army's interference in his legitimate business.

General Wright, a veteran campaigner against the Florida Seminoles and an Indian-hater, ordered Captain Hillyer's release. Had the general been aware of Hillyer's hoisting the *Union Jack*, he most likely would have ordered the pirate shot, for Wright hated the English even more than the Indians.

Hillyer enjoyed a short-lived victory, for the suit against Bensell was ignored, his charges against Simpson were dropped and the captain was barred from Yaquina Bay oysters until he complied with suitable payment. The disgruntled pirate captain left to oyster northern waters.

He returned the following September with a crew of roughnecks to lay claim to what he believed rightfully his. Again, Simpson summoned the army. The following day Captain Winant sailed into Yaquina Bay with a tougher crew of oystermen aboard the *Doyle*; the pirate beat a hasty retreat. Two weeks later, his schooner *Cornelia Terry* ran afoul of the bar and became a total loss.

One year later, Captain Winant and his schooner *Annie G. Doyle* went on the bar at the identical spot and she became a total loss. Meinert Wachsmuth, a cast-ashore survivor, abandoned the sea for the relative safety of oystering; this lucky turn of events led him into acquiring large holdings in the oyster fields and the establishment of Portland's famous Dan & Louis Oyster Bar.[9]

Oyster pirate Captain Hillyer faded into history, never to be heard from again, but not so the others. Corporal Royal A. Bensell, a young soldier whose thirty-one months as a volunteer in Company D, Fourth California Infantry was spent, with the exception of the Yaquina Bay Oyster War, in total frustrating isolation in Oregon while the Civil War raged in the east, wrote a delightful book on army life titled *All Quiet on the Yamhill*. Bensell went into lumbering and built the 3-masted, 200-ton schooner *Elinorah*.[10] He was a member of the Oregon Legislature and later served four terms as mayor of Newport. He died at the age of eighty-three in 1921, a Yaquina Bay legend.

Captain Solomon Dodge, a Maine man, founded Oysterville in 1863; he and Captain Winant founded their oyster business in 1851. One day, after the short-lived Oyster War had become part of Oregon history, Captain Dodge spotted clouds building up off the stern of the *Fanny* and recognizing them as the dark kind that brought night much sooner than expected, piled on all sail to race for the shelter of Shoalwater Bay, but the fast-advancing storm dismasted the helpless ship. When sighted in the morning, she struggled to keep afloat. The steamer *Pacific*[11] attempted to take the crew from the waterlogged wreck but in so doing, accidentally rammed the foundering vessel and hastened her demise. The doughty old captain survived only to be lost in the wreck of the *Champion* off Peacock Spit in 1870.

Captain J. J. Winant, born in upper New York in 1838, enjoyed an adventuresome life that included trading for pearls amongst the South Pacific cannibals, hunting walrus in the Arctic and whales off Siberia. He barely escaped a murderous attempt on his life while he and his partners slept a drugged sleep

---

[8] General George Wright, wife and staff perished the following year in the wreck of the *Brother Jonathan*. Approximately 190 lives were lost.

[9] In addition to the excellent cuisine, the restaurant has on display the wheel of the wrecked *Brother Jonathan*.

[10] Sunk in an 1897 collision 50 miles west of Cape Mendocino.

[11] Sunk in a collision with sail ship *Orpheus* near Cape Flattery on November 4, 1875...only one out of 230 people survived.

aboard the schooner *Robert Bruce* as she lay at anchor in Willapa Bay. The cook, irate over a fancied wrong, laced their dinner with laudanum, fired the ship and departed in the only boat. A logger, Bill McCarty, and Indians spotted the flames, rowed out to the burning vessel and carried the drugged men ashore. The *Robert Bruce* was a total loss. Winant lost another vessel to the treacherous Yaquina bar when his anchor failed to hold in an east wind and his schooner *Lizzie* went ashore on the south beach. In 1877 Winant sailed to Acapulco to salvage the treasure off the wrecked *City of San Francisco*; he succeeded in recovering $22,000 in gold. He died in the wreck of the *Bandorille* on Umpqua bar in 1895.

COASTAL DESCRIPTION
From the Umpqua River
to the Yachats River[12]

Umpqua River is entered 20 miles north of Cape Arago Light. Lumber, sand and rock are barged on the river but usually commercial traffic is very light.

The south point at the entrance to the river is marked by sand dunes, partly covered by trees, that reach elevations of 300 feet. About a mile below the entrance is a bright bare spot in the dunes that shows prominently through the trees. Shifting sand dunes about 100 feet high are on the spit on the north side of the entrance.

Umpqua River Light, 43°39.8'N and 124°11.9'W, is 165 feet above the water and shows from a 65' tower just to the south of the river; a marker radiobeacon is at the light. Trees surround the light but the lantern shows over the tops.

The entrance to the river is protected by jetties. The south jetty extends 1,200 yards seaward from the shoreline. About 160 yards of the outer end *is submerged*; a lighted sea-

sonal gong buoy is 300 yards off the end. A seasonal fog signal is on the end of the middle jetty, and just inside the entrance at light 4 is another fog signal. The north jetty extends 1,100 yards seaward from the shoreline. A lighted whistle buoy is 0.8 mile west of the end of the N jetty. The channels are marked with lighted ranges, lights and buoys.

The channel over the bar is reported shoalest usually during September. But later in the season the river cuts deeper through the bar. Depths in the channel and basin range vary considerably between dredging operations. Gasoline, diesel, water and groceries may be obtained at Reedsport. A machine shop at the town and a hoist for 100 tons can be used in emergency, but most hull and engine repairs for small craft can be made at Salmon Harbor.

Salmon Harbor is a small boat harbor on the east side of the Umpqua 1.5 miles above the entrance. It is entered through a dredged channel from the main river channel to a turning basin in the harbor located about 0.4 mile above the entrance. The channel is marked at the entrance by two lights and a 159° directional light that is shown from the top of a cannery building on the east side of the turning basin. A seasonal fog signal is at the west entrance light. In April, 1976 the channel had a controlling depth of seven feet to the turning basin, thence 10 feet to the basin. Depths of four to seven feet are found elsewhere in the harbor. Berths with electricity, gasoline, diesel, water, ice, launching ramps and marine supplies can be found in the harbor. A Coast Guard station is on the NE side of the harbor. At high tide the Umpqua River is navigable by vessels of six foot draft to Scottsburg, 14.8 miles above Reedsport.

From the Umpqua for 21 miles to the Siuslaw River the coast is straight and consists of sand dunes broken only by the mouths of Threemile Creek, Tahkenitch Creek, Siltcoos River and the stream from Cleawox Lake.

---

[12] Consult nautical charts 18580, 18583 and 18584.

Siuslaw River is entered 43 miles north of Cape Arago Light and 7.5 miles south of Heceta Head Light. Prominent from offshore is wooded Cannery Hill, on the east side of the river 1.4 miles above the entrance. The customs port of entry is at *Coos Bay.*

The river is entered through a dredged channel between two jetties and leads south to a turning point/basin off the town of Florence, 4.4 miles above the entrance, thence east for about two miles to Cushman. A light and fog signal, and a Coast Guard lookout station are on the north jetty. The channel is marked by a 094° lighted entrance range that favors the north side of the channel, and by other ranges and navigational aids to one mile above Florence. In August, 1977, the controlling depths were 11 feet at midchannel across the bar to the turning basin at Florence, thence 11 to 16 feet in the basin except for shoaling to two feet in the south quarter, thence eight feet to Cushman. The bar is narrow, and the depths *vary greatly* because of storms and freshets.

The Coast Guard has a "Rough Bar" advisory sign 37 feet above the water, visible from the channel looking seaward, on the Coast Guard lookout tower on the north jetty. The sign is diamond-shaped, painted white with international orange border and the words "Rough Bar" in black letters. The sign is equipped with alternating flashing amber lights that are activated when the seas are four feet and considered hazardous for small boats. However, if the lights are *not* flashing it is *no guarantee* that sea conditions are favorable.

A Coast Guard station is on the east side of the river 1.6 miles above the entrance. A marina, on the east bank 0.4 miles above the Coast Guard pier, has about 125 berths with water, gasoline, diesel, marine supplies and two 7-ton hoists.

Florence is a small town on the north bank of the Siuslaw River 4.4 miles above the entrance. A bascule highway bridge with a clearance of 17 feet crosses the river from Florence to Glenada, a small town on the south bank of the river opposite Florence.

A cannery wharf, marina and a small port operated boat basin, locally known as Holiday Harbor, are at Florence; fish are shipped by truck. The marina, about 0.5 mile west of the bridge, has about 80 berths with fuel and supplies available. There is a two-ton hoist, and small repairs can be made. Holiday Harbor, about 0.3 mile east of the bridge, has 250 berths with fuel, water and launching ramps.

From Siuslaw River for 7.5 miles to Heceta Head, the coast is composed of sand dunes that are quite conspicuous in contrast with the dark trees partly covering them.

Heceta Head, 28.5 miles north of Umpqua River Light, has a seaward face 2.5 miles long with nearly vertical cliffs 100 to 200 feet high. The summit of the head reaches an elevation of 1,000 feet covered with grass and a few pines. A sharp black conical rock, 180 feet high, marks the extreme west and north part of the head, and is easily made out from either north or south. Cox Rock, 1.5 miles south of the south part of the head, is conical in shape and sort of white on top from what the birds leave.

Heceta Head Light, 44°08.3′N, 124°07.6′W is 205 feet above the water, atop a 56 foot white tower, on a bench cut in the side of the high bluff near the west extremity. Because of the high bluff north of the light, vessels from the north will not make out the tower or the buildings until abreast of the station.

Heceta Bank, 70 miles NNW of Cape Blanco and 30 miles offshore west of Heceta Head, covers an irregular area about 30 miles long and 10 miles wide. The least depth on the bank is 25 fathoms with irregular bottom; depths are considerably more north and south of the bank. From Heceta Head to Cape Perpetua, a distance of nine miles, the coast consists of high broken rocky cliffs, except for the first two miles which are composed of much lower sloping sandy cliffs, backed by a strip of clear land. The hills behind reach an elevation of over 800 feet in less than one-half mile from the beach, and are heavily wooded.

Tenmile Creek, five miles north of Heceta Head, is marked by a sand beach about 0.3

mile long at its mouth. Cape Perpetua, 9 miles north of Heceta Head, consists of two projecting points, the north of which is the bolder. It reaches a height of 800 feet a short distance from the beach and 1,000 feet at a distance of 0.8 mile. The rocky cliff forming the face of the north point is reddish. A few rocks that uncover are close to its face.

Yachats River, navigable only for canoes, breaks through the coast hills immediately north from Cape Perpetua. The coast for 2.5 miles north of Cape Perpetua consists of cliffs, 15 to 30 feet high, with a narrow strip of grassy land 0.2 to 1 mile wide behind them. Thence for 5.5 miles to Alsea Bay there are low bluffs, with a broad sand beach in front and comparatively low wooded country behind them.

Table Mountain, 11 miles NE of the mouth of Alsea Bay, is flat topped, covered with trees and looks sort of white. Another summit is 0.6 mile SW of Table Mountain. Marys Peak is a prominent mountain 24 miles E of the entrance to Yaquina Bay; it is wooded on both sides but the top is covered with grass.

COASTAL DESCRIPTION
From Alsea Bay to Salmon River[13]

Alsea Bay is 68 miles north of Cape Arago. The north point is low, broad and sandy, but the south point is an abrupt sandstone cliff about 100 feet high and covered with trees. The entrance has a shifting bar with a depth of about six feet. With a rising tide the bar fills with sand and the full effect of the tide cannot be counted on. There is considerable fishing and crabbing in the bay and river, but the boats rarely cross the bar. Waldport, a mile inside the entrance, is the principal settlement. A marina with about 100 berths has fuel and water and is on the NE side of town. The river is navigable by small craft to about 10 miles above the mouth. There are several

marinas above the town and all have fuel and groceries, and small engine repairs can be made. The fixed bridge of the Oregon Coast Highway crossing Alsea Bay, a mile inside the entrance, has a clearance of 63 feet.

The 11.5 mile coast between Alsea Bay and Yaquina Bay is nearly straight and consists of a low sandy beach backed by dunes at each end with bluffs up to 100 feet high between; the land behind is low and wooded with areas of second growth timber. Rocks covered 2 to 4 fathoms extend almost 2 miles offshore. Seal Rocks, abreast the highest part of the bluffs about five miles north of Alsea Bay entrance, extend up to 0.5 mile offshore for about two miles; the tallest is 20 feet high.

Stonewall Bank, 14 miles offshore and 17 SW of Yaquina Head Light, is nine miles long in a northerly direction and 2.5 miles wide. Depths begin at 13 fathoms.

Yaquina Head, 32.5 miles north of Heceta Head, is distinguished by two conical hills covered with grass. The outer one is 356 feet high and the inner 390, with a low saddle between. The extremity of the point, which projects about a mile from the general trend of the coast is broken and rocky, but comparatively low. One mile inland from the point, the grass-covered land changes to a dense forest and the hills rise rapidly. Two covered ledges lie north of the point 0.65 mile from the beach. There is a kelp covered rock and considerable kelp about a mile south of the point. A patch of rocks that uncovers eight feet is about a mile north of Yaquina Head Light. South to Yaquina Bay, the coast consists of broken yellow cliffs, bordered on the south part by broad sand beaches.

Yaquina Head Light, 44°40.6′N, 124°04.7′W, is 162 feet above the water on a 93 foot white tower, at the west extremity of the head; a radiobeacon is at the station.

Yaquina Reef and its continuation north is a ridge of hard sand and rock covered from 5 to 30 feet. The reef extends from the outer end of the north jetty and parallel to the shore to

---

[13] Consult nautical charts numbers 18561, 18581 and 18520.

Yaquina Head. The wreck of the concrete ship *John Aspin* uncovers 5½ feet on the reef 0.65 mile from the outer end of the north jetty.

South Reef, covered 11 feet, is a southern continuation of Yaquina Reef, the two being separated by the entrance channel.

Yaquina Bay entrance is four miles south to Yaquina Head Light. The bay is a tidal estuary, the harbor itself being merely a widening of the Yaquina River.

The north point of Yaquina Bay entrance is a sandy bluff 120 feet high. An abandoned lighthouse and a Coast Guard lookout tower are on the high part. When viewed from the NW, the circular lighthouse tower on the roof of a two-story frame dwelling obscures the lower portion of the lookout tower. The south entrance point is a low sand beach backed by dunes rising to 150 feet.

The entrance to Yaquina Bay is protected by jetties 330 yards apart. The long north jetty extends out to Yaquina Reef. The other 125 yards of the north jetty *is submerged*. The outer visible end of the north jetty is marked by a light and a seasonal fog signal. A lighted whistle buoy is 1.5 miles SW of the entrance. The channels are marked by lighted ranges, lights, and buoys. A fog signal is sounded at the entrance range front light. Two rocks awash, about 100 yards apart, are about 50 yards south of the submerged end of the north jetty.

During the summer, when the swell is approximately parallel with the coast, the bar is fairly smooth, being partially sheltered by Yaquina Head. In winter, however, the heavy west swell will make the bar very rough. A smooth bar and a favorable tide are necessary for large vessels leaving Yaquina Bay.

The Coast Guard has established a rough bar advisory sign, 25 feet above the water, visible from the channel looking seaward, on the west end of the Coast Guard pier. The sign is diamond-shaped, white and has an international orange border. The words "Rough Bar" appear in the center. The sign is equipped with two alternating flashing amber lights that are activated when the seas

exceed four feet in height. However, if the lights are not flashing it is *no guarantee* that sea conditions are favorable.

In these, as in all directions in this book, use caution and use your head.

Controlling depths may vary considerably from projected depths provided by a Federal project so it would be wise to consult *Notice to Mariners* latest edition for up-to-date information. Strangers desiring to enter Yaquina Bay and river should employ a pilot or a man with local knowledge. At the entrance the buoys *cannot be relied upon* to indicate the best water, and in the river the depths are subject to *frequent change*.

Newport, just inside the north entrance point, is the principal town on the bay and river. The town has a considerable fishing industry with several small fish processing plants. Lumber, logs and paper are barged from up river to the wharves at McLean Point, just east of Newport.

The mean range of tides at Newport is 6.0 feet. The range between mean lower and mean higher high water is 8.0 feet. The current velocity is about 2.4 knots, on the flood, and 2.3 knots, on the ebb, in Yaquina Bay entrance. Near Newport docks the velocity is about 0.5 knot. Off Yaquina and one mile south of Toledo, the velocities are about 1 to 1.4 knots.

The Port of Yaquina Bay operates a small craft marina 0.7 mile above the highway bridge on the north shore. The moorage area is protected from the main channel by a breakwater, and has berths, with electricity, for about 620 craft. Gas, diesel, water, ice and groceries are available. There is also a launching ramp. There are several marine repair facilities on the river above Newport and a railway at Weiser Point can handle up to 50 tons and 50 feet. A large marina, just above Oneatta Point, 3.8 miles above the bridge at the entrance to the bay, has about 120 berths with electricity, fuel, water and marine supplies. Their hoist can handle 19 tons and 34 feet for hull and engine repairs.

From Yaquina Head to the mouth of Columbia River, the coast is fairly straight. The headlands are Cape Foulweather, Cascade

Head, Cape Lookout, Cape Meares, Cape Falcon and Tillamook Head. The 30 fathom curve follows the general trend of the coast 3.5 miles offshore, without indicating the several headlands. When opposite Tillamook Head, the curve swings west and is about 7.5 miles off the end of Clatsop Spit.

From Yaquina Head for 5.5 miles to Cape Foulweather, the coast consists of yellow and white sandstone cliffs, low and broken. Iron Mountain, 1.5 miles NE of Yaquina Head Light, is a 654-foot-high hill. When viewed from the south, the highest third of the hill is bare and composed of a red rock formation; the north side and lower part of the hill are covered with thick brush. A low flat rock, 8 feet high, is 0.4 mile offshore 2.8 miles north of Yaquina Head.

Otter Rock, 11 feet high, is 3.2 miles north of Yaquina Head and 0.6 mile offshore. Gull Rock, 56 feet high, is 1.2 miles north of Otter Rock and 0.4 mile offshore. In line between the two rocks is a kelp field with several covered rocks, with a few awash. Covered rocks that break are 0.5 mile to 1 mile north of Gull Rock.

Cape Foulweather is a prominent headland with about six miles of seaward face consisting of rocky cliffs over 60 feet high. The cape is formed by several grass-covered headlands, separated by densely wooded gulches. Near the middle of the cape is a strip of flat land, 0.5 mile long and 0.2 mile wide, bare of trees. The highest point of the cape is near the south part. A grassy patch is conspicuous on the SW slope. A white building with a red roof, 0.7 mile NNE of Gull Rock, is prominent on the high bluff just south of Cape Foulweather. About 0.9 mile SE of the extreme west point of the cape is a rocky point 445 feet high, and east of the point the hills rise to 1,100 feet in 0.6 mile.

Dangers extend for nearly two miles north of the north point of Cape Foulweather and about 600 yards offshore.

The Oregon Coast Highway follows the shoreline closely at Cape Foulweather.

Depoe Bay, eight miles north of Yaquina Head, has one of the best small boat shelters along this part of the coast. The bay proper has foul ground on both the north and south sides, but the channel leading to the narrow dredged channel to the inner basin is deep and well marked. The foul areas break in moderate seas and are marked by kelp. Prominent from seaward is the concrete arch bridge over the entrance to the basin. A lighted whistle buoy is 1.1 miles west of the entrance to the bay, and a bell buoy is farther inshore. In 1974 the controlling depth in the dredged channel to the inner basin was 5 feet, then 5 to 7½ feet in the basin. The fixed concrete bridge over the entrance is unusual in that it has a width of 30 feet; its clearance height is 42 feet. The 085°40′ lighted range at the south end of the bridge marks the entrance to the bay and the approach to the dredged channel to the basin; a fog signal is about 50 yards SW of the front range light. Floodlights, about 50 yards seaward of the bridge, illuminate the entrance to the inner basin. Be cautioned against the *dangerous surge* in the narrow entrance to the basin. Entry should not be attempted at night or in rough weather without local knowledge. A Coast Guard station is at the inner basin. There is a rough bar advisory sign, 25 feet above the water, visible from the channel looking seaward, on a building on the north side of the basin entrance channel. The sign is diamond-shaped, white, with international orange borders. The words "Rough Bar" appear in black letters. The sign is equipped with two alternating amber lights that flash when the seas exceed four feet in height and are considered hazardous for small boats. If the lights are not flashing, this is *no guarantee* that sea conditions are favorable.

The town of Depoe Bay is on the north side of the basin. The basin has a concrete bulkhead, mooring floats, and a tidal grid for minor hull repairs. Also available are fuel, water and ice. Marine supplies can be had and there is a 3-ton hoist, and a launching ramp.

From Cape Foulweather for 9.5 miles to the entrance of Siletz Bay, the coast continues as yellow broken bluffs, 40 to 100 feet high, bordered by about three miles of sandy beaches. From the north point of the bluffs to the bay entrance are sand dunes covered with low brush.

The entrance to Siletz Bay is 15 miles north of Yaquina Head. The entrance channel is subject to *frequent change*, and drafts of four to five feet are considered the deepest that can be safely taken in at high water.

The north point at the entrance is a low bluff with a narrow sand beach. The south point is a low sandspit about 250 yards wide. The dunes on the spit are thinly wooded near the shore, but become thicker inland. Several houses are on the spit. The bay inside the entrance is shoal. Siletz River enters the bay at the southeast end.

Taft and Cutler City are communities on the bay; both are parts of Lincoln City, which is 1.8 miles north. There are several marinas on the bay; a facility just above the highway bridge at the mouth of the Siletz River has berths for about 65 craft; there is a launching ramp and fuel and marine supplies can be had. The bridge just below the marina has a clearance of 31 feet. An L-shaped pier is just inside the entrance to the bay on the north shore; in November of 1977, it was reported that no moorage was available due to silting.

From the north point of Siletz Bay the coast extends seven miles to the Salmon River. For 2.5 miles of this stretch to the outlet of Devils Lake, the yellow sandstone cliffs are 80 to 100 feet high. The lake is a large body of fresh water, 10 feet above sea level, that empties through a narrow stream. At 0.5 mile WSW of the mouth of the stream is a covered rock that generally breaks. For three miles north from the outlet of the lake, the bluffs are 20 to 60 feet high, rising to grassy hills. A broad beach and ledges of rocks are along the shore.

Salmon River empties at the south extremity of Cascade Head; the entrance is nearly closed by sandbars.

Immediately south of Salmon River is a rocky cliff whose seaward face is 0.6 mile long. The summit is a dome-shaped butte 510 feet high. From here a rolling grassy plateau with a few trees extends south and east to the river. A rock, 46 feet high, is 700 yards west of this cliff, and about a mile south is a covered rock 630 yards off the beach. Immediately south of and in line with Cascade Head, opposite the mouth of the river, are three grayish rocks about 765 yards offshore. These have heights of 56 feet on the north one, 25 on the center and 47 feet for the south.

SHIP DISASTERS
Umpqua River to Salmon River

*Admiral Nicholson 5/16/1924 Steam schooner, Admiral line freighter, one deck, two mast, steel, 678 tons, 141' × 27.2' × 18.7', built in 1908 at Seattle as the *Northland*. She stranded while towing the disabled *G.C. Lindauer*. The wreck was purchased by C. K. West and scrapped.

Alaskan 5/13/1889 Sidewheel steamer, built at Chester, Penn. in 1883, 260' × 40' × 12.5'. Captain R. E. Howes. Vertical surface condenser with walking-beam engine. En route Portland-San Francisco. See story, "The *Alaskan*."

Alice Kimball 10/12/1904 Two-masted schooner, 107 tons, built by T. H. Peterson in 1874 at Little River, California. Ship wrecked on the Siuslaw River bar.

Almira 1/9/1852 Brig. Captain Gibbs. Ship went ashore one mile above Umpqua City with a cargo of government supplies and 36 soldiers for Port Orford; all saved.

Alpha 2/3/1907 Schooner, 143', three mast, 300 tons, built by Emil Heuchendorff in 1903. She was one of 55 vessels built at the Simpson North Bend Yard, which was established in 1859. Re-named the

* Refloated or partially salvaged.

Governor Tilden and later the *Walter*. She wrecked nine miles north of the Umpqua.

Annie Doyle 3/11/1865 Schooner. Wrecked on Yaquina bar; see story "Tough Breed...."

Anvil 4/11/1913 Siuslaw. NFI.

Atalanta 11/17/1898 Clipper, British, 1753 tons carrying 92,405 bushels of wheat valued at $65,000. It is said this ship was a good sailer and once covered 950 miles in three days. She was reported as having an unusual rig with a main skysail above her double topgallant yards, but I'll be darned if I can figure out that one. Built at Greenock, Scotland in 1886, she sailed 320 and 325 miles in two consecutive days on her trials. Captain McBride made a first-arrival bet with two other ships bound for the same African port. The other ships left two days ahead of McBride and, in order to gain time, he "coasted," a deadly game of hugging the shore. The *Atalanta* struck a reef where the rocks extend some two miles offshore near Seal Rocks, five miles north of Alsea. The captain paid with his life for the error, as did 22 others; only three lived. The ship is also listed as 1½ miles out from the mouth of Big Creek.

Bandorille 11/21/1895 Coastal steamer, ex-*George H. Chance*, re-built in 1893, 104' × 21' × 8', engine 8½" & 16" × 12". Wrecked on the Umpqua bar, crew and one passenger rescued by Life Saving Service. One dead.

Beda 3/17/1886 Steam schooner, 300 tons, built at North Bend by John Kruse in 1883. While bound from Knappton to San Francisco with Captain P. Halley in command, the ship began taking on water some 40 miles west of Cape Perpetua. The pumps failed and the rising water doused her fires. The crew jettisoned the deck load to no avail. At 3:20 in the stormy afternoon, 18 men put off in three boats. At first they connected their boats with lines, but those quickly chaffed. Two men in one boat died from exposure and two in the second boat drowned when it capsized in the surf. The third boat simply disappeared.

Bella 11/25/1905 Schooner, three masts, 180 tons, built at Acme, Oregon, by William Kyle. Ship was totalled at Ocean Beach, Oregon.

Berwick 3/13/1908 Two mast, 100-ton schooner, gas. Built by M. Turner at Benicia in 1887. A total loss at the Siuslaw.

Blanco 1864 Supposedly this vessel was the first brig built at Coos Bay. Simpson completed the job in 1859. She registered 284 tons, two masts, square rigged. The 125' vessel capsized off the Siletz River and drifted in keel-up with her masts gone, deck broken and hull split from rail to keel. The local Indians claimed ignorance of the wreck, but had in their possession five sheets of zinc, two kegs of nails, an oilskin coat, a calico dress, seven pairs of garters, two pair of boots and a lot of sail and rope. The crew was never found.

Bobolink 10/1873 Schooner, 170 tons, two masts.

She struck the Umpqua bar, but was salvaged only to be lost at Mendocino in 1898. See *California Shipwrecks*.

Bostonian 10/1/1850 Captain Coffin, with supercargo George Snelling (nephew of Boston merchant and owner Mr. Gardiner), sailed the vessel from Boston to the Pacific Northwest. She wrecked at the mouth of the Umpqua. Some of her cargo was removed and a sail-tent city set up. A portion of the ship's stores went upriver to Levi Scott, who founded Scottsburg. The wreck floated around the bay for some time before eventually grounding opposite the present site of Gardiner; much of her went into the early construction of that town.

Bully Washington 12/12/1857 Iron-hulled, steamer, built in 1850 at San Francisco by Captain Alex S. Murray. She was shipped to the Columbia aboard the bark *Success*, then re-assembled above Oregon City and ran between Canemah and the mouth of the Yamhill; her first run was June 6, 1851. She later sold to Allen McKinley & Co. for $3,000 and taken below the falls for Oregon City-Portland service. She again sold, this time to Captain Sylvester Hinsdale who brought her to the Scottsburg-Gardiner run on the Umpqua. Just after leaving the dock at Scottsburg, she suffered a fire and explosion. The hull was moved to the north side of the Umpqua just below the highway bridge at Scottsburg, filled with rocks and converted into a dock.

Captain Ludvig 6/25/1953 Oil screw, 54 tons, built in 1945. Burned off Newport.

Caroline Medeau 4/5/1876 Schooner, 73.32 tons. The vessel, valued at $8,200 and cargo at $1,800 became the victim of an "Irish Hurricane" (no wind). Her anchor failed to hold in the current and she was lost on the Yaquina bar. Captain Madison. The wreck sold for $200.

Charles Nelson 11/1903 Steam schooner. Foundered off Heceta Head. The derelict was later salvaged. 36 people saved.

Condor 11/17/1912 60-ton motor vessel under Captain W. H. Douty went on the rocks of the north jetty at Alsea. Douty and his three crewmen were saved, but the ship was totalled. Three Finnish fishermen began her construction in Astoria in anticipation of using the 56-footer for the Yukon gold rush. The men were determined to build her extra strong, so strong, in fact, that they did not complete her until nine years later and long after the gold rush ended. She was eventually sold as a freighter, but always managed to get into trouble; lifesavers were called into action five times in her six years of life.

Cornelia Terry 10/13/1864 Oyster schooner owned by Ludlum & Co. En route Yaquina-San Francisco and wrecked upon the Yaquina bar for a total loss. See story, "A Tough Breed...."

Dorothy Joan 9/13/1945 Oil screw, 50 tons, built in 1927. Foundered at Yaquina Head.

Emma Utter 12/1886 Ashore at Siuslaw. NFI.

Enterprise 2/20/1873 Sternwheeler, 247 tons, 119' × 22' × 4', built at Gardiner in 1870, owned by Merchants & Farmers Navigation Co. Captain French sailed the steamboat to Portland and, while crossing the Umpqua bar, the vessel broke a steam-pipe, lost power and drifted into the breakers to become a total wreck. Her engines were salvaged and installed in the *Beaver*.

Etta Kay 12/11/1946 Schooner, two mast, clipper-bowed fisher. Owned by Phillip and James Bowden. En route Newport-Alaska when an engine room explosion set the ship afire. The vessel went down off Yaquina bar; three man crew rescued.

Fawn 11/21/1856 Brig, re-rigged from schooner. En route San Francisco-Coos Bay. Four died in the wreck. Captain Bunker, four crew and three passengers were rescued by the Indians. None of the "valuable" cargo was saved. Captain Tichenor gave the location as the "Sinsclaw" (Siuslaw), five miles south of Cape Perpetua and 19 miles north of Umpqua.

Fearless 11/20/1889 Steam tug, 78 tons, 53' × 19.5' × 10'. Vessel also wrecked in 1873 when crossing the Coos bar. She was the oldest ship on the west coast connected with the Merchant Marine. Owned by North Bend Mill Co. and under Captain James Hill. The teak-hulled vessel was built in Shanghai in 1844 for use as an opium clipper and was rigged as a hermaphrodite brig named *Star of China*. She arrived at San Francisco in 1852 and was promptly seized for violation of revenue laws. She sold to General James M. Estill, who was part owner of the *Hartford*. He installed the engines of the latter into the *Star of China* and changed her name to *Fearless*. The ship performed any number of tasks, including carrying coal for Flanagan & Rogers' Westport Coal mine. Her loss was not discovered until the following day when debris washed up on the north spit of the Umpqua bar and a crewman crawled ashore. Unfortunately he died before revealing the cause of her demise. Captain Hill left a widow, formerly Annie Palmer of the Scottsburg Palmer House Hotel. Seven others died with the captain.

Frederick 4/14/1914 A barge of 319 tons. Wrecked on the Siuslaw bar.

G. C. Lindauer 5/16/1924 Steam schooner, 453 tons with 400 hp, built by Lindstrom at Aberdeen in 1901. Bound for Reedsport-San Francisco, she became a total loss on the Umpqua River bar. It was probably just as well, for after her launching, she ran into Point Sur in California, sank in San Francisco Bay in 1919, wrecked at Point Arena in 1912 and in 1923 was caught with six sacks of booze squirreled away amongst the 50 sacks of coal in her hold.

Graywood 10/2/1915 Steam schooner, 915 tons, ex-*Harold Dollar*, built by Bendixson at Fairhaven, California, in 1904. Foundered off Umpqua near a lightship??

Helori 12/21/1949 Oil screw, 79 tons. Burned off the mouth of the Umpqua.

Hugh Hogan 4/28/1914 Three mast schooner. Ashore on spit near Florence at Siuslaw. Broadside to the breakers, Captain Hill lost the tow by *L. Roscoe*. Ship was salvaged. See *Osmo, Ozmo*.

J. Marhoffer 5/19/1910 Steam schooner, 608 tons, built by Lindstrom at Aberdeen in 1907. One soul was lost when she burned off Yaquina Bay and drifted into what is now called Boiler Bay, due to the obvious reason.

John Aspin 4/22/1948 A concrete ship, decommissioned U.S. Army transport of 5000 tons, built in 1944 at Tampa, Florida, 365' × 26'. In tow from Cathlamet to Newport to be used as a revetment for a new dock. She broke from the tow and crashed into the Yaquina Reef where she sank. Portions of her hull are still visible at low tide. She lies 0.65 mile off the outer end of North Yaquina Bay jetty on the Yaquina Reef.

John Hunter 1873 Yaquina Bay. NFI.

Joseph Warren 11/25/1853 Peruvian bark, 250 tons. En route in ballast San Francisco-Vancouver when a giant sea knocked the ship over and swept her clean. Four drowned; the rest drifted 13 days before rescue. The wreck came ashore below Yaquina Bay.

Juliet 3/1852 Schooner. En route San Francisco-Columbia under Captain Collins; she came ashore two miles south of Yaquina. Crew was saved. See story "A State of Confusion."

L. H. Coolidge 8/20/1951 Coast-wise tug, 126', owned by Upper River Towing Co. and valued at $300,000. She went on the rocks at Bandon; the *Salvage Chief* pulled her off. While under tow to Columbia, the 282-ton ship went down 6.7 miles off Yachats.

Lizzie 2/16/1876 Schooner, 63.93 tons, built by Titus & Lee of Alsea. Valued at $7,500, oyster cargo at $1,500. She failed to hold anchor in an east wind and went on the Yaquina bar at South Beach. Captain J. J. Winant sold the wreck for $510.00.

Maggie Ross 12/8/1891 Steamer, 115', built at Pleasant Point by J. Ross in 1888. With a cargo of lumber and under the command of Captain Marshall, the ship sailed en route Coos Bay-San Francisco. A high sea carried off boats, smokestack and stove-in the house, killing the steward. The second officer drowned in the flooded engine room. The *Annie Gee* rescued the crew and towed in the battered, wrecked ship to Yaquina Bay.

Mary Gilbert 12/17/1894 Schooner. Captain J. W. Dodge. The ship carried general merchandise when she was totalled on the south head of Alsea Bay.

Meldon 3/16/1873 Schooner, cargo of lumber when the ship went ashore on the Umpqua bar. NFI.

Nassau 7/22/1852 Schooner. Captain Peter Johnson. A total wreck on south spit of Umpqua. NFI.

Nettie Sundberg 12/28/1902 Schooner. En route San Francisco-Siuslaw River when she wrecked at Siuslaw. NFI.

North Bend 9/23/1940 Four masted schooner, last vessel of this type built on the west coast, 981 tons. In the spring of 1926, the schooner was the last vessel to sail under wind-power over the bar and up-river to Astoria. She was converted to a barge and stranded on Coos Bay bar. Salvaged and scrapped.

Ocean Spray 11/20/1903 Schooner wrecked at Siuslaw River. Wreck sold for $150. NFI.

Oliva Schultze 4/28/1880 Schooner. En route San Francisco-Siuslaw. Wrecked at the Siuslaw River with no survivors and no witnesses.

Ona 9/26/1883 Steam schooner. This vessel made the first trip up Tillamook as far as Lincoln. She was lost on the Yaquina bar under Captain F. H. Treat.

Ork 11/24/1864 Bark. Lost on Ork Reef at the mouth of Umpqua at Lat. 43°41′, Lon. 124°11′. NFI.

Parker #2 2/26/1935 Dredge, 76 tons, built in 1908. Foundered at Yaquina Bay. Two dead.

Phil Sheridan 9/15/1878 Schooner, two mast, 158 tons. She was run down and sunk by the steamer *Ancon* 15 miles off Umpqua bar. The crew was saved. Excerpt from *The Daily Astorian*, November 30, 1878: "The hull seen by the ship McNear is supposed to be that of the Phil Sheridan wrecked sometime since in a collision with the steamer Ancon."

Phoebe Fay 4/16/1883 Schooner. En route Port Discovery-San Francisco. Ship was abandoned off Cape Foulweather. Steamer *Mississippi* rescued the crew.

Pilgrim 1912 Sloop wrecked near Cape Foulweather, five dead. NFI.

Quickstep 11/24/1904 Barkentine, 402 tons, built by Hall Bros. at Port Ludlow in 1876. Three masts, 149′ × 34′ × 13.5′. Foundered south of Yaquina Head.

Roanoke 2/2/1853 Brig. En route with general cargo San Francisco-Umpqua under Captain Barrett when she totalled on the Umpqua bar. A portion of her cargo was saved.

Samuel Roberts 8/6/1850 Schooner of the Klamath Exploring Expedition Co. Aground on Brandy Bar, Umpqua River; the explorers carried a quantity of brandy in the ship's locker and were forced to await high tide to free the ship. It was a beautiful day, so . . . .

Sea Eagle 11/20/1922 Tug. En route Honolulu-Coos Bay with the schooner *Ecola* in tow. The tug foundered in a heavy gale and lost all hands; the *Ecola* survived. The wreck drifted ashore nine days later and settled on the north side of the reef just off Sunset Beach at the entrance to Coos Bay. Five dead.

Sea Otter 8/22/1808 See story, "The Mysterious Wreck of 1808."

Sparrow 12/4/1875 Schooner, 197 tons. Ran ashore at Umpqua due to navigational error. Three dead. NFI.

St. Charles 5/17/1892 American ship en route Nanaimo-San Francisco. 100 miles NW of Cape Foulweather, the ship suffered a tremendous explosion from excessive dust in her cargo of coal; Captain M. Chapman was seriously injured. She went to the bottom almost immediately.

Struan 12/25/1890 Norwegian ship, wood, 1510 tons, built by S. Fraser at St. Johns & owned by E. Lindoe of Haugesund, Norway. Abandoned at sea; remains washed ashore south of Sand Lake on Lookout Beach near the Boy Scouts' Camp Meriwether. See story, "Struan."

Tacoma 1/29/1883 Steamer. A new ship launched the first of the year. Captain George D. Koatz. While taking 3,500 tons of coal from Tacoma to San Francisco, a faulty compass caused the vessel to run aground four miles north of the Umpqua. At first, the ship sat easy; the captain and a few men went for aid. The tugs *Fearless*, *Escort* and *Sol Thomas* raced to assist, but the sea was running high, so high, in fact, that the Life Station keeper refused aid . . . one of the few cases on record of such an act; however, a volunteer group was organized and 18 lives were saved. Engineer Grant was forced to pull a pistol to maintain order on the ship; after all had been saved, his was the last boat to leave the disintegrating vessel. Grant's boat became caught in the surf and capsized. Grant and nine others drowned.

Truckee 11/18/1897 Steamer. En route Tillamook-San Francisco. Ship sprang a leak in a gale and ran for cover at Umpqua. She stranded on the north spit at the entrance for a total loss.

Volante 3/7/1896 Propeller steamer, built at Oneatta in 1892. Burned at Newport. NFI.

Washtucna 8/17/1922 Barge, 710 tons, built at Portland for Columbia Contract Co., 180′ × 42′ × 12′, 2 masts. Lost at Umpqua River entrance.

Wilhelmina 1/22/1911 Gas schooner. En route Coos Bay-Gardiner. Aground on south spit at Umpqua mouth.

Yaquina 2/20/1935 Coast Guard Patrol Boat, valued at $20,000. The boat, true to the tradition of the United States Coast Guard, attempted to aid a disabled barge caught in the fierce breakers off the Yaquina bar. Numerous approaches were made toward the disabled, battered wreck. Finally, the smaller boat managed at great peril to work to the lee. At that moment a "widow maker" swept both vessels. The two seamen were washed away and the Coast Guard boat badly holed. Deadly floating planks, some broken and jagged, slammed and punched at the floundering men. George Elkins, George Meadows and William Stults of the Coast Guard lost their lives as did Vern Jackson and one unknown man from Astoria.

Yaquina Bay 12/9/1888 Steam schooner, 257′ × 34′ × 21′, built by Cramp & Sons in 1881 as the *Caracas*. While under tow, the hawser parted and she went ashore at Yaquina.

Yaquina City 12/4/1887 Steamer, owned by Oregon Development Co. This ship and the *Yaquina Bay* went ashore at the same place, a year apart. The wreck of the *Yaquina City* was caused by broken wheel chains. The loss of the two ships was more than the new company could absorb and the Oregon Development Co. went belly up.

1910 wreck of the J. Marhoffer. *Her discarded machinery gave Boiler Bay its name.*

Interesting debris, much of it, no doubt, from wrecks other than the Mary Gilbert *shown here just south of Alsea.*　　　　　　　　　　　　　　　　　　　　　*(University of Oregon)*

4

Cascade Head to Nehalem River

THE SHARK + THE ORIOLE =
THE MORNING STAR

Early pioneers descended into the lush valleys of the Tillamook and worked mightily to tame the fertile soil. The promise of trade, growth and prosperity in this virgin wilderness inspired the hardy farmers to endure the hardships of total isolation that all too soon left them bereft of the barest of necessities so basic to their survival.

Coffee, tea, sugar, tools, dry goods...all lay in abundance just beyond their reach in Portland and the inner cities, but a wall of high mountains and thick forests stood as an impenetrable barrier between the farmer's harvest and the city's trade goods.

Only the sea offered an avenue of salvation for the dying community. A group of desperate pioneers met on September 24, 1854, at the home of Warren Vaughn to discuss the building of a small trading schooner, the one last hope of securing their settlement's future. The inexperienced, but determined, farmers formed a company to undertake the project and accepted Warren Vaughn, Charles Hendrickson, Peter Morgan and O. S. Thomas as primary stockholders. Handshakes sealed the bargain.

Workers hewed out the ship's stern post and keel, then dragged the pieces to Vaughn's landing at the bay. Using the mud flats as their drawing board, the farmers scratched

out their calculations and ship design plans and, in spite of the collective inexperience of the group, a trim little ship of some 30 tons,[1] 37½ feet at the keel and a hold of 6½ feet miraculously began to take shape. Lumber for the vessel posed no problem, for the area yielded an excess, but a dire shortage of iron, followed by a scarcity of cordage and sail cloth threatened to put the company out of business. John Hobson of Clatsop came to the rescue with the information that the British[2] Man-of-War *Shark* lay wrecked upon the Columbia bar with pieces of her deck and hull, all heavy with iron, washed-up on the beach near Arch Cape.

Thomas and Vaughn, with five of Thomas' horses, set out for the northwest corner of Tillamook County and the site of the precious flotsam. The expedition was without proper pack saddles, but the men improvised with materials available and headed back over Neahkahnie Mountain with a full load of valuable iron fittings. At the narrowest point of the treacherous trail and at the edge of a high bluff, a cinch strap broke and a pack of iron swung under the horse's belly. The terrified animal, its hind legs over the edge of the escarpment, bellowed and thrashed. Vaughn described the tense moment, "...causing no end of excitment, he snorted and jumped

---

[1] Roughly the same size as Astoria's *Dolly/Jane*.
[2] He was mistaken. The wreck was not a Britisher; it was the American sloop *Shark*, lost September 6, 1846.

around frightening the other horses and we surely had a circus for a few minutes. Thomas had just got over his narrow part of the trail, I called to him for help and talked as pretty as I could to my horse to keep him from moving. . . ."

Thomas rushed in and, while Vaughn pulled on the halter to keep the beast from going over the edge, cut the rest of the restraining tie-straps. Working in unison, the men pulled the horse to safety. They proceeded to Tillamook with no further trouble, but made sure they used proper pack saddles for the succeeding four trips. They packed-out only usable iron, bolts, knees and nails and left two ship's cannon where they laid at the mouth of a little creek near a hemlock tree.

The farmers quickly built a blacksmith's shop and converted left-over ship's lumber into charcoal. Local settler Clark became the town's blacksmith and began re-shaping the *Shark*'s iron. He stated he never knew a ship carried so much iron and when he finished this job, he just might forget farming and head for Portland to supply ships. . . he would most certainly have the necessary experience.

A new avenue of supplies opened to the intrepid shipbuilders when friendly Indians brought word of another wreck ashore near Netarts. Providentially, the ship turned out to be the bark *Oriole* laden with supplies for building a lighthouse at Fort Canby. She ran afoul of the dreaded Clatsop spit on September 18, 1853 and sank in 5½ fathoms, a total wreck. Wave action broke her hull in half and drove ashore near the Netarts bay entrance that half filled with paint, ship blocks, standing mizzen and numerous other valuable ship's items. The Indians, anxious to be of service to their neighbors' shipbuilding project, collected the prized flotsam and offered the entire bonanza for a mere $10.

With all the necessary supplies now on hand, the farmers rushed to finish the project as quickly as possible. Dan Pike's farm supplied lumber; Charles West and John Saunders whipsawed every plank by hand and cut an average of 300 feet per day. Families spent their evening cutting the wrecked *Oriole*'s rigging into six inch lengths, soaking off the tar in hot water and separating the fibers for caulking oakum. The women ground winter wheat in coffee mills, browned it and added chicory to fashion cups of hot brew to soothe sore backs, fingers and sagging spirits. The working men's meals consisted of cheese and cream, for flour supplies had been depleted long ago and the settlers were now running in short supply of sugar and tea.

The little ship promised to be ready for launching on New Year's day, 1855, and all joined forces to celebrate the occasion with a grand feast. Eager hands emptied every pantry and root cellar. Elbridge Trask, Dougherty and Lyman supplied wheat. Mrs. Hiram Smith surrendered some eggs. Necessity became the mother of invention as finely diced and browned potatoes were brewed into a flavorful coffee.

By December, workers secured the last of the ship's planking and made fast her beaming and carlings.[3] Three Indians volunteered to take five horses to Leonard and Green's store in Astoria to purchase pitch and running gear. In a week's time they returned safe and sound with the goods, plus an added bonus of a few pounds of sugar. . . the first of which the settlers had seen in some time.

The line salvaged from the wrecked *Oriole* proved too heavy for the smaller vessel. Peter Morgan, experienced in rope walking, constructed a machine and a rope walk[4] that enabled him to take the heart of the larger lines to produce the needed rigging. Masts and bowsprit were dressed out and raised. Saunders and West completed the rigging while workers sewed sail.

Launching day approached. Some thirty settlers arrived from Hoquarten, Southprairie and Quick's and Trask's farms; Indians arrived from all directions. The enticing aroma of ersatz coffee beckoned one and all to partake of a feast table groaning under the

---

[3] Short pieces of timber, ranging fore and aft between beams, which served to strengthen beams and deck.

[4] The rope walk was located in front of Geinger's home with its entry in the prairie toward Kilchis Point.

Replica of the Morning Star, *first ship of Tillamook County.* Morning Star II, *engineered by Clarence Sessions and built by eager Tillamook citizens for Oregon's centennial celebration of 1959, is now on display at Tillamook County Creamer Association. The original* Morning Star *was constructed from the remains of earlier Oregon shipwrecks.* (Marshall collection)

weight of bread baked from hoarded wheat flour, cheeses and creams.

At the last moment and much to the celebrants' dismay, the farmers discovered they lacked the necessary grease for the ship's launching ways. Although their cattle survived upon the valley's lush grasses, only grain, depleted long ago, produced the fat from which tallow was made. Henderson suggested substituting old-fashioned bay silt, which was in plentiful supply. Thomas and Vaughn voiced serious doubts. Henderson promptly smeared the slippery goo upon two boards, placed one atop the other and jumped upon the two. One of the planks shot from under him and he lay flat upon his back, a painful but effective illustration to prove his point. Thomas remained unconvinced, explaining the weight of the ship pressed all moisture from between the hull and the ways

to leave only dry residue which would lock the ship in place.

The group opted to use bay silt and although not one in ten had ever seen a vessel launched, all hands fell to applying sediment by the shovel-full in their anxiety to christen the bay's water with their proud little ship.

At ten o'clock, January 1, 1855, Tillamook settlers and Indians gathered at the bay's edge to celebrate the auspicious event. George Scott of Hoquarten eulogized and after a fine address, closed with, "Ladies and Gentlemen, it has fallen to my share in the program to name this sturdy craft; we hail it as the blessing of a new Tillamook County. We therefore name this schooner the Morning Star of Tillamook." He broke a bottle of water across her bow, in lieu of non-existent wine. Amid deafening roars of the assemblage and the slamming blows of hammers knocking blocks away, the *Morning Star of Tillamook* shuddered, settled and refused to budge an inch.

Only one solution remained for the stout-hearted farmers. Regardless of the lean qualities of their cattle, a steer must be sacrificed; they must make whatever little tallow they gleaned from the beast suffice for greasing the skids. Trask volunteered one of his steers for the project. Soon, the poor animal's meager remains graced the ways for Tillamook's first vessel to broach the bay's placid waters.

The *Morning Star*, with the spirit of two fine American vessels deep within her bowels, performed beautifully. Soon the beleaguered settlers enjoyed a thriving trade in sugar, coffee, cloth, tools, flour and a multitude of necessities so vital to their continued existence.

MIMI

Beneath the rippling waters of Nehalem a deadly web of sands hungrily awaited the approaching iron-hulled German barque. A low, sticky, February fog camouflaged the danger as the *Mimi*'s Prussian skipper struggled to gain his bearings on this leg of the ship's journey from Callao. His precision-trained German crew leaped to his fog-shrouded commands. The blinded vessel plowed northward past the Nehalem jetty. A mile and a half later, she became firmly embedded upon the north spit.

The contract to re-float the *Mimi* was awarded to the Fisher Engineering and Construction Company. Captain Fisher took command of the situation and, much against the advice of Captain Farley of the Garibaldi Life Saving Station, ordered an unwarranted amount of ballast removed.

Ship, captain and crew remained stranded on the spit for the next two months while the Aryan seamen labored mightily to unload 1300 tons of ballast; all but 900 tons went by the board. The crew positioned two four-ton anchors at sea with attached lines to two barges and readied the ship's donkey engines

for the task of pulling in slack from the lines in order to slowly inch the *Mimi* into deep water. As their preparations neared completion, one of the mates dreamed of the *Mimi* under water, a hotel for the dead, with bloated, seaweed-entangled corpses bobbing in and out of submerged hatches. The mate related his nightmare to his companions; the first, second and third mates immediately deserted ship.[5] Their foolish talk started superstitious grumblings among the common crew and Captain Westphal now found it necessary to use a pistol to enforce his orders and to keep the restless sailors aboard.

At a signal given at high tide on April 6th, the donkey engines began winching the huge hawsers against the anchors on one side, tightening the lines to the stranded *Mimi*. Inch-by-inch the vessel rose and slid from her sandy cradle; each inch pulled her into a more precarious position. The ocean suddenly grew angry at these puny mortals who so brazenly thumped each other's backs in anticipated success of robbing her of her prize. A sea larger than the rest slammed the ship in a foaming rage, twisted her sideways and dumped her, masts shoreward, on her side.

Rank after rank of white-sheeted surf marched up and over the capsized *Mimi* to pluck struggling men from the canted deck. The ocean's heaving chest tumbled her human victims into a mass of twisted spars, broken masts and deadly, snaking rigging. Farley and his life-saving crew raced toward the stricken vessel. They tried again and again to approach from the lee side, but entangled wreckage blocked their access to the screaming, trapped men. One by one, the sea devoured her prey.

Fourteen of the German crew, some trapped within the *Mimi*'s bowels, perished one and one-half miles north of the Nehalem jetty, 800 feet out on the north spit, directly west of where Brighton now stands. Salvors Russell Blackburn and Captain Crowe, along with two of their men, died. Only Fisher, Westphal and two of the *Mimi*'s crew survived.

---

[5] The rate of desertions on French and German sail ships was much lower than that of the British and American Merchant Marine; a mere 2% for the former as compared to 30% for both the latter.

Hotel of Death *is what her first mate dreamed the German bark* Mimi *was to become — she did too, within a few days of the photo. Note men in rigging.*   *(Oregon Historical Society)*

The hull of the capsized German bark Mimi *off Neahkahnie Beach, 18 died.* (*Oregon Historical Society*)

FRIENDLY ENEMIES

The enormity of a shipwreck and its tragic results seldom fails to elicit a sense of the most profound pity from nearly all concerned. People from miles around will rush to the beachfront, mobilize and go to heroic proportions to rescue distressed seamen.

Seamen, who just a few moments prior were mortal enemies blasting each other with tons of hot iron and lead, will strain muscle and sinew against oars in a race to save those escaping a shot-shattered, sinking ship.

The following missives directed to former enemies, along with those letters from friends, give proof of this all-encompassing sense of administering aid to those victims of that electrifying phenomenon...shipwreck!

Fort Vancouver, Sept. 11, 1846

Dear Sir: We have just heard of the unfortunate accident which has befallen the Shark on the bar of this river, and we beg to offer our sincere condolence on the distressing event. We also beg to offer every assistance we can render in your present destitute state, and hope you will accept of the few things sent by this conveyance. Captain Baillie having dispatched bread and tea by the Modeste's pinnance anticipated our intention of sending such things. Have the goodness to apply to Mr. Peers for any articles of food or clothing you may want, and they will be at your service if he has them in store. As the people of Clatsop can furnish abundance of beef and potatoes, we are not anxious about your suffering any privation of food. If otherwise, Mr. Peers will do his utmost to supply your wants.

With kind remembrance to the officers, we remain, dear sir, yours truly,

Peter Skeen Ogden,
James Douglass
Neil Howison, &c., &c.

Her Majesty's Sloop Modeste,
Fort Vancouver, Columbia River, Sept. 13, 1846

Sir: It was with the greatest regret that I this morning received information of your vessel being on the sands at the mouth of the Columbia. From the hurried information I have received, I much fear my boat will be too late to render any assistance in saving your vessel; but in the possibility of your not having been able to save provisions, &c., I beg to offer for your acceptance a few of such articles as are not likely to be obtained at Clatsop.

I have the honor to be, sir, your most obedient servant,

Thos. Baillie, Commander
Lieut. Howison,
Commanding U.S. Schooner Shark

Oregon City, September 15, 1846

Dear Sir: Last night we heard the melancholy tidings that the schooner Shark was lost on the South spit. It was very painful intelligence, particularly as we are yet in doubt as to the safety of yourself, officers, and crew. The letter we received at this place state that the probability is, all were saved; which I sincerely hope may be the case; but until we hear of the safety of all, we will be in an unhappy state of suspense. My first feeling was to leave all here, and reach Clatsop as soon as possible, but I am situated in such a way, just at this time, that I cannot leave. Should you not make arrangements to get away in the Mariposa, we have your room in readiness for you, and will be very happy to have you make one of our family, as long as you may remain in the country, and any officers that you may choose for the other room. I perceive the Modeste's launch was to leave with a supply of provisions for you for the present. If you wish anything that I have, let me know, and I will send it down immediately. I have plenty of flour, and I have no doubt but plenty of beef and pork can be obtained here for the crew.

It will give me great pleasure to be of any service to you. Hoping to hear from you soon, and that yourself, officers, and crew are all safe on shore, and in good health,

I remain, dear sir, yours, very truly,
George Abernethy
Captain Neil Howison,
&c., &c., &c.

September 19, 1846

Should a vessel arrive belonging to the firm, I think you will have no difficulty in chartering her to go to California. I shall be happy to render you all the assistance that lies in my power. Should you wish any assistance as it regards money, or anything that I can obtain for you in Oregon, please inform me, and I will at the earliest date endeavor to procure it for you. Please accept my kindest regards to yourself and officers.

Yours truly,
John H. Couch
Capt. Neil Howison

Baker's Bay, Friday, November 9

Sir: I much regret the melancholy disaster which befell your vessel on Wednesday evening, and also my inability to render you any assistance at that time. The Indians tell me there are several lives lost, but I hope such is not true.

I am informed you wish to occupy part of the house at Astoria, it is at your service, as also anything else there in the shape of food or clothing, and I must, at some time apologize for offering you such poor accomodations. I sent off a dispatch to Vancouver yesterday morning, to acquaint them of your distress, and expect an answer Sunday morning.

I remain, sir, yours, most respectfully,
Henry Peers,
Port Agent of Hudson's Bay Company
To Captain Howison,
&c., &c., &c.

Baker's Bay, Columbia River,
December 1, 1846

Dear Governor: One of the few articles preserved from the ship-wreck of the late United States schooner Shark was her stand of colors. To display this national emblem, and cheer our citizens in this distant territory by its presence, was a principle [sic] object of the Shark's visit to the Columbia; and it appears to me, therefore, highly proper that it should henceforth remain with you, as a memento of parental regard from the general government.

With the fullest confidence that it will be received and duly appreciated as such by our countrymen here, I do myself the honor of transmitting the flags (an ensign and union-jack) to your address; nor can I omit the occasion to express my gratification and pride that this relic of my late command should be emphatically the first *United States* flag to wave over the undisputed and purely American territory of Oregon.

With consideration of high respect, I remain your obedient servant,

Neil M. Howison
Lieutenant Commanding United States Navy

Oregon City, December 21, 1846

Dear Sir. I received your esteemed favor of the 1st December, accompanied with the flags of the late U.S. schooner "Shark," (an ensign and union-jack) as a "memento of parental regard from the general government" to the citizens of this Territory.

Please accept my thanks and the thanks of this community for the (to us) very valuable present. We will fling it to the breeze on every suitable occasion, and rejoice under the emblem of our country's glory. Sincerely hoping that the "star-spangled banner" may ever wave over this portion of the United States, I remain, dear sir, yours truly,

Geo. Abernethy

Neil Howison,
Lieutenant commanding, &c., &c.

Thus, through the medium of a shipwreck, friendships were cemented, rivalries forgotten and all concerned returned to the business of developing this grand, primeval land. Ironically, the wrecked *Shark*'s flag, the first to fly over undisputed Oregon, has been misplaced, lost or destroyed. Hopefully, someday it will be found and restored to its rightful place in Oregon history.

THE INCREDIBLE DRIFT

The American wooden bark, *Emily Reed*, stood in much too close to the sands of Nehalem and much too late to wear ship[6] on the night of February 14, 1908. The weather held typically dark and overcast for several days off the coasts of California and Oregon; Captain Kessel charted the *Reed*'s course, unaware of the inaccuracy of his chronometer.

The ship sailed 102 days out of Newcastle, New South Wales with a load of coal for Portland's hungry industries. The skipper anxiously scanned the sea for the comforting arm of light from the Tillamook Lighthouse sweeping through the darkness.

The blinded bark drove through the breakers bow-on at high tide and hit the beach. Her back broke almost instantly under the weight of her load of coal; her forward section listed to port and the men there were swept into the sea. Captain Kessel, his wife, Second Mate Charles Thompson, seamen Barney Sullivan, H. Franchez and Herman Bertell clung to the sea-washed poop deck until low tide, then made their way through the receding surf to shore. All assumed the missing ship's boat had capsized or disintegrated in the welter of broken masts and tangled lines littering the dead ship. Reports stated that eleven men perished in the tragic episode.

Three days later and 200 miles to the north, the six-ton sloop *Tecla* lay anchored in Neah Bay, Washington. Her crew, aroused by a weak voice hailing their vessel, came to the rescue of Fred Zube and two other survivors from the *Emily Reed*. Seaman Zube nursed a broken arm; all three suffered from exposure and extreme thirst. In the boat with the three men lay the body of the ship's cook; unable to slake his thirst, the unfortunate mariner became delirious and drank sea water.

The ship's loss of life was reduced to eight when news of this incredible 200 mile drift covering more than sixty-six miles per day in a damaged boat with only one oar and no food, water or emergency supplies was flashed to surprised officials at Astoria.

ARGO #1

The twin-screwed steamer *Argo #1* was as uninteresting a little ship as was ever built in 1898. Her 130-foot length fitted easily into any one of a dozen 210-tonners launched during the era of the Alaskan gold rush.

As thousands of gold-fevered sourdoughs stampeded in a frenzied race for Alaskan shores, Ballard and Murphy (formerly the Cleveland Ohio Shipbuilding Co. and now known as Cleveland Alaska Gold Mining Co.) grasped this golden once-in-a-lifetime opportunity to corner Alaskan transportation. They quickly built and launched a coastal trader, *Argo #1* and a river steamer, *Argo #2*.

Argo #1 with *Argo #2* in tow sailed north to lay the foundation for Ballard and Murphy's coveted monopoly. Unfortunately *#2* broke loose en route and foundered off Dixon's Entrance.

---

[6] The *Reed* was on a port tack, the spanker and mizzen staysail would have to be taken in, the helm put to weather and the mainyard squared, with the spanker in her head would fly to leeward. From this position she would be running downwind; her foresails would be braced around and her jibs sheeted to port. The ship would still be in danger as she would be running parallel to the beach and would have to claw off. She would be brought around to a starboard tack, set her spanker and staysail and bring the head into the wind. The mainyard would be braced round and she would now pull on the starboard with all sails trimmed and drawing.

Collapsed stern section of the Emily G. Reed.   *(Wayne Jensen, Jr. collection)*

The Emily G. Reed, *30 years later.*   *(Tillamook County Pioneer Museum)*

Built for Alaskan waters, the hard working Argo *went down off Tillamook with the loss of several lives.*
(Tillamook County Pioneer Museum)

All too soon the gold rush fever of the Klondike slowed to a snail's pace and after only a few years of operation the company and the steamer route between the far north and San Francisco became a financial disaster. The now defunct company sold *Argo #1* to the Tillamook Steam Navigation Company... they shortened her name to just plain *Argo* and her route to Portland, Astoria, Tillamook and return.

The hard-working ship soon earned a reputation for comfort, speed, economy and safety ...until that fateful day of November 26, 1909. She left Astoria at 5:15 a.m. under the able hand of Captain Levi Snyder and sailed over the Columbia Bar en route for Tillamook Bay. The *Argo* arrived off the bay at 2:30 p.m. Worsening weather and deathly seasick passengers clouded the captain's judgment

and prompted his ordering the ship across the bar at dangerous half tide.

What exactly caused the port screw to snap will never be known, but snap it did. The unexpected thrust of the starboard wheel broached the wooden steamer into the concrete-like north spit with a jarring shock which snapped the vital steam pipe between the boiler and the throttle valve. Chief Engineer J. H. Snyder and his assistant, Thomas Russell, struggled mightily against the hissing cloud of live steam to couple the break. The surging current captured the wounded vessel and carried her past the mouth of the Tillamook, then slammed her onto the south spit with a crashing shock more violent than the first. The two men were hurled to the oil-slicked deck as the vessel began grinding to death. Swirls of water lashed at the men's feet. Snyder alerted the captain, "...not sure, captain, but it looks like her bilge keels ripped out. We got water pouring from behind the bunkers. I think her bottom planks and garboard strakes are sprung!"

Captain Snyder quickly ordered all crew topside and, with an ingenuity typical to Oregon steam-schoonermen, sent all hands scrambling up the rigging to set sails on both the main and mizzen masts to the onshore gale. He alternately luffed and trimmed to bring her off the deadly bar with nose up to the wind. Then, with as much luff as possible, he spilled the wind and ordered a hard starboard spin on the wheel. He again set his ship to the wind and successfully brought the gutted vessel into safer, deeper water.

Capt. Farley and his men at Garibaldi Life Station watched this daring piece of seamanship and realized the ship had, except for the sails, lost all power. Within minutes they launched a rescue boat and, pulling hard at the oars, raced to the stricken ship.

Loading the *Argo*'s passengers into the lifeboat progressed with a minimum of difficulty; as the surge raised the surf boat even with the deck of the *Argo*, men and women quickly jumped in and held on while the receding wave plunged their smaller boat below the moss covered waterline of the larger ship. As the surfmen prepared to push off, a surge of sea threw their boat against the wale of the larger ship, severely damaging it. Captain Farley, fearful of a swamping, ordered eight male passengers to return to the wallowing *Argo*. Lightened but leaking, the small craft made an erratic run for the beach, but when caught by the boiling surf, the lifeboat refused to answer the helm. End over end she tumbled, spilling line, survival gear, oars and screaming occupants into the slashing, pounding waves. Mrs. Jennie King of Tillamook recalled, "After the first great breaker struck us and the water pulled us down, we could see each other floating around. We all tried to get to the boat and right it, but another mighty breaker struck us and we were whirled in every direction.

"Before each breaker struck I would fill my lungs with air, close my mouth and hold my breath until it roared over me. Then I would strike out and try to paddle to shore. When we first got into the boat Captain Farley made us change the life jackets we were wearing for the better cork jackets in the surf boat. He said our jackets were no good; they were stuffed with tule.[7] The shore was so far, far away, then Captain Farley was thrown near me by the rollers. He said, 'Take hold of my hand and I will guide you to the boat, but do not pull on my arm as it is broken.'

"I told him I had better not take hold of you at all. But he said just to lock my little finger with his and we would get there all right. We got to the boat with three others but just then the next wave came along and washed us all away. One of the three was the little girl who drowned."

The cold threshing sea claimed the souls of 6-year-old Nellie Hunt of Napa, California, Mrs. L. A. Holdredge, Portland and Garibaldi surfman Henry Wickman. The others staggered ashore drenched but uninjured. Captain Farley was pulled unconscious from the sea with serious internal injuries in addition to his broken arm.

Meanwhile, Captain Snyder abandoned all hope of saving the waterlogged *Argo* and ordered the two lifeboats launched. He took charge of one and assigned his first mate A. A. Johnson to command the other. A last minute frantic search of the ship failed to locate passenger Tony Riggoletti who boarded at Astoria and the ship's fireman, Martin Anderson; the captain presumed both men washed overboard.

Mate Johnson's boat with its ten passengers headed for the beach. En route, they were met and rescued by the steamer *Oshkosh*.

Captain Snyder, in hopes of locating the missing men, directed his boat and its nine survivors to continue circling the drifting *Argo*, all the while "Hallooing" in anticipation of hearing a response. The exercise proved fruitless for the cold, dead ship merely stared back with sightless, broken window

---

[7] A swamp reed, buoyant for only a short time before it becomes waterlogged and heavy.

eyes, pitched and plunged, then awkwardly sank beneath the surrounding shroud of icy, green sea.

Ensuing darkness and a rising wind enjoined Captain Snyder to surrender his command of the frail craft to John Wodhouse, one of his most valued crewmen. Wodhouse previously served through the ranks of surfman; his last position, before signing onboard a ship in hopes of gaining his captain's stripes, was that of #4 in the tough Cape Disappointment rescue team. The crewman-now-captain skillfully counted a strength-saving cadence for the rowing men as he guided the boat through some thirty miles of wind and waves to the welcome safety of the ever-present *Columbia Light Ship #50.* Eager hands and Mate Nelson (in charge of the Light Ship during Captain Rasmussen's absence) cared for the half-frozen survivors during the next four days while the storm blew itself out.

The *Golden Gate,* a wooden tug bought from an Astoria fish company and rebuilt, replaced the lost *Argo.* Captain Snyder's indiscretion cost him a year's suspension of his license. That should be the end of the *Argo's* story, but wait....

A week following the disaster a group of some 200 angry citizens presented a petition to local officials asserting that one victim of the accident, a Mrs. Holdredge, was *alive* at the time of her interment. The damning document declared that all signators agreed to the apparent limpness of her wrist and hands and rosiness of her cheeks as she lay in the coffin and after discussing this evidence amongst themselves decided there was a distinct possibility of her being alive and they now sought legal assistance in exhuming her.

The beleaguered city officials quickly contacted the county coroner and dumped this hot potato into his lap. His reply, delivered with a modicum of sagacity and with no disrespect, agreed with the plaintiffs and their request of exhumation. Of course, he added, he was certain the lady was dead when he examined the body but, if any doubts remained, then by all means dig her up.

Howsomever, if she were not dead at the time of the burial, she sure-as-shooting would be by now, a full week after the fact.

It took a bit of time for his Solomonic advice to sink home, but when it did, logic prevailed among the petitioners. They allowed that if the funeral really did pre-empt death, well, after all, it was a nice funeral. One sage opined, "Just ain't no sense in undoing what's been done. Let's just put the whole matter to rest, so to speak."

And so they did.

SUNKEN SUBMARINES MYTHS

An alarming number of inhabitants along the western shores of the United States have become victims of an infectious, sometimes harmless, ailment known as the "Submarine Syndrome," a regional disease prevalent in saloons, dive shops and tourist centers.

During WW II western American coastal areas experienced minimal enemy submarine activity; the potential was there but Japan's hesitation to commit her excellent submersibles and highly trained crews to an all-out offensive attack became a leading factor in her ultimate defeat.

Japan assigned nine submarines to patrol the American western coast at the beginning of WW II. Seven of these ships designated "I"[8] were of the type "B" or I-25 class, while two, the I 9 and I 10, were of the "A" class and designated as headquarters submarines. The I 8, of the I 7 or type "J" class originally reported off the United States coast, stayed with SubRon 3 as flagship for the Pearl Harbor operation.

Confusing? Well, that is the very nature of submarine operations. In the latter part of November, 1941, Japan ordered her SubRons (Submarine Squadrons) 1 through 7 to disperse from their bases of Kure and Yokosuka and reassemble at their designated station by December 1. SubRons 4 and 5 (14 vessels) left to patrol the China Seas; SubRon 6 (4 mine laying submarines) mined the Philippine and Singapore waters, then proceeded to Aus-

---

[8] First letter in the Japanese phonetic alphabet meaning 1st class.

tralia to pick off shipping there; 9 short-range RO boats began their operations off Wake Island and the surrounding area.

The remaining SubRons 1, 2 and 3 (30 of Japan's finest, 20 of which carried airplanes and 5 carried midget 2-man subs) screened Vice Admiral Chuichi Nagumo's strike force en route to Pearl Harbor, with 12 subs arranged in two arcs to the south of Oahu and the five midgets' carriers stationed closest to Pearl Harbor.

The remaining subs patrolled as follows: I 10, San Diego; I 19, Los Angeles; I 21, Estero Bay; I 23, Monterey Bay; I 15, San Francisco; I 17, Cape Mendocino; I 9, Cape Blanco; I 25, Columbia River; I 26, Cape Flattery.

Immediately following Japan's attack on Pearl Harbor, war-crazed Californians, Oregonians and Washingtonians reported enemy submarine activity in a fervor of patriotic enthusiasm...through the ensuing years their tales of downed submarines persist with appropriate verification by:

"...A guy who comes in here every night. He'll tell you about it."

"...There's this diver who was out looking for abalone and found this Japanese sub right there...."

"...This old guy that lives right down the street; he actually watched the planes drop depth charges on it. He watched the bow go up in the air and saw the crew scramble up on deck and then it sank, right out there...."

Interesting stories, to be sure, but time and documented evidence prove them pure fantasy and in most cases harmless, but not always.

Californians claim the following submarines as their contribution to the war effort:

One lies off Catalina; one at Redondo Beach; one off San Pedro with tons of mercury as ballast; two off Monterey, one of which is a mini sub; one lies in the cold waters of San Francisco's fabulous gate, a victim of a ramming by a garbage scow; a Nazi U-Boat on the bottom off Newport.

Quite an impressive list and undoubtedly more subs will be added as the years go by. Aside from the known fate of all submarines Japan assigned to work in eastern Pacific wa-

ters, some common sense facts must be explored and logic must prevail.

Water is the primary ballast in submarines. The main ballast tanks allow controlled diving and surfacing of the vessel and are arranged in groups with some designated as fuel ballast tanks. These latter tanks remain empty while the submarine is surfaced, then are flooded for diving and used in conjunction with the main ballast tanks. In addition to the above named tanks there are the standard fuel tanks, a collecting tank, expansion tank, clean fuel oil tank, main sump pump tanks, reduction gear sump tanks, fresh water tanks, battery fresh water tanks, sanitary tanks, trimming tanks, and "water around torpedo tanks." Mercury exists aboard a submarine *only* in barometrical instruments, pharmacopia or certain types of blasting caps.

Unfortunately, in 1953, five Santa Barbara men drowned in a futile search for the mythical San Pedro sub and its fabulous tons of mercury ballast.

Just how, when or why a Nazi U-Boat managed to sink at Newport remains unanswered, but the story persists that the vessel and crew lie somewhere "out there." No U-Boats traveled eastern Pacific waters during WW II.

The Japanese sub and its mini counterpart rumored off Monterey are a product of overworked imaginations. In reality, the "mini" is a large rusted portion of sewer pipe.

Oregonians claim subs off of Newport (mercury ballast), Pacific City boasts of a sub with an eleven man crew, and Astorians will speak with smug pride of the sunken enemy raider at the mouth of the Columbia River that managed to land a four man invasion team prior to its watery demise at the hands of an attacking formation of B-24s.

The real mystery of Pacific City's tall tale is how did the original bearer of the news of a sunken Japanese sub know it carried exactly eleven men to the bottom?

Excluding the minis, the Japanese manned only two types of undersea boats with such small crews. One was the foreign built #6 boat which sank April 14, 1910 under the command of Lt. Tsutomu Sakuma and is now a national memorial to all Japanese submarinemen. The other eleven man crew vessels were the class #71 boats. This style proved too clumsy and complicated to handle; the Japanese dismantled all of them long before the onset of WW II.

More modest in their claims to total destruction of the enemy task force in those early years of sheer terror punctuated by short periods of absolute panic are the citizens of Washington. They claim only one...a straggler, no doubt, in search of its sister submarine and managed, though no one can say exactly how, to sink just outside of Seattle.

Not a single enemy submarine went to the bottom off America's western coastline during WW I or WW II.

RULES OF THE ROAD

Steamers meeting fair on end
three lights open, mast on one
in such a case have naught to fear
each ports her helm and passes clear.

If on your starboard bow or beam
a Steamer's red port light should gleam.
Be prompt to act without delay,
yours is the ship that should give way.

To every vessel under sail
a Steamer gives way without fail,
unless a case comes into view
of a sailing ship overtaking you.

When on crossing port bow you sight
a Steamer's crossing starboard light,
be cautious when you go ahead
while her green light shows on your red.

When you are approaching to,
a ship that should keep clear of you
this rule then comes into force
that you are to change your course.

If in a special case you see
that you can save a casualty,
then by these rules you are not bound
but exercise a judgment sound.

It is not by these rules advised
to part from custom recognized,
mind the lights, bright green and red
the land, the log, lookout and lead.

If you are bilious, take Dr. Pierce's "Pleasant Purgative Pellets" the original "Little Liver Pills" of all druggists.

Daily Astorian
April, 1883

OH, YEAH!

A man died at sea and the funeral was set for an early hour the next morning. The captain, of course, was to read the service.

At the appointed hour the vessel was hove to and all hands came aft to attend the solemn rites. The sheeted and shotted body lay on its plank, all heads were uncovered, all hearts brimming with emotion; but no skipper appeared. After waiting a long time the surgeon undertook to read the service, and advancing to the head of the corpse, prayer-book in hand, began: "I am the resurrection and the life...." Tardy skipper (emerging from below): "I'll be damned if you are! *I* am the resurrection and the life!"

Daily Astorian
October 11, 1883

B-A-R SPELLS DANGER!

The most dangerous condition — when a swift ebb tide current meets heavy rolling seas coming in from the vast Pacific at a shallow river entrance (in other words, the *bar*) — when this occurs, the water "piles up" and "breaks." Even on calm days, a swift ebb tide may create a bar condition that is too rough for small craft (any boat under 65'). Cross from harbor to ocean only on slack water, flood tides or when the sea is calm.

If you are inside, remain inside. If you are trapped outside a rough bar on an ebb current, *wait a few hours* until the flood.

Sands, spits and shoals are shallow areas at river entrances where waves build up. These areas are dangerous and should be avoided at all times.

In a bar area, sea conditions can change rapidly and without warning. Always cross with caution.

Have you checked the weather reports and tides?

READING THE BAROMETER

Barometer rising:

28.8 to 29.2 inches — Clearing, high winds and cool wave.
29.2 to 29.6 inches — High winds, cool wave preceded by squalls.
29.6 to 29.9 inches — Fair weather, fresh winds during next 24 hours.
29.9 to 30.2 inches — Fair weather, brisk winds diminishing.
30.2 to 30.5 inches — Fair weather, cooler, variable winds.
30.5 to 30.8 inches — Continued cool, clear weather, light winds.
30.8 to 31.0 inches — High winds, southeast with rains.

Barometer falling:

30.8 to 30.5 inches — Fair, warmer, followed by rain and wind.
30.5 to 30.2 inches — Approaching storm.
30.2 to 29.9 inches — Cloudy, warmer, unsettled weather.
29.9 to 29.3 inches — Squally, clearing, fair and cooler weather.
29.3 to 29.0 inches — Clearing, high winds with squalls and cooler weather.
29.0 to 28.7 inches — Stormy weather.

Get your weather reports on 162.4 KHz.

INTERNATIONAL DISTRESS SIGNALS

In the daytime:

1. A gun fired at intervals of one minute.
2. The international Flag Code Signal of distress indicated by NC.
3. The distress signal, consisting of a square flag, having either above or below it a ball, or anything resembling a ball.

4. Rockets or shells as prescribed for use at night.
5. Continuous sounding with a steam whistle or any fog signalling apparatus.

At night:

1. A gun fired at intervals of one minute.
2. Flames on the vessel, as from a burning tar barrel, oil barrel, etc. *Use extreme caution.*
3. Rockets or shells bursting in the air with a loud report and throwing stars of any color or description; fire one at a time at short intervals.
4. A continuous sounding with a steam whistle or any fog signal apparatus.

All officers and men of the United States Coast Guard recognize any of these signals when seen or heard as *signals of distress* — and will proceed immediately to render all possible assistance.

Most important, keep updated on all charts, signals, safety features (seamanship or scuba diving), weather reports and any other factor that may endanger your life…do not try to save that extra buck; spend it and stay alive!

NAME OF NAMES

Mr. Lewis A. McArthur, B.S., M.A., L.L.D., author of *Oregon Geographic Names*, upon whom I heavily relied and without his tome available, would have been virtually lost in a sea of names, breaks Oregon geographic names into six periods ranging from early Indian to modern.

The second and sixth periods are, for the purpose of *Oregon Shipwrecks*, the most interesting. The period of exploration along Oregon's coast left names of Spanish and English origin. Modern time's contribution added real estate phraseology.

To search for ships or place significant events would be virtually impossible without doing one's homework. For instance, Pete Peldo, a delightful ancient-mariner-type Astorian, tells of when he was a lad of many years ago. He remembered when he and his father hiked across Strawberry Hill and discovered a bank of sand broken away from its parent and slid downhill to expose a weathered, wrecked port-bow of a long-forgotten wooden vessel.

"Where is Strawberry Hill?"

"Well, I really don't remember just now, but it's someplace around Warrenton or Fort Stevens...or was it Gearheart?"

This encompassed an area of some fifty or so square miles. Although we never found Strawberry Hill and the ancient wreck, we had a good time talking about it.

Even the name Oregon and its origin are wrapped in the shroud of time. Major Robert Rogers is credited with the first mention of the name Oregon when, around 1760, he marched to capture the French fort at Mackinac in the Canadian wilderness. He became obsessed with a theory of a direct river route to the Pacific and called it, "...the great River Ourigan...." He claims to have received the somewhat accurate information from the Indians, but could he have received this information directly from a survivor from the wrecked Spanish ship of the Nehalem area? One castaway is known to have left his son, Soto, with the Indians of the Dalles. Could the survivor's name have been Obregon, a tongue-twister to the Indians who corrupted it to Oregon? Was it a phonetical spelling of names like Aragon, Ouragan or Aurigan?

There are those who say the word Oregon is simply an Algonquin word meaning "rainy country." Probably the most simplistic, matter-of-fact explanation, in spite of the hundreds of thousands of words written on the subject, was offered by Amalia Sher, whose delightful letter to the editor appeared in the April 15th, 1982 issue of the *Oregonian*:

To the Editor,
Having just completed my first year in your state, I understand why it is named Oregon.
When someone asks what the weather is going to be, the standard reply is, "Well, it could rain, or again, it could snow, or again, it could shine, or again...."

A few examples follow:

Arago — Halls Prairie
Astoria — Fort George, Union Town (West Astoria 1880), Alderbrook (Upper Astoria)
Bald Mountain — Bald Peak, Pilot Knob, Chussuggel
Bay City — Down the Bay
Bayocean — Barnegat
Big Creek — Tilly Ann, Tilly Jane, Tle-las-qua
Boiler Bay — Briggs Landing
Brandy Bay — Umpqua River
Brush Creek — Euchre Creek, Savage Creek 1889
Bunker Hill — Isthmus, Coalbank
Cannibal Mountain — Cannonball Mountain, Canniber Mountain
Cannon Beach — Elk Creek, Ecola 1922
Cape Arago — Cape Gregory 1778, Cabo Toledo 1775
Cape Arago Lighthouse — Gregory Point
Cape Blanco — Cabo Deligensias 1775, Cape Orford 1792
Cape Falcon — False Tillamook Head, Sierra de Montefalcon 1775
Cape Kiwanda — Sand Cape, Haystack Point
Cape Lookout — Cape Meares
Cape Meares — Cape Lookout 1850, La Mesa 1775
Cathlamet Bay — Swan Bay
Cathlamet Point — Aldrich Point
Chetco — Chetko, Chitco
Columbia River — River of the West 1767, Bahia de la Asuncion 1775, Ensenada de Hecata, San Roque 1788, Deception Bay 1788, Great River of the West 1817, Cabo Frondoso
Coos Bay — Marshfield 1944, Cahoose, Cowis 1837, Cowes, Koo-as, Koos, Coose 1851, Kowes
Coquille — Scoquel 1854, Coquette 1851, Nes-sa-til-cut
Delmar — Kings Landing
Depoe Bay — Depot Slough, Depoe Slough
Euchre Creek — Savage Creek 1889
Face Rock — Graystone
Fashion Reef — Multnomah Falls
Floras Creek, Flores Lake — Florey Creek 1855
Fort Clatsop — Port Clatsop 1852
Fort Miner — Citizens Fort 1856, Miners Fort
Glasgo Point — Jordan Point
Gold Beach — Ellensburg
Hammond — Kindred, Ne-ahk-stow
Hardtack, Ross & Toe Island — Hartack Island
Haynes Inlet — Haines Inlet
Hinton Point — Point Virtue, Idaho Point
Hood River — Dog River
Hook — Squally Hook
Humbug Mountain — Sugar Loaf, Tichenor's Humbug, Franklin 1853, Me-tus
Iowa Slough — Deadman Slough
Isthmus Slough — Wapello Slough
Karlson Island — Carlson, Carlesen
Kelly Point — Belle Vue
Kilchis Point — Jawbone
King Slough — Hinton Slough

Knappa — Tle-las-qua
Lakeport — Pacific City
Lemon Island — Lemmon's Island
Lewis & Clark River — Netul River
Libby — Eastport
Lint Slough — Indian Slough
Lookout Rock — Nog-gi-sa
Macklyn Cove — Macklin Cove 1864
McCaffery Slough — Johnson Slough
Memaloose Island — Memaloost, Memalust
Miami River — Mi-me-chuck, Mi-mie
Mount Emily — Mount Emery, Chetco Peak, Emney
Neahkahnie Mountain — Ne-a-karny, Ne-kah-ni
Necanicum — Push
Necanicum River — Nekonikon, Latty Creek
Nehalem — Naalem 1852, Ne-ay-lem
Nestucca River — Nea-stocka 1841
Netarts Bay — Na-ta-at, Oyster Bay 1899
Nice — Alsea Bay, Drift Creek 1874, Collins 1876 & 1882, Waldport 1881, Lutgens 1890 & 1897, Stanford 1893
North Bend — Bangor
Olalla Slough — Olallie
Oregon — Aragon, Ouragan
Pacific Ocean — Mar del Sur 1513, Great Western Ocean 1805-6
Phoca Rock — Hermit Islet
Pilot Knob — Bald Mountain
Point Adams — Cabo Frondoso
Port Orford — Ewing Harbor 1851, Indian Bay, Fort Orford, Ewing Bay
Redmans Tooth — Bucktooth Creek, Dead Indian Creek
Rogue River — Les Coquins 1820, La Riviere aux Coquins 1820, River Coquin 1833, Rascally River 1841, Gold River 1854, Trashit
Rogue River (town) — Woodville
Roosevelt Beach — Heceta, Samaria
Ross Island — Oak Islands, Toe Island, Island #3
Saint Helens — Plymouth 1845, New Plymouth 1849, Kasenau, Cassino 1850
Salmon River — Nechesne
Sauvie Island — Wappato, Wappatoo 1805, Wyeth Island 1834, Multnomah Island, Souvies Island 1852
Seal Rocks — Seal Illahe
Seaside — Ne-co-tat, Summer House 1871, Seaside House 1873
Shell Rock — Collins Landing
Silver Point — Sylvan Point, Point Cliff 1894, Sylvan Park
Sixes River — Sikhs River 1851, Sequalchin River, Sa-qua-mi, Sik-ses-tene
Skipanon River — Skipanarwin 1805, Skeppernawin Creek, Skipanon Creek 1925, Skippenon Creek 1856

Smith Point — O-wa-pun-pun, Point George, Youngs Point
Smugglers Cove — Short Sand Beach, Treasure Cove
Snake River — Lewis, Shoshone, Nes Perce, Sahaptin, Kimeonim, Louis
Southbeach — Harborton 1916
Tansy Point — Raccoon Point 1813
Techumtas Island (now under water) — Switzler Island, McComas Island
Tenasillahe Island — Kathlamet Island
Ten Miles Rapids — Little Narrows, Short Narrows, Les Petites Dalles
The Dalles — Dalles 1814, Dalls 1825, Great Dalles, Long Narrows, Quenett, Que-nett (Lewis & Clark 1805), Rockfort Camp 1806
Three Arch Rocks — Three Brothers 1787
Tillamook — Lincoln, Hoquarton, The Landing, Tillamook Landing
Tillamook Bay — Quicksand Bay 1788, Murderers Harbor 1788
Tillamook Head — Clarks Point of View 1806, Nah-se-u-su
Tongue Point — Point Williams 1805, Secomeetsivc
Umatilla River — Youmalolam, You-matella, Umatallow, Utalla, Ewmitilly, Eu-o-tal-la, Umatilah, Umatella
Umpqua River — Umptqua, Arguilas 1825, Umkwa 1846, Umquah 1833, Umpqua 1845, Umpquas 1846
Vingle Creek — Divinity Creek
Wallace Island — Yapats Island, Kotsi Island
Warrenton — Lexington 1848, Skipanon Station, Skipanon 1889, Upper Landing
Warrenton/Hammond — Flavel, Konapee
Willamette — Wallamette, Walamet, Wal-lamt, Wilhamet
Willamette Bar — Post Office Bar
Winchuck Rover — Neh-jaw
Yaquina Bay — Iakon, Aquinna, Yakone, Youlkeones, Youkone, Yacone
Youngs River — Meriwether Bay, Kilhowanahkle River

COASTAL DESCRIPTION
From Cascade Head to Nehalem River[9]

Cascade Head, 23 miles north of Yaquina Head, is very jagged and heavily wooded. The face of the cliff is three miles long, is over 700 feet high in places, and is cut by several deep gorges through which the waters of three creeks are discharged in cascades 60 to

[9] Consult nautical charts numbers 18520, 18556 and 18558.

93

80 feet high. Several rocks are about 0.1 mile offshore.

Two Arches, 30 feet high, is a rock 0.9 mile north of the south point of Cascade Head. The arches are visible from the north; the inner is the larger.

From Cascade Head for 9.5 miles to Cape Kiwanda, the coast is a low sand beach with a narrow marsh behind the south part. Rolling hilltops, occasionally wooded, rise to an elevation of 500 feet behind the beach.

Neskowin Rock, at the high water line about 0.3 mile north of the north extremity of the cliffs marking Cascade Head, rises abruptly from the sand beach to 113 feet in height. The rock is dark brown and wooded on top.

North of Neskowin Rock the Oregon Coast Highway is about one-half mile inland. At night the headlights of automobiles traveling this road cause *intermittent flashes* as they make the turns and might be mistaken for vessels.

Nestucca River empties into Nestucca Bay 5.5 miles north of Cascade Head. The channel over the bar changes frequently in position and depth. Only light draft vessels with local knowledge are able to cross safely.

A fixed highway bridge at Pacific City has a clearance of 10 feet. The river has many snags that change the depths and shift the channel. Even in moderate sea, the bar is *extremely dangerous*.

The point on the south side of the entrance consists of several low-rolling, grassy hillocks about 400 to 500 feet high, which approach very close to the beach. The north point is the south extremity of the sandspit and dunes that extend to Cape Kiwanda.

Pacific City, a summer resort three miles above the entrance to Nestucca Bay, has a general store. Small quantities of fuel and other items may be purchased.

Haystack Rock (do not confuse with the more northerly Haystack Rock), 327 feet high, 0.5 mile SW of Cape Kiwanda and 0.5 mile offshore, is a prominent landmark. The rock is conical and dark for about half its height, and in the summer the birds go to

work on it again. A lighted seasonal whistle buoy is just NW of the rock.

Cape Kiwanda, 33 miles north of Yaquina Head, is a rocky point, low and yellow; it is much broken and eroded. It projects about 0.5 mile from the general trend of the coast. Behind the cape are bright sand dunes, 500 feet high, which are prominent from seaward. Just to the south of Cape Kiwanda is a beach resort area; a public launching ramp is here. A radio beacon is about 0.5 mile SW of the cape.

From Cape Kiwanda the coast extends 7.5 miles in a general northerly direction to Cape Lookout. It is broken about halfway by the entrance to Sand Lake, which is shallow and not navigable. The coast consists of sand beaches and dunes until about a mile north of Sand Lake where it changes to vertical sandstone cliffs, 50 to 100 feet high. These continue to Cape Lookout.

Cape Lookout, 40 miles north of Yaquina Head, projects west for 1.5 miles, forming a narrow rocky promontory 432 feet in height at its seaward extremity. The south face is nearly straight, and its precipitous cliffs have numerous caves. The north face is sloping and covered with a thick growth of timber. The ridge that forms the cape runs at about right angles to the coast, reaching an elevation of some 2,000 feet, 3.8 miles inland. The north face of the cape is smooth and bald for the first mile, and then is much broken. It is marked by caves and several cascades. Fair shelter in NW winds may be had under the south side of the cape in 6 to 8 fathoms, sandy bottom. A lighted whistle buoy is about 0.5 mile off the cape.

North of Cape Lookout for 4.5 miles, the land falls to a low narrow sandy peninsula, separating Netarts Bay from the ocean. The sand dunes on the peninsula are visible for 10 or 12 miles.

Netarts Bay is a shallow lagoon most of which is bare at low water; a whistle buoy off the entrance marks the approach. The village of Netarts is on the north shore a mile inside the entrance. Only light-draft vessels with local knowledge should enter. A small-boat basin and launching ramp are at Netarts. North of the entrance to Netarts Bay, for 1.5 miles to the rocks forming the south side of Cape Meares, the coast is a sandy beach, backed by cliffs 50 to 120 feet high. These cliffs are topped by sand dunes varying in height from 150 to 200 feet. They are good landmarks.

Cape Meares, 48 miles north of Yaquina Head, is a high and rocky spot with a two-mile-long seaward face. The north part is the higher, with nearly vertical cliffs 640 feet high. The west point is narrow, covered with fern and brush, and terminates seaward in a cliff 200 feet high.

Three Arch Rocks are the largest of a cluster extending 350 yards off the south point of the cape. They range in height from 204 to 275 feet. The largest arch is in the middle of the lowest rock, and about half the height of the rock above water. The rocks are a favorite resort of sea lions, whose barking can be heard a considerable distance with a favorable wind.

Cape Meares Light, 45°29.2′N, 123°58.6′W, 232 feet above the water, is shown from a 17 foot white masonry building on the summit of the cliff.

Pillar Rock, 75 feet high, is 0.2 mile NW of Cape Meares Light, and 0.4 mile farther NW is Pyramid Rock, 110 feet high, which leans seaward.

From Cape Meares to Kincheloe Point, the coast is a low partly wooded sandspit, with dunes 40 to 50 feet high. It forms the west shore of Tillamook Bay. A sand dike prevents a breakthrough north of Cape Meares, at Pitcher Point.

Tillamook Bay entrance is 42 miles south of the Columbia River, 22.5 miles south of Tillamook Rock Light, and five miles north of Cape Meares Light. The bay has a tidal basin of 13 square miles, most of which, at low tide, presents a succession of sand and mud flats. There is no commercial traffic in the bay except for fishing boats and pleasure craft.

Kincheloe Point is low and sandy and appears to be an island from a distance to the north. The north side of the entrance is a termination of a wooded ridge extending between the bay and Nehalem River. Green Hill, opposite Kincheloe Point, is a 400-foot spur that terminates in a bluff rounded point. The prominent hill is covered by ferns, grass and dense brush, with trees on the top.

In 1976 a jetty, extending from Kincheloe Point in a NW direction, was under construction. A Coast Guard station is on the north shore, west of Garibaldi. A lookout tower is near the intersection of the entrance jetty and the beachline.

The north side of the entrance to Tillamook Bay is protected by an 800 yard jetty, marked near the seaward end by a light and a seasonal fog signal. A lighted whistle buoy is 1.1 miles west of the end of the jetty. The channel to Garibaldi is marked by a lighted range, lights, and buoys. The bar sometimes makes out across the range from the north during the summer or whenever there have been any periods of extended northwest winds.

In August of 1977, a depth of 20 feet could be carried the east side of Tillamook Bay to the south end where it continues through narrow and crooked Hoquarten Slough to Tillamook, 11 miles above Tillamook Bay entrance. The channel has a depth of about six feet to Bay City, 4.4 miles above Tillamook Bay entrance, but south of this point depths are less than three feet to Tillamook. During the freshets, snags are carried into the upper part of the bay where they form a menace to navigation.

Tillamook River empties into the south part of Tillamook Bay just west of the entrance to Hoquarten Slough. A fixed highway bridge with a clearance of 15 feet crosses the river about 0.7 mile above the mouth. A small marina is just south of the bridge; berths and fuel are available, small repairs can be made. It is open only in the summer.

From Tillamook Bay to Nehalem River, the coast is nearly straight for about five miles. Several lakes in this stretch are separated from the beach by wooded sand dunes. The heavily wooded hills begin to rise 0.5 mile to 0.8 mile from the beach and in one mile reach an elevation of 1,000 to 1,600 feet.

Twin Rocks are 700 yards offshore and two miles north of the entrance to Tillamook Bay. Their bases are so close together that they usually look like one rock. The south, and larger, has an arch in it.

Nehalem River, 5 miles north of Tillamook Bay entrance, is tidal for about 10 miles from the entrance. Above this point the river is a mountain stream full of riffles and obstructed by boulders.

Nehalem Beach, the north point at the entrance, is a narrow sandspit, bare of trees, and with dunes of moderate elevation over the north part. The south side of the entrance is a low broad sand beach, backed by wooded country rising to elevations of 400 feet.

The entrance is protected by jetties extending 600 yards from the shoreline, though there are a number of breaks in the jetties. A whistle buoy is nearly a mile west of the entrance. The channel is marked by an entrance range, daybeacons, and buoys; the aids are privately maintained. In July of '73 the range was reported obstructed by trees. The controlling depths on the bar is variable around four feet with three to eight feet to Wheeler. The channel is changeable.

Several marinas are at Jetty, on the east side of the river just inside the entrance, and along the river to Wheeler, 4.7 miles above the entrance. Berths and supplies are available. The Coast Guard usually maintains a summer patrol station on the river between May 1 and October 1, and storm warning signals are displayed.

Brighton is a small settlement on the east shore, a mile inside the entrance to the river. Wheeler, 4.7 miles above the entrance, has an abandoned sawmill and wharf in ruins.

Nehalem is a small settlement on the west shore of the river, 6.3 miles above the entrance. A highway bridge over the river just below Nehalem has a swing span clearance of 21 feet. The bridge is kept in a closed position. A surfaced launching ramp is on the east side of the river 0.3 mile below the highway bridge.

The coast is low and sandy for about 3 miles north of the Nehalem River entrance, then a dense forest begins which rises gradually to the south slope of Neahkahnie Mountain. There are grassy hillocks, 40 to 100 feet high, in the vicinity of the beach.

SHIP DISASTERS
Cascade Head to Nehalem River

Antelope 9/30/1907 Schooner, 123 tons, two masts, built by M. Turner at Benicia in 1887. Vessel went ashore between Nehalem and Rockaway and was completely forgotten until 1940, at which time the wind blew the sand away to expose the ship's musty hull.

Argo 11/26/1909 Steamer, 110', 210 tons. See story "Argo #1."

Brant 1862 Schooner, 50 tons. Captain Ben Olney drowned when the *Brant* capsized at Tillamook. NFI.

Carmathan Castle 12/2/1886 Ship, British, iron, 1407 tons. Ship sailed en route San Pedro-Portland in ballast and was on dead reckoning for several days due to thick, glue-like weather. Captain William Richards, try as he may, was unable to get a sighting.

She struck south of Nestucca Bay and became a total loss. The skipper and crew of 27 were saved but, while proceeding to Tillamook on a borrowed horse and as the old saying goes, "...a seaman on horseback...," the captain's steed stumbled, fell into a creek and nearly drowned the rider.

Charles H. Merchant 8/11/1902 Schooner, three mast, 340 tons, 120' long, built by H. Reed at Marshfield in 1877. The vessel ran on the beach at Nehalem and was eventually salvaged and scrapped.

C. T. Hill 7/30/1912 Schooner, 140 tons, built by Alex Hay at San Francisco. Ashore on Nehalem bar.

Detroit 12/25/1855 Brig, 141 tons, 84' × 21' × 9', built at Guilford, Conn. in 1836. Leaving the Columbia, the ship bumped heavily and sprung her planks. She took seven feet of water; the crew hailed the pilot boat and were taken aboard after they

---

* Refloated or partially salvaged.

lashed the *Detroit's* helm and squared her yards. Looking her best, the doomed ship sailed for 24 hours before going to a lonely death ashore at Tillamook.

Ellen 4/20/1870 Schooner built for the Tillamook-Shoalwater run by Captain Quick in 1865. She was lost at some undisclosed location between Tillamook and Shoalwater.

Emily Reed 2/14/1908 Bark, American, wooden, 1564 tons, 215' × 40.6' × 24.1', built at Waldboro, Maine in 1880, owned by Hind-Rolph & Co. See story "The Incredible Drift." The ship's ribs were uncovered in the sands by the winds in 1938. She and her cargo of coal were a total loss. Eight died. Because of this and other wrecks in the area, a Life Saving Station was established under Captain Farley with a crew of eight men on stand-by.

Garcia 12/12/1893 Schooner, two masts, 116 tons, built by Matthew Turner of San Francisco in 1882. Lost at Cape Meares. NFI.

Gem 2/15/1904 Schooner, two masts, 120 tons, built at Parkersburg, Oregon in 1865 by S. Danielson. She was lost near a double-headed rock between the jetty and the town of Barview.

George R. Vosberg 5/3/1912 Steamer, screw, built at Portland in 1900, 75 net tons and 106 gross, 75' × 20' × 8.7', propeller. A bay rock, or "Bay Rock" punched a hole in her hull. The crew jammed a spare gasoline tank into the cavity to stop the flow of water, but it proved ineffectual. The Wheeler Lumber Co. vessel, specially rigged for heavy weather, became hampered by the tow of the *Nehalem*. Although the crew was saved, the ship was a total loss on the south spit of the Nehalem bar.

Gerald C. 5/10/1907 Gas screw, lumber cargo. Captain Tabell. A total loss on the north spit entrance to Nestucca. Built in 1895 with two masts, 58' × 18' × 5'.

Hill 6/17/1908 Nehalem bar. NFI.

Ida Schnauer 6/17/1908 Schooner, three masts, 215 tons, built by Hall Bros. at Port Ludlow in 1875. En route Hobsonville-Redondo. She anchored near Bayocean awaiting a tug when the wind shifted from SW to W and her anchor cable parted. She went on the Tillamook bar for a total loss. She wrecked only three weeks after the establishment of the Life Saving Station there.

Kate L. Heron 4/27/1881 Schooner, two masts, 50' × 18' × 4'. Only 26 tons, but mentioned here because after she missed stays and broke up at Tillamook, parts of her washed ashore at Nehalem and have been mistaken for the wreckage of the famous *Beeswax* ship. The *Kate L. Heron* sailed under Captain Charles Yarnberg; she carried a cargo of wool.

Laguna 7/17/1900 Steamer, aground at Tillamook. A week later, she ran aground near the Klamath River for a total loss. NFI.

Lifeline 1923 This little ship, under zealot Captain Lund, ran up and down the coast for the Baptist Missionary Society saving the souls of erring seamen and longshoremen alike. After a long and healthy life of do-gooding, she ran ashore just south of Neahkahnie. Long forgotten, the little vessel was uncovered by a bulldozer in 1949.

Lila and Mattie 1897/1900 Schooner, two masts, 150 tons, built at Albion River, California in 1887 by John Peterson. Wrecked at Tillamook on one of the above two dates, take your pick.

Millie Bond 1871 Struck Tillamook bar and apparently salvaged, for she is shown as a wreck at Rogue River, November 21, 1875. NFI.

Mimi 2/13/1913 through 4/6/1913 Bark, four masts, 1984 tons, ex-*Glencova*, owned by H. H. Schmidt of Hamburg, Germany. See story, "Mimi."

Oakland 3/22/1916 Schooner, three masts, 393 tons, built by W. F. Stone & Sons of Oakland, California. Ship was abandoned at sea and drifted ashore at Brighton Beach. She was re-floated in 1918 and re-named the *Mary Hanlon*; foundered off Mendocino, California on 6/24/1924.

Occident 3/12/1897 Steam tug. A total loss at Nehalem River. NFI.

Phoenix 11/5/1923 Gas schooner. Out of Astoria, she attempted to enter Tillamook in rough seas. She tried to turn back, but became caught in a trough and capsized. Captain Farley and his lifesaving crew came alongside in 20 minutes. They chopped a hole in the bottom of the *Phoenix* thinking someone may still be alive, but the noise they heard was not a signal, merely loose gear slapping against the bulkhead with each roll of the ship. They found no one alive. Four died. The wreck drifted to the north side of the bay near the jetty.

Pilots Bride 8/1/1881 A sloop under Captain C. H. Lewis bound for Portland from Nestucca. She wrecked, for a total loss, on the Nestucca bar. NFI.

Pioneer 12/17/1900 Schooner, three masts, cargo of lumber. The ship sailed en route Knappton-San Francisco and lost her rudder off Nestucca Beach. She went ashore just below Pacific City. Some 500,000 feet of her lumber cargo was bought by John & Leonard Krebs and Howard Kellow of Pacific City for use in building the *Della*, a gas boat that worked Tillamook for many years. The stem and ribs of the old *Pioneer* can still be seen during certain times of beach erosions.

Queen of the Bay 11/11/1887 Schooner, two masts, 107 tons, built at Portland in 1883, 95' × 24' × 6'. The vessel was delivering supplies to Kinney Cannery; Captain Brazil Grounds lost his ship at the mouth of the Nehalem River.

Sagamore 1/14/1934 A 2600 ton steamer bound for Portland-New York, ex-*Fedora*, built Lorain, Ohio in 1920. The ship reportedly ripped her bottom out on Corwin Rocks, wherever they are, was then driven full speed to the beach at Prout's Neck, wherever that is. All hands rescued—the ship was pounded to pieces.

Sea Island 2/7/1932 A rum-runner of which very little is known, but she was large enough to carry at least 51 drums, 3 barrels and 289 cases of whiskey when she went down after striking the boulder that sticks out from the south reef that lies near the entrance of Whale Cove. Jim White, in his *Diving for Northwest Relics* (Binford & Mort 1979), tells more of this adventure.

*Tyee 4/3/1933 Tug, 90', owned by F. P. & A. G. Hubble of Hoquiam, Wash. Under Captain Fowler, she went aground on the south portion of Nehalem jetty.

*Tyee 12/6/1940. Tug, diesel. At 7 a.m. one stormy day, the heavy tug worked the Tillamook bar. A large sizzling breaker slammed into her and ripped off the pilothouse. Subsequent seas battered the cripple, jamming her rudder and causing her to run in circles until she rolled. Two men were swept off and lost. The remainder found some relief when the huge diesel engine weighing some 40 tons tore from its mounts and fell through the overhead of the inverted vessel to plunge to the bottom. Considerably lightened, the ship and the remainder of the crew drifted to shore. The engine, located later by its oil slick, was recovered and the ship was repaired.

Venus 1923 Not much of a description except she was 40' × 12'. The vessel was pooped and capsized on the Nestucca bar, but then something occurred that went unnoticed at the time, but proved interesting upon later examination. Captain Adolph Konisger and his engineer, Olaf Bowman, fought clear of the wreck and swam for shore. About 100' from safety, the captain felt a violent tug on his foot, a tug that nearly pulled him under and away from his companion. A vigorous kick freed him from this new and unknown peril. Imagine his surprise, and those on shore who cheered him on, when he found fully one half of his boot missing! Captain Konisger thus became, as the ripping teeth-marks indicated, the first recorded victim of a shark attack in Oregon. Miraculously, he was unhurt.

Vida 4/28/1912 Gas schooner. This two-masted, 60 footer attempted to brazen the bar when returning from a successful fishing run. Under Captain Nelson, who was anxious to return to Tillamook with his load of halibut, the ship fought high winds with ease until she lost her rudder. Finished, the *Vida* was carried onto the north spit where she broke to pieces. The captain and his crew of six were saved by the Life Saving crew.

Second time aground in a week, the Laguna *couldn't take any more.*   *(Wayne Jensen, Jr. collection)*

Tough and determined, men of the Life Saving crew faced death daily. Their deeds are heroic almost beyond belief.
(Tillamook County Pioneer Museum)

Schooner Ida Schnauer *went aground only three weeks after the establishment of the Garibaldi Life Saving service.*
(Oregon Historical Society)

Vida *on the north spit of Garibaldi.* *(Wayne Jensen, Jr. collection)*

The unlucky Oakland *in one of her numerous mishaps, this one off Brighton. She was eventually lost in California waters.* *(Tillamook County Pioneer Museum)*

5

Cape Falcon to Cape Disappointment

THE *PETER IREDALE*
(A study in whimsy)

Coastguardsman Robert Farley had just about completed his early morning beach patrol along the Clatsop Spit when his faithful companion, a non-descript mutt named Riley, drew his attention seaward with a high-pitched staccatoed barking as he raced toward the surf line on each ebbing wave, then danced back in retreating hops as the frothy liquid of the Pacific advanced up the sandy beach. Surfman Farley squinted through the thick coastal haze and caught a glimpse of a large mist-shrouded mass of creaking hull and twisted rigging.

"C'mon, Riley, we'll go wake up the boys." With this laconic comment, young Farley spun on his heel and double-timed it back along the two and one-half mile route to the Point Adams Lifesaving Station to summon help for what, in time, would become one of the most famous shipwrecks on the Pacific coast.

The broaching of the *Peter Iredale* on a coast described with many a grim countenance as the "Graveyard" produced the most singularly unexciting shipwreck scenario in maritime history. The four-masted barque simply grounded; the crew abandoned ship via breaches buoy, but had they waited for low tide, they could have easily waded ashore.

A few adventuresome boys played hookey from school, Huckleberry Finn-style, but even that proved unnecessary for the prin-

cipal dismissed classes later in the day so the entire school could view the wreck. Thus, a total lack of a dramatic rescue or legendary heroism caused the entire affair to become rather drab.

The only excitement connected to the wreck occurred the next day when Malcolm Grider, of nearby Warrenton, attempted to row around the *Iredale* in his small boat, fell overboard and drowned. Railroad officials ran a special excursion train to the now tranquil wreck scene of the land-locked vessel. It ran on Sundays only and, of course, after church services.

The *Peter Iredale*, majestic in her day, gradually fell into a slumber disturbed only by the distant cawing of local gulls and the snap, snap, snapping of George Eastman's famous little black box, the "Kodak."

Some fifty-four years later, dark clouds, far more ominous than the ones that steered the *Iredale* to her final resting place, suddenly loomed over the tranquil scene and its nearby communities. It came in the form of a letter dated June 2, 1960, directed to Leonard Lindas, Chief Counsel for the Oregon Highway Commission. The missive, originating from the desk of Oregon City Attorney Jack Caldwell, stated in simple terms that his client, Cliff Hendricks, held legal title to the remains of the *Peter Iredale* and intended to take immediate possession of his property. Alarmed, Chief Counsel Lindas quickly contacted Guy

Boyington, District Judge of Clatsop County. Judge Boyington flew into a rage and burned up the wires to City Manager E. R. Baldwin, of Warrenton.

Although Warrenton is a small community, its city boundaries are as legendary as those of Los Angeles. Everyone knows that when the beach recedes, Warrenton's city lines recede, but when the sand is continually added to by forces of nature or a man-made device like the huge rock-jetty on the nearby Columbia River, then the area claimed by the energetic little town grows substantially larger. These antics have been undisputed since the turn of the century and the total area now claimed by the city now safely includes the remains of the old four-masted barque. Yes, Sir, no doubt about it; Warrenton owned the ship and no "dry-land foreigner is going to have anything to do with her"...the terminology "foreigner" referring to anyone born outside of an approximate five mile radius of the sleepy little coastal town. Ergo, Oregon City lay an unacceptable one hundred and four miles inland and, in spite of its locale on the beautiful Willamette River, it was and still is considered "dry land."

Hendricks remained adamant regarding his claim of ownership to the rusty hulk...the property he inherited from his deceased father included legal title to the ship as purchased in 1908. He felt an obligation to carry out the original intent of his father, that of scrapping out the remains of the *Peter Iredale*.

Even the most meek jolted screaming to their feet at this electrifying news. Citizens from far away Astoria (six miles) congregated on street corners to, at first, mutter amongst themselves, then to vehemently agree with soap-box orators who harangued them into action. Fred Andrus, editor of the *Astoria Daily Budget*, wasted no time in his race for the Clatsop County Courthouse to begin a detailed, albeit frantic, search of all records denoting sales for the year of 1908. He found nothing in regard to the ship *Peter Iredale*.

The following day, Thursday, June 4, the *Daily Budget* smugly announced the upstart's claim *invalid* and confidently assured its readership that the tempest was over. A grand sigh of relief could be heard all over the county, until the next day....

An overly efficient clerk in the County Records Office (some people held that he was a spy placed in that position years before by Oregon City) did not halt his search with the year 1908, but continued on into 1909, 1910, 1911, methodically plowing his way through the dusty tomes to June of 1917 and lo-and-behold, there on the 14th, the late Mr. Hendricks did indeed record his purchase of the wreck in question for a paltry $25, adding insult to injury to this now priceless relic.

"Foul," screamed the Warrentonites. "Tampered records," claimed the legal minds of Clatsop County.

"*Alerte! Aux Armes! Aux Armes!*" once again rang through the old fur trapper's post of Astoria.

Judge Boyington, acutely aware of the county's weakened legal position, smoothed over his prior thundering threats of jail and referred to *Mr.* Hendricks in a more gracious manner. "Perhaps," he stated, "if Mr. Hendricks would donate his ship to the people of Oregon, the county would mount a plaque with his name on the wreck, and," he added as an afterthought, "Saint Peter [of Iredale?] would smile favorably when they meet," which seemed a definite possibility not too far in the future, according to a number of authoritative sources.

Offers of salvation flooded Clatsop County. Portland businessman Mike DeCicco, in order to keep the *Iredale* on the beach, generously agreed to meet any price a salvage firm might pay for the rusting hulk. An organization called the Oregon Coast Ad Club wished to purchase the wreck and remove it in sections to "20 Miracle Miles" near Lincoln City, there to re-assemble and preserve the *Peter Iredale* as a tourist attraction.

As tempers and emotions rose to a fever-pitch, perhaps the unkindest cut of all came from Cliff Hendricks' own attorney, Jack Caldwell. He flatly stated, "...my client has a valid claim, even though the state and county have both exercised the Right of Ownership without actually owning the ship.

Probably the most photographed wreck in the world. The Peter Iredale *is visited daily by hundreds of camera buffs.*
(Oregon Historical Society S.P.&S. Collection)

They have neither been interested enough to preserve the hulk or even inform the people and," he continued, "if Mr. Hendricks decides not to salvage the ship, I am going to suggest that he give it to *Clackamas County*. At least we, in this county, have taken adequate steps to preserve our historical monuments. We can put it right in front of the courthouse."

The June 5th edition of Oregon City's *Enterprise-Courier* dutifully reported the rumor of a twenty-four hour machine gun watch posted on Clatsop Beach near the wreck.

When Mr. Hendricks opined he wished to visit *his* property, Judge Boyington distastefully issued orders to County Sheriff Carl Bondietti requesting the proper protection for the alleged ship owner and, as he had been informed, a party of engineers and salvage experts expected to accompany the unwanted transgressor. Then, with an unexpected twinge of compassion toward Mr. Hendricks, the good judge directed an admonition: "...we won't shoot you, but the people of Clatsop County will lay down their lives for this vessel. Of course I would accompany you *if I had the time*, but for your own protection you had better keep your intentions to yourself until you are safely out of the county."

Enterprise-Courier, June 7: "...survey will be by landing party from the sea. A corps of lawyers working for the Highway Department have begun a search of not only the records of the various transfers of the *Peter Iredale*, but the state abandonment laws, the admiralty laws and the states rights of any property over which it has exercised jurisdiction."

Lindas, in charge of this august group, stated the first order of business was to establish ownership before granting permission to move the wreck across state property.

"Now," said State Park Superintendent C. H. Armstrong, "since the State owns the Fort Stevens State Park where the wreck is located and the State owns the beach, if the moving of the hulk affects the park in any way, I shall recommend against its removal!"

City Manager Baldwin stated flatly, "The *Iredale* is in the City Limits—the town will resist."

Fred Andrus of the *Astoria Budget* let loose with a broadside in his editorial...if Hendricks owned the ship as he claimed then it was obvious that he owed some fifty-four years of property taxes to the state in addition to fines and rental for abandoning a vehicle (the ship) on a public highway (the beach) and occupying that space for the last five decades!

The issue became further clouded when Judge Boyington, while thumbing through an old family album, came across a long-forgotten incident some thirty years prior when *he* and William Larson laid claim to the *Iredale*, posted a "No Trespassing" sign and photographed it to legalize their claim against a band of junkies who intended to cut up the ship for scrap metal. Of course, just exactly what authority the two men evoked was not rightly remembered, but no doubt it must be legal. Besides, if Mr. Hendricks believed himself to be the owner, then why, by thunder, didn't he say so *then*?

Cliff Hendricks maintained a stoic aplomb throughout the mounting storms of protest and cold-heartedly proclaimed, "Once it is clear, the State, the County of Clatsop, and the City of Warrenton have *assumed private property*, then I shall instruct my attorneys to submit our ownership claim and we will proceed with whatever plans I might have for *my* ship."

Oh, the ignominy of it all.

But wait, take heart. That obscure little clerk in the County Courthouse, the one who waited until darkness fell before venturing from the safety of the fortress-like stone confines of his place of employment, the one who scurried rat-like from shadow to shadow and pillar to post seeking the sanctuary of his humble home against the slings and barbs of former friends, found the instrument with which to redeem his social standing and to verily elevate him to the status of sainthood amongst his fellow Clatsopites.

Through that same devotion to duty with which he persevered in uncovering that odious Document of Sale of a treasured monument for $25 to Mr. Hendricks, he now walked forth among the people, fearing not their hoots and boos, for he clutched firmly in his upraised fist a *second* Bill of Sale, dated three days after that first treacherous document, transferring ownership of the wreck from Mr. R. E. Hendricks to an unknown person by the name of J. A. Moshor for the magnificent and face-saving sum of $325.00! Standing before the multitudes, he raised both arms toward the heavens and proclaimed the bones of the *Peter Iredale* would, for all eternity, remain undisturbed upon the gentle sands of Clatsop Beach. The crisis was ended.

At last the weary citizens could now direct their attentions to the mundane problems of everyday living...President Eisenhower's

Happy couple cavorting on the wrecked Peter Iredale. *View from 'midship forward.*

(Wayne Jensen, Jr. collection)

Another view of the famous Peter Iredale.

(Oregon Historical Society)

trouble with Red China and Gary Powers' abortive U-2 flight over the USSR. Mr. Hendricks, the sheriff and Judge Boyington could sit back and laugh uproariously over the practical joke they had so successfully pulled off and all would be quiet again.

. . . until the descendants of the unknown Mr. J. A. Moshor appear on the scene.

WILLIAM AND ANN

Journal and letters of David Douglas.[1] Letter to Sir William J. Hooker, Sept. 14, 1829:

. . . Did you hear of the total wreck of the Hudson's Bay Company's ship on the sand bar at the entrance of the Columbia River, with the loss of every individual on board, forty six in number, on the 11th of March last?

It was the vessel in which Dr. Scouler and I went out in 1824, when the late Captain was First Mate. It is stated that those who escaped from the wreck were destroyed by my old friends, the Chenooks [sic].

This may be true, though I confess I entertain some doubts, for I have lived among those people for weeks and months. . . .

THE FIRST COLUMBIA PILOT

Dangers of the Columbia Bar were readily apparent from the time Robert Gray discovered the river in 1792; the eventual arrival of the Astor party proved it all too certainly with their loss of eight men embarked to sound the channel for the *Tonquin*.

The Chinooks' Chief Concomly was the first to guide ships over the bar on a business basis, but even then the only safe method involved sounding ahead in small boats to lay out a channel.

Lt. William Slacum, USN, charted the first reliable survey of the entrance in 1837, but river run-offs decreed it only a temporary finding. A legislative act by the territory in 1846 provided for an examination and subsequent licensing of pilots for the bar and river clear to the head of navigation.

The first pilot to prove competent was S. C. Reeves. He received high praise for his ability but suffered dismissal due to false charges of deliberately wrecking and looting the brig *Vancouver*. Reeves left in 1847 for San Francisco and there drowned in a boating accident.

The lack of competent pilots caused ships much delay and, in one case, the brig *Sequin* used up fifty-four days tacking back and forth in the river while en route from Astoria to Portland. Service was re-established on Christmas Day, 1849, when two New York harbor pilots, Captains J. G. Hustler and Cornelius White, anchored their sixty-foot eastern pilot schooner *Mary Taylor*[2] in Astoria.

Business to the fast-growing towns upriver soon surpassed the capabilities of these two captains. Competition in the form of Captain George Flavel, who passed his pilot examination in 1850, put them to task. As the first licensed branch pilot, one approved to pilot both river and bar, Flavel enjoyed a decided edge in the rate war that soon followed.

Captain Paul Corno arrived in 1865 with a steam tug and, for a while, captured much of the business from the wind-bound Flavel. The idea of towing ships across the bar, rather than relying upon capricious winds, intrigued Flavel; he promptly purchased a speedier and larger tug.

Corno's business lagged and soon Flavel monopolized the field and set his rates accordingly. The gradual advent of steamships rendered the bar tugs obsolete. Rates fell and Flavel eventually sold his interests to Asa Simpson. Steam soon allowed a pilot to bring in a ship under its own power. Sail-power faded. With towing jobs no longer necessary, tugs turned to other duties along the mighty Columbia.

---

[1] David Douglas (1798-1834), for whom the Douglas Spruce is named, was a Scottish botanist who arrived in Oregon in 1823. As a collector for the Royal Horticultural Society he discovered many new species of plants, trees and birds and travelled extensively through the northwest states including California and British Columbia. He died in the Sandwich Islands, the victim of a wild bull.

[2] Later sold to Capt. J. J. Winant of Shoalwater for use in his oyster operations.

...Mere description can give little idea of the terrors of the bar of the Columbia: all who have seen it have spoken of the wildness of the scene, and the incessant roar of the waters, representing it as one of the most fearful sights that can possibly meet the eye of the sailor.

from the report of the first official survey of the river by the United States Navy under the guidance of Lieutenant Charles Wilkes and his expedition of 1841

JOEL MUNSON, BUSINESS – LIFESAVING

It just seemed natural for Joel Munson to be in the business of lifesaving, which proved fortunate for those unlucky souls who wrecked at the mouth of the Columbia River.

The Munson family lived near the old town of Lexington alongside the Skipanon River west of Young's Bay. Munson, the lighthouse keeper at Cape Disappointment when the bark *Industry* met her fate in 1865 and seventeen lost their lives, found amongst the tons of wreckage washed up on the beach a beat-up but still watertight metallic lifeboat. It became the nucleus of his private lifesaving business.

This unsung hero raised money for additional equipment with several Astoria dances at $2.50 per head. After talking the Lighthouse Department into building a shelter for the metallic lifeboat, he put out a call for volunteers. The government, taking his cue, established a station at Fort Canby and turned the boat over to that department. One year later the *W. B. Scranton* wrecked and Munson, as part of the crew of lifesavers, fought the currents in "his" boat to the successful rescue of thirteen persons. When the *Architect* ran afoul of the Columbia bar, ten more voyagers joined the ranks of those saved.

Munson built and operated the *Magnet*, a small steamer. In 1881 he received an appointment to the Point Adams Lighthouse which he held until 1898.[3]

---

[3] Located near the present site of Battery Russell.

CHILDAR

When it comes to the rescue of a ship in distress, an alert and ever-ready United States Coast Guard rushes to the scene regardless of weather, type of vessel, or national origin. One example of outstanding service performed by these able seamen occurred on the morning of May 4th, 1934 at 7:07 a.m.

"Sparks," the radioman aboard the United States Coast Guard cutter *Redwing* stationed at Astoria, sat tending his wireless. Through his bulky earphones S O S...S O S broke through the static of a heavy southerly gale. The distress call from a location not more than ten miles away electrified the *Redwing's* crew into instant action. As the seamen dove into their foulweather gear, "Sparks" received chilling news from the stricken ship, who identified herself as the Norwegian freighter *Childar*. She lay helplessly trapped in the smashing waves of the North Spit Bar at the entrance to the Columbia River...all hope of abandoning ship went by the boards as the gale-force winds, after tearing her lifeboats into matchwood, now threatened to force her aground.

The small but powerful cutter *Redwing* loosed her lines and headed into thick rain squalls, pea soup gales, and murderous seas. The mighty Columbia River, swollen by a strong spring runoff, forced the navigator to quickly adjust to a forty-five degree leeway from the seven degree heading he normally used during ebb tide to clear the bar. All eyes strained through zero visibility in hopes of sighting familiar bearings. A short break in the surrounding murk revealed the *Childar* rolling in the breakers in the center of North Spit near Buoy 5. Bone crushing seas crashed over the stricken ship's devastated deck in smothering waves.

As the *Redwing's* commander Lt. A. W. Davis maneuvered to close the gap between the two ships, the storm shut down all visibility. The *Redwing* stood by and rode the storm for four hours before sighting the *Childar* once again. This time the lumber-laden vessel lay on the other side of the spit, thrown there by the huge breakers.

The exhausted Norwegians lacked the strength to serve the steel hawser passed to them via a line fired from the *Redwing*. The combined muscle of the *Childar*'s crew failed along with the foundering ship's power to operate winches or capstan. The *Redwing* shot another line, this time passing a manila towing hawser which the Norwegian crew eventually secured to a bitt.

While the *Redwing* waged a superhuman battle against all odds, other Coast Guard units sprang into action. A power lifeboat under the guidance of Chief Boatswain Mate Lars Bjelland left Point Adams to fight its way across open seas. CBM Lee Woodworth and his crew set out from Cape Disappointment in their small power lifeboat.

A new radio message from the distressed Norwegian stated they lost the first mate, second mate, and steward over the side. The cook had been killed on board. Three crushed seamen were in serious condition. The two small power boats immediately bored in. After several abortive attempts the Point Adams lifeboat succeeded in rescuing two of the injured men; the Cape Disappointment boat managed to take aboard the third crushed seaman even though Bo's'n Woodworth, himself a casualty, suffered from several fractured ribs as a result of having been thrown against the engine compartment by a giant sea.

The smaller boats retreated and delivered their injured cargo to ambulances waiting in Astoria. The *Redwing* winched in the slack on the hawser towline so as to maneuver the broken *Childar* out of dangerous breakers. The freighter lay low in the water, a dead weight with her deckload torn off, superstructure smashed into kindling, boats gone, rails twisted, and bulkheads crushed.

In spite of the odds the smaller ship slowly hauled in the slack on the heavy line and she began to have an effect on the lumbering *Childar*. At a snail's pace, the two vessels inched toward the open sea. Suddenly, at about 1:30 in the afternoon, the *Redwing* shot forward as if launched from a giant catapult.

The *Childar*'s bitts, torn free from her battered deck, crashed, banged, and skidded toward the bow. Fortunately they became enmeshed in the forward chocks, thus saving the tow. But with her decks awash, the *Childar*'s keel would never clear the bar. The *Redwing* altered course for Puget Sound at about 4:30 p.m.

The two ships labored through mountainous crests and canyon-like troughs until 9 o'clock that night.

Once again, the Norwegian radioed an urgent message: "The ship is breaking in half at number 4 hold. Can you possibly remove the crew?"

The *Redwing* radioed Gray's Harbor Coast Guard Station to dispatch their power lifeboat. Skillful maneuvering brought the small boat alongside the stricken steamer. Eighteen men, two seriously injured, were removed without mishap and deposited aboard the *Redwing* where they received the best care possible under such adverse conditions.

The Gray's Harbor lifeboat returned to the freighter and stood by in the event the *Childar*'s captain ordered the engineer, pilot, third mate, and radioman to abandon ship. At dawn the Coast Guard cutter *Chelan* arrived to assist. That evening the tug *Roosevelt* hove into view. With the *Childar*'s number 4 hold flooded and her number 5 filling, the big ship was going down by the stern.

Constant yawing of the dead ship made towing increasingly difficult, but the little *Redwing* held fast with a vengeance. Water now moved up to the tanks of the *Childar*'s engine room; the shaft alley leaked badly. This combined weight strained the ill-secured tow line, foretelling all would soon be lost.

Salvation arrived with the chilly dawn... four ships stood into the comparative calm of the Straits of Juan de Fuca. The *Roosevelt* succeeded in securing a line to the crippled 4,138 ton ship and thus eased the back-breaking strain on the *Redwing*'s engines. The tug *Roosevelt* waited until 5:00 that night, then took over and completed the tow to Victoria, British Columbia.

Redwing cast off and headed for Port Angeles where her bone-weary crew enjoyed a well deserved rest, thus closing another very routine chapter in the annals of the United States Coast Guard...almost.

Two months later, two members of the Norwegian consul stepped ashore at Astoria. After receiving directions to the Coast Guard station, the representatives entered its office and requested Lieutenant Davis and the crew of the *Redwing* to present themselves immediately. The seamen arrived, the Scandinavians opened a package stamped with the seal of a diplomatic courier. They presented the brave and tenacious Coastguardsmen with a beautifully engraved silver cup bearing a message of appreciation from the grateful people of Norway on behalf of the crew of the *Childar*.

As gallant a fight as had ever been made against the old man of the sea turned out to be all in vain for he was determined not to be cheated. After months of repair, Captain Matthisen, his crew and the *Childar* set out on their original course, South Africa, never to arrive and never to be heard of again.

PEACOCK

A fine name, the *Peacock*, and it aptly suited this proud and beautiful sloop-of-war. The U.S. Navy selected her name in commemoration of their 1812 engagement against HMS *Peacock*, Britannic Majesty George III's frigate that ran afoul of the U.S. warship *Hornet*. The English erred by concentrating their fire high into the *Hornet*'s rigging while the Americans slammed tons of iron directly into their enemy's hull. Thirty-eight Englishmen and the HMS *Peacock* died on the spot. A jubilant U.S. Navy immediately contracted with the firm of Adams and Brown for a new sloop-of-war; when completed in 1813, she set her course as a defiant British reminder that the *Peacock* loyally carried America's stars and stripes to all corners of the world.

She spanked down the Atlantic seaboard to Florida where, with her 117 feet of fighting trim, she celebrated her maiden voyage in a

Beautiful St. Mary, *a sister ship to the lost* Peacock *and typical of the sloop-of-war class vessel of the U.S.*　　　　　　*(Marshall collection)*

baptism of fire under the command of Captain Lewis Warrington. The *Peacock*'s twenty-two guns and 140 crew soundly trounced HMS *Epervier*'s eighteen guns and 128 men. Victoriously blooded, she scudded for the Sunda Straits to sniff out HMS *Nautilus*. Her discovery of the unsuspecting Britisher between Sumatra and Borneo proved deceptively easy. Spoiling for another fight, she ran down and challenged the easy-sailing ship, at which time the British warship informed the Americans that the war was ended.

Captain Lewis Warrington, ever suspicious of English motives, hauled up within range and, with bristling cannon, demanded the British strike. The *Nautilus*'s commander refused the popinjay Yankee captain's challenge and, after receiving two thundering broadsides through his ship's hull and rigging, ruefully submitted. Captain Warrington triumphantly boarded the enemy vessel to receive the defeated commander's sword. Much to his chagrin he received instead a copy of the cessation of hostilities from a more than slightly irate British officer. With red-faced abject apologies, the crestfallen American ordered his beautiful *Peacock* to tuck in her soiled feathers and fly for home.

The *Peacock*, unable to abide peaceful inactivity, soon sailed for engagement in the Mediterranean, followed by a patrol in the West Indies to suppress piracy and slavery. She emerged eminently successful in both endeavors. She returned to the South Pacific to show her colors for the benefit of the American whaling fleet. On her return to South America from Hawaii the ship was rammed by a whale, which caused serious damage. Nevertheless she reached Callao; from there she departed for New York. Then she was stripped down to her bare bones.

The new *Peacock* that emerged was just a tad larger at 559 tons, almost a foot longer and 12 inches less in her draught. Her armament was changed also to 8 20-pounders and 2 9-pounders.

Under Commander C. K. Stribling, she cruised the Persian Gulf where, for a brief time, an uncharted reef held her captive. The crew heaved her big guns by the board and she gained her freedom.

With Lt. William Hudson in command, the ship was assigned to the South Seas exploration expedition of the extremely competent, but hot-headed, Lt. Charles Wilkes. She scudded through southern waters and into the forbidding ice-flows of the cold Antarctic

where she batted around for a considerable time before skipping back to the port of Oahu in the tropical Sandwich Islands to disembark her sick and take on supplies. She left immediately for the dangerous Samoas where, for 228 days, she charted the waters as far west as the Pescadores.

The *Peacock* returned to Oahu; Hudson received a package of sailing orders from Lt. Wilkes, since departed for the Straits of Juan de Fuca. He directed the vessel to chart the mighty Columbia River and there await his arrival. While still in port at Oahu, Lt. Hudson met Captain Spaulding, fresh from Ft. George (Astoria). The American master of the *Lausanne*, a veteran of many crossings of the Columbia River bar, gladly furnished Lt. Hudson with directions of entry into the Columbia.

The *Peacock* arrived off the bar the morning of July 17, 1841. She spent her first day flapping around in a thick fog with only an intermittent light breeze nudging against the yardarm's slack-draped canvas. The day following this ominous welcome, Hudson stationed himself on the ship's fo'c's'l, placed a fellow officer high in the foresail top-yard to watch for hidden dangers and, armed with Spaulding's written directions, ordered all hands to work the ship into the river. He brought Cape Disappointment to bear NE by ¼ E by compass and Chinook Point to bear ENE. He saw crashing breakers directly in front of the *Peacock*'s course.[4] Assuming he lay too far south, Hudson ordered his helm about to put the *Peacock* up to clear the white water. The ship's maneuver missed the channel; the gallant ship struck.

The young commander ordered helm alee to bring her into the wind and haul off. She struck again. The crew furled sails and dropped anchor. Lt. George F. Emmons launched the ship's cutter and pushed off from the wallowing ship to sound the area.

Increasing winds blasted from the north and west. The mainmast continually punched holes in the low-riding, leaden storm

---

[4] Considered a normal condition on the bar.

clouds blanketing the stricken ship. A strong ebb tide embraced the deadly thrust of the river. Eternally wedded, nature's forces raced into the Pacific breakers to give birth to a deadly "Widow Maker"...the towering waves smashed with unexpected, tremendous violence against the obstruction in their malevolent path. The poking, probing finger of the main mast punctured a weak spot in the blackened clouds and, with a wrenching, twisting thrust, released a torrent of hail, sleet and rain. Emmons and his boat crew pitted themselves against the storm's fury, just barely making it back to the dubious safety of the crippled *Peacock*.

Each incoming swell lifted the ship from its deadly cradle, then, with a passing rush, slammed her into the spit's concrete-hard sands. Shouting officers ordered barefoot seamen to lower royal and top-gallant yards and masts. Gunners trussed marker buoys and lines to their heavy ordnance for easy recovery after jettisoning. Pumps, continually manned, yielded little; cascading water swept the decks and forced the pump crew to abandon their stations.

The crew hauled iron shot from the stern lockers and fed it to the sand-filled waves. The lightened stern swung, thus allowing the bow to knife the onrush of waves. A crashing, cross-current wall of water tore away the rudder's iron-strapped tiller. The freed rudder acted like a giant paddle swinging back and forth administering a deadly spanking; it smashed and tore at the weakened stern. The *Peacock*'s bower lay off to larboard with forty-five fathoms of anchor chain; each heave of the tortured vessel carried away her link stoppers. The sudden loud snap of the strained anchor chain heralded the end of the *Peacock*'s anguish. The battered links slipped from the hawsehole and the ship broadsided, striking so hard that all hands thought she would break up on the spot.

The crew let go another anchor, if only to delay the inevitable. It eased the situation to a degree and, with the combined force of high water, the ship's head faced the incoming waves again. The ebb began its insidious work and the terrible cycle repeated in spite

of a stream anchor dropped from the stern. By morning's light, a final watery fist slammed open the larboard port bulwarks and flooded the spar decks. Water gained from ankle depth to over the top of the shot lockers, completely thwarting the pump crew's efforts. Passed Midshipman Alonzo Davis wrote a terse log entry, "We have no hope, but of saving the crew."

A slight calming, the first in twenty-four hours, occurred about 7 a.m. Hudson ordered all charts, papers and information pertinent to the scientific discoveries of the voyage be carried ashore and instructed all hands, including scientists and officers, to abandon ship with only the clothes on their backs. Marines took their muskets and shot pouches, nothing else.

The vessel lay only one and a half miles from shore, but conditions forced the ship's boats to travel four miles to a safe landing. Evacuating the vessel took most of the day. The last members of the expedition reached shore after sunset.

The following morning Lt. Hudson returned to the wreck scene in vain hope of retrieving further items. All that remained of his late command was the tip of the *Peacock*'s bowsprit reaching for salvation from the clutch of the unforgiving bar but that, too, was denied and all trace of the gallant sloop-of-war soon disappeared. The sandy tomb of the proud vessel is now known as Peacock Spit.

Launch of the *Peacock*

The captain of the *Peacock*, in memory of the tragic loss of his sloop-of-war, generously donated his vessel's sturdy launch to George Gear and Robert Alexander for use as a pilot boat to guide ships safely across the Columbia's treacherous bar and through the river's dangerous currents.

Both men honored the captain's wishes; however, when business across the bar became slow, the enterprising mariners developed an alcoholic beverage that became known as "Blue Ruin," a name that aptly described the vile fluid. The seamen boiled potatoes in a cast iron pot covered by an oaken lid and collected the steam in a coiled, old iron pipe, then fed the blue-tinged liquid into various containers, bottles or otherwise. It was said that the resulting product was strong enough to fry the liver of a brass monkey.

Robert Alexander soon tired of the piloting and moonshine partnership and departed for the American River where he ended his career on the receiving end of an Indian tomahawk.

George Gear continued producing and selling the company's gut-rotting product to whomever would buy, including the local Indians. All too soon, the crazed aborigines' drunken war-cries and menacing staggers terrorized the community's women and children to the degree that Astorian and Clatsop settlers requested Gear to immediately cease his wholesale sales and tend strictly to piloting.

Gear declined to comply on the grounds that he was one of his own best customers. A gathering of irate citizens, incensed by Gear's haughty attitude, promptly tossed the offender into the Columbia's chilling waters with the threat that they would soon set him to dancing on air if he persisted manufacturing "Blue Ruin." Gear opted to leave the area.

The *Peacock*'s launch, a fine little sailer, went into service carrying a number of passengers to San Francisco.

E INOA O KANALOA
Glory to Kanaloa, God of the Sea

The solemn file of dusky Hawaiians slowly wound through the emerald-green somber forest of giant fir trees on a desolate point of the Oregon Territory.[5] Their quest was to give proper burial to their fellow Hawaiian who had drowned yesterday in a boating accident while sounding the channel for his ship, the *Tonquin*. The date was March 24, 1811. The interment of this unknown seaman would be the first *recorded* burial in the Northwest Territory.

A setting sun lengthened the forest shadows before the group of Islanders and two Englishmen[6] located the small sandy beach where an earlier search crew suspended the native's body from a high tree to keep it safe from wild animals.

The Hawaiians embedded the butts of their pine-knot and oil torches into the sand in the form of a large circle. They quickly set to work, each seeming to know exactly what to do. They dug a hole in the center of the torch-rimmed circle, collected rocks, then lovingly placed their dead shipmate in the newly-dug hole. Naukane[7] gently positioned a ship's biscuit under the cadaver's arm, some lard under its chin and tucked a few precious tobacco leaves under the genitals.

The Sandwich Islanders stood in a single line on each side of the grave. As one, on an unseen, unheard signal, they knelt facing east. With brown hands placed palm down on each thigh, they bowed their heads and began their lament for the dead, the doleful yet primitively beautiful *Kanikau.*

Auwe auwe, the group intoned (Alas, alas)
E inoa o Kane (Glory to the name of Kane [Giver of Life])
E Lohe hookupu, chanted Naukane (Glory to the name of Kanaloa [God of the Sea])
E Lohe hookupu, came the antiphon (O hear this, gift giver)

Naukane sprinkled the lost soul with water dipped from the sea.

---

[5] On May 18, 1792, Captain Robert Gray named the headland of the bay Point Adams and the northern point Point Hancock. John Meares searched in vain for the mouth of the Columbia River in 1788 and consequently named the location Deception Bay and Cape Disappointment. Vancouver, in 1792 (a few months after Gray) changed Hancock to Disappointment on his charts, the name it retains today.

[6] Benjamin Pillet and Gabriel Franchere.

[7] One of King Kamehameha's favorite subjects and a member of the royal household assigned by the King to accompany the group as a royal observer. Naukane later became known as John Coxe, supposedly due to his resemblance to one of the crew by that name. Since none of the crew or passengers bore such a name, it is likely he was dubbed that by the crew of the *Tonquin*. John Cox or Tom Cox was a slang term to indicate one who by artful dodging is able to avoid all work yet still give the appearance of accomplishment. Today they are known as "gold brickers." Naukane, as a royal observer, would most certainly fit into this category.

Laniakea kanaka aniani (Gently beckon this man to the boundless heaven)
Hale aniani auwe auwe, they chanted (Gently beckon home, alas, alas)

The soulful chant vibrated across the small sandy beach and became lost in the hush of the silent forest and as the deep tones of the song continued, a dark-skinned native piled rocks atop his shipmate's body. As the light from the flickering torches wrestled with the darkening shadows of an ending day, a muted sound found its way between the words of the intonation . . . the soft thump of shoveled sand falling into the hole.

The interment completed, the men arose. Each lifted his torch and fell into line. Looking neither to the right nor to the left, they began their long, silent procession through the night-shrouded forest. Under the most difficult of circumstances, this small group of aliens in a cold and distant land adhered as best they could to the ancient and established beautiful obsequies of their tropical Hawaiian Islands.

A few drops of rain fell from the darkened sky and their heartbeats quickened in joy for this was a sure sign that Kanaloa, the God of the Sea, accepted the soul of their dead brother and that he would live forever in *Kappa-hanau-moku*, the beautiful land of peace.

RAILROAD TO THE RESCUE

Jetty foreman J. C. Tenbrook turned from his paper-strewn layout table, noted the raging storm through his construction shack window and commented to Al Sifert, engineer on the Columbia River jetty railroad system, "Al, this storm obviously will prevent us from dumping any rock this morning and, from the looks of it, for the next few days . . . the waves'll be too high. Do you think you can keep the men busy in the yard until it slacks off?"

"No problem. We have a lot of gondola and flat car shuffling to do, and. . . ." The engineer paused, took a sip of hot coffee, then continued, "O'Neil's building up steam on Number 4 right now. We want to get that pile driver in the shed and. . . ." The harsh jangle of the wall-mounted telephone cut his words short.

The other man reached for the receiver. "Jetty office, Tenbrook speaking. Yes. . .no, our watchman hasn't reported a thing. Too stormy; can't see more than a hundred feet. Is that right?" The speaker paused long enough to glance at his pocket watch, then continued with his one-sided conversation. "Oscar, it's 8:45 now . . . we'll be ready as soon as you get here." Replacing the earpiece on its hook, Tenbrook turned excitedly and ordered, "Get your slicker on, Al. That was Oscar Wicklund, Point Adams Life Station. He says Cape D[8] just picked up a wireless from the steamer *W. S. Porter* reporting a four-master in trouble on the South Jetty. Have O'Neil bring that engine out as soon as Wicklund gets here. Looks like we're going for a ride!"

The lookout clung to the slippery wave-washed deck of the *Admiral* and shouted in terror, "Breakers ahead!" He not only interrupted Captain Joseph Bender's breakfast with his wife and four year old son, but sent the veteran seaman racing from his cabin.

"Breakers," the captain muttered to himself as he ran for the open deck. "That cussed fool couldn't have seen breakers. Confound it, we're sixty miles out to sea!"

Long strides propelled him three steps at a time toward the upper deck of the four-masted, 683 ton schooner. Seventy mile-per-hour wind and spray slammed him full in the face as he emerged from the companionway. Racing forward, he suddenly stopped and stared in horror at a long line of jagged rocks jutting seaward just off the ship's lee bow. The mammoth rust-colored boulders, as if held in a giant, invisible fist, thrust and parried at the onslaught of mountainous seas that attacked from every direction. A gale-force wind from

---

[8] Point Adams Life Station lies on the south side of the Columbia River; Cape Disappointment, or Cape D station is situated on the north bank of the entrance. J. C. Tenbrook later became Mayor of Astoria.

the port quarter aft drove the reefed, jib-set schooner full on into that deadly maelstrom.

Captain Bender ordered the helm hard-up in an attempt to broadside his ship against the spray-lashed line of slavering dragon teeth. Ironically, with only a hundred more feet of forward drive, the ship could have safely cleared the rocks, but now she lost all headway. The laboring vessel lurched with a grinding crunch into the wooden railroad trestle that ran parallel to the jetty.[9] The surging sea mercilessly dumped the doomed *Admiral* onto the two-foot-thick standing bents;[10] they snapped off like matchwood, then impaled the struggling vessel upon their splintered stumps.

Frantic crewmen dodged falling railroad ties as they fought for footing on the wildly pitching deck. Iron spikes, explosively wrenched from their wooden sheaths, sailed like deadly missiles across the wreckage-strewn deck. Steel rails, shorn of their bonds, whipped back and forth in the driving gale, slashing sails and tearing rigging from the schooner's chainplates. The roaring violence drowned out Bender's shouted orders, but no matter, the crew was powerless to obey.

In spite of the *Admiral's* dire peril, the sturdy schooner carried an incredible amount of luck with her on that final day. She struck the one place along the entire seven mile long jetty that had yet to receive its full complement of rocks.[11] Mountainous waves grabbed the trembling ship, twisted her in mid-air, then threw her stern-first through the frothing, twenty-yard-wide crevasse. The sledge-hammer momentum slammed Captain Bender into the deckhouse.

"Save yourselves!" he gasped, ". . . save yourselves," he moaned and slowly sank to the deck.

First Mate Andy Anderson fought his way below where a helpless woman and child lay trapped in the captain's cabin. Their home would soon disintegrate into mere floating wreckage upon the frothy brine. Anderson, with the Bender boy tucked tightly under his arm, the now-recovered captain, Mrs. Bender and the ship's cook struggled to assist each other escape from the wave-lashed deck of the dying ship to the dubious safety of a splintered, swaying, wind-lacerated railroad trestle.

Each time the ship heaved up and rocked to starboard, the 'midship's railing became almost level to the bed of the trestle. Anderson leaped across first, waited for the ship to rise on its return roll, then extended his arms over the undulating chasm and snatched Mrs. Bender to safety. He seated the shivering, nightgown-clad woman on the ties between the rails. The doughty First Mate nearly lost his balance when he reached across again and grabbed the little boy just as the ship slammed into another bent and jarred the weakened trestle. He handed the terrified child into Mrs. Bender's outstretched arms, then, while struggling against rock-hard, wind-driven salt spray, helped the captain and ship's cook scramble onto the elevated roadbed. . . on the schooner's return roll, the cook's toes were crushed between the lee rail and the remaining stanchions, although he did not discover the injury until later.

The five survivors huddled in misery on the swaying trestle while roaring seas attacked them from every quarter and gale winds threatened to thrust them into a seething cauldron of icy water.

The feeble headlight of Engine #4, a little 0-4-2, H. E. Porter construction engine, dimly lit the tracks through a thick veil of furious wind and sea. Engineer Sifert, his eyes blinded by salt and spray from seas punching the ungiving rocks below, gingerly inched his puffing machine over the trembling, wave-washed jetty tracks. High seas crashed against the struggling engine, wrapping the rescuers in great clouds of steam.

"There! There. . .in front of us!" O'Neil

---

[9] Built for the purpose of dumping huge boulders for the body of the seawall.

[10] Upright posts or pilings.

[11] A common practice of leap-frogging and returning at a later date to fill in. This allowed engineers to study currents while at the same time lessening the strain upon the new wall.

shouted above the raging wind of a Pacific hurricane. "Somebody's crawling along the tracks."

Sifert eased back the throttle and applied the brakes. Wicklund and Tenbrook quickly jumped out of the cab, hugged against the engine as they felt their way along the edge of the ties toward a barely-discernible sopping figure kneeling on the roadbed. They found Anderson half-frozen, almost unconscious from the wet and cold, with a little boy clutched under his rough-knit, soaked, wool sweater. "The others," he gasped, barely able to summon enough strength to hand over the frightened four year old. "The others are still back there."

The men gently lifted Anderson and the child into the tiny, overcrowded cab; the warm haven somewhat revived the violently shivering seaman.

Sifert eased his throttle forward; once again the engine inched along the narrow, spume-covered roadbed. Within a shivering mile they found the three survivors, all suffer-

ing from severe hypothermia. Captain Bender reported others, who abandoned ship in the same manner as he, awaited rescue on the outer portion of the severed trestle.

Wicklund, unable to see more than a few feet through the storm, ordered the train's cautious retreat to the mainland where, by pre-arrangement, his surfmen stood by with a horse-drawn beach wagon loaded with rescue equipment.

Jetty foreman Tenbrook took the five shipwreck victims into the warm confines of his construction shack, then telephoned for added assistance in rescuing the remaining survivors.

The Point Adams Life Crew loaded two flatcars with a Lyle gun and breeches buoy. Sifert moved the engine forward along the track to the siding where the flatcars, now crowded with men and life saving gear, were waiting. He picked the cars up on his front coupler and raced through the crashing waves toward the wreck and what now could be called "End of track." Within thirty minutes

The crew of old number 4 (minus her lamp) participated in one of the strangest shipwreck operations ever!
(Fort Stevens Historical Center)

Captain Wicklund and his efficient crew effected a safe breeches buoy rescue of the seven stranded seamen.[12]

Shortly after the *Admiral* struck the trestle, thundering seas forced the abandoned vessel through the jagged jetty opening and into the river's mouth. In spite of attempted towing by the tug *Wallula*, the *Admiral* drifted until she broke up.

The Woman's National Relief Association supplied warm clothing to the survivors, then arranged for their transportation to various destinations of their choice. Most all of the shipwreck victims lived long enough to tell open-mouthed grandchildren the unlikely tale of their rescue from a storm-battered, sinking vessel-at-sea by a *railroad train*.

"IF I LIVE, I WILL RETURN ...AFTER BREAKFAST"

Captain George Flavel carefully maneuvered the 309 ton propeller-steamer *General Warren* through the bar's breakers on January 28, 1852, handed over the ship's command to Captain George Charles Thompson and then embarked to his pilot boat *California*. The seasoned pilot-captain watched the eight-year-old steamer, with her full load of wheat and hogs and a number of passengers bound for San Francisco, slowly buck toward the south as her bow bit into the waves of an increasing gale.

Twin mishaps struck the *General Warren* around midnight...her foremast, carried away by a heavy southwest sea, sprang the mast-curlings which, in turn, strained her step, keelson and futtock. The wrenching ship's hold began to take on a steady flow of sea water. Captain Thompson immediately ordered the vessel's pumps into action, but a shifted, wheat-cargo's loose, floating, swollen golden grains completely clogged the overworked pumps. He ordered the ship to return to Astoria for repairs.

The crippled steamer lay off the mouth of the Columbia at dawn, but heavy weather prevented contact with Flavel's pilot schooner until midafternoon. Captain Block, of the pilot service, shouted across angry seas that he was coming aboard; Captain Thompson yelled back that he preferred Flavel's assistance. Flavel complied and immediately boarded the struggling ship.

Thompson quickly took Flavel aside to report three feet of water in the hold, more coming in every second and the pumps hopelessly clogged. "We won't live until morning unless we get into the Columbia. You'll have to take us in."

Flavel, pointing out the breakers crashing across the bar, refused. "It's out of the question. You haven't enough steam to cross before dark; you will have to ride out the storm. Possibly by morning I can take you in."

"Look," desperate urgency rang in Thompson's plea, "I will fire up a lot of fat bacon and dry stuff to make steam. You *must* take us in!"

The pilot shook his head. "I know the bar. A heavy ebb is running. We'll never make it...it's suicide."

Nervous passengers crowded around the two arguing captains and one of them accused Flavel of cowardice. Flavel capitulated, his face flushed by the insult. "All right, if you insist. I will take you in, but will not be held responsible for the consequences."

After ordering his boat crew to return to the *California* and follow in the schooner, Flavel turned the steamer's bow at 5:00 p.m. toward the river's darkening, roaring entrance. Suddenly the wind died and the sail-powered schooner fell behind in a helpless wallow.

The *General Warren*, with a poorly responding rudder and tons of sloshing sea in her belly, rode painfully low in the water. Heavy seas rolled over the stricken steamer, sending the water level dangerously close to her fires. Progress against the ebb proved impossible.

---

[12] Captain Oscar Wicklund prided himself on using only 2½ ounces of powder for hurling the Lyle projectile and its #9 braided line across the foaming abyss; he succeeded on the first try. Surf wagons were normally pulled by hand; on this occasion, however, because of conditions, a horse was rented from a local farmer. The Life Service received a bill for $5.00.

"We'll have to beach her if we're going to save your passengers."

Another heavy sea carried away all but one of the ship's boats; blinding rain turned into a snow storm. The pilot steered for Clatsop spit. Within a few moments, the *General Warren* struck and began to break up. Captain Thompson rolled out a keg of whiskey and, as a defense against the bitter cold, ordered crew and passengers alike to help themselves.

Captain Flavel, a teetotaler, tossed the offending brew over the side. "Captain, we need clear heads if we are to save those aboard." The passengers began to pray.

Flavel stood near the ship's bell as Captain Thompson approached to point out the one remaining ship's boat and ask, "Pilot, do you think you can make it to Astoria and get help for us?"

"I am willing to try, but I don't think we can make it through the breakers."

Thompson called his crew together. "The following men will man the boat with Captain Flavel. First Officer Edward Beverly, Second Mate William Irons, Seaman James Murray, Seaman Isaac Sparrow, passengers E. L. Finch, Henry Marsh and Matt and James Nolan."

Flavel spotted a husky-built man and asked him if he could handle an oar; J. C. Wall joined the crew. The men successfully lowered the ship's boat into the raging sea and with much effort pulled away from the drowning vessel.

Captain Thompson shouted against the roaring wind, "Pilot, you will come back?"

Flavel bellowed back over the clamor of the breaking ship, "If I live, I shall return." The struggling crew and ship's boat disappeared into the gloom.

Only by constant bailing were the men able to keep the wooden boat afloat through the snow-filled night. A grey dawn found them off Scarborough Head. Recognizing the landmark, they pulled southward toward Astoria.

The bark *George and Martha* lay in the stream; Captain Beard immediately complied with Flavel's request for assistance and placed a large whaleboat and men from his own crew at the pilot's disposal. The rescue group headed for the *General Warren* but, strangely enough, Flavel ordered the mission interrupted in order for him to partake of breakfast at Kindred's farmhouse.[13] When the rescuers eventually arrived at the scene of the disaster, all that remained of the *General Warren* was surf-tossed wreckage.

Forty-five bodies and eight hundred hog carcasses washed ashore between Clatsop Spit and Seaside.

To Honbl. the commissioners of Clatsop County—the undersigned citizens of Clatsop County having found upon the sea beach in said county thirteen dead human bodies to the undersigned unknown which bodies were all buried by us in as good a manner as circumstances would allow, some of them were buried in boxes or sheets others were buried without coffins, etc. The dates of burying the same were Feb. 1, 2 persons, on the 10th one, on the 11th two, the 15th one, 21st six, 22nd one. The undersigned were occupied in time as well as expense by hiring Indians etc., All of which we humbly submit to your Honors: for adjustment on the bodies of the above persons were found the following amount of money and watches to-wit, —$197.70 cash, 1 gold watch and silver chain, one silver watch all of which is hereby presented to your Honors.

> *Signed* James Cook, M. S. Smith,
> N. Dougherty, and R. W. Morrison

Recd. April 5th 1852, of the board of County Commissioners one hundred and twenty five dollars for services rendered for burying bodies washed on the beach from the steamer "General Warren".

Report of F. Ketchum for interring bodies:

I was told by the Indians that there was a body on the beach near my house on three different occasions. Myself, and two Indians who were living with me went and dug a grave for each of three bodies which came ashore into which we put them without coffins or winding-sheets or other cover-

---

[13] B. C. Kindred, an early pioneer, and his family lived at the present site of Fort Stevens. In later years he donated land near Hammond for the establishment of a Life Saving Station.

ing except their clothing. I not having any lumber for making coffins, nor any cloths for shrouds. We buried the bodies near the beach above high water mark. There was nothing on the bodies except their clothing, with the exception of one hair brush. Their clothing was of no value and buried with them.

signed: Frederic Ketchum
April 7th 1852

Recd. April 7 1852 of the Board of County Commissioners fifteen Dollars for services in burying the bodies washed ashore from the wreck of the "General Warren".

signed: Frederic Ketchum

Captain George Flavel received a medal on which was engraved, "Presented by the citizens of Portland to Captain George Flavel for his praiseworthy exertion in rendering assistance to the passengers and crew of the steamship General Warren at the mouth of the Columbia on the 31st of January, 1852." The reverse side of the medal featured a picture of a whaleboat leaving a sinking vessel with the inscription, "If I live I shall return."

James Swan discovered the vessel's stern section in 1854 at Copalis, Washington, forty miles north of the wreck scene. The actions and conversation of Capt. Flavel, Capt. Thompson and the others aboard the doomed vessel are as told by Mrs. George Flavel to historian Fred Lockley. The story appeared in the *Portland Daily Journal*, September 8, 9, 10, 1922.

ROSECRANS

"We are rapidly breaking to pieces on the bar.... Good-bye." That terse message marked the demise of one of the unluckiest ships afloat; it also gave notice that thirty-three seamen aboard the *Rosecrans*, ex-*Methven Castle*,[14] were within minutes of finding

a watery grave at the mouth of the mighty Columbia.

The *Methven Castle*, too slow to remain in the Castle Mail Service, was sold to the United States in 1898 for use as a troop transport during the Spanish-American War. She proved totally unsatisfactory in that capacity and, with the end of hostilities, found herself on the auction block. Associated Oil Company bought the vessel, converted her into a tanker, and put her into service as the *Rosecrans*.

While sailing off the coast of California, she became unmanageable in a gale and was tossed ashore; her quartermaster and carpenter lost their lives. Although she was listed as a total loss, Associated Oil Company refloated the vessel and ordered her towed to San Francisco for re-building. Five months later, as she lay tied to a California landing, the *Rosecrans* caught fire while loading oil; once again, the company re-built her.

While en route to Portland with 19,000 barrels of oil, she approached the Columbia River bar under gale-force winds and a blinding, foggy sleet. The 2nd Officer on the bridge mistook the North Head Light for that of the Lightship. Evidence indicates that the 2,976 ton tanker bore head-on, up and over the south jetty, for paint scrapings and torn hull plates were found more than midway out on the rocks several days following the tragedy.

The mortally wounded ship lay on the bottom of the Peacock Spit with her decks barely above water...each passing breaker split her asunder. By seven o'clock the next morning, little remained of the *Rosecrans*.

The 3rd quartermaster clung to a splintered plank and washed ashore seven miles distant from the wreck. Three seamen hung to the *Rosecrans*'s rigging for five hours and, to keep circulation going, ran the ratlines, even though one of them suffered a broken leg. He died, as did thirty-two others.

---

[14] The *Methven Castle* began her spotted career in Glasgow, Scotland in 1883, just one year after several misguided Irish Nationalist dynamiters committed the notorious Phoenix Park murders. Lord Charles Cavendish's assassination prompted the English government to bring the plotters to a swift and sure justice. Carey, one of the assassins, turned state's evidence and thus beat the noose, but not death. He became fearful for his life and, with coat collar turned up and suspicious of every strange sound, surreptitiously booked passage for Cape Town, South Africa on the new vessel. An Irish "Death to Informers" squad gunned him down the minute he stepped off the gangplank.

A COMPANION OF FELONS

As a result of an overwhelming popular vote, Americans saw an 18th Amendment[15] officially added to their constitution on January 16, 1919. On that same day, they also saw the unofficial inauguration of a Bacchanalian Navy[16]...a dedicated group of seafaring men determined to out-run, out-smart and out-maneuver the United States Coast Guard.

Canadians and Mexicans looked upon the Volstead Act as absolute proof of American insanity, especially so when they learned of the Yankee whiskey-lover's suffering and humiliation in swilling down rot-gut, blinding, bathtub-gin along with a variety of concoctions equally dangerous. They immediately organized a relief program to deliver unlimited quantities of good Canadian whiskey and Mexican tequila, thus providing an instant and permanent cure for what they considered a national American health hazard. Supply and demand soon cemented firm relationships between Canadian and Mexican exporters and the Bacchanalian Navy.

Smuggling, bootlegging and rum-running sailed rampant; a nefarious and criminal activity according to those who were "dry," but brave and honorable to those who were "wet." Regardless of personal sentiments during prohibition days, dealing in whiskey was definitely illegal and therefore dangerous.

Bacchanalian captains John Vosper, C. H. Hudson, George Ford and Robert Pamphlet, to name only a few, shared in the wealth of exchanged information regarding dog holes, bays, mud flats, caves or camouflaged quays where stored, hidden, buried or sunk contraband goods could be traded in relative safety from the watchful eye of the United States Coast Guard. These wily captains transported cargos of wine, gin, scotch, bourbon and champagne with bills-of-lading for goods loaded in Canada and consigned for delivery to grand hotels in Baja California or Acapulco; conversely, goods originating in Mexico were labeled for delivery in Vancouver and Victoria. The short stop, of course, became the territorial waters of the United States. This subterfuge of paper ports lent a note of legitimacy to the validity of a ship's cargo should the vessel be intercepted while sailing coastal waters. High profits and high risks were the name of the game, as Robert Pamphlet, captain of the 100 ton, 2-masted, ex-sealing schooner *Pescawah*, soon discovered.

February 1, 1925 dawned in a grey bluster so typical of the Pacific Northwest. The American steam schooner *Caoba* left the confines of Willapa Bay to make a run to San Francisco. A sea, somewhat larger than the rest, rose on the starboard side of the *Caoba*, surveyed this insignificant gnat crawling on its chest, then mournfuly sighed across the deck, leaving tons of its watery self rolling behind the scuppers before passing on. The little steamer shook herself and continued on as the inclement weather worsened. That swell, the same one it seemed, grew perceptibly more vicious as it returned again and again.

The *Caoba*'s loading boom broke from its tethers and, with each roll of the ship, the huge flail smashed everything in its path. Ripped-loose deck cargo plunged through the bulwarks and added wreckage to the oil slick trailing from sprung tanks. The steam schooner's upper works suffered, too. Smashed doors and broken windows allowed searching fingers of cold water to enter; charts, papers, cushions and numerous other items sloshed back and forth in foot-tangling disarray. The situation deteriorated and, with the ship's helm unable to answer, Captain A. Sandvig reluctantly ordered his radio man "Sparks" to send out their position and request assistance. He told his seventeen men to take to the boats.

A nearby tug, the *John Cudahy*, crawled to the scene; the abandoned *Caoba* wallowed helplessly and seemed ready to go down at any moment. Their forty-eight hour search

---

[15] The Volstead Act, more commonly known as the "Noble experiment," i.e. prohibition.
[16] Rum-runners.

for the crew ended in partial success when they discovered one boat containing nine of the luckless ship's men.

The *Forest King* steamed toward the distress call and discovered the *Caoba* some twelve miles south of the Columbia Lightship. Ignoring the peril of those seamen still adrift, the *Forest King* made several attempts at a salvage tow, but the derelict kept breaking away. By the time the U.S.C.G. cutter *Algonquin* arrived, the *Forest King* had continued on her way and another ship, the *Thomas P. Beal*, held a tow on the waterlogged wreck until heavy sea forced them to part company. In this mad scramble for salvage rights any concern for the castaways seemed long forgotten, except for Captain Robert Pamphlet of the rum-runner *Pescawah*.

The sturdy ex-sealing schooner lay safely outside the prohibited twelve-mile line and rode out the storm, bow on, little worse for wear. Her captain scanned the radio channels with an alert but ever-cautious ear. He realized the rescue of only nine men from a steamer the size of the *Caoba* did not comprise the entire crew and surely there must be another lifeboat adrift. Pamphlet pored over wind velocity, tide charts and current directions to ascertain where, if at all, the remaining crew rode the seas.

Captain William P. Wilshaar of the United States Coast Guard also tried to plot the lost seamen's course. At 4:00 p.m. on the 3rd of February, the cutter *Algonquin* arrived at the location[17] in time to spot a sleek, all black, sinister-appearing, two-masted schooner scooting under taut canvas due west. Swift as the smaller craft was, she proved no match for the *Algonquin*, which drew abreast of her within several hours. Wilshaar ordered a shot fired across the sailship's bow.

"Don't fire!" called the pursued captain when he saw the gun crew pull the protective covering from the one-pounder on the cutter's foredeck. "I have shipwrecked seamen aboard."

Examination of Pamphlet's papers showed no manifest for some 1,000 cases of Scotch whiskey stored in the hold. This oversight, much to his regret, was to cost him dearly, for the Coast Guard decreed he sailed within the twelve-mile limit.

Captain Wilshaar ordered a towing hawser attached to the *Pescawah*, but, with all due respect, Captain Pamphlet refused. Left with no other choice, Wilshaar ordered a prize crew aboard the vessel; Warrant Officer Floyd Overhauser took command of the errant rum-runner and encountered no resistance from her captain.

Pamphlet, always a gentleman, later explained to the customs commissioner and the press, "I want to express my thanks to you, the custom commissioner, and the other officers with whom I have had dealings. I have been well and kindly treated. I have felt that in my own interests I should maintain an aloofness and 'laissez faire' policy. I had to tell Captain Wilshaar that I had no manifest and I declined to make his hawser fast to my vessel, not from desire to impede him but because I wanted to do nothing prejudiced to my interest and those of my men."

When the two ships tied up at Astoria, the local citizens, along with Captain Sandvig and his grateful crew, wildly cheered the captured and chained crew of the *Pescawah* as the United States Coast Guard led them ashore.

District Immigration Officer R. P. Bonham, piqued by Astorians' spontaneous gesture of good will, disregarded the fact that the captain and crew stepped upon Astoria's shores as prisoners under the guns of an American warship. Bonham immediately wired for and received warrants of arrest on each of the captives for *entering a U.S. port without inspection* and *failing to have proper visas in their possession.*

The rescued crew of the *Caoba* testified in the U.S. Federal Court in Portland that they sailed well outside the twelve-mile limit at the time of their rescue by the *Pescawah*. The

---

[17] Estimated independently by both captains.

judge disregarded their statements on the grounds that they were shipwrecked and adrift with no means of knowing just exactly where they were; the Federal Court ignored all pleas for clemency by citizens across the United States and Canada.

"They treated us like kings," Captain Sandvig testified. "Everything on board was ours. They gave us their food, their clothes, their bunks and their booze. We cannot help but feel that they are now prisoners because of their humanity to us. Where a big freighter [the *Forest King*] refused to stop long enough to save 9 men, a booze runner picked us up and was seized as a result. They may be bootleggers *but they are men!*"

Captain Robert Pamphlet, Mate S. Bridges, G. H. Rex, William Tickle, J. Silverson and Pete Kenny went to Federal Prison with a stoicism found only in those who follow the sea; their only comment, "Don't feel bad, mates, we did it and we'd do it again to save a seaman's life."

The *Pescawah* languished for the next eight years tied to a Portland dock. Her cargo, it was rumored, gradually disappeared in spite of the watchman's bloodshot eyes. The government sold her once, but only on paper, for they immediately reclaimed her when payment was not forthcoming. In 1927 MGM studios showed an interest in using her for a film about rum-running, but the idea never came to fruition.

Eventually Victor H. Riley of Oregon City purchased the old ship. Riley sailed well in inland waters (just a few years prior he rescued a pilot who, after losing his engine in mid-air, crashed in the Columbia), but he dreamed of hunting whales in the seas of the Arctic. Riley convinced nine Portland College students[18] to crew the *Pescawah* on an Arctic expedition.

A lot of used whaling equipment was purchased, although no one knew how to use it. A few rotted boards of the *Pescawah*'s deck were caulked and a wheezy Maxwell automobile engine was installed as a power plant . . . all fair enough for dreaming, but obviously not adequate for high seas adventure.

Whales happened to be scarce that year so the resolute group held a meeting and, in lieu of Arctic whaling, agreed to fish the prosaic waters of Newport, Oregon.

The old and, until now, reliable *Pescawah* with her ancient engine misfiring, attempted to leave the sanctuary of the Columbia. She slammed into the north jetty; the worn pintles in her rudder simply fell apart. The largest piece of her to reach shore was her wooden wheel. The young men managed to swim, claw and crawl through and out of the surf. Riley's body washed up three days later in Dead Man's Cove.

Thus ended the saga of a ship and her master, both broken and cast aside. Pamphlet died shortly following his release from Federal Prison. His epitaph, as it appeared in the *Vancouver Daily Province*, described the man for what he was, "He is gone now, a sailor home from the sea for the last time. They ought to have found a better way of dealing with him than to make him a companion of felons, but we like to think that the memory of it, hard as it must have been for a man like him, was nothing beside the consolation he had — THAT HE HAD BEEN TRUE TO THE CODE OF THE GOOD SEAMAN, and that he had kept the honor of the sea."

He was fifty-nine.

OSHKOSH

The 89-foot, 123-ton *Oshkosh* had been battling an 80-mile gale for the last twenty-four hours. Captain Thomas Latham and his seven man crew were bone tired. Not a hot meal or even a cup of coffee in all those hours; one of the first great waves had carried the lifeboat into the deckhouse and ripped apart the galley, the stove, and destroyed or carried

---

[18] Harold Norman, Bill Thomas, J. W. Powley, Fred Norton and Claus Versteeg of Portland. Wayne Potter of Beaverton, M. G. Chambers of Stevenson, Washington, Ed Anderson of N. Dakota and Martin Zimmerman of Kansas. Tom Hyskell, the only person with even a little knowledge of the sea, shipped on as 1st Mate.

away all watercasks. Forward, much of the rigging lay in a tangled, surging mass that moved in all directions with each mountain of water that swirled across the deck. Men labored with axes to rid their ship of the deadly tentacles. Another jackhammer wave assaulted the crippled schooner and then another; below decks Engineer George May sweated over his 200 hp gasoline engine to keep up enough revolutions to give the ship headway into the wind.

Without warning, a white-sheeted comber bore down and with one mighty wrench swept the deck clean of wreckage, pilothouse and men. If any of the six lost souls had time to scream a warning, May never heard it, for he suddenly found himself in a roller-coaster engine room that lifted high into the air, then suddenly turned and slammed him into the bulkhead with a crushing blow. A table fell heavily on top of him. Clumsy wrenches danced about as they clanged within inches of his head. A drawer, crammed with nuts, bolts, fixtures, short pieces of pipe and thousands upon thousands of other items so necessary to an engine room, shot out of its casement and plowed through the air directly at him. He struggled to get out of the way and just barely succeeded as it crashed with stunning finality into the steel wall at his side. May crawled painfully across steel carlings toward the feeble glow of the caged engine room light. He reached one skinned, oil-covered hand toward the dimming globe. A choking sob wrenched from his throat; he realized with a stab of terror that he was on the ceiling, the overhead. The ship had turned turtle.

The engines gave one final roar of freedom, threshing the propeller in a wild frenzy against the cold air above the moss-covered hull of the inverted ship. Then, with a gurgling sigh, the twin monsters stopped, choking for want of their life-giving fuel. Hot oil dribbled from the filler pipes while dirty bilge water hissed and danced amid little volcanic spumes of oily smoke against the hot manifold.

The yellow glow of light flickered, then extinguished. The battered engineer lay his bleeding head on one arm, only to feel rising water lap against his cheek in the stygian darkness. He clutched frantically at inverted bulkhead fittings, using the unknown projections to climb toward the. . .floor.

For the next four hours, the battered engineer clutched and clawed for a firm hold while the unrelenting ocean, little by little, tore away portions of the ship. Many times May called out against the terrible crashing of the outside fury, hoping against hope to hear a human voice reply. Then, just when his aching muscles could stand the constant motion no longer, the shrieking wind died to a low moan, the jerking of the cubicle slowed to a gentle sway. The storm had passed.

George May thought he saw a thin gleam of light; looking hard, down and to the front, he saw it again, barely perceptible at first, then brighter. It faded and he lay in inky darkness again. No, wait! There it was again. . .it *was* light coming through the companionway. He felt the boat bump as she stranded close enough to shore for the fresh-washed sunlight to reflect off the clear, sandy bottom.

The urge to crawl through that narrow passage nearly overpowered the battered seaman, but a jarring jolt prevented any thought of escape. If he managed to get out of the inverted hatch, he would be in the water and have to fight surge and current to avoid being crushed between the ship and the bottom. He wisely decided to wait.

Hours passed with his prison alternately lighting and dimming like a cheap hotel room with a neon sign just outside the window. Then, a dozen bone-jarring crashes in swift succession, a huge lift and one final jamming descent ended George May's ordeal.

The battered *Oshkosh* lay high and dry on the sands of Clatsop, propped up upon her own wreckage. George stepped from under the ship without even bending his head to be greeted by amazed lifesaving men who had gathered on the beach to watch the derelict come in through the surf.

COASTAL DESCRIPTION
From Cape Falcon
to Cape Disappointment[19]

Cape Falcon, 17 miles north of Cape Meares and 10 miles south of Tillamook Rock, projects about two miles from the general trend of the coast. The seaward face, less than 0.5 mile in extent, is very jagged with numerous rocks under the cliffs. The SW point of the cape is composed of nearly vertical cliffs, 200 feet high, and is partially timbered. Falcon Rock, 0.7 mile west of the cape, is small and not very conspicuous.

Smuggler Cove, a small bight just south of Cape Falcon, is an excellent anchorage for small boats. The best anchorage is close to the north shore in four to five fathoms, protected from all except SW winds. Care should be taken to avoid two rocks, bare at extreme low water, that are about 150 yards from the north shore of the cove and rise abruptly from deep water.

Neahkahnie Mountain, 2.8 miles inland of Cape Falcon, is a prominent landmark, and the most important feature for locating Nehalem River. The west summit of the double-headed mountain is rounded and 1,900 feet high, but the east summit is serrated and divided into three peaks of nearly equal height. The entire SE slope is bare of timber, but is covered with grass and fern. The seaward face terminates in rocky broken cliffs over 500 feet high, and there are a few rocks about 100 feet from the beach. The two summits are visible from the south; from the north, the west summit hides the east and is very conspicuous.

Northeast from Cape Falcon, and two to three miles back from the shoreline, is a group of peaks; the highest and most prominent has a rounded summit, with a very gentle slope to the south and a more marked and abrupt drop to the north. It is very conspicuous from the west in clear weather.

Arch Cape, rocky and precipitous, projects slightly from the general trend of the coast. It is the termination of a mountain ridge rising to 2,775 feet about three miles east. The cape is bare of timber. A high rock is close to the cape and connected with it at low water. A smaller rock is about 100 yards seaward of the larger. There are several high rocks in the vicinity.

Castle Rock derives its name from its remarkable resemblance to a medieval castle with two towers, the taller of which is on the seaward end. It is about 0.8 mile west of the highest part of Arch Cape, and is the outermost bare rock. On the upper part the birds went to work again and it shows up very distinctly in the sunlight. A rock awash is about 0.9 mile off the cape and 0.4 mile SW of Castle Rock; another rock, bare at low tide, is 0.5 mile offshore and one mile south of Castle Rock.

Hug Point is a small cliff close to the beach, 1.8 miles north of Arch Cape; the cliffs in its vicinity are above 180 feet in height.

Double Peak, halfway between Cape Falcon and Tillamook Head, is the seaward end of a ridge extending east that reaches a height of 1,050 feet in less than 0.7 mile from the shore. It is heavily wooded and pitches abruptly into the sea, ending in a rocky broken cliff 100 feet high and 0.2 mile long. A rock is close to and abreast the south end of the cliff; another rock is close to and abreast the north end. A ledge, with two rocks that uncover about four feet, is about a mile WSW of the highest part of the cliff.

From Double Peak, the coast extends north for 2.7 miles to the mouth of Ecola Creek, and then turns sharply NW for the same distance to the west point of Tillamook Head. The coast is high and wooded with broken cliffs bordered by numerous rocks, except at Cannon Beach at the mouth of Ecola Creek.

Haystack Rock (do not confuse with the one to the south), 1.5 miles north of Double

---

[19] Chart #18520 and 18521.

Peak, is the largest of a cluster of rocks stretching from the low water line to ten fathoms. A rock awash at low water and surrounded by about nine fathoms is 0.8 mile SW of Haystack Rock.

Tillamook Head, 76 miles north of Yaquina Head, ends in two points which are 0.5 mile apart. The cliffs are 560 feet high at the south point and 1,000 feet high at the north point. A pinnacle rock is at the foot of the north cliffs, and extending offshore from it for 300 yards is a cluster of rocks, 45 to 140 feet high, the outer one being the lowest. The summit of the head is flat and densely wooded, with slightly lower land behind it.

Tillamook Rock, nearly 1.2 miles west of the south point of Tillamook Head, has an abandoned lighthouse and buildings on it. The west face leans a little seaward. A rock awash is between Tillamook Rock and the nearest part of Tillamook Head.

North of Tillamook Head the coast is a broad sand beach extending for 17 miles to Clatsop Spit, on the south side of the entrance of the Columbia River. Low sandy ridges, covered with grass, fern, and brush, extend parallel with and back of the beach.

Necanicum River, a small stream, empties at the summer resort of Seaside, 2.5 miles from the north side of Tillamook Head.

Saddle Mountain, double-headed and 3,283 feet high, is the landfall for the approach to the Columbia River. The mountain is visible for 50 miles offshore and is 14 miles east of Tillamook Rock. From the NW the mountain appears to be triple-headed; the NE peak appears cone-shaped, sharp, and lowest; the middle peak is irregularly cone-shaped; and the south and highest peak is a flat-topped cone.

Clatsop Spit, on the south side of the Columbia River entrance, is a low sandy beach, extending about 2.5 miles NW from Point Adams. There is a tendency for the shoal north of the spit to build up to the NW because of spring freshets and NW storms; vessels are cautioned to keep informed about conditions at the spit. A Coast Guard lookout tower, on the NW end of the spit, is prominent from the entrance.

Point Adams, just inside the spit, is a low sandy point covered with fir and undergrowth to the edge of the sand beach and low dunes. The point usually shows well from seaward, particularly if it is hazy inside.

Cape Disappointment, the rugged north point at the Columbia River entrance, is the first major headland along the 20 miles of sand beach north from Tillamook Head. It comprises a group of rounding hills covering an area 2.5 miles long and 1 mile wide, divided by a narrow valley extending NNW. The seaward faces of these hills are precipitous cliffs with jagged, rocky points and small strips of sand beach.

Cape Disappointment Light, 46°16.6′N, 124°03.1′W, 220 feet above the water, is shown from a 53 foot white conical tower with a black horizontal stripe, on the extreme SE point of the cape; a radiobeacon is at the station. A Coast Guard station is at Fort Canby on the east side of the cape. The Public Health Service maintains a contract physician's office at Long Beach about 4 miles NW of Fort Canby.

From the south the cape shows as three low knobs, separated by low flat ridges. North Head Light shows on the west slope of the west knob. From the west the cape is not prominent, but it stands out when there is fog, haze or smoke inside the cape. From the NW, the cape appears as a flat island with a slight depression in the center and a timbered knob at each end. From this direction, a low, flat hill with gently sloping side between the cape and high ridges appears as an island from a distance.

Special Note

The lights at the entrance and at Willapa Bay 28 miles north, are distinguishing marks for determining a vessel's position and subsequent shaping of her course. In thick weather, *great caution* is essential on the approach *from any direction*. The currents are variable and uncertain. Velocities of 3 to 3.5 knots have been observed from Blunts Reef and through to Swiftsure Bank, and velocities considerably in excess of those amounts have been reported. Under such conditions, vessels should keep outside the 30-fathom curve until the light-buoy (the lightship has just recently been replaced by a light-buoy) has been made. Care should be taken *not to mistake* the low *sand beach north* of Cape Disappointment for that of *Point Adams*. Nearly all the vessels which have gone ashore attempting the entrance have been wrecked north of the mouth, in the vicinity of Peacock Spit!

In clear weather, vessels should have no difficulty in entering the river as the aids to navigation are numerous. In thick weather, however, when aids cannot be seen, strangers should not attempt to enter without a pilot.

Local vessels entering in thick weather and with a rising tide, as a rule, do not attempt to pass beyond Desdemona Sands Light, because of the difficulty under such circumstances of avoiding vessels anchored in the narrow channel above the light. Strangers should not attempt to navigate the river at night.

Dredges will usually be found at work in the channels; these dredges should be passed with caution and reduced speed.

An estimate of bar conditions, visibility, and weather may be obtained by radio from the Coast Guard station at Cape Disappointment.

Mean ranges of tides on the Columbia River range from 6.7 feet at Youngs Bay, west of Astoria, to 3.3 feet at Longview, Washington, to 1.3 feet at Vancouver, Washington.

The Columbia River bar is very dangerous because of sudden and unpredictable changes in the currents often accompanied by breakers. It is reported that ebb currents on the north side of the bar attain velocities of *6 to 8 knots*, and that strong NW winds sometimes cause currents that set north or against the wind in the area outside the jetties.

In the entrance the currents are variable, and at times reach a velocity of over 5 knots on the ebb; on the flood they seldom exceed a velocity of 4 knots. The current is always modified both as to velocity and time of slack water by the river discharge. On the flood there is a *dangerous set* toward Clatsop Spit, its direction being approximately ESE; on the

ebb the current sets along the line of buoys. *Heavy breakers* have been reported as far inside the entrance as Buoy 12, south of Sand Island.

On the Columbia River, the freshet flow causes some shoaling in the dredged cuts, but re-dredging is done to maintain project depths.

Since logging is one of the main industries of the region, free floating logs and submerged deadheads or sinkers are a constant source of danger in the Columbia and Willamette Rivers. The danger is increased during the spring freshets. Deadheads or sinkers are logs which have come adrift from rafts or booms. One end of the sinker will settle toward the bottom while the other end floats, just awash, rising or falling with the tide.

Baker Bay is a shoal open bight, east of Cape Disappointment formed by the cape and the recession of the land north. Sand Island, low and flat, fronts the bay on the SW side.

A dredged channel leads north from the Columbia River along the west side of Sand Island, thence to the Port of Ilwaco mooring basin about three miles above the entrance. The spur dike, on the east side of the entrance, and the west jetty are marked by lights. The channel is marked by lights and daybeacons.

In September, 1977, the centerline controlling the depth was five feet from the entrance to Fort Canby; thence in 1976, nine feet at midchannel to the Port of Ilwaco mooring basin. There is about a ten foot depth in the basin. The entrance is subject to continual change. As there is usually a swell here, the channel should be navigated only at high tide with local knowledge. The rest of Baker Bay is covered with shoals and abandoned fishtraps.

Ilwaco is the base for a large commercial and sport fishing fleet. Almost all marine supplies are available, as is fuel. The marine railway can handle 100 tons and 65 feet. There are marine and carpentry shops here.

Desdemona Sands, a shoal area extending from just inside the entrance of the Columbia River for eight or nine miles SE, divides the river into the main channel to the south and a secondary channel to the north. Desdemona

Sands Light, 46°13.5′N, 123°57.2′W, 23 feet above the water, is shown from a dolphin with red and white diamond-shaped daymark.

Fort Stevens Wharf, at Mile 7.3 (8.4) on the Oregon side, is marked by a light and fog signal on a dolphin off the end. A special radio direction finder calibration station is at the light. The wharf is in ruins. A boat basin is at Hammond, 0.2 mile SE of the wharf. Its entrance is marked by a light and a daybeacon on the east and west jetties, respectively. Depths inside are about six feet, berths for about 200 craft, gasoline, diesel, water and ice are available, as are groceries and a launching ramp.

Warrenton, on the Skipanon Waterway at Mile 9.5 (11) is the base of a large *sportfishing* fleet. The largest marine railway here can handle 150 tons, 115 feet and 12 foot draft for hull and engine repairs. Several marinas are on the water way, and a mooring basin is on the east part of the waterway about 1.4 miles above the entrance. Floats for about 300 craft, fuel, water, groceries and marine supplies are available.

Scarboro Hill, 820 feet high, is on the Washington side about seven (eight) miles east of Cape Disappointment. It is a long, gradually rising ridge, covered with grass, fern and some trees. A number of conspicuous light-colored buildings of the historical Fort Columbia State Park may be seen near the base of the hill.

A dredged channel leads from the Columbia River near the east end of Baker Bay to a basin at Chinook, on the Washington side. In January, 1978, the midchannel controlling depth was five feet except for shoaling to bare in the SE half of the channel in the vicinity of light 2. In 1973 there were depths of ten feet in the basin. Supplies and fuel are available, and a five ton hoist.

Youngs Bay is a shoal body of water just west of Smith Point. It receives the waters of Youngs River and Lewis and Clark River. The docks of a marine repair yard are 0.5 mile above the highway bridge crossing the Lewis and Clark River. The yards can handle vessels up to 400 tons and 33 feet wide with 15 foot draft for hull and engine repairs.

Point Ellice, on the Washington side 11 (12.7) miles inside the entrance, is the termination of a spur from the mountain ridge back of Scarboro Hill. The point is rounding and rocky, but not high. Two hillocks lie behind the point. In this area there are many abandoned fish traps and pile structures that extend into the river.

Astoria, at Mile 12 (14) on the Oregon side, extends from Youngs Bay to Tongue Point. It is the principal city on the Columbia River below Longview, Washington. It connects with the interior both by rail and highway. General anchorages are north and west of Tongue Point. Harbor regulations prohibit vessels from anchoring more than one hour within an area bounded on the south by the Astoria waterfront and on the north by the main channel buoys. Temporary anchorage may be had by any vessel of suitable draft just east of buoy 19, NW of Desdemona Sands Light. Astoria is a nice place to visit.

The mean range of the tide at Astoria is 6.5 feet. The range between mean lower low water and mean higher high is 8.2 feet. A range of 12 feet may occur at the maximum tides.

Currents above Astoria are 1 to 3 knots except during the freshet period when increased water comes from the mountains; however, this will not affect navigation seriously.

Astoria's perennially verdant landscape is hemmed by rather low mountains on the north, east, and south. On the west it is open to the Pacific over four miles or more of low green dunelands and the last ten miles of the Columbia River.

Weather hazards occasionally occur. Storms may sink or wreck ships. *Even in fair weather*, wind and wave may combine to produce a type of breaker known as the *"widow maker"* and swamp a boat.

Heavy rains inundate lowlands, and high tides aggravated by gales may push seawater across highways and up the beaches. Rains may cause earthslides, mostly in highway cuts. Storms may fell trees or break power lines or poles. Lightning strikes seldom occur. Showers of small hail may briefly whiten the ground during many of the months. Occasionally in winter there may be rather brief periods of freezing temperatures, with snow or ice.

The climate is generally healthful, except for dampness and a feeling of isolation in winter. The local wags maintain if you can see the Washington mountains, it is going to rain, and if you can't, it is raining. Even then, the gloomy spells of cloud and driving rain may be broken by an occasional ray of sunshine, which of course brings a rejoinder of "Astorians don't tan, they rust." Alike relaxing are the cool breezes, waters, fog, and warm sands of summer; and the roaring seas and storms with their rainy balmy nights in winter join hand in hand to build *men*. Heat waves are uncommon and usually brief. The washed atmosphere stays remarkably clean and fresh.

Two mooring basins for small craft and fishing vessels are maintained by the Port of Astoria; 0.3 mile west of the south end of the Astoria Bridge is the West Basin, with a reported 15 feet through the entrance and about 6-foot depths at the floats. About 425 berths with electricity, gasoline, diesel, water, ice, and marine supplies are available. Engine repairs can be made at several private firms on the basin. A 10-ton hoist at a packing plant just west of the basin can handle small craft in emergencies. The East Basin, two (2.3) miles east of the Astoria Bridge, has berths for about 50 small craft and a launching ramp; however, no services are available. Reported depths of 15 feet through the entrance and 10 feet at the floats are available.

SHIP DISASTERS
Cape Falcon to Cape Disappointment

Admiral 1/13/1912 Schooner, four masts, 683 tons, 173', built by Simpson and K. V. Kruse at North Bend in 1899. See story, "Railroad to the Rescue."

Admiral Benson 2/15/1930 Steamer, passenger, 3049 tons, 299.6' × 45' × 22.5', one deck, two masts, built at Wilmington, Delaware for Baltimore & Caroline SS Co. Ship could accommodate 200 passengers and 60 crew. Purchased by the Admiral Line in 1927, she was the former *Tipton*, ex-*Ester Weems*. Watch officers used the remains of the *Laurel*, wrecked eight months prior, as a range buoy and thus computed from false bearings. As late as 1979, another vessel struck the remains of the *Benson* and would have sunk, but for the efforts of the Coast Guard.

Alice McDonald 12/30/1906 Schooner. Wrecked on Clatsop Spit. NFI.

*Alsternixe 2/9/1903 Bark, German, four masts. Stranded on Peacock Spit and was one of the few vessels to escape.

Amak 10/16/1942 Tuna and drag boat, 70'. Near buoy 10, Captain Charles Ellis looked up just in time to see a freak sea rising from out of nowhere. A choking shout of surprise was all the warning he could give. Three of the crew managed to climb to the top of the deckhouse while the captain and one other dove below deck. When the huge, smothering wall of water passed over, the three men on the deckhouse were surprised to see their ship, minus the portion they rode, wallowing over 75' away in the foaming sea. A passing boat threw the men a line and took them aboard, then secured the decapitated *Amak* and towed it to safety. The deckhouse was later brought in by the Coast Guard. Captain Charles Ellis, John Vogg, Thor Wika, Chris Wika and Duke Williams will never forget that day at the mouth of the Columbia.

Americana 2/28/1918 Schooner of 900 tons, built in 1892. Foundered at the mouth of the Columbia. 13 dead.

Architect 3/10/1875 Listed as a bark and a schooner, also listed as lost on the 28th of March, not only on the Clatsop Spit, but in the Columbia River as well. She sailed apparently in ballast under Captain Mertage en route San Francisco-Cementville (Knappton) when she filled and settled. The crew climbed to the rigging of the 20 year old Rockland, Maine built vessel and stayed there all day until rescued. She was

---

* Refloated or partially salvaged.

valued at $8,247; the wreck sold for $52.

Ariel 1866 Schooner. Wrecked on Clatsop Spit. May possibly be the same as next listed vessel.

Ariel 1886 Schooner. Wrecked on Clatsop Spit. May possibly be the same vessel as previously listed.

Barges 1/18/1947 Two ocean-going barges in tow of tug *Teton* and en route for Honolulu with 1,400,000' of lumber. The barges drifted when strong winds forced the tug to release her tow lines in fear of being dragged onto the spit. Owned by Portland Tug & Barge Co., the two barges were insured for $50,000 each.

Battle Abbey 12/18/1914 Bark, British. She burned at sea off the Columbia River. A German ship rescued the crew. The *Battle Abbey* was owned by James Rolph, Jr.

Bordeaux 12/13/1852 Brig. En route San Francisco-Puget Sound, the ship broke from her temporary anchorage at the bar and was totalled on Clatsop Spit.

Broderick Castle 12/1908 British grain ship., Wrecked on Peacock Spit.

Buster 10/17/1940 Barge, 230 tons, built in 1920. Foundered on the Columbia bar.

Cairnsmore 9/27/1883 Bark, British, three-masted, 1300 tons gross. Captain B. Gibbs sailed her en route London-Portland with 7,500 barrels of cement and some machinery. The $48,000 ship and her $18,000 cargo became lost in the fog. A huge swell caught her and, by the time the men heard the surf, it was too late to put back. The steamer *Queen of the Pacific* saved the crew. The sea drove the ship higher upon the sand; she lies just a few hundred yards due west of the south end of Coffenbury Lake at Fort Stevens Park. The huge ship was visible as late as 1914; Warrenton children used to play in her rigging during school picnics.

C. A. Klose 3/21/1905 Schooner. Ashore, bottom-up, on North Beach peninsula after grounding near the Coquille Lighthouse in 1903.

Calmar 1/1949 Steamer. Struck by a huge sea, the "Biggest I've ever seen in all my years at sea!" exclaimed Captain R. B. Hughes. Two of the *Calmar's* crew died; one was washed overboard, the other was slammed into the deckhouse. Thrown on her beam ends, the ship was salvaged only by good seamanship.

Caoba 2/1/1925 Steam schooner, ex-coaster, 579 tons, built by Lindstrom at Aberdeen in 1905. See story, "A Companion of Felons."

Cavour 12/8/1903 Bark, square-rigged, Italian, ex-*Avonmore*. She earned the dubious honor of being the first Italian vessel wrecked on the Columbia bar. Built at Nova Scotia in 1881, 1,354 tons. Under Captain Telemore Sofianos, she carried 1,030,000 feet of lumber bound for South Africa.

Champion 4/15/1870 Schooner aka *Joe Champion*. Built by Capt. Quick of Tillamook in 1865. Captain Dodge (see "A Tough Breed . . ."), his son, Mr. B.

Stevens, and an Indian boy were aboard. The Indian survived by tying himself to the capsized lifeboat which drifted ashore near Oysterville. Three dead. This wreck is variously reported as occurring at Shoalwater bar and Columbia.

Chatham 10/20/1792 Tender, British. Grounded on Peacock Spit (it was not known by that name until years later) and reported as the first known grounding on the Columbia. No damage, no lives lost, the ship was worked off.

Childar 5/3/1934 Motor ship, Norwegian. See story, "Childar."

City of Dublin 10/8/1878 Ship, British, 814 tons, en route Port Chalmers-New Zealand-Columbia River. Captain David Steven. In 1880 the *Weekly Astorian* reported parts of the *City of Dublin* had washed through the woods and were now lying behind the Fort Stevens garrison quarters. "Rigging and other fixtures of the wreck were sold Dec. 1, 1878. The sale was well attended, $500 more was brought in than was expected" — *Daily Astorian*, Dec. 1878.

Columbia River Light Ship #50 11/29/1899 Ship drove ashore and salvaged in a very spectacular and successful recovery at Cape Disappointment.

Corsica 2/21/1882 Bark, British, 778 ton, a wooden vessel 13 years old, 170' × 31' × 21'. She struck heavily on the bar while leaving for England with 43,867 bushels of wheat. Vessel was valued at $32,000 and the cargo at $40,838. The tug *Fearless* stood by while the *Corsica's* crew fought a losing battle. They were rescued; the ship vanished beneath the waves 12 miles south of the river. Capt. W. H. Vessey.

Curacao 7/12/1940 Steamer, ex-*Helenic Skipper*, 1548 tons, steel with 2 masts, 2 decks, 214.3' × 38' × 16.3', built in 1895 with a 47 crew and 100 passenger capacity. An explosion sent her to the bottom off the Columbia. Everyone saved.

Daisy Freeman 10/11/1912 Steam schooner. Struck Columbia bar and salvaged

Delharrie 3/10/1880 Bark, British, 1293 tons. En route Astoria-Queensland when she failed to answer the helm and went ashore on the north entrance of the Columbia. Ship was valued at $65,000, cargo at $78,000. Total loss, crew saved.

Devonshire 1884 NFI.

Dolphin 1852 Brig. Wrecked at the mouth of the Columbia. NFI.

Dreadnaught 2/1876 Sloop, built at Tillamook on Hiram Smith's place, the present site of Bay City. Under Captain William Terwilliger, she went on Clatsop Spit shortly after her completion. Seven dead.

Drumcraig 1906 Bark, foundered at sea west of the Columbia.

Drexel Victory 1/21/1947 A victory ship of 10,500 tons gross, 7607 net. Launched 4/7/1945 by Kaiser at Richmond, Ca. Outbound for Yokohama, the ship struck the Columbia bar and began breaking between holds 4 and 5. Captain Canute Rommerdahl did his best for Olson & Co. and the U.S. Maritime Commission, but his ship drifted and sank due west of buoy #6, ¼ mile out in 210', losing a grain cargo of more than 5,000 tons.

Edith Lorne 11/17/1881 Bark, British, 803 tons with a cargo of grain when she was lost on the bar while en route to Queenstown. Captain William Watt said the ship was valued at $60,000, the cargo at $44,000. Ship and cargo a total loss, the crew was saved.

Electra 1/26/1944 Diesel troller, 72 tons. Lost on Clatsop Spit.

*Emily Stephens 2/8/1881 Schooner, 68 tons, built at Westport by W. J. Stephens, 77' × 21' × 7'. Wrecked on Clatsop Spit.

Emma Claudine 11/19/1906 Schooner was in a bad way during a severe blow and foundered on Clatsop Spit. Captain Stream tied his trusting wife to a spar after signaling the barkentine *Winkleman* to stand close. With the two ships running side-by-side, he cast a line to the other ship, rigged a snatch-block and butt-sling and sent Mrs. Stream dousing through the water to safety. The fight to save the ship, however, was a losing one and the crew finally were forced to abandon ship. They were picked up by the *Minnie E. Caine*.

Fern Glen 10/16/1881 Ship, British, iron, 818 tons. Captain F. Budd was unaware of the new Tillamook Light and the change of color in the Point Adams Light. As a result, he drove his ship directly into the Clatsop Spit.

Flora 3/26/1954 Troller. Wrecked just outside of Peacock Spit. Two dead.

Francis H. Leggett 9/18/1914 Steam schooner en route Grays Harbor-San Francisco. The vessel encountered difficulties in heavy weather when a deckload of ties canted off the deck of the 1606 ton ship. She listed to starboard and took great gulps of water down her torn hatch covers. Captain C. Maro had little time to prepare his passengers for what was to come. At the same time as the distressed 11 year old ship began to plunge to the bottom, the 3000 ton Japanese cruiser *Idzumi* happened by. Using the excuse they sailed on a search-and-destroy mission against the *Leipzig* of the Imperial German Navy, the warship refused to halt and aid the survivors and sent, instead, a garbled and misleading wireless as she steamed past. Out of the 37 passengers and 25 crew, only James Farrell of Seattle and George Pullman of Winnipeg survived. They were picked from the choppy seas by the *Beaver* and the *Frank Buck*. The ship is believed to have gone down in an area just south of the Columbia. A body, that of a woman, washed ashore on Manzanita Beach. Captain Jens Jenson, a survivor from the *Nokomis* wreck on Clipperton Island a few weeks prior, was also lost.

Frank W. Howe 2/22/1904 The schooner, with her cargo of railroad ties, was a total loss on the North Head of the Columbia.

Foss #2 1931 Scow, 495 tons. Lost while under tow near Tillamook Head.

Galena 11/13/1906 Bark, four masts, 2294 tons, 292' × 43' × 24', built at Dundee, Scotland by A. Stephens & Sons in 1890. The ship, in ballast from Junin, Chile, was 59 days en route to Portland for grain. Captain J. J. Howell reported to her owner Thomas Shute in Liverpool an occurrence very similar to that of Captain Laurence of the *Peter Iredale*, lost just 18 days previously a few miles north. Poor visibility caused the *Galena* to go ashore at Surfpines. Her remains are presently under some new homes in the dunes about three miles north of Seaside and some 600' from the surf.

Gamecock 6/28/1898 Sternwheeler northbound under tow with the *Staghound*. Both ships ran into foul weather and became severely damaged while being towed by the *Elihu Thompson*. Only the *Gamecock's* cargo of wood kept her afloat long enough to bring her into the safety of the Columbia.

General Warren 1/30/1852 Steamer, 309 tons, built at Portland, Maine in 1844. Grounded and lost on the Clatsop Spit. See story, "If I Live. . . ."

George W. Prescott 3/9/1902 Schooner, ex-*Irondale*. Foundered at sea off the Columbia. One dead, NFI.

Glenmorag 12/19/1896 Ship, British. Grounded on North Beach. Not all bad for the stranded Captain Turnbull, for he met and married Miss Agnes Garretson of Ocean Park.

Glenesslin 10/1/1913 Square-rigger, three masts, steel hull, 1818 gross tons. It was a clear, calm day, so calm, in fact, it could have been called an "Irish Hurricane" when this Glasgow-built ship went ashore. Having sailed the seas since 1885, the beautiful ship came to a sad end when, after years of losing money, she struck at the foot of Neah-Kah-Nie Mountain. Captain Owen Williams, who had been drinking, left his vessel in charge of inexperienced hands. The captain lost his license for three months; the 2nd mate, John Colefield, lost his for six months, but the insurance paid off anyway. The ship's value was set at $30,000. The wreck sold for $560, but when the buyers took another look, they sold it on the spot for $100. The new owners removed most of her deck gear and made a substantial profit, but much of her hull still remains and is easily found in the water along the rocky shore below the pinnacles of the mountain.

Governor Moody 9/20/1890 Pilot Schooner built at Astoria in 1885, 61 tons, 83' × 21' × 10', two masts, owned by A. M. Montgomery. At 4:15 a.m. she hit thick weather and went ashore on the north head of the Columbia. Some of her rigging was saved.

Grace Roberts 12/8/1887 Barkentine. The old and tender vessel, under Captain M. Larsen, became lost in heavy fog and ran on the north beach of the Columbia. The wreck was bought by Martin Foard.

*Hazard 1798 American brig, commanded by Cap-

tain Ben Swift, who lost his chief officer and four men when he ordered them to sound the Columbia bar in a small boat. This incident may have been the one to which the first officer of the *Tonquin* referred when he said, "I go to lay my bones alongside those of my uncle who died here some years ago," when Capt. Jonathan Thorn ordered him to sound the bar; Ebenezer D. Fox and seven others of the *Tonquin* perished.

I. Merrithew 1/12/1853 Bark, 128 tons, general cargo. The ship, under Captain Samuel Kissam, stood off the bar waiting for a pilot. When none appeared, the captain entered in good weather and on a flood tide. As he reached the red buoy near the Clatsop Spit, the wind died. Capt. Kissam anchored, the ship dragged to the middle sands, bumped and went on her beam ends. The masts were cut away, but the seas continued to break over her. At 9:00 a.m. the pilot boat happened by and rescued the crew. The ship broke up, her hull drifted to Cape "D."

Industry 3/15/1865 Bark, built at Stockton, Maine in 1858 and owned by Paul Corno. The vessel stood offshore two weeks waiting to clear the bar; stores and water were in short supply. The ship attempted to enter under Captain I. Lewis. Once inside the bar, the wind lulled and the anchor was dropped. The wind freshened, rose and the anchor was raised, but the ship missed stays. The skipper tried to tack a second time and again she missed stays, this time bumping on the middle shoals and unshipping her rudder. A boat was launched, but it upset; 1st mate Cavines drowned. 23 passengers and crew took to the rigging for the rest of the day and night after heavy seas took the ship's upper works, cabins and boats. The SS *Oregon* from San Francisco crossed the bar, spotted the *Industry*, but was unable to render assistance. The following morning two rafts were built from the wreckage and people climbed aboard both. The first raft drifted into the south channel where the riders were rescued by a lifeboat manned by soldiers from the fort. Captain Lewis and three others remained with the ship, but 14 others drowned. Because of this wreck, Joel Munson started the first Life Service at the bar. See "Joel Munson. . . ." Also, visit the Columbia River Maritime Museum in Astoria to seek Shark Rock with its inscriptions carved by the survivors.

Intrepid 2/16/1954 Bark, 1800 tons. Originally built as a training ship for the Navy, she accommodated 330 officers and men and was armed with six 4-inchers and several smaller guns. She had steam engines for auxiliary power, but relied primarily upon sail. Constructed in 1904, the ship never really fulfilled her intended purpose and served simply as a drill ship, a receiving ship and a barracks in San Francisco until 1921. The beautiful ship was then sold, cut down to a barge and used commercially until she wrecked on the north beach of the Columbia.

Inveravon 10/1914 Bark, British. En route Callao-Portland. She was last sighted off the Columbia bar; missing with all hands.

Iowa 1/12/1936 Steel freighter, 8800 tons, Captain Edgar L. Yates. Owned by the States Line. En route Astoria-New York with general cargo. Ship left the river in the face of a fierce, 76 mph gale. One faint SOS was heard and the CG Cutter *Onandaga* put out immediately in search of the distressed vessel. She was located within a few hours, broken in half with only her masts above water. The storm's terrific power broke off her metal stanchions and cast them ashore nearly three miles away. Six bodies were recovered; a total of 34 died.

Jane A. Falkenburg 1872 Aground on Clatsop Spit. Hauled off with no danger.

J. C. Cousins 10/7/1883 Schooner, two masts with topsail, 49 tons, 66' × 20' × 8', built at San Francisco as a sleek yacht in 1863. The vessel was purchased by pilots Welch, Wood, Doig and Olsen for use in competition against the Flavel Pilot Co. The little sloop arrived in 1881 and, though she took away some of Flavel's business, she never really posed a serious threat, at least not enough to blame Flavel for the mysterious chain of events that soon occurred when the little ship came under the charge of boat-keeper Zeiber (no one remembered his first name, which served to further arouse everyone's suspicions). The boat sailed to Astoria for her usual supplies, then returned to her station off the Columbia bar. The crew aboard the *Mary Taylor* observed her exit, run off, tack and stand in; all seemed normal and when night fell, they thought no more of it. Bright and early the next morning, the *J. C. Cousins* was observed tacking three miles offshore. At approximately 1:00 p.m., her one set sail caught, filled and brought her directly toward the foaming breakers on Clatsop Spit. Observers from shore knew her four man crew would veer from such a dangerous course, but were puzzled by her strange antics. At 2:15 p.m., she clumsily plowed through the surf some 10 miles below Point Adams Lighthouse, directly in front of West Packard's farm. There was no one on board; no bodies were ever found. Rumor held George Flavel responsible for ordering the *Cousins* crew murdered by Zeiber, who then escaped to the Orient. This, of course, was pure nonsense, for Flavel controlled the pilotage and most certainly would not have gone to such great lengths in eliminating an ineffectual competitor. Nevertheless, the mystery remains.

Jenny Ford 1/29/1864 Barkentine, American. Under Captain McCarty she sailed en route Puget Sound-San Francisco and became a total wreck on the North Head; passenger Osgood drowned.

Jenny Jones 5/14/1864 Schooner wrecked on Clatsop Spit.

Josephine 1849 Bark. She carried a cargo of 16,760' of hewn and 53,450' sawn lumber for Kilborn & Co.,

29,000′ for Charter Co. and 12,000′ sawn lumber for Charter and Oregon City Co. She also carried 201 sacks of potatoes. She left Astoria December 14th and, in spite of a drunken Indian pilot, made it to Baker Bay. There, the ebb pulled her into the current where the anchor failed to hold. She drifted to the south channel and struck Point Adams bar. Her masts were cut away to lessen the load; she drifted in a leaking condition until abandoned as she went under at a point on a straight line between Cape "D" and Tillamook Head.

Laurel 6/16/1929 Freighter, 5759 tons, en route for New York with a lumber cargo. She encountered a gale while exiting the Columbia. Her steering went haywire and she broke in two when she struck the sands. A huge sea carried off 19 year old Russel Smith of Dorchester, Mass., who had been standing on the *bridge*. The ship was totalled; Captain Louis Johnson lost his license for 90 days for failure to use his emergency steering gear.

Lupata aka *Lupatia* 1/3/1881 Bark, iron, 1400 tons gross, 1039 net. Built in 1875 at Harrington, England by Williamson. Owned by J. H. Clark. She sailed en route Japan-Portland in ballast. The ship was spoken the day before at a point some 40 miles off the Columbia by a skipper who expected to be hailed by his old friend, Captain Irvine. He learned that Captain Irvine had died at sea a few weeks out of Antwerp and First Mate B. H. Raven was now in command of the *Lupata*. Able as Raven was, he could not control the weather and what was first a gentle breeze soon worked into a full-blown southeast gale. While Raven fought the storm, a construction crew under Captain H. S. Wheeler (one of the most famous of lighthouse builders on the west coast) was busy chopping out a pad on the grim, deadly, bottom-ripping, rocky projection and hidden reef known as "The Tillamook." At about 8:00 p.m., Wheeler and his men heard the creaking slap of a ship under way in the pitch-black, gusty, cold night. A voice called from the stygian gloom, "Hard aport!" Wasting no time, the construction crew lit every lantern available and threw kerosene on a pile of driftwood. Little time remained for the big ship as she loomed, ghost-like, into the feeble light supplied by those on the rock. "Meet her . . . meet her" (reverse the helm, she's swinging too far) was the last command heard. A howl of wind drowned the screeching of her iron bottom as it knifed into the reef behind Tillamook. Wheeler and his men were helpless to do more; the next morning before the men continued work on the belated lighthouse, they anxiously scanned the shoreline, fearing the worst. There it was, inshore beyond the reef, the mizzen of this proud grainship jutted from the water to mark the graves of 16 lost souls.. Lon. 124°01′06″, Lat. 45°56′12″; Loran C 100kHz, 9940 − W:12208.82; X:28021.99, Y:43921.87.

Maine 8/25/1848 Whaling bark. Astorian colonists pressured New Bedford, Maine and Massachusetts to consider using their little town as the western terminus of the great whaling industry. The owners of the *Maine* ordered her to put in for supplies at Astoria and survey the town's possibilities. The ship sailed two years out of Fairhaven with a hard-earned cargo of 1,400 barrels whale oil, 150 barrels sperm oil and 14,000 pounds of bone. Heavy weather prevented Astoria's pilot Hawkes from boarding the whaler to bring her into port; the *Maine*'s impatient captain foolishly elected to enter by sounding with a small boat. The capricious winds fell to a fizzle at the crucial moment and the bark drifted helplessly onto Clatsop. Along with the ship, the pounding waves crushed Astoria's dream of being the "Nantucket of the Pacific." John Hobson managed to salvage the ship's cooper shop, but the balance of her cargo was an enormous loss. The ship's first and third mates, perhaps not too anxious to face their eastern employers, remained in Oregon to learn piloting. The remainder of the crew and their captain took the ship's longboat to San Francisco and from there returned to the east coast.

Makah 10/24/1888 Barkentine, 699 tons, built in 1882 at Port Blakeley by Hall Bros. En route Portland-Australia under Captain Larsen. She was found bottom-up off Tillamook Head. 11 dead.

Marie 11/19/1852 Brig en route San Francisco-Shoalwater Bay. Wrecked on North Beach, Cape Disappointment. Two saved, nine died.

Mauna Ala 12/10/1941 Freighter, 6256 tons, 420′ in length, owned by Matson Lines. Ordered to return due to the Japanese attack at Pearl Harbor on December 7, 1941, the vessel ran aground on Clatsop just south of the old *Peter Iredale*. She was loaded with all kinds of Christmas goodies for the Hawaiian Islanders. The ship was a total loss, but is still fondly remembered by those people of Warrenton and surrounding communities who enjoyed her cargo of turkey, chicken, butter and other good things including Christmas trees washed in from her wreck. Had the *Mauna Ala* not wrecked on Oregon shores, she no doubt would have fallen prey to Captain Megii Tagami's submarine I 25.

Mizpah 6/3/1951 Troller. Lost at sea off the Columbia. One dead.

Monitor 3/24/1901 Barkentine, three masts, built in 1862 at San Francisco for John Kentfield by Domingo Marcucci. Foundered off the Columbia.

Neptune 11/16/1948 Tug. Rammed and sunk by *Herald of the Morning* at the mouth of the Columbia. One dead.

*Nightingale 12/26/1941 Minesweeper. She struck a buoy and sank at the mouth of the Columbia, later raised.

Nimbus 12/29/1877 American ship, 1302 tons, built at Bath, Maine in 1869. Under Captain Leonard, the oak and pine ship left Astoria for Cork. She thumped heavily on the bar and began to leak. In spite of her pumps, the water rose and her crew was taken off by the *Aberystwith Castle*. The *Nimbus* went under at 12:55 a.m., 25 miles off the Columbia. On November 28, 1878, the Revenue Cutter *Thomas Corwin* investigated a bottom-up wreck floating off False Tillamook and determined that it was the *Nimbus*, her bursting cargo having forced the ship to surface.

Nisqually 3/26/1938 Brig. Lost at Clatsop Spit, in the old channel. NFI.

North Bend 1/15/1928 Schooner, 981 tons. Ashore on Peacock Spit, this vessel became unique in the annals of shipping. The *North Bend* "walked" across the spit on a 13 month journey. With a minimum of human help, she was safely launched into the bay's deep water. She was converted into a barge and eventually lost after striking Guano Rock at Coos Bay. She was burned for scrap in 1942.

Oleum 1/12/1951 Tanker for American Oil, 10,048 tons. She cracked while crossing the bar and spilled oil all the way to Portland, which definitely did not make any points with the ecologists. Her 19 plates were replaced at a cost of $118,700. Built in Portland in 1945, she was owned by Union Oil Co.

Oriole 9/18/1853 Bark. Captain Lewis H. Lentz. Bound for Astoria from San Francisco carrying light-house material for Fort Canby. The wind died as she entered on the ebb. Dragging anchor, she struck on the south sands in three fathoms. Her rudder un-shipped and the cargo shifted when the ship put off to sea. She went under in approximately 5½ fathoms with only her topsail exposed. Captain George Flavel saved the 32 on board.

Orion 10/4/1897 Schooner, two masts, 117 tons, built by Bendixson and Peterson at Humboldt Bay in 1878. Cut in two by the German ship *Peru* near the Columbia Lightship; Captain Nelson and crew were saved.

Oshkosh 2/13/1911 Gas schooner, 123 tons, built in North Bend by Kruse & Banks in 1909, 89' × 24' × 7', equipped with twin 200 hp engines. See story, "*Oshkosh*."

Peacock 7/18/1841 U.S. Sloop of War. See story, "*Peacock*."

Pescawah 2/24/1933 Schooner. See story, "A Companion of Felons."

Peter Iredale 10/25/1906 Bark, four masts. See story, "The *Peter Iredale*."

Pinmore 1901 British bark, 2358 tons, 310' in length. She became distressed while attempting to enter the Columbia en route Santa Rosalia, Mexico. Apparently her ballast shifted and panicked the captain. After abandoning the ship to the elements, the crew were picked up by a passing steamer and taken to Astoria where they became the laughing stock of the town for there, bigger than life, waited the *Pinmore*. She had been spotted and towed in with little effort. The salvager's fees were enormous. She eventually met a much grimmer fate in the Atlantic. The four-master, built in 1882, seemed plagued with in-

eptitude despite being one of the best of her type of ship. Count Felix von Luckner, as a runaway lad using the assumed name of Phelax Luedige, signed her articles for a disastrous 285 day journey from Vancouver to Liverpool in which he contracted scurvy when the ship ran out of food off Cape Horn. On February 19, 1917, the world's most famous German sea-raider sighted her again. Count von Luckner's own ship, the *Sea Adler*, was in need of supplies, and the intrepid German captain brazenly sailed the *Pinmore* into Rio de Janeiro. There, under the very noses of the British warships *Glasgow* and *Amethyst*, he took aboard the necessary items while, at the same time, listened to well-meaning HMS officers caution him to "...be alert for that 'Sea Devil' von Luckner who is prowling the area...." Well satisfied with the success of his charade, the wily German returned to his own vessel at sea and, with tears in his eyes, reluctantly ordered the sinking of the *Pinmore* before making his escape.

Potomac 1852 Brig. Lost at the mouth of the Columbia. NFI.

Potrimpos 12/19/1896 Bark, German. Sailed out of Hamburg for Manzanillo, Mexico, then to the Columbia to pick up a cargo of grain. Under Captain Hellwegge, who waited in vain for a pilot boat to assist him across the bar, a failing wind caused the ship to drift helplessly to the north beach sands where she went aground and eventually became a total loss.

Primrose 1882 Supposedly on the Clatsop Spit. NFI.

Protection 1/1/1899 Steamer, 281 tons, built at San Francisco in 1888. While bound for San Francisco from Seattle, the vessel ran into trouble off the Columbia. 14 of her crew were rescued by the British bark *Colgate* before the *Protection* went under with one man.

PT&B 1684 & 1685 1/18/1947 Barges, each 1700 tons. They went on Peacock Spit loaded with $70,000 worth of lumber. Both were a total loss.

Queen 2/17/1904 Steamship, 1700 tons, built by William Cramp & Sons of Philadelphia in 1882 as *Queen of the Pacific*. She was a single screw, 330' × 38.5' vessel with an engine of 45 " × 90 " × 48 ". She ran onto Clatsop Spit in 1883 after being blinded by the smoke of a forest fire. In 1888, she quietly sank at Port Harford. In May, 1890, for unknown reasons, her name was shortened to *Queen*. It was 1901 before the next accident befell this hard-working vessel; she displaced some rocks that were attached to a reef in Alaska. Recovering from that mishap, she earned the distinction of becoming the first Puget Sound ship to be equipped with electric lights. Her next mishap occurred on February 17, 1904, when fire broke out in the aft portion of the ship. Capt. N. E. Cousins and his crew valiantly fought the stubborn blaze while the ship wallowed in the swells just off Tillamook Head but, in spite of their best efforts, 14 lives were forfeited. The ship was eventually scrapped in Japan in 1935.

Raccoon 12/31/1813 British, sloop of war, grounded on Columbia River bar and lost a portion of her keel, which is now on display at the Columbia River Maritime Museum in Astoria. See story, "Raccoon."

Rambler 12/1859 En route Neah Bay-San Francisco with a cargo of oil and peltries under Captain A. J. Tuthill. The schooner came ashore on Clatsop Spit in March; no trace of her captain or crew of four was ever found.

Republic 2/7/1945 Troller, shark boat. Lost at sea off Cape Disappointment. Four dead.

Ricky 7/22/1949 Fishing boat lost on Peacock Spit.

Rival 9/13/1881 Bark, American, three masts, built at Baltimore in 1869, 299 tons, 130' × 31' × 12'. Ship left harbor with Captain Thomas B. Adams en route San Francisco-Knappton under pilot Hansen. The ship and her cargo of shingles and hay were a total loss on Peacock Spit.

Roanoke 1911 Steamer, iron, three decks and two masts, 2354 tons, 267' × 40.5' × 16.4', built in 1882 at Chester, Pennsylvania and operated by North Pacific SS Co. Carrying passengers and freight, she ran on the bar at the Columbia; one life was lost. In May of 1916, she turned turtle off Port San Luis, Ca., where 47 out of 50 people lost their lives. See *California Shipwrecks*.

Rose Ann 2/8/1948 Fish dragger, built in 1946 at Jensen's Boatyard in Seattle. Captain Roy Collins. Vessel foundered in a fierce storm east of the Columbia Lightship. Four dead.

Rosecrans 1/7/1913 Tanker. Wrecked on the Columbia bar. See story, "Rosecrans."

S. D. Lewis 3/16/1865 Brig lost at the entrance to the Columbia River. NFI.

Sea Thrush 12/4/1932 Freighter, 5538 tons, 8800 deadweight, built by Northwest Steel Co. in 1918 at Portland and owned by Shepard SS Co. Ex-*West Cherow* and ex-*Westland*. Under Captain Ernest J. Landstrom and en route Puget Sound to Vancouver, Wash., the vessel ran aground due to faulty charts. Thirty-one crewmen, one female passenger and one stowaway were rescued by the U.S.C.G. *Redwing* and some $50,000 in cargo was salvaged before the ship broke in two near the south jetty and was swallowed by the sands.

Shark 9/10/1846 U.S. Sloop of War, schooner rigged, 184 tons, built in 1821 on the east coast at the cost of $23,627. Her 12 guns consisted of 10 carronades and 2 long-toms, all 32 pounders. See stories "Friendly Enemies" and "The *Shark* + The *Oriole* = The *Morning Star*."

Staghound 6/28/1898 Steamer, sternwheel, built at Portland in 1898. While under tow 30 miles off the Columbia River, she was severely damaged. Her hull was re-built into the river tug *Hercules*, which later sank at Three Mile Rapids on the Washington side of the Columbia.

Sulphur 1839 HMS, 300 tons. This British warship stranded briefly at the mouth of the Columbia and for many years Clatsop Spit was known as Sulphur Spit.

Strathblane 11/3/1891 British grain ship, 1300 tons. Under Capt. George Cuthell, the vessel, 19 days from Honolulu, missed the entrance to the Columbia and became a total loss on the north beach. An erratic chronometer was the cause of the disaster. Seven people, including the captain, were drowned. Captain J. D. Murray was aboard and survived to marry Miss Frances D. Taylor of Pacific County, while Charles A. Payne, an apprentice seaman, took heed of his narrow escape to eventually become editor of the *Chinook Observer*.

Susan 1/11/1952 Cannery tender, 52 tons. She became unmanageable and was abandoned west of the Columbia River. She eventually washed ashore on Peacock Spit about 500 yards west of the jetty.

Tillamook 2/1876 She and her crew of seven were lost on Clatsop Spit. NFI.

Tokuyo Maru 5/3/1921 Steamer. On fire 60 miles SW of Columbia. A total loss included the ship, her cargo of sodium nitrates en route to Japan and eight of her crew.

Tonquin 3/22/1811 Ship, American, 269 tons. She brought part of the Astor party on their expedition to settle the west coast. Eight men drowned trying to sound the bar; the following day, two more met with the same fate. Throughout history, Captain Jonathan Thorn has been unjustly chastised for supposedly causing the deaths of these seamen. See story, "E Inoa O Kanaloa" and the loss of the *Hazard* crewmen.

Unknown 2/1876 Sloop, built at Tillamook a few months earlier and probably named *Dreadnaught*. Under the guidance of her builder and with a crew of five (all *over eighty years* of age with the exception of one), she went on the Clatsop Spit for a total loss. Dead: Captain William Terwilliger, 80; Joseph Centen (builder), 83; Indian George (pilot), 85; Richard Hall, 83; William Bailey, 86; and James Forest, a mere 20.

U. S. Grant 12/19/1871 Propeller steamer, built at East Portland by Clinton Kelly in 1865, used to carry passengers and mail between Astoria and Ilwaco. 55 tons, 70' × 15' × 6'. While Skipper J. D. Gray and his crewman brother A. W. Gray were below decks, she broke from her moorings at Fort Canby and grounded on Sand Island. The men were saved, the ship wasn't.

Vancouver 5/8/1848 Bark, British, 400 tons and under charter to the Hudson Bay Co. En route London-Vancouver, Washington, Captain Mouatt turned his vessel over to pilot S. C. Reeves, the first of many pilots on the bar of the Columbia. Reeves, for whatever reasons, struck the sands around the middle of the river; some accused him of plotting to pillage the wreck. Although these charges were never proved, Reeves resigned his position as a pilot. The ship was a total loss, as were much of the vitally needed supplies she carried for the fort at Vancouver.

Vandalia 1/9/1853 Bark. Bound San Francisco-Columbia. She was spoken the previous day by the *Grecian* off the Columbia. The *Vandalia* was discovered bottom-up near McKenzies Head. People from Pacific City (Ilwaco) raced to the wreck scene where Holman, Meldrum, Scudder and Colonel Stewart of that town held off the Indians who were intent upon plundering not only the wreck, but the three bodies that washed up as well. The ship's dead captain, E. N. Beard, washed into a small defile now known as Beard's Hollow. Three other bodies were recovered. It is believed between 9 and 12 people were drowned in the wreck.

Vazlav Vorovsky 4/3/1941 Freighter, Russian, British-built at Sunderland, England in 1912. 2672 net tons, 365′ × 52′ × 27.8′, ex-*Meskinan Maskinonge*. En route for the USSR under Captain Simon Tocareff and in the hands of bar pilot George Conway. The vessel lost her rudder control and immediately went aground on the north side of the river, 300 yards west of jetty "A" and ½ mile from Cape "D" lighthouse. The captain made a valiant but futile attempt to save his ship and his honor by refusing to abandon. Finally, he was forced to leave due to his ship's rapid disintegration. The disheartened man found little solace upon returning to his homeland where, it is rumored, he lost his life by the orders of Josef Stalin and thus became the shipwreck's sole casualty.

Virginia Vessel was mentioned in the *Alta California* of March 16, 1880, which was most likely in error and actually meant to refer to the *Vandalia*. The supposed captain was named Bird and the paper reported 10 died on the Columbia bar.

Wallula 10/10/1912 This bar tug is a very famous one in the history of the Columbia bar, but whatever happened on this date apparently wasn't much, as NFI was given.

Washington 11/13/1911 Steam schooner, 539 tons, built at Seattle in 1906. When she ran aground, the newspapers felt so sure that the Columbia River bar sands would swallow the stricken vessel, they ran headlines "Forty Eight Doomed" and "Schooner Washington Driven Ashore," but much to everyone's surprise and relief, Captain Buck Bailey came along in his big tug *Tatoosh* and effected a dramatically successful rescue.

W. B. Scranton 5/5/1866 Bark, 810 tons of cargo supposedly carried in her holds. Somewhere in the neighborhood of $200,000, according to records, was lost when the ship, owned by Captain Paul Corno, went ashore on the Columbia bar. The only cargo saved were two threshing machines which washed ashore.

*Webfoot 11/21/1904 Variously rigged as a schooner and a barkentine, she sailed en route Coos Bay-San Francisco and became waterlogged off Tillamook Rock. She was dismasted and three of her crew drowned. The wreck was towed to Astoria. She was built at North Bend in 1869 by J. Kruse.

Whistler 1883 American bark ashore on Long Beach. NFI.

*Whitney Olson 12/16/1940 Steamer wrecked on Clatsop Spit. NFI.

William & Ann 3/11/1829 Supply vessel for Hudson Bay Fur Co. Under Captain Swan, she ran ashore on Clatsop Spit. None of her passengers or crew survived, supposedly murdered by the Indians (see story, "William & Ann"). Records suggest this was not true, for Dr. John McLoughlin sent a schooner from Vancouver to recover the various bits of flotsam salvaged by the Indians, but never did he demand the tribe to *produce the murderers*. This controversial action, long denounced in history, was further complicated by the rash act of shelling the Indian village and killing the chief and two others, all for the recovery of a lifeboat and some oars. Most certainly McLoughlin did not order that done; nor did the Indians kill any of the *William & Ann*'s survivors.

William H. Bessie 7/25/1886 Bark, built at Bath, Maine in 1873, 1027 tons, 179.9′ × 36′ × 36.2′, valued at $31,500. Under Captain Gibbs, she sailed en route from New York with a cargo of railroad iron. She came up on the Clatsop Spit and began to fill almost immediately. The wreck lies 1½ miles out from the Lighthouse bearing E by N. Gibbs used an old chart and was minus the services of a pilot. There is a buoy at the wreck site now, aptly named "Bessie Buoy." All hands were saved.

*William Nottingham 10/9/1911 Schooner, built at Ballard, Washington in 1902 and registered 1204 tons. The crew was picked up by the *David Evans*; the *Wallula* towed her in. At one time during her career (1908), she left New York with a cargo of coal and was 340 leaky days coming by way of the Cape of Good Hope. She put in at Melbourne for repairs, but the bone-tired crew under Captain Lowery continued to work the pumps for 120 days before reaching San Francisco.

Woodpecker 5/10/1861 Schooner, aka *Barkanteen*, sailed for Portland from Victoria. She was built in England for the Barclay Sound Mill Co. and stayed on as a coaster. Beating over the bar, she missed stays and grounded. 104 cattle and 200 to 300 tons of flour in 50-pound sacks were thrown overboard. Only one of the animals survived, a cow rescued by William Chance of Ilwaco. She lived a long life and was a good producer, except Chance claimed her milk always tasted of salt water. The waterlogged sacks of flour were recovered and, with their water-hardened shell knocked off, supplied Astorians with bread for several months.

29C8221 5/19/1944 Troller lost on Clatsop. Two dead.

29P859 10/13/1948 Troller lost west of Clatsop. Two dead.

It was rather windy when Mrs. W. Wahlgren, 80, of Astoria climbed down to the lifeboat from the Admiral Benson. *Her only comment, "If the men in the boat hadn't been so busy with other things, they would have seen more pink bloomers than they've seen in years. Our dresses were up around our necks most of the time."*
(Oregon Historical Society)

Sucked almost out of sight, the British Cairnsmore *was for years a swinging play ground for local youngsters.*
(Columbia River Maritime Museum)

Sucked in by the sands, the 1882 wreck of the Cairnsmore *lies just to the west and south of Coffenbury Lake on Clatsop Spit.*   *(Oregon Historical Society)*

Too close for comfort, the C.A. Klose *was salvaged from this one near the Coquille Light. She met her end off the mighty Columbia River two years later.*   *(Coos-Curry Museum)*

Frank W. Howe *near Seaview, Wash.* (Oregon Historical Society)

Determined photographer and his box camera about to get a surprise at the wreck of the Glenesslin.
(Tillamook Pioneer Museum)

Unusual view of the lovely Glenesslin.   *(Wayne Jensen, Jr. collection)*

How such a beautiful ship, under full sail, on a clear calm day, managed to run smack dab into such a big mountain has never been figured out. She became a total loss. Portions of the Glenesslin *can still be found in the rocks at the base of Neahkahnie Mountain.*

(*Wayne Jensen, Jr. collection*)

Some of the Glenesslin *was salvaged in the first weeks after the wreck but then the sea took over.*
(*Wayne Jensen, Jr. collection*)

Too late now, whatever there was to be salvaged, long ago has been removed.

(Wayne Jensen, Jr. collection)

The final scene, Glenesslin *three weeks later.*   *(Tillamook Pioneer Museum)*

Wreck of the Glenmorag, *December 19, 1896. Its final chapter ended in romance when her captain married a local girl. Maybe it was the moonlight glinting off the hull.* (Oregon Historical Society)

Sporting a popular symbol of the 1930s the 8800-ton swastika marked Iowa *attempted to cross the Columbia Bar in the teeth of a 75 mph gale. She had time to make only one faint distress call.*

(Oregon Historical Society)

Only the swirling sea and a pair of masts mark the spot where 34 died, 28 still entombed in the Iowa.
(Oregon Historical Society)

Little in the way of salvage and only six bodies of the Iowa's *crew were recovered. 28 others lie beneath the chill waters of the Columbia Bar.*
(Columbia River Maritime Museum)

The steamer Laurel *aground on Peacock Spit, June, 1929.*   *(Oregon Historical Society)*

Potrimpos *near Long Beach. Salvage efforts failed and she capsized. No one was injured but 17 years later, 18 were lost when the* Mimi *rolled in an identical mishap.*   *(Oregon Historical Society)*

144

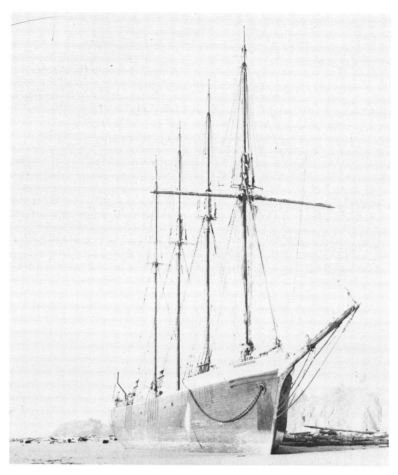

Beached but upright, the 981 ton schooner North Bend *walked herself across Peacock Spit without human aid and launched herself 13 months later in Bakers Bay, little worse for wear.*

(Oregon Historical Society)

She never made it to Alaska but, believe it or not, the hull was rebuilt into the tug Hercules *and worked the river for another 35 years until wrecked at Three Mile Rapids.*　　*(University of Oregon)*

The inset shows the beached Sea Thrush *in one piece; 25 days later she was broken in half.*
(Oregon Historical Society)

Huge seas soon reduced the 4793 gross ton Vazlav Vorovsky *to a heap of rusting, torn junk.*
(Columbia River Maritime Museum)

6

Cape Disappointment to Tongue Point

The mighty Columbia, River of the West, that long-sought mystery of yesteryear, serves the entire Northwest as the most important marine trade route in the United States, second only to the Mississippi.

Prior to Captain Robert Gray's 1792 discovery of this liquid highway, much had been written of its suspected existence; it even appeared in charts in a crude, yet somewhat believable, manner. Itinerant Indians reported the river in rather vague terms to Jesuit priests in 1725. Sieur de la Verendrye compiled a map in 1730 from a crude sketch by Chief Ochagach.

A large river appears on most Spanish maps drawn between 1750 and 1775; a Russian named Tobenkoff shows it on his chart of 1760. None of these men actually entered the Columbia's mouth to explore or traverse its mighty waterway.

Thomas Jeffrey's map of 1764 and Bruno Heceta's charts of 1775 mark the river's approximate location. Jonathan Carver, mistakenly credited with naming Oregon, records the Columbia in 1778.

To further confuse the issue, a variety of names has identified this magnificent river. The Spanish referred to it in 1603 as Rio d'Aguilar. Later, the name changed to Rio de los Etrechos, then, in succession, it was known as Bahia de la Asuncion, Thegaya River, Wauna, Estrada de la Ceta, Ensenada de Heceta, Senora de Asuncion, Ensenada de la Nuestra, San Roc, San Rogue, Deception Bay, Pe-Koo-on (Cayuse meaning Bigwater),

Auragan, Oragan, Origan, Oregan, Oregon (U.S. Naval maps 1825-1840) and, of course, the Columbia.

RACCOON

Captain Cook's accidental discovery of lucrative profits in Canton, China from the few sea otter skins he picked up as a curiosity during his exploration of the Pacific Northwest resulted in a stampede of enterprising companies and individuals to the virgin wilderness. The English-owned Hudson's Bay Company and North West Fur Company, John Jacob Astor's American Fur Company, explorer-traders Alexander Mackenzie, Simon Fraser, David Thompson and Jediah Smith scrambled in bitter rivalry over trade monopolies; the "fustest with the mostest" (meaning gunpowder) usually held all the aces.

Americans, in spite of their feeble navy and inexperienced government, held the upper hand in this new market. Unlike their English cousins, they enjoyed unrestricted free trade privileges throughout the world. England, with her limited charter policy, restricted the North West Company from infringing upon Hudson's Bay territory, forbade the company's trading in Canton where the East India Company held a charter and, vice-versa. America's free-wheeling policy soon became intolerable to British interests in this tiny corner of unclaimed territory.[1]

---

[1] British Columbia, Oregon and Washington

A loyal Britisher and employee of the English-owned North West Company, Alexander Henry Jr., wrote a succinct yet candid journal which evolved into a historical milestone. His day-by-day writings of a roving life during North American expansion abruptly began with his entry, "Autumn, 1799. While building At Riviere Terre Blanche, near the foot of Fort Dauphin mountain, my Russia sheeting tent was pitched in a low place on the lower branch of the little river, sheltered from the wind, among some tall elms and oaks. I was accustomed to sit up late, with a candle burning in my tent, for some time after the fires had been put out. . . ." And thus he continued, by burning candle, to write of events great and small for the next fifteen years, ending with his equally abrupt entry, ". . . the weather cleared up. . . ."

Alexander Henry's remarkable diary reveals not only the daily life of early voyageurs, but more importantly records the transition of Fort Astoria to Fort George and the subsequent comic-opera events from the earliest shipwreck of the area to a tragic misunderstanding the day before his untimely death. These events, though peripheral, set the future pace for a seemingly constant out-of-step little town called Astoria.

June of 1812 marked the beginning of a highly unpopular war between the United States and Great Britain. England, smarting over the loss of her American colonies, determined to return every Englishman, Americanized or not, to the fold and thus introduced a new factor into the intense rivalry between the English-owned North West Fur Company and the Pacific branch of John Jacob Astor's American Fur Company. Business competition turned to all-out war.

Nor'westers, anxious to upstage their countrymen, the Hudson's Bay Company, plotted a three-pronged attack upon Astor's struggling little colony at the mouth of the Columbia River. J. G. McTavish commanded the overland expedition while Duncan McDougall and his group of voyagers infiltrated Astor's ranks. The third assault team, aided by the British navy, planned to attack by sea; Donald McTavish and John McDonald of Garth, both proprietors of the North West Company, acted as spokesmen to the Lords Commissioners of the Admiralty. They reached an agreement whereby the *Phoebe*[2] was to accompany the *Isaac Todd*[3] in a raid upon Astor's newly established fort and sweep their isolated enemy from the land and sea.

The ships departed upon their highly secret mission from Portsmouth on March 25, 1813. Following a rough Atlantic crossing they arrived at Rio de Janeiro on June 10, only to discover that their secret mission was quite the reverse, due in large part to McDonald's and McTavish's vociferous indiscretions when they successfully induced a comely, young Portsmouth barmaid, Jane Barnes, to accompany them aboard the *Isaac Todd*.

They immediately formulated new plans, not only because of the "leak" in security, but their discovery that the *Todd* proved a very poor sailer with her heavy deck-cargo of guns, poor loading and an overload of top hamper. Fearful of the vessel's dangerous clumsiness, seven crewmen jumped ship at Rio. The captains of both ships ordered a close watch on the remaining seamen to thwart their taking unauthorized leave. In spite of the increased security, two officers made good their escape.

News of the activities of the 40-gun U.S. frigate *Essex*, Commander David Porter, added a further complication for the Nor'westers. The *Essex*'s powerful guns had challenged British whalers in the South Pacific and she had captured numerous prizes. Rear Admiral Manly Dixon ordered the sloops *Cherub*,[4] 18 guns, and the *Raccoon*, 26 guns, to join the mission. In order to assist the *Todd*'s sailing capabilities, her government stores were transferred to the warships and two new officers were assigned to control the malcontent crew. Secret orders, opened four

---

[2] A frigate of 36 guns commanded by Captain James Hillyar.

[3] A 20 gun vessel belonging to the company. She carried a Letter-of-Marque authorizing her to capture enemy merchant ships.

[4] After departing Rio, the *Cherub* and the *Phoebe* eventually left the convoy to strike out on their own and, after a fierce battle off Valparaiso, Chile, captured the *Essex*.

days out from Rio, read in part, ". . . totally annihilate any settlements which the Americans may have formed either on the Columbia River or on the neighboring coasts."

The four ships stopped long enough at Juan Fernandez to transfer various stores and John McDonald of Garth to the *Raccoon* under command of Captain William Black. En route to the Northwest, the bumbling *Isaac Todd*, unable to keep pace, quickly fell behind. The *Raccoon* was now on its own to capture and/or annihilate all American forces on the Columbia and surrounding coasts.

The British *Raccoon* raced northward, all the while engaging in gunnery practice in anticipation of a glorious victory and rich spoils from an enemy fur-trading fort. During the scaling of the guns, a tremendous black-powder explosion roared along the deck from gun to gun and powder horn to powder horn in the ranks of the marines, ripping abdomens, damaging guns, deck and rigging. Seven men died and numerous others suffered horribly from burns, among them was John McDonald of Garth who lost his famous flowing red beard.

The crippled *Raccoon* limped across the Columbia bar on November 30, 1813 and anchored behind Cape Disappointment at Baker's Bay. Unbeknown to the Britisher, Fort Astoria had quietly changed ownership through the not-so-aboveboard machinations of one of John Jacob Astor's partners, Mr. Duncan McDougall.[5] Mr. Alexander Henry Jr., now in charge of the newly-acquired English fort and its contingent of fur trappers, fired three shots from the four-pounders as a welcome to the unidentified ship anchored in Baker's Bay. Receiving no answering sally, he concluded the Columbia's waters had now been broached by an enemy vessel. He immediately ordered the fort's supplies and cache of furs taken up river and sent McDougall and Mr. J. C. Halsey (recent ex-employee of Astor's Pacific Fur Company) to spy out the identity of the heavily-armed alien warship.

Henry's tense vigil over the fort's safety ended at 9:30 that night when Halsey returned in a water-logged canoe oared by a rowdy group of drunken, singing seamen to report the suspect vessel was the English sloop-of-war HMS *Raccoon*. His partner, McDougall, three sheets in the wind, remained aboard His Majesty's Ship. Halsey's slurred report further revealed that the *Raccoon* had planned to land a force of eighty marines in three boats to take the fort by storm, but McDougall and Halsey successfully convinced the captain that Fort Astoria, through a peaceful purchase by British interests, was no longer enemy territory. Captain Black and crew, understandably disappointed by the furrier's private negotiations, drowned their blighted, grand-attack hopes in fine Tenerife wine. No longer required to fight for England's honor, the ship remained at anchor while captain and crew explored the cape.

Henry, in dire need of supplies, kept his men busy running back and forth to the *Raccoon* in the little two-masted *Dolly*, a thirty-ton general utility coaster Astor had built in New York, disassembled and shipped to Astoria aboard the *Tonquin*. Booming cannon from ship and shore announced each arrival and departure between HMS *Raccoon* and the fort. The constant reverberation of ignited gun powder impressed the local band of aborigines, but failed to intimidate the remaining loyal Americans.

John McDonald of Garth left the *Raccoon* on December 7th; five rounds from the four-pounder welcomed him as he stepped ashore at Fort Astoria.

Captain Black swallowed his pride over Fort Astoria's peaceful take-over and boarded the *Dolly* on December 12th to pay his respects to the tiny English settlement. Rather than fight the Columbia's current, he and his contingent of men anchored the schooner in

---

[5] McDougall, whose loyalties unquestionably lay with the Northwest Fur Co., sold out his partner and benefactor in one of the most controversial deals ever pulled in the Northwest. A million dollar's worth of furs and a fort (such as it was) sold for the paltry sum of $58,291.02, with Astor eventually receiving a little over $40,000. The balance was claimed as wages due by McDougall and the junior partners, even though Astor trustingly accepted them into his Pacific venture; out of all his partners, only one, Gabriel Franchere, refused to switch his allegiance to the Northwest Fur Co.

Young's Bay. The night turned black and stormy as the fort-dispatched canoe picked them up and on its return trip ran into Point George and holed, forcing a disgruntled Captain Black, A. Stuart and Mr. Clarke[6] to stumble the rest of the way over driftwood, slippery stones and water-filled potholes. They arrived at the fort with sore feet, skinned knees and bruised shins and retired at 2 a.m. in understandable ill-humor. Not all of Captain Black's pique dissipated when he arose the next morning and examined the fort which England had sent him to capture. He tersely proclaimed, "Is this the fort about which I have heard so much talking? Damn me, but I'd batter it down in two hours with a four-pounder!" The fort's seven guns, fired in his honor, punctuated the captain's churlish observation.

That afternoon the marines, seamen, northwesters and officers stood at attention in parade formation. The captain, in full uniform, saluted the raising of the Union Jack over the post, renamed the settlement Fort George in honor of King George III and claimed it and the country as English territory. The ceremonies were concluded with his breaking a bottle of Madeira wine upon the base of the flag staff. Three cheers echoed around the few loyal Americans as they languished about in relaxed nonchalant poses; three rounds of musketry finished off the ritual and almost finished off one of the marines whose musket discharged upon grounding and nearly blew off his head.

The celebrants drank to the health of His Majesty, fired eleven salvos from the four-pounder, listened to Mr. Franchere's speech to Casacas, son of Chief Concomly, and drank their final toast to a festive day.

The next morning the party canoed to the old headquarters of Lewis and Clark. Now that the territory lay in the safe hands of England, all admired the excellent choice of location for Fort Clatsop, both for security and hunting. Later in the day Fort George fired two guns; the *Raccoon* answered with three.

Captain Black presented Chief Concomly with a fine suit of clothes on December 15th, boarded the *Dolly* and returned to his ship under a five-gun salute. The *Raccoon* answered with one. Three more guns announced the *Dolly*'s anchoring to lee of the *Raccoon*. An evening gun proclaimed day's end and, in the morning, another ushered in the rising of the sun. At 9 p.m. a boat arrived from the sloop-of-war with Master Stevens, the purser, the doctor, a midshipman and six seamen . . . all very drunk after seven hours en route to the fort.

Henry entered in his journal on the 17th, "After breakfast the master and the midshipman went to sound the river. At 3 p.m. they returned; the tide was too far spent for them to return on board to-day. Famous fellows for grog they are!"

Gunfire greeted the light of day on the 18th. The cutter delivered numerous items for sailing, passengers and five hogs to the ship but, in spite of fine bar-crossing conditions and top gallants shook loose, the *Raccoon* remained at anchor.

The evening gun signaled the close of day.

Master Clark, the gunner, a midshipman and ten oarsmen manned the *Raccoon*'s pinnance on the 21st to fetch papers left at Fort George by the captain. Blinded by drink, the thirteen seamen made four stumbling attempts to land at Astoria before finally accomplishing the act.

Alexander Henry watched His Majesty's sloop-of-war *Raccoon* weave in a drunken stagger through the Columbia breakers on December 31st and disappear toward the south; in joyous relief he fired a seven-gun salute.

Captain Black, his mission completed, retired to his cabin to reflect upon the message he dispatched overland, "Country and fort I have taken possession of in name and for Brit-

---

[6] John Clarke, a man who switched sides in the fur business as often as he changed clothes, worked first for the N. W. Co., then Astor's P. F. Co., again for the N. W. Co. and finally switched to the H. B. Co. While with the P. F. Co., he committed an incredibly stupid blunder by hanging an Indian (the first necktie party on the N.W. coast) for a minor offense of theft of an already returned goblet. Expecting praise for his "brave" act, Clarke was cursed by all he met, for his contemporaries knew they would eventually pay with their lives, and so they did shortly thereafter when a war party massacred a group of whites.

ish Majesty; latter I have named Fort George and left in possession and charge of North West Company.

"Enemy's party quite broke up; they have no settlement whatever on this river or coast.

"Enemy's vessels said on coast and about islands; while provisions last, shall endeavour to destroy them . . ."

Henry, however, enjoyed a slightly different opinion as to the value of the *Raccoon's* appearance upon the scene, for he later wrote, "Indeed with the exception of Captain Black, the Officers of the Raccoon are not those vigilant, careful, active and fine enterprising fellows so much talked of and admired by all the World, as the main prop of Great Britain. The Navy, were all His Majesty's Naval Officers of the same stamp as those we saw here, England would not long have it in her power to boast of her Wooden Walls."

Indeed not, for upon crossing the bar the *Raccoon* bumped so heavily as to leave a large portion of her false keel driven deep into the bar's sands.[7] The damaged vessel, shipping seven feet of water in her hold, barely managed to reach the Spanish settlement at San Francisco. Black and his officers considered abandoning the ship and returning to England via Mexico, but word reached them that the wayward *Isaac Todd* languished at the sleepy little pueblo of Monterey, just a few miles south. The *Todd*, her passengers and crew were rudely prodded into immediate action by an order from one of His Majesty's Naval Officers to render all possible assistance to the stricken *Raccoon*.

They careened her on Angel Island and by January 19th she was fully functional to proceed to the Sandwich Islands in search of American prey.

As a shipwreck, the *Raccoon* played a minor historical role, but as a warship she engendered enormous problems on the northwest coast and the Columbia River in particular. Were McDougall's actions sly, cunning, devious or just plain stupid? The Americans of Astor's company considered him craven for his sell-out to the English. Others thought of

him as merely the most unfit man in the world for Astor to have chosen to head an expedition or command men. J. C. McTavish, of the opposing company, proved equally as disastrous by aiding and abetting a known enemy of his country when he bought all of Pacific Fur's assets more than a year after England declared war upon America. Captain Black's declaration, ". . . Country and fort *I have taken possession of* in name of country and for British Majesty . . ." further complicated the legality of Great Britain's claim to *country*. What were its boundaries, from what shore to what shore?

No, Captain Black was not happy with the actions of the Northwesters, nor were they with him. Obviously Black hoped to influence the Admiralty Court with the claim of capture; the value of such held promise of a handsome reward for him and his ship's company.

In spite of these complications, Hillyar enjoyed a double success in that the entire Northwest coast belonged to England and the *Essex*, America's first and only navy warship in the Pacific, had been captured.

The North West Fur Company, smug in its assumption that Fort George remained secured for Britain, increased fortification of the area and, with clandestine aplomb, began shipping furs to China. Little were they aware of Astoria's uncanny habit of snatching defeat from the jaws of victory.

The signing of the Treaty of Ghent on December 14, 1814 officially ended the hostilities between England and America. Article One directed all properties taken from one side by the other be returned. Simple enough, yet in this case, Earl Bathhurst, Secretary for War and the Colonies, preferred to ignore through oversight any reference to Fort George. This left the Nor'westers up the Columbia without a paddle regarding their claim of legal purchase of Fort George and the continuing necessity of England's protection.

The United States Secretary of State, James Monroe, informed the British that Captain Black's claim cancelled the sale; the United States intended to move into the fort without

---

[7] Recovered in 1973 by David W. McGrath of Gearhart and donated to the Columbia River Maritime Museum, Astoria, Oregon.

delay. Monroe then addressed a missive to Anthony St. John Baker, British Minister-in-Residence, requesting him to direct the British Naval Commander in the Pacific to return the fort. Baker replied he believed the abandoned fort to be in ruins and suggested Monroe contact Sir Manley Dixon, Commander in Chief of warships in the Pacific. The British Minister wrote in secret to Dixon to inform him of a possible American takeover and admonished him that England would not recognize any American possession on the west coast. Manley, having learned of the sale and considering it legal, took no action . . . just as well, for not one single United States ship was available to back up all this big talk coming from Washington.

In 1817 the United States sloop-of-war *Ontario* and her twenty guns sailed on a not-so-secret mission to take possession of Astoria. When the Northwest Company learned of the mission, they appealed to Sir Charles Bagot, British Chargé d'Affairs in Washington. Sir Bagot immediately stormed into John Quincy Adams' office, slammed his fist upon the Secretary of State's desk and demanded to know if the accusations were valid.

"Uh-huh," admitted the highly embarrassed Adams, "but only to assert American sovereignty, not to destroy the trade of your Northwest Company."

Bagot, hot-headed and dissatisfied, ordered the Governor General of Canada to send an overland party to warn the Nor'westers of an impending takeover. Even the Commander-in-Chief of the West African coast learned of the *Ontario*'s mission and quickly reported the Americans contained a restless and hostile spirit with plans to capture islands and territories in the Pacific.

England wished no further involvement in a war against her former colony, but hotheaded quarreling in Washington fast approached a point of no return. Foreign Secretary Viscount Castlereagh threw cooling waters upon the political bonfire by presenting to the cabinet that although he had personal knowledge of the North Wester's purchase of Astoria, Captain Black's claim that he captured the fort meant England must honor the Treaty of Ghent's Article One and return *status quo ante bellum* all conquest-of-war territories. Thus, ". . . to cultivate the arts of peace" he relinquished the post to America with the proviso that his action would neither recognize the American claim nor invalidate the rights of the English. The British flag was lowered and the American raised in a symbolic gesture for, although the Americans now owned the fort, the Nor'westers occupied it rent free. The utterly confused fur traders of Astoria prepared to defend the post, but none were sure against whom . . . things just never seemed to go smoothly for very long in Astoria. Total confusion reigned supreme when the Nor'westers sold out to the Hudson's Bay Company in 1825; who owned what now?

In any event, the mere presence of the *Ontario* in the Columbia River convinced the British to call for a sit-down meeting to resolve the peace-threatened territory. Thus, the Anglo-American Convention of 1818 found the English proposing an international boundary along the Columbia River which placed Astoria on the American side. The United States rejected the proposal in its entirety.

War-weary England now sought to come to the best terms possible by suggesting a joint occupancy of the Oregon Territory. The adoption of this haphazard arrangement thoroughly confused the already confused trappers, ship's captains, settlers, diplomats of the newly-emerging South American nations and the seasoned veterans who represented France, Spain, Russia, Hawaii and Mexico.

For the next twenty-eight years American and British ships snapped and growled at one another as they passed in and out of the mighty Columbia. American vessels suffered the worst of these crossings, not through hostilities, but by losing two out of three warships[8] on the bar as against the English only damaging four out of five of their ships.[9]

---

[8] *Peacock* and *Shark*
[9] *Sulpher, Starling, Modeste* and *Raccoon*

Westward immigration over the Oregon Trail brought a multitude of loyal Americans to the territory who, in 1843, formalized their own provisional government. Western states rallied to the Oregonians' cause and demanded United States' recognition of the Oregon Territory. The Democratic convention of 1844 forced an answer with the campaign slogan of "Fifty-four Forty or Fight" that resulted in the compromise Treaty of 1846[10] which fixed the present-day boundary of the United States and Canada.

THE TROUBLE WITH JANE

A big man with a shock of flaming red hair, a beard to match and a booming voice was John McDonald of Garth; his band of tough Canadian voyageurs nicknamed him *Bras Croche* in honor of his crippled left arm, but all men jumped to his bellowing orders in the knowledge that John McDonald not only loved a good fight, but insured his victory with the constant companionship of a brace of pistols.

McDonald and his canny Scot partners in the Northwest Fur Company formulated ambitious plans for monopolizing trade in America's Northwest Territories; their first order of business and the key maneuver to the entire scheme depended upon capturing John Jacob Astor's tiny American settlement in Astoria. With great foresight, the group had already infiltrated Astor's ranks with their own men to await the attack of a land expedition which was in the process of crossing the continent, but their ace-in-the-hole was John McDonald and Donald McTavish who, with an assist of the English Government and the War of 1812, would mount an assault from the sea.

While the Northwest Fur Company confidently congratulated itself for such foolproof plans, the fickle finger of Fate steered John McDonald's path across that of . . . Jane Barnes. Bras Croche was, of course, not the first to fall under the young, sensuous, English belle's spell, nor would he be the last.

The company's ship, *Isaac Todd*, lay tied up at a Portsmouth quay where partners McDonald and McTavish appeared on a daily basis to oversee the proper lading and manning of the vessel. Following their day's attention to the thousand and one details involved in an expedition of this magnitude, *Bras Croche* and Donald McTavish retired to the local waterfront pub for a bit of relaxation, as was their custom. During one of their sojourns, Fate exposed the two men to the charms of Miss Jane, a Portsmouth barmaid. Indeed, her good nature, beauty and generosity of physical attributes captured the hearts of these two-fisted, hard-hitting, penny-pinching Scotsmen. John McDonald quickly staked his claim by offering the young damsel an unbelievable all-expense-paid cruise to the far corners of the world.

Portsmouth, 15 March 1813

A gentleman who spoke to you today has given me your address. If you first intend to make a sea voyage, I promise you good treatment and the necessary articles of dress and on your return I shall pay or cause to be paid you at the rate A/C of Twenty-five or Thirty pounds per annum for which this note will be sufficient security. I intend going to sea, though not a sea going man, the first change of wind but I should wish you to embark tomorrow noon, I lodge at the Crown Inn and will expect your answer with your decision by 9 o'clock tomorrow morning. If you inquire or address your note to James Edmond he will deliver it.

J McDonald

Miss Jane Barnes

Jane, never one to pass up such an enticing offer, leaped at the opportunity to improve her station with a contract that guaranteed her a generous salary, good treatment *and* a new wardrobe.[11]

Portsmouth, 16 March 1813

---

[10] See the wreck of the *Shark*.

[11] In later writings Miss Jane was described as ". . . flaxen haired, blue-eyed daughter of Albion" and as one who ". . . always managed to display her figure to the best advantage." Jane was a daughter-of-the-times, for England suffered from a very real man shortage, as verified in the 1801 census. The Napoleonic Wars devastated the male population to such a degree that economists of the period advocated polygamy; Protestant bibliolaters and Deists delighted in pointing out polygamy's acceptance in Mosaic law.

I am extremely sorry that I was not at my lodging last evening and this morning when you came. I wish absolutely you go on board tomorrow morning and should wish to see you. If you will go, it will be necessary to get some things for you, make me a memorandum of them and I shall take care to procure them and let me know at what time you will go on board. My servant is the Bearer. Your determination is expected. I shall be at home till 9 o'clock,

I am yours truely
J. McDonald

The red-haired giant, consumed with infatuation for the comely barmaid, threw all caution to the winds. Never in his life had *Bras Croche* signed "I am yours truely," much less authorized a *carte blanche* for feminine frills. Quite obviously Jane reaped the benefit of her ardent benefactor's addled emotions and it now fell to the love-sick entrepreneur to justify to the Northwest Fur Company and his frugal partners the necessity of enlisting Jane Barnes' services in an expedition that intended to wage war upon an American fort.

John must have labored mightily throughout the night to resolve the problem. The private expedition, sponsored by the gentlemen of the Company and in cooperation with the English government, comprised a working group of company clerks, rough-hewn woodsmen, Canadian voyageurs, a twenty-gun licensed privateer *Isaac Todd*, the twenty-six gun warship *Raccoon* and some three hundred sailors and marines prepared to wage war half-way around the world, but their plan lacked a very essential element necessary to its success...they needed a *seamstress*. *Bras Croche* took quill in hand and wrote,

Articles of Agreement entered upon before witness, between Mr. John McDonald for himself and on behalf of the Northwest Company on this one part and Miss Jane Barnes of Portsmouth on the other part. The said Jane Barnes consents to do any needle work that may be necessary on the passage and elsewhere when nothing happens to prevent such.

The said John McDonald for himself and the Northwest Company binds and obliges himself to pay or cause to be paid the sum of Thirty pounds sterling yearly to the foresaid Jane Barnes and every necessary articles of clothing suitable for the Country, in consideration of the above services or one half at the expiration of every six months should she require the same. He further binds himself that her treatment shall be as good as circumstances will admit and to procure her a passage home when suitable to both parties.

Portsmouth 17 March 1813
J McDonald

In presence of Mr. McTavish
J. C. McTavish
witness

With that problem nicely tucked away, the *Isaac Todd* set her sails to catch the wind that would take her crew of argonauts and a smugly-satisfied couple on a long journey to the faraway Oregon coast.

The *Isaac Todd* and the *Raccoon* hove-to a month later near Rio; John McDonald of Garth transferred to the *Raccoon* with the rationalization he wished to lessen the chance of capture of both company officers during a possible American encounter. More likely, *Bras Croche*, after a month's exposure to that sensuous, ever-eager, bouncing Jane, opted to take refuge aboard a warship. Portly, wealthy, retired-merchant Donald McTavish eagerly offered his services for the remainder of the voyage as protectorate of the company seamstress's care and virtue.

The two ships rounded the Horn, then became separated. The *Raccoon* raced ahead in anticipation of a richer haul by their single-handed capture of the American fort. The *Todd*, ambling along with many stops here and there, seemed perfectly content to let her sister ship speed onward to capture all the glory.[12]

John McDonald nervously paced the confines of Fort George, ex-Fort Astor, in agi-

---

[12] Captain Black and his swashbucklers "captured" Fort Astoria following its peaceful sale to his own countrymen. Upon leaving the Columbia, the *Raccoon* struck heavily upon the bar, sustaining severe damage. The warship limped south to San Francisco where Captain Black discovered, to his great delight, that the *Isaac Todd* lay at anchor just a few miles south enjoying the generous hospitality of the Alcalde of Monterey. Black promptly commandeered the services of Captain Smith and his crew in the repair of the 26-gun *Raccoon*. During the next three months of refurbishing the warship, the Alcalde of San Francisco played the gallant host to McTavish and his fascinating Miss Barnes.

tated anticipation of the arrival of the *Isaac Todd* and Jane Barnes; he fortuitously discovered pressing business demanded his presence in the interior and promptly departed with a band of trappers.

Alexander Henry, Master of Fort George, anxiously awaited the arrival of essential men and equipment aboard the supply ship *Isaac Todd*, which had departed Portsmouth thirteen months prior. Dire thoughts of the vessel's capture or shipwreck haunted Henry day and night, for the entire territorial future of the Northwest Fur Company hinged upon the *Todd* safely reaching her destination. But then, the harried Master of Fort George knew not that the craft sailed with beautiful Jane Barnes aboard.

The armed black and yellow ship dropped anchor across from Fort George in Baker's Bay on the 17th of April, 1814. Henry, fearing her an American raider, ordered the fort's valuable equipment and furs packed and shipped upriver for safe keeping. For most of that day, the alien ship lay quietly at anchor and made no effort to identify herself. When the local natives reported a *woman with yellow hair* aboard the unknown vessel, Henry suspected some type of Chinook chicanery afoot due to unrest amongst the tribe following the English take-over of the fort.

Henry ordered Duncan McDougall to reconnoiter; hours later he returned to say he feared getting too close to the ship and thus had nothing to report. Toward evening, the strange vessel fired three guns. Fort George replied with three, but still remained ignorant of the ship's identity. At 10:00 o'clock the next morning, the fort hoisted her flag; a half-hour later the vessel's foretop showed a white flag and two guns thundered from her ports. Henry exhaled a long sigh of relief at the recognition signal of the long-awaited *Isaac Todd*.

Post Master Alexander Henry received a note at noon via the Indian Ramsey that stated McDougall was aboard the *Todd* and

invited Henry to do the same. Henry ordered the Union Jack hoisted and five guns fired; the *Isaac Todd* answered with eleven and sent the junior company representative J. C. McTavish ashore.

The following morning Henry dressed in his Sunday best and ordered his men to paddle him to the supply ship. As he approached, he noted the absence of crew and officers on deck and, upon boarding, found himself quite alone with critical resentments against this highly improper greeting for a company official.[13] After several intolerable minutes of silent isolation on deck, Henry detected a slight, silken-like rustling behind him and turned to gaze directly into two limpid pools of azure loveliness. . .the eyes of Jane Barnes!

Donald McTavish assisted Jane across the companionway's sill and introduced her to Henry who, from that moment on, became a man captured in a delicious whirlwind of exquisite feminine grace and charm. The besmitten fur man's few remaining days of life were to be filled as they had never been before. She became the fort's rays of sunshine scattering away the ominous grey clouds of the great northwest. Henry turned her visits from the ship into festive holidays, much to everyone's dismay and much to Henry's delight. McTavish immediately ordered the name of the fort's ship changed from *Dolly*[14] to *Jane*.

Jane, with her effervescent personality, captivated nearly every male heart on the entire west coast. "The Indians daily thronged in numbers to our fort," wrote Alexander Ross in describing her effect upon the aboriginal population. Jane, ever appreciative of such avid attention, deemed it only proper to repay in kind. Each day she donned a different gown, carefully chosen from her extensive wardrobe purchased by McDonald. Mindful of her effect upon the fluttering hearts pounding in every male chest, she alternated her attire between a high collar demurely covering her ivory throat to a plunging neckline's revelation of her abundant

---

[13] It remains a mystery as to whether McTavish deliberately planned the moment to impress Henry or if the lack of protocol was due to malcontent amongst the vessel's passengers.

[14] A 30-ton schooner Astor named after his daughter and ordered shipped to Astoria in the hold of the ill-fated *Tonquin*.

"upper rigging" or "top hamper," as gawking, open-mouthed seamen were quick to note. White man and redskin alike raced for the water's edge when the *Todd's* boat carried Jane to Astoria's shore; eager male heads bobbed to gain an unobstructed view as she graciously repeated her ritual of deftly lifting her skirts above a well-turned ankle to bless the damp sands with her dainty foot. Speculation ran wild as to which style she would coif her spectacular golden hair...would the silken tresses be tucked under a wide-brimmed, flowered bonnet or would her golden fleece flow free in the gentle breezes?

Her overall effect upon the fort became, in a few days, as devastating as it was during her thirteen-month tenure aboard the *Todd* where the crew became unable to concentrate on their duties while the company's junior clerks set pens aside and followed her like a pack of frolicking puppies. Rivalry for the touch of her smile or a glance from her cornflower-blue eyes set man against his brother. Voyageurs Duchene and Le Prine quarreled with the *Todd's* sailors when they came ashore, then set after the mariners in a canoe and severely boxed their ears. Cassacas, the pointy-headed son of Chief Comcomly, declared he would never again bring his whale-oil anointed body within the confines of the fort in a peeved fit over Jane's rejection of his offer of marriage which included a generous dowry of slaves, furs, smoked/dried salmon and a life of ease among his four other wives. Quite secretly, though, he and his piscatorially aromatic buddies plotted to kidnap Jane during one of her traditional evening strolls along Astoria's beach. Chief Comcomly, still angry over McDougall's sale of the fort to the English and miffed at his son's rejection by an Englishwoman, demanded the full balance of payment for his daughter's hand in marriage to McDougall, whom he now called his cowardly son-in-law. The argument between company clerks Pillet and Montour ended in a duel; Astorian Pillet received a hole in his coat collar while the Northwester Montour sustained one in his trouser leg. Ross Cox noted, "...the tailor speedily healed their wounds."

In spite of Henry's dire warnings, the *Isaac*

Todd's crew "...begin to feel the effects of their communications with the Chinook ladies; several of them are laid up already." McTavish and his fur company partner, William Henry, quarreled violently. Joseph Cartier, clerk, called off his impending marriage upon discovering the extent of his bride-to-be's infectious disease.

McDougall ineptly demonstrated the operation of a blunderbuss to Chief Comcomly by blowing away a goodly portion of the Chief's robe; the Chief raced from the fort in a panic, but not before a sentry, alerted by the shot, aimed, fired at and missed the fleeing Indian Chief. Confusion erupted when the sentry yelled an alarm and the redskin yelled bloody murder. Everyone, Chinooks included, assumed one side had attacked the other and formed their respective battle lines. Eventually cooler heads prevailed, but it seemed that affairs never went smoothly in Astoria.

Events progressed badly aboard the *Isaac Todd*, too. Captain Smith threatened to place his First and Third Mates in irons. The First Officer refused to dine at the Officer's Mess and ate only with the crew, who barely tolerated him and hated the captain. All aboard were only too eager to kill McTavish who, realizing his peril and totally exhausted, struck a bargain with Alexander Henry in which the latter gratefully agreed to become Miss Jane's cavalier. (Henry notes in his journal that Jane was the first white woman he had seen in fifteen years and implies that he was already madly in love with her.) McTavish, immensely relieved to be rid of Jane, immediately began shopping around to replace her with a less rambunctious, Indian, female companion.

Jane cheerfully agreed to the new arrangement and within a few days her well-being was turned over to the keeping of the besmitten fur trader. Henry prepared for the moving day by throwing drunk voyageurs and Indians out of the fort. He tidied up the area and re-stored the smelly furs at the far end of the compound. Jane completed her arrangements by requesting her things taken from the ship and deposited in Henry's bedroom.

Jane settled in with Henry and seemed perfectly content, even though Henry's journal entry suggests some dared challenge Henry's claim upon Jane,

"Mr. McTavish and myself came to an understanding for future arrangements. We differ on some points, but my course is clear to me, though it may not be so to others. However, this, as far as it may concern a certain person, shall not affect our general interests; but, in every other respect, I am determined to support what I conceive my rights, even at the displeasure of every person on the Columbia."

Henry's blissful state negated his usual worry over the Chiehilth war party on the other side of the river; their differences lay with the Chinooks, not the Northwest people. For the moment, all seemed to go well even though the vitriolic Captain Smith refused moving the *Isaac Todd* to the Astoria side of the river. Relaying messages and stores across the Columbia's expanse in the *Jane* and the ship's long boat remained an inconvenience, but was tolerable. Mr. Bethune, Mr. William Henry and Joseph Cartier, their primeval instincts aroused by Jane's presence, chose redskinned Chinook ladies for their brides. Even old man McTavish felt a surge of generosity toward the happy threesome and offered his clean bed and room for the night's nuptials while he slept on a table in the Indian hall. He awoke after a long night of interruptions with people talking, snoring, dogs barking, cats yowling, a too-hot fire, a hard bed and no pillow; he informed the entire fort that from now on, all would be awakened to the ear-rending beat of a drum.

Every day the jolly boat, under the direction of the captain's nephew, or the *Jane*, manned by the Northwest men, carried passengers and supplies back and forth between the fort and the distant ship. The men man-handled a half-dozen long six-pounders across the river for the tiny fort's defense. Peas and powder, vegetable seeds, medicines, McTavish's luggage, porter and wine and casks of beef moved across the long distance of the flowing Columbia...a distance that would soon prove fatal.

The ecstatic Alexander Henry was oblivious to all but his beguiling Jane. He wrote a candid journal entry in which he gently chided McTavish for draping his flat-headed Indian wife in fine black broadcloth which cost twenty-three shillings sterling a yard. Yet Henry, in a burst of generosity foreign to the Scot blood coursing through his veins, gathered his men together, offered them a dram apiece, gave them one hundred pounds of flour, fifty pounds of grease, eighty pounds of beef, forty pounds of tallow, five pounds of molasses, eight gallons of rum and a half box of biscuits. Mr. Bethune delivered a suitable speech on behalf of Henry. Indeed, Jane's presence seems to have loosened her ardent admirer's purse-strings.

On the 21st of May, Henry packed away some beeswax and whale tusks traded from the Clatsops, mused the possible chastising of Blacksmith Roussel for his drunken hurrahing of the Americans and loud damning of the British, backed off from a quarrel between McTavish and his nephew William Henry and conferred with Coniah, the Clatsop chief, who showed him a rather interesting paper signed by two American explorers, Lewis and Clark. The document listed the names of their entire party, with the dates of arrival and departure. Perhaps Henry felt irritation with Captain Smith for his continuing refusal to anchor the *Todd* nearer Fort George. Possibly, Henry wished to forget anything American, for he then threw the offending paper into the fire. Later that evening, Henry sat at his candle-lit desk and, as was his habit, entered the day's observations in his journal, "...finished examining the goods, arranging the garret, etc. Now all is in readiness and order, and the bedstead put up. The longboat came over under sail with a letter from Captain Smith, saying he could not bring the ship, there being only 13 to 18 feet of water at half-tide for 2½ miles, and the ship drawing 13 feet aft and 12½ feet forward. There had been a misunderstanding on board the ship with Mr. McKay, regarding the bread given out to the crew, and an appeal made to the captain. The weather cleared up..."

Cut short in mid-sentence, Alexander Henry would write nevermore. Perhaps Jane, with an impatient toss of her golden curls, interrupted the preoccupied writer's quill-scratching by brushing her ruby lips against his ear and playfully pulling a smiling, indulgent Henry into the comforts of their downy bed.

The following stormy evening Alexander Henry, Donald McTavish and six men boarded the *Todd*'s longboat for another arduous river crossing; at mid-stream Henry's short, but extremely happy, romantic interlude came to a choking end in the mighty Columbia's treacherous, silt-laden waters. Carpenter John Little, sole survivor, wrote of the tragic event, "We pushed from the wharf at 5:00 o'clock in the afternoon, the wind blowing a gale at the time, and the tide setting in. The boat was ballasted with stone, we were eight on board and a heavy surf, about two miles out in the stream she filled and sank like a stone. A terrible shriek closed the scene! The top of the mast was still above the surface of the water, I got hold of it, but the first or second swell swept me away. In a moment nothing was to be either heard or seen but the rolling waves and whistling winds. Jack, a young sailor lad, and I took to swimming and with great exertions reached a dry sand bank in the channel, about three-quarters of a mile ahead of us; but the tide flowing at the time and forced by the gale soon set us afloat again. Here we shook hands, bade each other farewell, and took to swimming again. At the distance of a mile we reached another flat sandbank, but the tide got there nearly as soon as ourselves and we were again soon afloat. Jack was much exhausted, I was little better, and the wet and cold had so benumbed us that we scarcely had any feeling or strength. We now shook hands again, anxiously looking for relief towards the fort. Here poor Jack began to cry like a child and refused for some time to let go my hand. I told him to take courage and pointing to a stump ahead of us said to him, 'if we get there we shall be safe.' Then bidding each other *adieu* we once more took to swimming in hopes of reaching the stump I had pointed to, being better than half a mile off. I reached and grasped it with almost my last breath; but poor Jack although within ten yards of it could not do so, it was too much for him and I could render him no more assistance. Here he struggled and sank, and I saw him no more. I had been grasping the stump with the grasp of despair for more than half an hour when fortunately a little before dark an Indian canoe, passing along shore, discovered my situation and saved my life.[15] The water had reached my middle, and I was insensible."

Both Jane and McTavish's Indian woman suffered a double bereavement, Jane with her loss of McTavish and Henry and Mrs. McTavish, if she may be called that, with the loss of Donald and her prior paramour, B. Clapp of Astor's Pacific Fur Company.[16]

Following the death of Alexander Henry, history reveals only a few recorded clues as to the whereabouts of the enigmatic Miss Barnes. Most certainly she did not leave Astoria aboard the *Isaac Todd*, whose domineering Captain Smith caused the deaths of seven men, including his own nephew. More likely she secured passage aboard the 185 ton schooner *Columbia*, a ten-gun vessel owned by Inglis-Ellis and McTavish-Fraser Companies. Peter Corney, Chief Officer under Captain Anthony Robson, left some tantalizing hints when he wrote of the ship's entry into the Columbia after an abortive mutiny off Cape Orford. The *Columbia* anchored off Fort George in July of 1814 to put the mutineers ashore in irons and pick up supplies; they were informed of the deaths of Governor McTavish, Chief Factor Henry and of the sole survivor John Little. Although several bodies were recovered, the rescuers anticipated Indian trouble and hastily buried McTavish's body where they found it on Cape Disappointment.

---

[15] The American carpenter came closer to death than he realized. The Indians, at first thinking he was a seal, had taken a bead on him with their rifles.

[16] Benjamine Clapp arrived on the ship *Beaver* from New York on May 9, 1812. He took up with the Indian woman until October when he left with the Franchere expedition. He then entered the U.S. naval service as a midshipman and by coincidence was captured in the *Essex* incident by the *Phoebe* and *Cherub*.

The *Columbia* left Fort George and, after nearly swamping while crossing the Columbia bar, made her first stop at Queen Charlotte's Island. She proceeded on to the Prince of Wales Archipelago, Norfolk Sound, to the Russian Fort of Governor Baranoff where, after taking on a load of furs, everyone managed to become roundly drunk. It would seem Jane were aboard.

In September the ship sailed for the Columbia and, on arrival, found the *Isaac Todd* had departed a few days prior. Corney disinterred Donald McTavish's corpse for proper burial on the Astoria side of the river. Captain Robson read the solemn service as McTavish was laid to rest behind the northeast bastion of Fort George. Presumably Jane, dressed in mourning (if her extensive wardrobe allowed) dutifully attended the ceremony and daintily dabbed at a wayward tear.

Captain Robson topped off his cargo of furs and set sail for Monterey, California. Jane, no doubt, enjoyed visiting old acquaintances while the captain restocked his ship's provisions. At the next port-of-call, Robson engaged in trade with the tiny Russian settle-

Headstone of Donald McTavish, early victim of the Columbia, is located at 15th and Exchange and is considered by some to be Astoria's oldest and most precious relic. Unfortunately it is fast falling prey to vandals and the elements.

(Marshall photo)

ment at Bodega Bay, then broached the Pacific's wide expanse for Hawaii and ultimately Macao. The Chief Officer's journal entry offers an enticing clue suggesting Jane's continued presence aboard the *Columbia*, "On the 9th (March, 1815) we ran into the Macao roads, and came to in 3 fathoms water, bottom of soft mud. Captain Robson went on shore in a Chinese boat; in the evening he returned, and the next day took the young woman on shore, the Chinese not allowing her to proceed to Canton in the schooner. On the 17th of March, we got a pilot on board, weighed, and stood up the river; we were three days in our passsage up to Wampoa." How disappointing for Jane to be denied the pleasure of sightseeing and shopping in the Orient's most fascinating trade center, but not even Jane's feminine wiles could sway the well-established Chinese law that denied entry to firearms and Western women.

Captain Robson, up to now, seemed well content with his ship-captain career as he sailed the Northwest coast of America, Spanish California, the beautiful Sandwich Islands and Oriental waters. Without explanation, he requested he be relieved of his command that he might return to merry old England. With company permission, he relinquished his post to Captain John Jennings and immediately booked passage for himself and Jane aboard the England-bound brig *Javas Road*.

Upon their arrival in London, it appears Jane and her captain conspired to enhance their fortune by presenting a bill for transportation of Jane Barnes to Robson's company representatives. Inglis, Ellis and Company forwarded the couple's demands to Alexander McKenzie at the Northwest Fur Company's home office in Montreal.

Regarding Jane Barnes   May 18, 1816

Captain Robson having lately arrived from China, it became necessary to settle his accounts & in attempting to do this, we have met with great difficulty from the circumstance of a very heavy charge made by him for the expenses & passage of a female home from China, which forms a very large feature in them . . . It had been agreed to pay his own passage, when to our surprise a charge of £717:12/—was made, the greatest part of which sum was required for the expenses of the female we have alluded to. At the same time Capt. Robson acknowledges to have received on this account from Mr. Bethune in China £2000—at 6/ each being advanced expressly on account of his expenses home, in deduction of this claim, & we must leave the settlement of this extra demand, under these circumstances, amounting to £117:12/—to your decision. To enable you to give this, with some information on the equitable rights of all parties, we inclose by Capt. Robson's desire, copies of letters this woman has in her possession & an agreement entered into by the representative of the N. W. Compy., who went out in the *Isaac Todd*. He is now we understand in Montreal, & will enable you, by such further information as he can give you on the subject, to decide, as we are sure you will, upon the just merits of the claim. The poor woman further desires to know where and to whom she is to apply for the annuity promised her. We entreat your early answer, & instructions on these points.

The great John McDonald of Garth lamely justified his original involvement with Jane Barnes in his reply to the company,

N. B. The above mentioned female was taken on board of the *Isaac Todd* as seeing Trip and for Dept of Co. She was at her A/C found apt for it—When she expressed a wish to return to England, Mr. James McTavish gave about Thirty pounds as a compensation and she embarked with Captain Robertson *Javas Road*—with a promise from Captain Robertson to take her to England free from any charges. This my opinion anyway, to get the balance between the Thirty Pounds given her and the time she was absent at the rate of Twenty-five pounds per annum, this was the true necessity of the above agreement.

John McDonald

Did Jane Barnes become Mrs. Anthony Robson (Robertson) or did she, following her sojourn around the world, return to being a barmaid at her old place of employment in Portsmouth? Not likely...not Jane!

SYLVIA *de* GRASSE

California's early gold rush days brought fortune to many and ruin to many more. It is often said that the man who pursued the more mundane qualities of business invariably fared better than the gold-crazed adventurer. In some cases, yes, but there exists an exception when just plain cussed bad luck or excessive greed turns a fortune into a disaster.

William Gray, an enterprising east coast businessman, determined the value of any ship, regardless of its condition or age, capable of sailing to the west coast was literally worth its weight in gold. When news reached him of lumber fetching a high price of $500 per thousand feet in bawdy San Francisco, as compared to a mere $10 per thousand along the Columbia River, William Gray saw dollar signs when he scanned the heavily wooded northwest forests.

Gray purchased the *Sylvia de Grasse* from eastern merchants. The old girl, who had passed her fiftieth birthday, was well into an age where all concerned would have been better off to retire her, but she arrived on the Pacific coast ready to serve her new master.

The hungry-handed new owner loaded his ship to the gunnels and prepared to race southward with the precious lumber cargo.

Haste precluded sound judgement... through some *gaffe Sylvia de Grasse* became pinioned just off shore from the pioneer town of Astoria on an outcropping of rock. The grossly overloaded ship could not be worked from her stranded position; a shift in cargo served to cram her even tighter into her rocky crypt.

The envisioned loss of his ship and $50,000 worth of cargo forced the now almost defunct businessman to resort to desperate measures. He offered $10,000 in cash to a nearby vessel to take the entire shipment to its destination, but his generous bid was refused since that ship already sailed under charter.

The frantic William Gray finally managed to secure the services of three smaller vessels and crews at premium rates. Working day and night, the hired crews managed to offload the crippled parent ship and stow the lumber cargo aboard the sibling schooners. This, combined with the delay always met when exiting the Columbia River, plus the long passage to the Golden Gate, used up what little profit may have been gained...

lumber was now being shipped in from the redwood coast with prices dropped to a more reasonable level. All monies gained from the lumber sale went into the pockets of the masters of the three vessels and William Gray was left bankrupt. He suffered the total loss of the *Sylvia de Grasse* and, at last report, was still in debt . . . all due to excessive overloading and greed.

Before her demise, the old sailer *Sylvia de Grasse* left her mark on American shores . . . she brought the first news of the storming of the Bastille in 1789, which marked the beginning of the French Revolution.

IT JUST NEVER HAPPENED . . .

The great fishing-fleet disaster of May 4, 1880, that is. On that date a great storm arose out of the Pacific, struck the mouth of the Columbia River and, as the story goes, wiped out the entire fishing fleets of Astoria, Ilwaco, Chinook and all the other small communities in the area with a resultant loss of over two hundred fishermen.

Over the past one hundred years, this disaster has grown into epic proportions with the telling; today's historians readily accept this exaggerated tale as an actual event. Should a disaster of such monumental significance devastate any local area, surely a commemorative remembrance, column or plaque would attest to the recorded loss of over two hundred brave souls. None exist. Why? . . . because it just never happened.

True, a record-breaking storm vented its rage upon the northern Oregon coast on May 4, 1880 and, in its savage fury, claimed the lives of fishermen, but the death toll never climbed anywhere near the two hundred mark.

The day began just like any other day at the mouth of the Columbia. Perhaps the fish-

ermen were a bit more anxious than usual for it was their first day back after being idled by a strike and each anticipated a prize catch in compensation for lost time. They all noted the falling barometer, but with the tide running right the entire fleet of gillnetters, both private and those under contract to the canneries,[17] eagerly set out for a day of prime salmon fishing.

W. L. Harris, captain of a small steamer, stood by, but with a good steady wind blowing from the southwest, knew none of the small crafts required a tow. He watched the fleet as each vessel bounced out upon the slack tide with unfolded spritsails waving gaily to swooping gulls.

The prolific salmon crowded every inch of the Columbia River in their ancestral migration to the spawning grounds. The prized Pisces were herded by horses, herded by wiers[18] and herded by gill nets.[19] Each enterprising fisherman staked out a suitable portion of the river to net the wave of delectable pink flesh. The reapers of nature's harvest knew the annual millions of salmon breaching the mouth of the Columbia would never diminish in size or amount. A few die-hards preached moderation and conservation, but their admonitions fell upon deaf ears for there were fish to be caught and today was the day . . . barometer and harbingers of Judgement Day be damned.

Gillnetting areas ran sporadically from points inland toward the sea. On the Washington side, one ran roughly west from Jim Crow Point to about a mile past Pillar Rock; on the Oregon side, it followed the channel downstream from Woody Island to the lower tip of Long Island . . . another one encompassed the Cordell Channel. The largest gillnet area extended almost bank-to-bank between Gray's Bay and Point Adams.

Each 24′ boat carried a two-man crew, 13′ oars, a net up to 450′ long by 12′ deep, a sprit or tri sail and the all-important primus stove

---

[17] Over 34 in the Astoria-Ilwaco area.

[18] A large, funnel-shaped net.

[19] The top edge of the nets with floats attached remained on the surface. Lead weights pulled the lower edge toward the bottom. The mesh net's design allowed the fish's head to penetrate. If the salmon tried to back out, its gills became ensnared.

for coffee. During the week of salmon harvesting, a goodly number of fishermen slept on their boats nightly, using their downed sail as a tent. They hauled their daily catch to the parent cannery or the appropriate scow-boat for unloading. The Columbia River gillnetters were experts in handling their double-ended, V-bottom beamy boats under a small spread of sail, just enough to keep the boat moving as they played out their net. In lieu of wind, they put their oars to use.

Gillnetters usually avoided the seine-hauls (horse nets), the wiers and pound nets.[20] They captured their pink-fleshed harvest from deeper waters, but on May 4, 1880, the vagaries of wind, river and sea combined forces far beyond the control of mortal man.

Wind velocity increased and now a strong ebb current, the result of unseasonal 80° temperature in the snow country causing a massive run-off, carried the sturdy little boats over the bar through the breakers while, at the same time, other crafts, driven by an increasing southwest wind, found themselves stranded upon Chinook Point.

Old-timers marveled at the length of the ebb tide and the current's strength as it slammed into the Pacific at the mouth of the river. The breakers grew in intensity. Captain Harris, at anchor near Cape Disappointment, shouted to his crew, "Get up steam! Those fishermen out there need help and need it fast!"

Captain Turner of the steamer *Quickstep* observed two capsized boats...he managed to retrieve one body from the maelstrom. The in-coming *Edith* reported two overturned boats, most likely the same two observed by Turner.

The flood of incoming reports became garbled. The tide slacked, then turned. Its powerful pull dragged boats back through the surf...the surge drove four hapless vessels across Bakers Bay and swamped them beneath Scarboro Hill. Peter J. Blagan, an independent fisherman, was lost.

The barkentine, *Webfoot*, hanging on her anchor, observed desperate crewmen clinging to the slippery keels of two boats, bottoms up, tossed like toys in the boiling surf on the Washington side of the river.

An unusual amount of debris swept seaward along the river's channel. Drift logs, miniature mossy islands ripped from the river bank far upstream, cut timber and even portions of buildings caused false reports from citizens mistaking each piece of flotsam for another wrecked boat. One hysterical individual raced from Tongue Point to Astoria exclaiming that Big Mike's boat had just rescued four men from two capsized crafts and no sooner had he landed them into his boat than a log rammed them and all six drowned. No one in town knew Big Mike, but all felt the loss just the same.

Captain Harris, with a good head of steam fired up on the *Rip Van Winkle*, beat it around Sand Island and rescued the men clutching the bottom of their boats, then charged back through the raging fury of white foam. He threw lines to three helpless vessels and took them in tow.

Darkness descended and each minute brought more cold, more wind. Nick Manual lost his scow on Barney's Point with George Ethan, his crewman, drowned. Many of the gillnetters beat a hasty retreat to the refuge of the Chinook River; others spent a cold, miserable, wet night far out to sea. A sullen, grey dawn broke and, one by one, red-eyed salmon fishermen emerged from under their tarp-like sails. Soaked to the skin and bitterly cold, they surveyed the carnage.

Anglo-American Cannery lost one smashed boat which drifted out to sea. Captain W. P. Whitcomb of the mail packet *General Canby* reported four empty boats in Bakers Bay. *Joseph Hume* picked up one empty yellow and white boat...crewman George Adams drowned. A body washed ashore at Wallicut.

Hume Cannery found two more of their boats, #28 and #32, but lost Hans Hansen and

---

[20] A gillnet set between tide marks and supported by stakes. If the staked net acts as a leader into a circular enclosure, the net is then a pound net.

Henry Heinson. Megler reported boats #11 and #8 missing with their crewmen Dick Jones, Charles Harvey, a fisherman known only as Gus, and one other, name unknown.

One of Kinney's men, Peter Hakanson, became entangled in his net and was pulled under. Chris Christiansen, another of Hume's men, found himself and his boat #26 tangled in a net which a huge breaker picked up and threw across his boat's bow. Helpless, the craft smashed into boat #34, whose crewman was thrown into the sea. A high wave struck both ships and carried the net off, thus allowing James Hainson to crawl aboard. Christiansen's boat went under, but not before Christiansen made a grab for the painter of the other boat. Climbing and pulling with a herculean effort, he managed to get into #34 boat. Hainson, too frightened to assist, watched as another breaker caught Cristiansen, wrenched him free of the craft and threw him shoreward into the seething surf. He crawled through the crashing foam, then collapsed. Upon recovering his strength, he staggered toward Megler... along the way, he found boat #34 stranded upon the beach with its occupant, Hainson, dead.

The storm slacked for a few hours, just long enough for the battered fishermen to head for their home bases. Then, as if waiting to entice them into a vulnerable position, the vicious elements struck again.

The courageous, smoking, snorting steamer *Rip Van Winkle* chugged right out there in the middle of it again, racing back and forth plucking distressed fishermen from the sea's boiling cauldron and towing boats to safety. The *Webfoot* hoisted her distress signal as she fought for her life just off Sand Island. On the island itself, fisherman Kyle and a dozen others crawled upon its sandy strand from their capsized boats. The castaways remained isolated upon the island for two days before they were discovered and rescued.

Captain Harris, his little *Rip Van Winkle* loaded to the gun'ls, sighted another upside-down craft headed out the bar with two men riding its keel. High seas prevented the *Rip* from coming about or launching a rescue boat... the distance to the distressed men was too great for a life-line. The keel-riders, as if intending to spend the night at the opera instead of heading for the terrible crashing breakers of the Columbia bar and certain death, jauntily tipped their hats, waved and resumed their vise-like grip on the keel. They disappeared forever.

At long last the storm blew itself out. the Big Mike story proved a hoax. One fisherman staggered in four days later after the storm had cast him ashore near Oysterville. The final tally, including both sides of the river, counted 13 known dead out of a possible 18.

The grateful survivors passed a hat for Captain Harris and the plucky old *Rip*. Mr. Gus Forsberg placed an ad in the local paper to thank all those brave seamen who helped him when the storm smashed his *Warren* #9 into matchwood.

Yes, the great storm of May 4, 1880 took its toll of men and boats. It was a mighty storm and through the years has grown with the telling. Unfortunately, lives and equipment went to the bottom, but fortunately, the true tally was 18 (not 200) brave fishermen lost.

SHIP DISASTERS
Columbia Bar, inside Tongue Point

Abe Lincoln 1870 Schooner, built in 1861. For many years, the wreck was visible at low tide near a shipyard in Astoria.

*Allegiance 10/18/1879 Ship was wrecked on Old Sand Island. NFI.

Arrow #2 1/21/1949 Tug. An explosion and fire in Astoria took the life of Captain John Pemberton.

*Aurelia 8/1911 Steamer, screw, 162 feet, built at Prosper in 1902 by G. Ross. Ship stranded on Sand Island.

---

* Refloated or partially salvaged.

Columbia 10/22/1892 Barge, cargo of 550 tons of wheat in tow of *Ocklahama*. She swung too wide and struck a dock. Captain Marshall Short and John Peterson went inside to inspect for damage; she careened and sank, taking both men with her to the bottom. Two dead.

Desdemona 1/1/1857 Bark, three masts, 104′ × 25′ × 12.7′, owned by George Abernathy, built at Jonesboro, Maine in 1847. Carrying a general cargo under Captain Francis Williams, she attempted to cross the bar with a fair wind on a flood tide without a pilot. The lower buoy was adrift and when the captain stood for Astoria, the ship struck. The bark lay easy for a full 24 hours while a tug attempted to tow her off the Chinook Sands, as they were then known; try as she might, the *Joe Lane* met with failure. Eventually the ship bilged and the crew was forced to salvage her cargo via barges. By January 5, they were down to the last load when the unfortunate ship capsized, drowning seaman George Cartland. Moses Rogers offered $215 for whatever was left and it was accepted. He stripped much of her gear; the hull remained visible, stark and alone, on sentry duty for many years to warn others to beware her fate...thus the name *Desdemona Sands*.

Dilharree 1880 Wrecked on Sand Island, auctioned off on 3/18/1880.

Elfin 5/11/1937 Diesel freighter, 196 tons, 84′ in length. A total loss due to an engine room fire. Captain Alfred Babbidge and 10 of her crew were rescued by *C G Cape* "D" lifeboat.

Erria 12/20/1951 Motor, cargo, passenger vessel of the Danish East-Asiatic Line. In the road at Astoria with a fire caused by an electrical short. Within 10 minutes after the first fire alarm, Captain M. Agge ordered the 450′ ship cleared of her passengers. Out of the 83 crew and 31 passengers, eight passengers in cabins and three crewmen in #5 hold died.

Firefly 2/24/1854 Steam propeller tug, built at San Francisco in 1853 by Captain Hawkes. Vessel, towing logs from Youngs River to Welsh's sawmill, rounded the point and became caught in the ebb. She drifted with the tide until grounded near Point Stevens. High and dry, the *Firefly* lay there until an incoming tide swung the log raft, reversed its direction and, as it passed the tug at a furious rate, the tow line tightened and pulled the vessel in a scandalous, untug-like fashion across the flat and into deeper water off Tansey Point. Unable or unwilling to cast off the tow, Captain Hawkes, Purser Van Dyke Wiesenthal, Engineer Swasey and an Indian lad went to the bottom. Passenger Welsh climbed aboard the offending log raft, somehow managed to free it, and rode with the tide to Astoria where astounded citizens took him off before forming a rescue party. They raced to the scene of the disaster and found the tug in three fathoms of water, her smoke stack above

the rising tide with her fortunate fireman sitting placidly on top.

Gleaner 1/28/1888 Small river steamer under Captain Peter Jordan. She went to the bottom in a gale off Tongue Point. Passengers Jacob Rennell, Mary Holt and Hilda Wilmer drowned; 30 others escaped.

Great Republic 4/17/1879 Sidewheel steamer, 4750 tons, built for Pacific Mail S. S. Co. at Greenport, Long Island in 1866. She struck at high tide on Sand Island, which proved the undoing of the huge, bark-rigged ship that measured 378′ × 47′ × 30′ with four boilers and a vertical beam engine. Although expensive to run, her passengers soon discovered she provided better food and accommodations than what they could afford on shore, thus many citizens chose to share her sea-faring life. Pilot Thomas Doig was at a loss to explain to the angry 550 cabin passengers, 346 steerage travelers and ship's Captain James Carroll just exactly how he managed to run the *Great Republic* on the bar. Some of her 1059 tons of freight was saved and all the passengers were brought safely ashore. When her bow broke off in heavy weather, seven of the 27 horses on board managed to escape their stalls and swim to shore. The last boat off, containing 14 of the crew, broke a steering oar and overturned; 11 drowned. The ship was insured for $50,000, her freight for $75,000. George Flavel, J. H. D. Gray, W. S. Kinney and W. S. Gibson bought the wreck for $1,280, her cargo for $2,500. Doig's license was suspended for a year. Unable to face the town's citizens, he departed for South America where he became an Admiral of the Puerto Rican Navy which consisted of one ship, the *Yrazu*, ex-*Pelican*.

Henriette 12/27/1901 Bark, French, 735 tons. As she settled, her anchor punched a hole in her hull. She stayed on the bottom with her decks awash for several months. Daniel Kern refloated her and sold the vessel to MacKenzie Bros. of Vancouver, British Columbia. She was converted into a barge, but in 1905 her beautiful lines inspired her owners to convert and refit her as a twin-screw steamer for the Skagway, Alaska run. She was purchased by Captain Woodside of San Francisco in 1910 and rigged as a four-masted schooner. She was then sent to the Fiji Islands as a trader and wrecked there in 1922.

Isabella aka *Isabel* 5/2/1830 Brig, British, Hudson Bay supply ship under Captain Ryan. Taken from the log of the *Owhyhee*, "May 2 1830, arrived the English Brig Isabella, At 4 pm she struck on the point of the north breakers came to anchor and abandoned her..." Seemingly her small bump on Sand Island, in which the ship could have been worked off, turned into a major disaster when the crew panicked at the sight of naked savages gawking and laughing at the strange manner in which the ship arrived. Assuming the Indians were hostile, the crew fled in the ship's boat upriver to the safety of Fort Vancouver. Dr.

John McLoughlin was quite upset at such actions, for he felt the Indians would have helped rather than harrassed the seamen. A portion of her cargo was saved, but the ship broke up in a few days. The Hudson Bay committee was philosophical about the entire affair, for the ship and cargo were very well insured.

Leonese or possibly *Leonasa* 12/27/1860 No listing in official records of a ship by this name. Rumor has it that she was a bark under Captain Edward Howard that wrecked on the Desdemona Sands, nine dead.

*L'Etoile du Matin aka *The Morning Star* 7/11/1849 Ship, French. Sailed under Captain F. Menes with a cargo belonging to the V. Marzion & Co. of Le Havre. Her captain attempted to enter the river without the aid of a pilot and hung up his ship on Sand Island. Sweeping surf strained every timber in the vessel and hour after hour of working the pumps had little effect upon the water rising in her bowels. Alexander Lattie, an early Astorian and pilot, spotted the floundering *L'Etoile* and, with the aid of some Indians, rowed to the stricken ship to render assistance to the tired crew. A rudder was constructed to replace the one unshipped during her hard bumping. Enough repairs were effected that the ship, after being freed by a combination of high tide, wave action and just plain hard work, proceeded to Portland. Captain Menes, loyal to his employers and far and away above the duties of a seaman, opened a business he named "The French Store" and began selling the cargo of general merchandise to the locals. Business was so good that even John McLoughlin, the father of Oregon, bought a share of the partnership. The *L'Etoile du Matin* was declared a total constructive loss and sold as such.

Magnet 4/2/1883 Steam propeller, recently sold to two men, names unknown. She left Astoria with provisions for the Coleman, Tucker and Sales families who lived upstream on the Youngs River. Loaded with flour, bacon, lumber and miscellaneous household items, the little ship became somewhat of a mystery when she failed to make her scheduled delivery. Several weeks later, Tucker arrived in town to inquire at Wilson and Fisher's mercantile store as to the whereabouts of the supply ship. A search turned up a sack of flour, 2 brooms and some planks that had floated downstream to the tidal flats. All were identified as a portion of the *Magnet*'s cargo. More days passed; the puzzle deepened when word was received that the two new owners of the ship were seen heading on foot for Tillamook. Eventually hunters found the *Magnet*, stove in and sunk by a log snag. The finders secured the aid of the tug *General Custer*, towed the waterlogged ship in and claimed her for salvage. The owners' identity and whereabouts remain a mystery.

*Massachusetts 5/9/1849 U.S. troop transport of 750 tons, ship-rigged with a steam plant/Ericsson propeller. She was the heaviest vessel to cross over the bar up to that time. She carried 161 men of the First Artillery Battalion under the command of Brevet-Major John S. Hathaway. Recognized as the first official U.S. troops in Oregon, they traveled to take over Fort Vancouver from the Hudson Bay Co., as per the newly-enacted treaty between the United States and England. Alexander Lattie was pilot aboard the *Massachusetts* when she went on the Tongue Point sand spit and was worked off with no damage.

Mindora 1/12/1853 Bark. En route San Francisco-Portland under Captain George Staples. Conflicting reports cite her accident at Shoalwater Bay and at the middle sands. In any event, the *Mindora* lay off the Columbia for 28 days before able to enter, then she was forced to anchor when the wind died. The ebb tide drug her to the middle sands; she struck about 8:00 p.m. Mountainous sea built up around her; the crew abandoned ship. By morning light, the vessel had worked loose and drifted off. She eventually came ashore between Gray's Harbor and Shoalwater.

*Natoma 1/4/1938 Port of Astoria dredge sank while moored near Pier #1. Raised.

*Orbit 3/1850 Bark wrecked at southeast area of Old Sand Island.

Parker #1 1934 85-ton barge stranded near Astoria.

*Refuge 2/16/1948 Steamer, U.S. Navy hospital ship, ex-*President Garfield*, ex-*Kenmore* (AP62). While under tow to the scrap yard at Swan Island, she sprang a leak off Willapa and grounded heavily at the Columbia entrance. It seemed as if the old 1921 Dollar liner might end her days on the bar, but she was finally freed and scrapped as planned.

Rochelle 10/21/1914 Steam schooner, aka *Minnie E. Kelton*, 582 tons, 176' × 35', gained a reputation as a "voodoo" ship under Captain Kildahl. Pilot Captain H. A. Mathews in command when she wrecked on Clatsop Spit and Desdemona Sands for a total loss. See story, "The Ordeal of The Minnie E. Kelton."

Sylvia de Grasse 11/1849 Her wreckage still hung on the reef in 1895, according to the newspapers. Buoy #4 marks the location just north of the foot of 46th Street, Upper Astoria. See story, "*Sylvia de Grasse*."

*Telephone 11/20/1887 Sternwheel steamer, 386 tons, a favorite and fast ship on the Columbia. She was underway with Captain U. B. Scott, 140 passengers and crew. The alarm of "Fire!" prompted Captain U. B. Scott to head his vessel toward shore just below Tongue Point near Upper Astoria. The engineer opened the throttle all the way while the remaining crew fought the stubborn blaze. The mud-slick flats received the racing steamer; she struck at 20 mph and continued across the flats sustaining little damage to her hull. Astoria put out the alarm and the pumper put out the fire. One man burned to death. The hull was saved and rebuilt. She

eventually ended her days at San Francisco.
Thielbek 8/24/1913 Bark of German registry, ex-*Prince Robert*. Collided head-on with Norwegian *Thode Fagelund*. She sustained above-waterline damage.
Windward 12/23/1871 Ship went aground on Sand Island. NFI.

The United States Coast Guard and fire boats pour tons of water into the furiously burning Erria. *Eleven died.* (Clifford Hargand collection)

Great Republic *grounded on Sand Island, Columbia River. She was a total wreck and for years after the soldiers of Fort Canby used her boilers for target practice.* (Oregon Historical Society)

736 ton Henriette *on the bottom of the Columbia River.*   *(Columbia River Maritime Museum)*

A wet deck, Henriette's *reward for settling on her own anchor. City of Astoria in background. Salvage barge and unknown sternwheeler tied just to right.*   *(Columbia River Maritime Museum)*

167

7

Missing at Sea and Unknowns

KNOWN ONLY TO GOD

On April 25, 1865, three bodies rolled in the surf beneath the towering majesty of Tillamook Head. John Hobson and others brought the cadavers ashore and buried them above the tideline. Today, their graves, which can be seen along the beach road, are tenderly cared for by the local citizens. Who were these lost souls? No one knows or ever will know, nor can the ship from which they came be identified.

George Stevens, on January 18, 1880, discovered a ship's binnacle in good condition, with the exception of a broken glass, in front of his home on the beach at Newport. Later that same year, the wreckage of a sloop with the body of a man lashed to the wheel came ashore south of Seaside.

In 1906 the sea released a name-board, broken at both ends, with only the letters AR-RACO visible. Records indicated a sole ship with that combination of letters, the *Barracouta*, but she lay safely in port with name-board firmly attached. Cannon Beach citizens never solved this mystery.

Frank Stafford of Clatsop Beach discovered one blustery day a battered lifeboat lying on the beach opposite his farm. It was turned upside down, as though used for a shelter. Someone had knifed off splinters from the gunnels and attempted a fire in the sand, but no one was around nor did anyone ever show up to offer an explanation.

Indians, in 1848, found near the mouth of the Columbia a cask of brandy on the beach; further along they came across a bundle of shingles, some salmon in barrels and a jib-boom with a portion of sail attached. The ship's identity is unknown, though her fate can be surmised with grim finality.

Who knows the identity of the mysterious ship of Flores Lake or the vessel that washed ashore in Siletz Bay and wedged herself against the rocky islet where Drift Creek enters? She carried ample supplies, but no crew or identity. Her ribs were still visible in 1943.

These mysteries and that of the Beeswax ship forever add to the enigma of Oregon's rugged coast and her romantic past.

THE CHINA SHIP

"...we helped build the most western lighthouse on the American continent, knowing how many vessels have been lost at Yaquina. Jack Bamber told me that early in '49 a silk laden ship from China was wrecked there — the cargo drifted ashore and the coast Indians wore shawls that would have sold for $100 apiece in San Francisco. One Irishman got *1,800 yards* of silk...made a fortune. Yessir that Cape Foulweather light saved many a ship."

George Luther Boone of Yaquina, an early Oregonian and the grandson of that great frontiersman Daniel Boone, made the above statement.

SUNSHINE

The spanking new 326-ton three-master,

built at a cost of almost $100 per ton, slid into the water from the yard of Holden & Co. at Marshfield (now Coos Bay) in September, 1875. The gala launching of the stately vessel belied the grim fate that awaited her in a little more than a month's time.

Partial owner and full-time captain George Bennett charted his lumber-laden ship southward on her maiden voyage. The saucy lass arrived in San Francisco on the 8th of October; her proud crew of ten lost no time in off-loading and then taking on a general cargo of machinery plus other items bound for the northwest. The *Sunshine's* remarkable run south, combined with the clean-looking lines of a new ship, enticed northbound travelers aboard for her return voyage. On November 3rd First Mate John Thompson and Watch Officer Joseph Johnson ordered unfurling of fore-and-afts and the graceful ship cleared the Golden Gate. She sailed northward into. . .what?

Fifteen days later the *Sunshine*, bottom up, drifted in the swells off the mouth of the Columbia River. Her exposed planking, too new to collect the wispy green tendrils of seaweed enjoyed by older ships, left no shred of doubt as to the identity of the vessel. On November 22nd, her battered remains washed ashore on the North Beach peninsula of the Washington coast.

Records reveal that in addition to cargo valued at $18,000, the *Sunshine* carried $10,000 in gold coin being shipped by San Franciscans who purchased an interest in the vessel.

Rumors, as usual, popped up with the regularity so common to a mystery when gold is involved. The passengers who so eagerly boarded the ship at the Bay City were accused by many of being pirates who murdered the crew, abandoned the drifting ship, and rowed to shore in the ship's boat. Some audacious experts claimed they never did trust those shifty-eyed First Officers who obviously ran the *Sunshine* aground, then buried the gold 15 miles north of Coos Bay. The basis for this preposterous supposition and location has never been determined.

Only the twenty-five souls aboard the *Sun-shine* during the time disaster struck know the true story. Unfortunately no trace of them has ever been found.

A MYSTERY AT FLORAS LAKE

George Sypher, resident of a town now known as Langlois, strolled the beach of Floras Lake marveling at God's handiwork in blending an orange and pink spectrum of delicate sunrise hues. A stubbed toe rudely interrupted his reverie on this fine spring morning of 1886. . .George kicked the sand from the offending object and discovered a very large link of anchor chain lay embedded at his feet. Bending over, he brushed away the fine white sand and soon uncovered another eroded link. After careful inspection he detected a long chain of links lying in a direct line to the shore and into the breaking surf.

George Sypher reported his curious find to a number of friends in town. Together, they returned to the beach with shovels and a surf boat. Though they labored mightily for hours to retrieve the chain from the surf, it refused to yield. The tired and disheartened salvors returned to town, related their experience to the locals, and concluded the chain must be attached to a very large anchor lying far out to sea.

One old timer recalled as follows, "Yup, 'twas back in about 1867. We were all called down to the beach just north and west of Cape Blanco. Someone spotted a large barque in trouble out there. The sea was up and we couldn't get out, so we set up a watch. Well, she began to drift aimlessly, but we never saw any movement on deck nor any men in the rigging. She floated around for two days, all the while working in toward shore on a northerly set. Finally she struck and began breaking up. Her cathead snapped, the hook dropped. She worked toward shore and the chain just kept paying out with nothing to control it. Well, we never did learn her name or whatever happened to her crew 'cause we never saw a soul in all that time. . .even when she broke up. She was loaded with lumber and let me tell you, what come drifting ashore sure built a slew of houses around here."

THE GALLEON OF NEHALEM

The Spanish galleon *Magallanes* wearily threaded her way through Cavite Bay and the massed assortment of Malay *proas*, Chinese junks and native *vicorros* on a hot, muggy day in June, 1815. Few of the bored, rag-tag Filipino onlookers realized or cared that the *Magallanes'* anchoring marked the end of an era.

For two hundred and fifty years the life-blood of the Philippines and her Spanish masters depended upon the success of these annual Pacific crossings from this Castillian capital of the Philippine Islands to the arid shores of western Mexico, the new Spain of the American continent. Year-after-year these huge, heavily laden, lumbering ships transported the island's Oriental trade goods eastward across the Pacific; their west-bound return route brought home the profits . . . profits so huge and so necessary that the loss of a single vessel could plunge the colony into bankruptcy, break the Spanish trade capabilities with Oriental merchants and send the wealthiest of noblemen into starvation.

To all intents and purposes in this year of 1815, the line was economically dead. Rising dissension among Spain's colonies would soon lead to a dozen revolutions that would divert the mother country's attention to more pressing matters. Further, this once exclusively private trading enterprise faced problems compounded by hundreds of foreign merchants and exploration ships crossing and recrossing with impunity the secret routes of the vast sea once known to the world as the "Spanish Lake."

Exactly what was a Manila galleon? Why did Spain keep its very existence a secret from the rest of the world for so long? When the rest of the world finally discovered the galleon's covert journeys, why did Spain's many enemies and freebooters alike scheme to capture such a ship?

It all began over four hundred years ago when Miguel Lopez de Legaspi, " . . . a worthy and reliable man" was ordered by his king, Phillip II to, " . . . bring some spice, in order to make essay of that traffic." from the area of the western oceans for the purpose of breaking the Portuguese monopoly of the trade. Spices, highly prized in Europe for their taste-enhancing and food-preserving qualities, were literally worth their weight in gold. King Phillip further admonished Legaspi against any " . . . delay in trading or bartering and to return immediately" to New Spain, for " . . . the principal reason for this expedition is to ascertain the return route."

Legaspi deemed it essential he remain in the Philippines to establish the foundations of Spanish rule. He ordered his grandson, Felipe de Salcedo, and a veteran seaman turned monk, Andtes de Urdaneta, to command the expedition aboard the tiny *San Pablo*. Heading north from the Philippines, as per Legaspi's instructions, the little *San Pablo* poked her apple-nosed bow hesitantly toward the east to lighten the dark shadows that covered this vast expanse of open ocean. With each succeeding mile the galleon seemed to grow bolder and finally, with the loss of only sixteen men, reached Acapulco[1] in the incredibly short time of three and one-half months. Her second trip over the same route proved last; she wrecked in the Ladrones, the first of thirty-three wrecks the line was to suffer over the next two hundred and fifty years.

Within a few short years, the now-established route proved a boon to the Spanish economy. By avoiding the peril-filled route of the Indian Ocean, Cape of Good Hope and the long Atlantic run to Spain, the Crown moved vast amounts of merchandise in comparative secrecy to New Spain, traded with merchants of Mexico, Chile and Peru while off-loading at Acapulco, then transported the remaining cargoes overland to Vera Cruz for convoy shipment across the Caribbean and the Atlantic to mother Spain.

Philippine merchants, eager for cargo space aboard these Pacific ships, submitted

---

[1] Legaspi began his expedition with five ships and 400 men at Navidad, Mexico in November, 1564. Following the group's arrival in the Philippines, the 40-ton *patache San Lucas* (under Lope Martin) deserted to make her way across the Pacific in the west-east direction. This remarkable, but illegal, feat cost her and her crew a forfeiture of official recognition. All credit went to the *San Pablo*.

their bids to a special committee responsible for measuring each vessel's carrying capacity, dividing the space into square or rectangle *fardos* of eighteen to twenty square feet and then quartering the *fardos* into *piezas* with a decreed maximum limit of four thousand per ship. The galleons rarely followed the limitation; an average ship sailed with seven to eight thousand assigned *piezas* and, on one or two occasions, left port with as many as twelve thousand *piezas*.

A *boleta*, a ticket for a *fardos* or *piezas*, was sometimes allotted by committee, sometimes by chance or sometimes by whim or coercion. Widows usually received some space for shipment of goods, but merchants, politicians and the church managed to monopolize all remaining space. If the lucky holder of a *boleta* had nothing of value to ship, he could immediately convert it by sale into a considerable amount of cash. Soldiers and sailors almost always managed to augment their income by securing space, sometimes secretly, but usually openly on deck where bale upon bale continually interfered with the safe operation of the ship.

St. John's Day (June 24th) or St. Peter's Day (June 29th) were the preferred but seldom followed days set for departure from Manila. Captain and crew hoped to catch the monsoon winds and, with sails billowing, speed south down the island-dotted channel of the Embocadero, cross to the open ocean, then double back to capture the tradewinds for the long voyage across the Pacific. Their timing was essential for if a vessel were delayed only a few weeks in her departure, she became victim to terrible hurricanes that swept the ocean clean. One ferocious Pacific sea plucked thirty-six seamen from their ship's deck in 1676, but was considered only a minor mishap in comparison to the dangers of the Embocadero, known as the Strait of San Bernadino. The deadly Strait claimed a vessel for every step of the way.[2] Lubang, Calantas and Isla Verde marked the beginning of the passage leading to that fearful place between Capul and Luzon where, according to Carmelli (verified years later by the U.S.-Philippine Coast Pilot) numerous swirls and eddies rampaged in the channel; the water seemingly boils up from beneath, causing the center of the eddy to rise at least a foot higher than its edge.

Because of the high death rate during the arduous voyage, each galleon carried three or four pilots. Not only did disease create the necessity of continually training new men, but other factors caused complications as happened to the unfortunate pilot on duty when the *Nuestra Senora de la Vida*, only ninety miles from her starting point, struck a reef and stayed on Isla Verde; angry passengers felt the pilot's wage of seven hundred pesos per trip was entirely too much for such incompetence and promptly hanged the unfortunate man.

The *ruttier*, or route directions, of expert pilot Cabera Bueno describes the hazards, "... E eight leagues, with the dangerous Maranjos to starboard and the shoal of Calantas to port; NE by N and then ENE seven leagues around Cupal; NE with the Sorsogon coast to port and San Bernadino to starboard and N E by E seven leagues to the Embocadero, with San Bernadino now to port and the island of Biri to starboard. At this point," he candidly continues, "the rapid currents require skillful pilot work."

The Spanish king's decreed course now set northerly roughly between Japan and the Marianas, then easterly along a sliding route of thirty-one to forty-four degrees latitude. By now, six to eight weeks may have passed if the voyagers were lucky, months if they were not. In either case, food is no longer fresh and only a few wilted vegetables remain. Out of the depleted livestock, only a few precious chickens survive. Fresh water presents no problem, for long ago the Spaniards learned to drape mats of woven reed designed to catch rain in the shrouds and drained the precious

---

[2] The *San Jose*, 1694, 400 drowned; *San Nicolas*, 1621, 320 died; *Encarnacion* near Bulan claimed 150; at Catanduanes the *San Geronimo* returned after nine grueling months at sea only to strike a reef there with a mere eight survivors; the *Senora de la Vida* left her bones and those of her unlucky pilot on Isla Verde.

liquid into huge, cut sections of bamboo, nature's perfect rain barrel. These *bambones*, as large as a man's thigh, guaranteed fresh water for most of the voyage, or at least until the ship reached the parched coastline of Baja California, at which time the ship made use of an emergency supply of three to four thousand earthen water jugs stored in the ship's hold and/or suspended from the rigging.

During the first or second boring month the passenger's grumbling has not yet surfaced, but it soon will begin with complaints of cramped living quarters and ugly sanitary facilities. The gentry enjoy a private potty, but the common folk share a community slop bucket which is emptied only sporadically. During a ship-tossing storm, however, it may be emptied quite unexpectedly and disastrously should the hatches be dogged down.

Capricious tradewinds often forced the galleon northerly or southerly of her charted course between the thirty-first and forty-fourth latitudes. After the third month of endlessly rolling seas, passengers and crew eagerly scanned the horizon for Cape Mendocino, the hoped-for prominent landmark that signaled the beginning of the southward trek toward the lower latitudes to Acapulco. The landfall was a welcome sight for the battered and weary group; here they could, weather permitting, enjoy the antics of the *lobillos* (little wolves), the furry creatures with little paws who so deftly held abalone on their chest while hammering open the thick shell with a stone and all the while gaily waving at the ship as she lumbered by. Little did the argonauts realize the immense value of the sea otter and its eventual effect upon trade and the "Spanish Lake."

Lack of fresh food and fierce storms added to the now sickly crew's misery as they struggled to work the ship, haul in the huge yards or secure loosened cargo. The *Espiritu Santo* of 1604 sailed into a SW gale the 10th of November and for the next twelve days the desperate ship, barely able to hold her rigging, clawed and fought off the dangerous rocks of Cape Mendocino. On the 22nd, a cracking volley of two, razor-sharp lightning bolts struck and sheared off her four-foot thick mainmast. One bolt killed three men and severely injured eight. The second onslaught left sixteen men unconscious and speechless for the remainder of the day. For two more months the exhausted crew labored day and night to work the galleon south to Acapulco.

Passengers paid one thousand, five hundred pesos for fare to Acapulco...a princely sum for a five to seven month trip on a stench-filled vessel so crowded that walking was restricted to no more than twenty feet in any one direction. Clutter on deck, bales of goods, sleeping, off-watch seamen and soldiers, rigging and chain, gun carriages and guns, spars, sails and dozens of essential items littered the deck of the half-merchantman, half-warship galleon. Below deck was worse, much worse. Rank human odors mixed with those of the animals, tarred ropes and oakum decks added to the vile stench which, on hot, sun-burnt days, seared lungs, violated stomachs and watered eyes. Rats, yes, thousands of huge rats sent the numerous ship's cats fleeing from their onslaught of ferocious cleaving teeth. These voracious vermin violated at least one third of the ship's edible supplies by consumption and/or urine and fecal contamination. Rats on deck were a common sight and, if caught, served as shark bait. In emergencies, their captors ate them. The rats below fared better, for the vessel's swollen belly might contain as much as forty thousand pounds of biscuit, two thousand, three hundred pounds of salted fish, a ton and a half of dried or salt beef, four hundred bushels of rice and more of tea and sugar, along with wagon loads of coconuts and fruits. Far-sighted crew and passengers provided their own supply of fruit preserves and chocolate, which they jealously guarded.

All aboard prayed daily for a short, five-month voyage with the knowledge that six months presented unbearable hardships and seven months at sea proved deadly. In any event, the ship was committed to a completed journey...to turn back or to lose the galleon imperiled thousands of Philippine citizens whose daily bread depended upon the delivery of their goods in New Spain. The average

Spaniard of the day, though brave and adventurous, avoided physical labor with great diligence. If he lost his fortune, regardless of the reason, he turned to begging on the streets in lieu of seeking gainful employment. The problem, described in a royal decree issued in 1621, directed all viceroys to counsel indolent Spaniards to seek work; however such counseling, they were told, should be done "only with great adroitness and good humor."

The galleon *San Sabiniano* returned to Manila in 1663 after seven months of faulty navigation. One ship in 1655 and another in 1657 failed to reach their objective, as did four earlier ships of 1616-1617. Each time, the financial stability of the island fell into ruin. Day after long, boring day, week after toilsome week, this troublesome thought preyed upon the argonauts. Close confinement in cramped quarters with little room to turn and no room to stand erect caused tensions to mount. Gambling and most other forms of diversion were strictly forbidden. Dice and cards were a punishable offense; reading of certain books was permitted if one allowed for their space. Regulations limited luggage to two chests measuring three and one-half feet long, seventeen inches wide and fifteen inches high. Two bottle cases for wine were tolerated and ten jars could be carried for the storage of honey or oils. Each passenger supplied his own mattress.

During inclement weather, all fires were doused, all hatches and doors were closed and meals, if any, were served cold. If the galleon ran out of firewood, meals were cold and uncooked for the remainder of the trip. The ceaseless hammering of iron-hard waves demanding entry into the bowels of the wooden hull drove most people mad during their confinement to the dank, stench-ridden, dark hold where, it seemed, the world consisted of never-ending motion. There, in the ship's bowels, the sinister voice of doom screamed in a most silent way; prayers offered to the Almighty served to accentuate the moaning sobs of a dying passenger as he coughed up bloody and half-digested, wormy food.

Sunny days brought blessed relief; Dons and Ladies, officers and crew crowded to the deck to bask in the brightness of a new day. Imperceptibly, the voyagers sensed more deck space...some of the deck cargo went by the board in the high seas...and more shoulder room, too...after the funeral services. Conversation gave way to gasps of approval and astonishment when the passengers sighted a spouting whale or when a circling shark darted in with the speed of light to gobble an impaled rat, and, in turn, be gored by an iron hook. If a large shark, it provided fresh meat for supper. Shark fishing usually occurred before the dead were cast over the side, but sometimes this was especially difficult if a portion of the crew were Malay... three or four would be found dead every morning, killed by the cold of the higher latitudes. The scourge of scurvy took the largest toll. As late as 1755, eighty-two of the *Santisima Trinidad*'s four hundred and thirty-five died before reaching Cape San Lucas. In earlier years, the deaths were higher; one hundred and fourteen died on the two galleons of 1643; one hundred and five were slipped over the side during the voyage of 1629.

Life was cheap and death was commonplace, but travelers spoke in terror-hushed tones when they discussed the sad fate of the *San Jose*. When her sails were first sighted off the Acapulco coast in 1657, jubilation ran through the town, for now the yearly trade fair could start. But wait...something seemed amiss. The ship sent no signals; no flags flew from the masthead and no booming of her cannon signaled her arrival. The *San Jose* failed to heave-to or tack and continued sailing on down the coast. Small boats set out in pursuit and finally overtook the ship. The rescuers boarded, only to discover a ship-of-death carrying mummified passengers and crew. The *San Jose* had been at sea more than a year.

Passengers enjoyed smoking when the weather allowed; gentlemen excused themselves from the ladies and moved to an area above the waist of the ship and to the lee side. Absolutely no smoking was permitted in the berths or below decks. Violation of the fire regulations meant one year's service without pay aboard the ship. The *San Cristo de Burgos* disappeared in 1693; her charred timbers were found in the Marianas. Years later, two of the six survivors of the raging inferno were rescued from a lonely island...one was mad and the other broken in spirit from having dined off the flesh of dead companions.

Passengers sought amusement in various forms. Blinding sharks and tying their tails together before casting them alive into the sea helped pass idle hours. A more favored pastime involved tying a bladder to a shark's back before returning it to the sea. In spite of regulations against gambling, the voyagers bet on the slightest improvisation, though gambling debts were seldom recognized or honored unless, of course, owed to one of the ship's officers.

Experienced travelers considered certain areas of the ocean more unlucky than others and when traversing within that portion of the sea a certain solemnness prevailed. Just north of the Marianas passengers fell to praying instead of gambling, for it seemed as though an inordinate amount of deaths always occurred there. It mattered little though, for wherever the ships sailed, dreaded scurvy was sure to be a fellow passenger. Northern people claimed the disease came from the south, southerners said it was a northern curse, likewise east and west, hot or cold climates. It made little difference, for scurvy was known and feared the world over. Throughout the years, numerous clues as to its cause and cure popped up, but none were recognized. Hundreds of thousands died a slow, torturous death...they wasted away, unable to close their ulcerated mouths. Teeth, by their weight alone, fell from spongy, swollen gums. Mucous membranes oozed pus and blood. The victim's rotting skin remained depressed to the touch. Acidious fruit was the cure, but even after this was recognized and relief stations were set up at Monterey, San Bernabe and San Blas to aid the distressed, many galleon captains refused to make these ports-of-call in their haste to reach the profit-able Acapulco marketplace. In many cases the passengers were of the same ilk; their greed overcame their fear of death and they urged their captain to press on. Pedro Cubero Sebastian wrote that out of four hundred passengers who embarked from Manila on his ship, two hundred and eight died before they were able to take on fresh fruit at Navidad, Baja California.

Regulations prohibited common sailors from using space aboard ship for trade goods, but wages were so low (150 to 175 pesos per trip) that wise ship captains winked at violators in the knowledge that, in order to protect their own goods, the crew would fight disease, the raging elements and the very real possibility of capture by pirates.

A foolish captain who failed to allow seamen space for their illicit goods or refused to issue them arms faced the possibility of mass desertion; one unfortunate vessel commander arrived at Acapulco where the Indians, desiring to learn the art of wine-making, induced seventy-four out of seventy-five disgruntled sailors into deserting their ship and its niggardly captain.

A simple space or *piezas*, listed at a value of two hundred and fifty pesos, could conceivably return as much as two thousand, five hundred pesos or more. Commanders received their commissions via politics or payola with a salary of four thousand, three hundred and twenty-five pesos per trip. A cunning commander often realized a clear profit of twenty-five or thirty thousand pesos per trip on his personal goods and then would return his original ship's salary to the governor who appointed him to the post. A particularly astute captain might clear as much as fifty to one hundred thousand pesos via gratuities, commissions or percentages on unregistered cargoes.

Only four galleons were captured;[3] the rest beat off vicious attacks by Moros, Dutch, English and other freebooters of the western ocean. Following the loss of the *Santa Ana* in 1587, passengers were issued arquebuses,

---

[3] Santa Ana, captured by Thomas Cavendish in 1587; *Encarnacion*, captured by Woods Rogers in 1709; *Cavadonga*, captured by George Anson in 1743 and *Santisma Trinidad*, captured by Admiral Cornish in 1762.

swords and bucklers. Seamen received a sword each and the ship's soldiers or partisans were given pikes, powder, munitions, bombs and grenades. A trained gunner was provided for each piece of ordnance.

World traveler Gamelli Careri quite accurately described the longest and most dreaded voyage in the world,[4] "...vast ocean to be cross'd, being almost one half the Terraqueous Globe, with the Wind always a-head: as for the terrible Tempists that happen there, one upon another, and for the Diseases that seize people, in 7 or 8 months, lying at Sea sometimes near the Line, sometimes cold, sometimes temperate, and sometimes hot, which is enough to Destroy a man of Steel, much more Flesh and Blood..."

William Lytle Shurz, in his excellent book *The Manila Galleon*, estimates some sixty million pesos and untold thousands of people were lost on this ghastly route; yet, because of such vast profits, it continued for two hundred and fifty years. Ship losses were at an unbelievable minimum at thirty-three vessels during the entire life of the line with only ten ships listed as lost at "unknown locations."

What exactly were these ships, the galleons, to which people entrusted their very lives for so long and so difficult a journey? Most ships of the Philippine route were built in Manila. They were, during their time, the most advanced ocean-going vessels afloat and among the most successful warship, transport-type ships ever built. Cavite shipyards produced the greatest number, others were built at Mindoro and Bagato. One vessel was built in Japan. Casimiro Diaz enthusiastically exclaimed that the finest wood in the universe grew in the islands and, "...were it not for the quality and strength of their timbers the galleons could not make so dangerous a voyage." Only the earliest ships of the fleet were built in Mexico, due to the inferior quality of lumber from that area.

Teak wood from East India and Malaysia formed the massive frames; knees and keel were built of Philippine *molave*; *lanang*, a rather odd, rubbery wood able to withstand great shocks, made up the sheathing. The great *Santisima Trinidad*, cloaked in *lanang*, absorbed the shock of one thousand and eighty cannon balls of eighteen and twenty-four pounds before capture by the English in 1762. This occurred only after she had been dismasted and brutally beaten in a hurricane. After capture, she sailed for England, showing little in the way of adverse effects, even with tons of cannon balls embedded in her sides.

Regardless of the risk, the capture of a Spanish galleon meant wealth beyond reason. Tales of a Thousand and One Nights, Alladin's Magic Lamp and the Wealth of the Orient describes the cargoes stored deep within the dank, dark holds of these sturdy vessels. Pearls and precious stones from India, the diamonds of Narsinga and Goa, rubies, sapphires, topazes and cinnamon of Ceylon, pepper from Sumatra and Java, cloves, nutmegs and a myriad of valuable spices from the shores of the Moluccas and Banda, fine Persian silks, brown-eyed, sensuous slave girls, wools and carpets from Ormuz and Malabar, rich tapestries and bed coverings of Bengal, exotic beeswax for candles in adoration of the Christian God, turbaned eunuchs of Nubia, fine camphor of Borneo, balsam and ivory from Abada and Cambocia, civet for perfume, bolts of silk from Lequios and Great China woven in velvets and figured damasks, taffetas and other cloths of every texture, design and color, linens and cotton mantles, gilt-covered and decorated articles, embroideries, porcelains, curiosities of great value and esteem, Japanese amber, vari-colored silks, secretories, lacquered boxes, desks of precious inlaid woods and ornate silverware crossed the Pacific in a steady stream. An astonished Englishman once wrote enthusiastically of, "...a mariner that brought a

---

[4] Francisco Gamelli Careri, an Italian physician, satisfied an almost insatiable curiosity of the world by doing what few people of that day and age dared attempt...he circumnavigated the globe as a common tourist. Best of all, he recorded his experience aboard the *San Francisco Xavier* in 1697. He even mentioned the delay in the vessel's departure due to overloading which forced the ship to return to the quay and off-load numerous passengers and tons of *beeswax*!

pearle as big as a doves egge from thence, and a stone, for which the Viceroy would have given 3000 ducats."

All this and more composed the cargoes of these wallowing, half-warship, half-freighter type vessels, some of which were rated two thousand tons and capable of carrying two hundred crew along with four hundred passengers. More important, how did the numerous legends of pirate treasure, castaways and wrecked ships become so prominent on and about a small spit of sand at the mouth of the Nehalem River in northern Oregon?

The majority of losses during the two hundred and fifty year span of the galleon fleet occurred in or about the Philippines. The *San Juanillo* and the *San Juan* disappeared in 1578 and 1586, but they date too early, in view of later evidence, to qualify as the wreck at Nehalem Spit. Wreckage of the *San Antonio* floated onto the coast of Luzon and, of course, we know the *San Agustin* left her bones in Drakes Bay, California, in 1595. Charred wreckage of the *Cristo de Burgos* floated ashore on the island of Saipan and there is some evidence, though slight, of at least one galleon lost off the western coast of Baja California. The most intriguing and most publicized enigma is the mysterious wreck that many believe lies on that one and one-half mile-long strip of sand near the little town of Manzanita at the foot of Neahkahnie Mountain in northwestern Oregon. It is here, for the past two hundred years, sand and sea have allowed only a few tantalizing fragments of wood to peek through drifting dunes, wood that may or may not indicate the presence of a lost galleon. Occasionally the vagaries of wind and current release a few chunks of weathered, strangely marked beeswax.

History reveals unmistakable evidence of survivors of an ancient Spanish wreck in the area. Gabriel de la Franchere, an Astoria fur trapper, ventured up the Columbia River in 1811 and, near the Cascades, actually spoke to a first generation descendant of one of the castaway Spaniards. Using an interpreter, Franchere determined that the old and nearly blind man bore a typical Spanish or Latino name of Soto and was the son of one of the

four seamen who, after escaping the wreck, melted into the Indian culture. In time, the four castaways grew weary of the savages and elected to strike overland to the east in hopes of finding their own kind. According to Soto, he was a very small boy when his father and companions left, never to be heard from again.

Alexander Henry, fur trader and prolific chronicler of the age, wrote of trading with the Indians at Astoria for beeswax, "...which they collect on the coast to the S. where the Spanish ship was cast away some years ago...." He further mentioned a red-haired Indian who obviously was the second generation product of a slight ripple in the local genetic pool. Ross Cox, another early Astorian, mentions the same person, but gives a more detailed description in as much as he notes the subject bore the tattooed name *Jack Ramsey* upon his arm. Obviously, in this case, not a Spanish name, but that of a seaman who deserted an English ship and stayed long enough with the Indians to sire this red-headed son. Genetically speaking, the son had to be the product of a half-breed woman who, in turn, was the daughter of an *earlier* white man...most likely, the Spaniard, for without this combination, red hair would not have been possible.

An anonymous Spanish officer of the survey ship *Sutil* recorded his observations of an Indian tribe inhabiting the shoreline of Nunez Gaona, a small harbor in the Straits of Juan de Fuca. He described several women of the tribe and Chief Tetacus' wife, Maria, as being white. The name *Maria* was not a corruption of the local language, but totally Spanish with the proper inflection upon the syllables. Obviously, she was the product of a union that lasted longer than mere gestation.

As mentioned, the *Espiritu Santo* survived her ordeal off the American coast, but the *San Antonio* the year before, the *San Juanillo* in 1578 and the *San Francisco Xavier* of 1705 (whose Captain, Santiago Zabalburu, enjoyed a reputation for habitually overloading his ships) were entered into Spanish records as lost at unknown locations. In later years the captain of the ill-fated, overloaded *Pilar* ig-

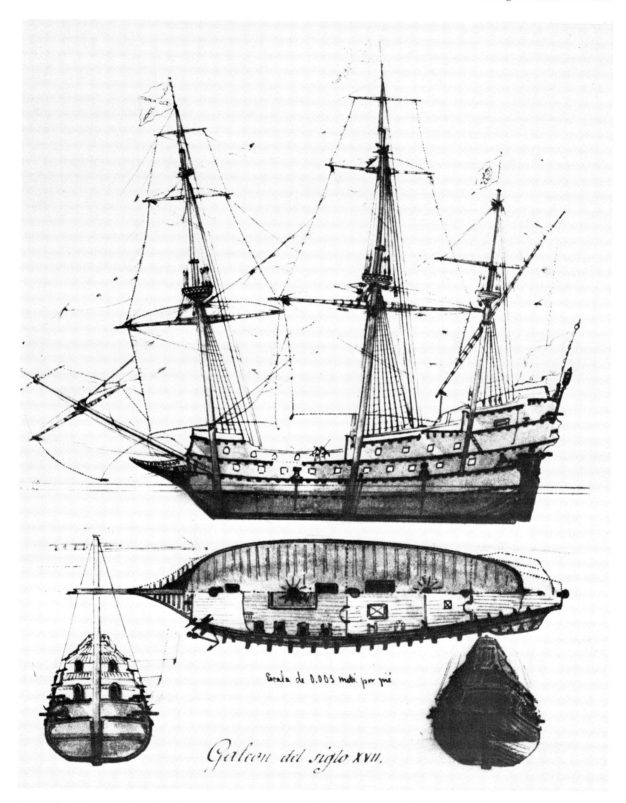

Galeon del siglo XVII.

Typical galleon of the Manila trade route, circa 1700. Does a vessel like this lie beneath the waters of Neahkahnie?

(California State Library)

nored the pleas of his worried passengers as they boarded ship and proclaimed, "...Acapulco or Purgatory!" Fate decreed the latter and for many long months, distressed Acapulco merchants vainly awaited her arrival.

The Nehalem shipwreck appears to be that of the *San Francisco Xavier*, for most of the evidence collected leans strongly in her direction. The old Chief Soto (interviewed by Franchere and previously mentioned) and second generation Jack Ramsey (mentioned by Henry and others) correctly places the time of the Nehalem wreck to correspond with the *San Francisco Xavier*'s recorded loss.

One may easily envision a battered galleon and her weakened crew blown northward, far off course, attempting to claw off the rugged rocks that abound around the Tillamook-Nehalem coast. Did the angry sea drive the vessel ashore on Nehalem's Spit, or did she capsize just offshore and break up?

Ships timbers have been found in the sand just south of Manzanita, the small and picturesque town in the area. Two coasting schooners, the *Milla Bond* and the *Kate L. Herron* did leave their mouldering bones on the spit, but the flotsam of at least one ship does consist of teakwood ribs. This portion of wreckage once was the center of casual investigation, but since its disappearance under the sand in the 1930's, interest and romanticism has intensified.

In the 1930's, Ben Lane, Mayor of Manzanita and somewhat of a craftsman, cut portions from the exposed wood and built a small table which is now on display at the Columbia River Maritime Museum in Astoria.

In 1970, through the determined efforts of E. W. Giesecke, historian, the wood table was tested at the Department of Wood Science and Technology, University of Washington, where Dr. L. Leney found the sample to be teak, possibly originating from the Philippine or Malaya region. Other pieces of this same wood are on display at the Tillamook Pioneer Museum in Tillamook, Oregon.

Does the presence of teak indicate a Spanish ship? Not necessarily. Exotic as it may sound, teak was a common type of lumber used in ship construction. *Lanang* or *molave* remnants would be a real clue, but no wood of that species has been found. The massive chunks of beeswax, however, are a totally different matter.

Alexander Henry, in 1813, was the first to chronicle the existence of beeswax flotsam from the area and since then an estimated twelve to twenty tons have been recovered. In the early years Indians traded the beeswax blocks for articles from the white man's fort at Astoria. As time went on, the chunks became valuable collector's items and museum pieces, particularly if they bore mysterious, man-made glyphs. These marks or brands were simply means of identifying cargo after its delivery to a designated port. A galleon's manifest listed the name of the consignor, the *boleta* number and the description of the consignment. Due to the similarity in Iberian names, the Spaniards devised a system of private brands to assure proper delivery of goods. Of course beeswax was not the only type of cargo to bear these identifying marks, but it has been the only cargo item to survive the wreck, boxes and bales having long since rotted away.

Tales of buried treasure from the "Beeswax ship" were noticeably absent prior to 1884. Certainly Henry, Ross, Cox and other pioneers of the region would have been told by the local tribes about a large ship whose white-skinned crew struggled up the side of a rugged mountain carrying a large, heavy treasure chest, burying one of their own men with it, then gaily sailing off into the glowing sunset. There is no such known incident in shipwreck history. If early settlers knew of such a tale, they never bothered to mention it in their chronicles. If the legend existed during their time, they would have found it impossible to suppress such interesting information.

What was the event that triggered rumors of buried treasure guarded by the mouldering bones of a slain pirate or tales of strange marks incised upon stones, supposedly indicating the imaginary "X" that marks the spot?

During the 1890's two literary works appeared in print and became immediate favor-

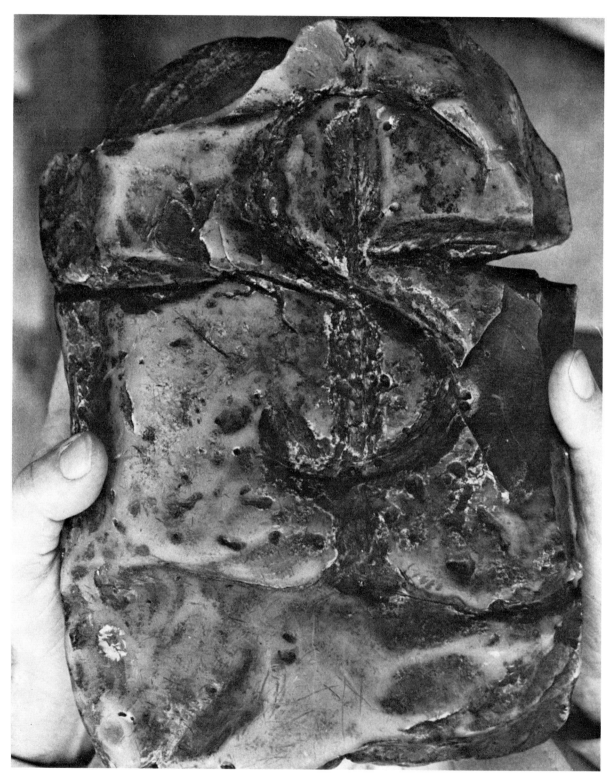

For almost three hundred years the ocean has cast up mysterious clues to a shipwreck. Beeswax on Manzanita beach. The incisions are probably ownership symbols.

(at Clatsop County Historical Museum, photo by Sam Foster)

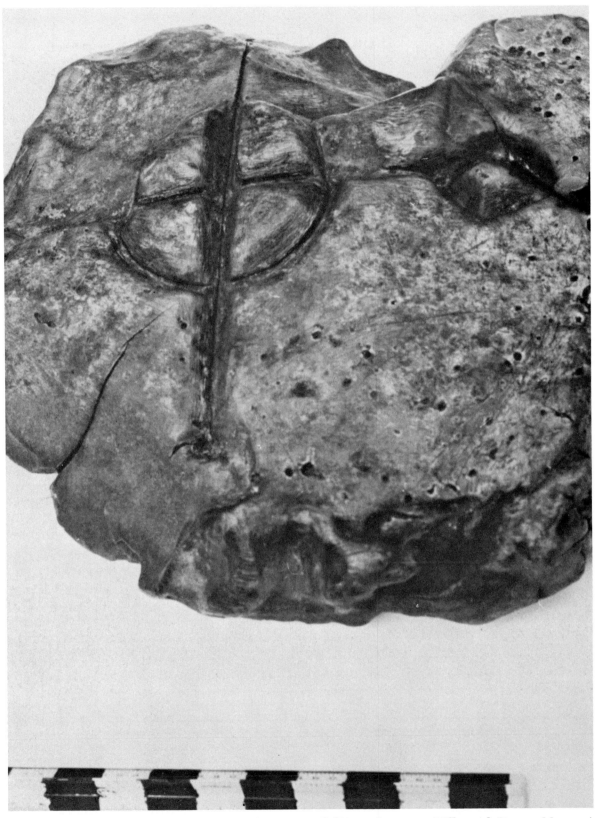

Another example of Oregon's oldest shipwreck mystery, Philippine beeswax. (Tillamook Pioneer Museum)

ites with those more inclined toward romanticism. One of these tales, *The Sea Cook*, later called *Treasure Island*, was written by Robert Louis Stevenson. The other, a somewhat older story and not really popular until serialized in the newspapers, was titled *The Gold Bug*. It was written by that master of mysteries, Edgar Allen Poe. The current Neahkahnie treasure tales are highly flavored with portions of both these adventurous childhood stories which appears to have resulted in fiction becoming fact through the medium of over-worked imaginations.

Tales of pirates, treasure chests, eight foot Negroes and an entire Spanish galleon lying on the beach can be summarily dismissed with a modicum of research and common sense.

Indians of the northwest prized iron above all other trade items and prior to the gigantic influx of the white man, eagerly searched the ocean sands for driftwood containing nails, bolts or other ferrous pieces that on occasion would float across the vast reaches of the Pacific from the Orient. Any aborigine so lucky as to retrieve such a windfall was considered unusually fortunate by his companions. Should a Manila galleon wash ashore in its entirety, the tribe claiming the beach area littered with tons of iron and brass already shaped in the form of cutlasses, pikes, axes and armor...to say nothing of countless other forms of merchandise...would immediately be elevated to the most powerful, feared and envied tribe on the coast and inland areas. Yet nothing in Indian legend or archeological studies support any type of hard core evidence of this nature. Only the beeswax remains, impervious to the ruinous nature of salt water and buoyant because of its waxy substance. Sometimes, as mentioned by Rev. Joseph H. Frost, an early pioneer/missionary, the flotsam drifts in when a SW wind blows.[5]

W. E. Warren wrote to Inspector of Hulls in 1895, "This packet or whatever it was, must have been at least 200 years old or it is a piece of a junk which had drifted across the Pacific. There were several sections of the junk washed in two years ago...I saw them while fishing one day, and yesterday I found one piece close to my place on the sand where I can get close to it with a team. The piece I refer to is 20 feet long, 14 feet wide and 6 inches thick...the boat was put together with nails and dogs and wooden pins. She was caulked with the bark of a tree. Altogether the craft must have been a peculiar one."

Would portions of a foreign wreck drift across the Pacific during a span of two years and come ashore at the same place? Not likely. But if a ship were breaking up, on the bottom, just offshore, the story would be different.

Numerous factors indicate only a portion of the *San Francisco Xavier*, if indeed it were her, lies on the spit at Nehalem. The remainder, with a fabulous cargo weighted down by tons of heavy ordnance, lies someplace offshore, possibly entangled in swaying seaweed and only occasionally releasing a chunk of buoyant beeswax to tantalize the unwary beachcomber and bewilder the historian.[6]

NEHALEM BEACH BEESWAX SYMBOLS

Years of probing by the author have produced numerous sketches and a few photos of the V-sunk enigmatic incisions found on the beeswax lumps discovered in the vicinity of Nehalem throughout the years.

Close examination reveals these owner's identification marks were not formed by the use of hot branding irons as formerly believed but were deftly carved into the wax with what sculptors call a "parting tool."

In addition to the beeswax bartered over the years by the Indians to the traders of Astoria, farmers in the area managed to come up with substantial amounts of the mysterious

---

[5] Lee and Frost, *Ten Years in Oregon*, Ye Galleon Press.

[6] In 1961, the Shell Oil Company laboratory performed a radio carbon test on a piece of this beeswax and dated it 1680 AD, plus or minus 110 years.

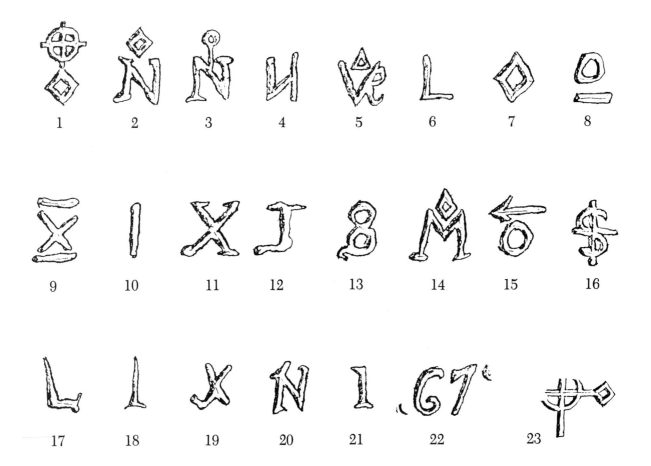

Nehalem Beach Beeswax Symbols: (1) Found by Waldemar H. Hollenstead in 1890 two miles below present site of Manzanita. (2) Illustration from Scott's History of Oregon Country. (3) Beeswax block measured 20" × 16" × 6". (4 through 8) Reported by Dr. Miller in the 1920's. (9 through 11) Tracings by D. S. Boyakin of Nehalem. (12) Reported by Prof. Davidson of University of Oregon, 1920's. (16) On display at Clatsop County Historical Museum (Sam Foster photo). (22) Found on Nehalem Beach in 1909 and donated by Mrs. A. C. Anderson to Tillamook County Pioneer Museum, where it is now on display. (23) Notice similarity of this fragment's design to that of #1. On display at Tillamook County Pioneer Museum.

substance. Six tons were recovered and shipped to Hawaii in 1847 and later another 450 pounds were plowed up by settler J. J. Gilbert. In 1867 the *J. C. Champion* carried several hundred pounds to Portland and a Mr. Edwards recovered three tons from the Nehalem sands in 1890. It has been estimated that between 12 and 20 tons may have been recovered thus far.

NEAHKAHNIE MOUNTAIN
ANCIENT SHIP TIMBERS

An ancient wreck visible at the foot of Neahkahnie Mountain but impossible to approach by beach or from the water because of its location in an extremely rough and wave tossed area was long thought to be that of the famous "Beeswax" ship. During an April storm of 1894 portions of the old wreck broke away and washed northward toward Arch Cape. Mr. Clutrie, a resident of the area picked up one of the timbers and brought it to the offices of the *Astoria Daily Budget* and on April 21, 1894 they published the above sketches with the following description. The planks were possibly of red cedar and were 14' long by 32" wide and 7" deep. The two planks were joined together on the edge by iron clamps, and nails and every four feet with square wooden pins. The nails were of a peculiar make (illustrated) and bent in such a manner that when driven the point turns about 6 inches below and is clinched. The head is sunk and covered with an inserted wooden block. The joined timbers had a tongue on each end which evidently fitted into a groove of a similar plank. Except for the drawings in the paper, it seems that neither were they photographed or preserved. Their whereabouts are unknown.

SHIP DISASTERS
Missing at sea

Alta 1/1904 Gas schooner lost at sea with all hands.

Alta 2/1923 Four masted barkentine, 1385 tons. Missing at sea en route San Pedro-Bellingham.

Americana 1913 Lumber schooner exited Columbia River en route Astoria-Australia. On her previous voyage of January 12, 1912, Captain Carl Benson was shot and killed by a disgruntled Japanese cook.

The captain had just relieved his first mate for insubordination; 2nd mate Francis Robinson brought the ship to port with the cook in irons. Vessel and crew simply vanished.

Andrada 12/11/1900 Four masted bark, 2,593 tons en route Santa Rosalia-Portland. Standing off the Columbia, she took Pilot Peter Cordiner aboard. She stood to sea under unfavorable weather conditions.

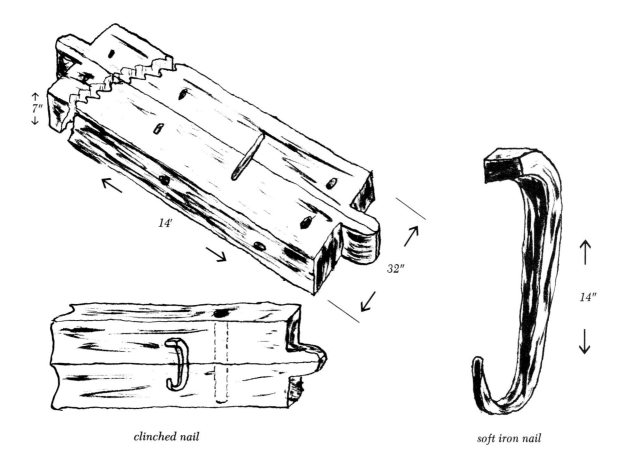

clinched nail

soft iron nail

Neahkahnie Mountain Ancient Ship Timbers: Clinched nail.

The vessel was never seen again. Seven years later, Captain Kennealy of the British 4 master *Jordan Hill* related he sighted the ship laying on her beam ends, flying signals of distress, but he had been unable to assist.

Anna 3/3/1901 Schooner missing, NFI.

Anna C. Anderson 1869 Schooner under Captain W. H. Stapleford en route Oysterville-San Francisco, owned by John & Thomas Crellin and John Morgan of San Francisco. Seven dead.

Arthur I 2/6/1898 Schooner, 129 tons. En route San Francisco-Tillamook. Disappeared at sea, six dead.

Bessie K 2/25/1907 Gas schooner, 98 gross tons, 84 net, 84' × 26' × 7', built at Alameda, California in 1893, owned by Charles C. Horton. This is the vessel that searched so long in vain for the missing *City of Rio de Janeiro* near San Francisco. The vessel, under Captain Louis Lazzarevich, carried 100,000' of lumber and 300,000 shingles when some mysterious occurrence caused the loss of her 10 man crew. The derelict drifted for several years and was sighted many times, a mute testimony to the vagaries of the sea.

Butcher Lat. 44°37'00"N, Lon. 124°06'00"W. NFI.

Bulwark 2/21/1881 British bark went under 300 miles off the coast while bound for Puget Sound from Yokohama. She sprang a serious leak shortly after leaving Japan. The skipper promised the crew he would put in at Honolulu for much-needed repair. The captain was the only navigator aboard and chose to say nothing when the ship passed the islands headed directly for the Sound. The ship went to the bottom suddenly. Three men managed to get into one boat, two in another. The three crewmen, after great difficulty and suffering, managed to gain the Oregon coast near Empire City. The other two mariners were picked up by the Britisher *Blackwell*. The rest died.

Cadzow Forest 1/4/1896 Bark, British. She picked up a Columbia pilot in anticipation of entering the river, but the sea rose and she beat it out to disappear with all hands.

Cape Wrath 1/15/1901 Bark, steel, four masts, 2140 tons. 75 days out from Callao en route Portland. Sighted off the Columbia bar, vanished without a trace. 15 lost.

Cordelia 1/19/1878 Steam tug, 59.52 tons, valued at $11,000. She left San Francisco for Coquille River. She was found on March 5, 1878 adrift, bottom-up, off Vancouver Island, British Columbia. 5 dead.

Cornelius 12/1892 Sloop left Victoria with a crew of six and about 40 Chinese. Destination unknown, but probably intending to debark illegal passengers at some hidden coastal cover. Captain, passengers and crew paid with their lives; the sloop was found in February, bottom-up, 100 miles south of the Columbia. 46 missing.

Courser 1892 Schooner, three masts, 357 tons, built in 1876 by Hall Bros. at Port Ludlow. She wrecked

once at Shoalwater in 1879 and was successfully salvaged, only to disappear off the Oregon coast in 1892.

Cowlitz 1/29/1893 Bark, American, 797 tons. Under Captain William Hansen, the ship sailed from Port Gamble to San Francisco. Ship, captain and crew of 14 were never seen again.

Dauntless 6/20/1899 Schooner en route Rogue River-Port Orford. She never arrived...anywhere.

Demerest 1880 Brig under Captain Collins en route New York-Columbia River. Missing at sea, 9 lost.

Discovery 1/1896 Barkentine, 415 tons, built by Charles Murray at Port Discovery, Washington in 1874. Bound from Port Gamble to San Francisco; vanished.

Douglas Dearborn 1/4/1890 Schooner en route San Francisco to Puget Sound. Discovered bottom-up off the Columbia bar. All hands lost.

Elida 12/1874 Schooner, two masts, 179 tons, built at Port Madison in 1868. Found abandoned, a total wreck, off the Oregon coast and taken in tow to Juan de Fuca.

Elnorah 12/22/1897 Schooner, three masts, 144 tons, built by James Monroe at Newport, Oregon in 1871. Disappeared off the Oregon coast.

Empire 7/24/1901 Bark, lost by fire at sea, NFI.

Florence 11/18/1875 Bark, 430 tons, built at Bath, Maine in 1836. The Duncan family were gathering firewood on the beach and found the name plate of the ship. A few days prior, Captain S. A. Dayton and his crew of eight had abandoned the ship in a fierce gale some 20 miles south of the Umpqua. They were bound Port Discovery-San Francisco. Most of the bodies of the dead crew were found near Cape Perpetua. The wooden vessel and her cargo proved a total loss to owner Isadore Burns. The name plate *Florence* was nailed to a post; the area has been known as Florence ever since.

Forest Queen 3/1898 Bark, 511 tons, built by Hiram Doncaster at Port Ludlow in 1869. Bound from Tacoma for San Francisco, Captain Basely, his crew of nine, 500,000 feet of lumber, 107,000 feet of laths and the ship vanished.

Fred Gower 2/22/1901 Schooner missing. NFI.

Glenbreck 9/1901 British ship missing off the Columbia. NFI.

Grace Darling 1/18/1878 Extreme clipper, 1042 tons, built in 1864. This beautiful vessel was named after Grace Darling, daughter of English lighthouse-keeper John Darling. The young girl won international fame for aiding her father in the perilous rescue of shipwreck victims on Farne Island off the coast of Scotland. The ship left Victoria for San Francisco on the 3rd with a cargo of coal. The Britisher *Melancthon* sighted her on the 18th in a heavy gale, hove to off the Columbia. None of her wreckage was ever found. 18 dead.

Great Admiral 12/6/1906 Fully rigged ship, built at Boston in 1869. En route under Captain E. R. Sterling, Mukilteo-San Francisco with a cargo of lumber. The ship went under. Three days later the British ship *Barcore*, sailing some 200 miles off the mouth of the Columbia, came across some wreckage, including the roof of the cabin; clinging to it were a portion of the crew, two of whom were dead, and Mrs. Catherine Martin, wife of the 1st mate. The backboard of the captain's gig, with the name *Great Admiral* carved into it, was found some years later tacked to a native hen-house in Hawaii.

Ida McKay 2/2/1912 Schooner, 187 tons, built in 1880. She went under in the vicinity Lat. 40°59'00"W, Lon. 130°41'00"N.

Ivanhoe 11/1894 American ship, 1563 tons, built at Belfast, Maine, 202' × 39' × 27', owned by the Black Diamond Coal Co., bound from Seattle under Captain Edward D. Griffin. The ship went missing in a hurricane off the Columbia River. Lost with the ship were Frederick J. Grant, editor and part-owner of the *Seatle Post Intelligencer*; mates James J. Toohig and Charles Christianson; carpenter William Andolin; Hans Stephenson; M. Stewart; Frank Saariner; H. Johnson; Emil Lowenroth; George Cordner; Sam Hart; J. Johanesson; McGunderson; Lenart Holm; W. Herman; John Anderson; Martin Jacobson; two Chinese cooks and three unknown passengers.

Jane Falkenburg 11/1899 Barkentine, 137' × 29.7' × 11.9'. Built at New Bedford in 1854, she came west the following year. The trip took 115 days and gave the captain an idea as to how fast she really was. She made her first trip to Manila in 39 days, beating the famous clipper *Flying Fish* by 7 days. Captain Falkenburg was killed in San Francisco in February, 1856 and the ship was purchased by Captain George Flavel of Astoria. In 1861 he expertly guided her in a fantastic run of 3½ days from Astoria to San Francisco. She collided once with the *Brother Jonathan* on that ship's last trip on the Columbia just prior to her loss. The *Jane Falkenburg* was a hard-working ship and a great money-maker. On her last voyage from Port Hadlock to San Francisco, the 45 year old vessel just had to give up and quietly slip forever into the encompassing arms of the sea.

Johanna M. Brock aka *Hannah M. Brock* 1/20/1878 Schooner, two masts, 134.35 tons, built in 1876 at Little River, California. En route San Francisco-Humboldt, her capsized hull was sighted on 3/3/1878 at Lat. 41°09'00"N, Lon. 125°34'00"W, and again about 12 miles off Port Orford. Eventually the schooner was driven onto the Rogue River Reef. No trace was ever found of her six crewmen.

John McDonald 6/20/1901 Ship burned at sea. NFI.

Joseph and Henry 1/3/1901 Schooner, two masts, 95', built at Benicia by Matt Turner in 1892, owned by Joe Harder and Henry Steffins of San Francisco. The vessel was found on above date, washed ashore six miles south of Alsea, Oregon. There are bones of

an unknown vessel that uncover every few years just off Highway 101 at the mouth of Big Creek, between Waldport and Yachats; they may be those of the *Joseph and Henry*. The crew was never found.

Laurel Bank 2/1/1899 Bark, four masts. Went missing en route Shanghai-Astoria. NFI.

Lottie 4/1892 Sealing schooner en route Victoria for who-knows-where. Captain Butler, Charles Rafferty and Gus Erickson were running 28 contraband Chinese to some out-of-the-way cove on the coast. The ship was found bottom-up off Tillamook and towed to Astoria. Maybe they made it, maybe they didn't.

Maid of Oregon 9/1896 Wood, propeller, two masts, 92' × 55' × 6', built at Astoria in 1888. Brazil Grounds was her owner and captain. She was lost someplace off southern Oregon.

Manchester 9/1901 British grain ship went missing off the Columbia. NFI.

Maria E. Smith 7/12/1904 Schooner, three masts, 365 tons, built by Hall Bros. at Port Blakeley in 1881. Missing at sea.

Merrithew 1852 Under Captain Kissam and with 100 tons of general merchandise, she went missing off the Oregon coast.

Michigone 11/20/1852 Schooner en route Astoria-San Francisco under Captain I. H. Simpson. The ship is believed to have foundered just west of Clatsop Spit. Captain Simpson was the half-brother of Asa Simpson, the famous lumberman of Coos Bay. Simpson's ships were never insured and by 1892 he had lost over $500,000 in 34 separate shipping mishaps. The cargo of the *Michigone* was, of course, lumber. Mate Lem Small, nine other crewmen and the ship disappeared without a trace.

Nabob 3/4/1876 Bark, British grain fleet, under Captain Fetherson. The ship disappeared just off Clatsop Spit.

Nomad 12/1897 Schooner, four masts, 565 tons, built by Hall Bros. at Port Blakeley in 1897. This beautiful ship went missing off the Columbia the same year she was built.

North Star 4/1887 Brig, bound Seattle-San Diego under Captain Williams. Found bottom-up near Portland Point, a location I have been unable to pinpoint.

Ocean Bird 4/3/1864 Bark, American, built at Augusta, Maine in 1847. The gold rush brought the ship to San Francisco where the crew, like so many others, deserted. Purchased by General M. M. McCarver, Sampson, White, Berryman Jennings and Dolp Hannah, who also purchased the *Carib* and *Keoka* at very little cost. The ship ran profitably between Milwaukie and San Francisco until her disappearance.

Ocean Pearl 1878 Schooner, two masts, 195 tons, built and owned by J. G. Wall, survivor of the *General Warren* wreck. The vessel went missing with all hands.

Rathdown 3/18/1901 Ship went missing with all hands off the Columbia. NFI.

Red Rover 1941 Troller, a former rum-runner of the 1920's went missing with no survivors. Debris came ashore (in one of Fate's grimmer jokes) at Whiskey Run, between Coos Bay and Bandon.

Reliance 11/20/1901 Schooner, 64 tons, 69′ × 24′ × 6′, built in 1886 and owned by George Kneass. Vessel, under Captain Franz, went missing on a run from Coquille River to San Francisco.

Romp 1875 Schooner, 50.42 tons, valued at $2,000. Missing with three persons en route San Francisco-Oregon.

Samaria 3/19/1897 An American ship bound Seattle-San Francisco. Her gig, a lifebuoy and portions of her deckhouse floated ashore at Cape Disappointment on April 24th. NFI.

Sonny Boy 2/5/1939 Seiner. Sailed into a rain squall with a crew of eight. Last seen off Yaquina Head.

South Coast 9/18/1930 Steam schooner, 301 tons, built by White at Seattle in 1887. She carried a cargo of 100,000 feet of cedar and a crew of 19. The vessel left Crescent City for Coos Bay and was never seen again. She was one of the oldest boats in the coastwise service, owned by Hobbs Wall & Co. Captain Stanley Sorenson was an able seaman who knew the coast well. The tanker *Tejon* sighted the *South Coast*'s deckhouse off Port Orford. Other ships reported seeing an empty lifeboat, numerous floating logs and miscellaneous debris SW of Cape Blanco. She is believed to have foundered on Port Orford Reef; there is much kelp in the area. A possible location of her wreck site Lat. 42°44′00″N, Lon. 124°36′05″W. Loran C 100 kHz W:13849.28; X:27673.35; Y:43908.91.

Star King 1872 Steamer left San Francisco for Coos Bay with Captain Parker Butler of North Bend, Oregon, a well-known captain of the tugs *Fearless* and *Escort*. Ship, crew and passengers were never seen again.

Surprise 1/31/1901 Schooner missing. NFI.

Sunshine 11/18/1875 Bark, may have been schooner-rigged. Missing off the Columbia. 25 dead. See story, "Sunshine."

Truxillo 7/3/1932 Caught in a trough at an unknown location. Five saved, nine dead.

Uncle Sam 2/27/1876 Schooner, two masts, 113.32 tons, valued at $14,000, built by T. H. Peterson at Big River, California in 1873. The ghostly wreck drifted from the fog one gloomy morning and onto the shore about 12 miles north of Cape Foulweather at an Indian reservation. Her masts had been cut away, a tangle of gear lay on and around the ship and a dead man was found in the cabin. No one was ever able to tell what grim fate befell the unfortunate vessel or crew.

Urania 12/29/1876 Schooner, en route Kodiak-San Francisco. Captain Thomas Lee, wife, two year old son and eleven others missing.

Wachusett 5/13/1900 American ship en route Hawaii-Columbia River. Missing with all hands. NFI.

Western Belle 1867 Barkentine, 275 tons, built by E. & H. Cousins at Eureka in 1867. Disappeared with all hands on her maiden voyage en route to Columbia River.

Yarora 2/20/1901 British grain ship, missing off the Columbia.

UNKNOWN SPANISH VESSEL Most likely the *San Francisco Xavier*. She failed to arrive at Acapulco in 1705; her intended route followed a portion of the Oregon coast. See story, "The Galleon of Nehalem."

This beautiful Grecian lady found in 1957 by beachcomber Eve Blunt in the rocks at the surf line of Lone Ranch Beach. Cast iron is not typical of ship's ornamentation or figureheads. The heavily corroded mystery measures about 16" in height.
(Chetco Valley Historical Society)

Found on Clatsop Spit, this carved trail board is a treasure for the Oregon beachcomber. It was donated to the Clatsop County Historical Society by Jerry Kirsch and Sid Zetosch. *(Marshall photo)*

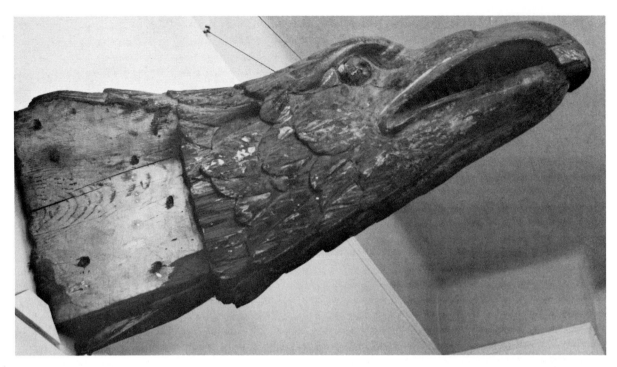

Beautiful carved figurehead. This eagle, from an unknown ship, is nearly five feet long. It washed ashore near Waldport, Oregon, some years ago. (Columbia River Maritime Museum)

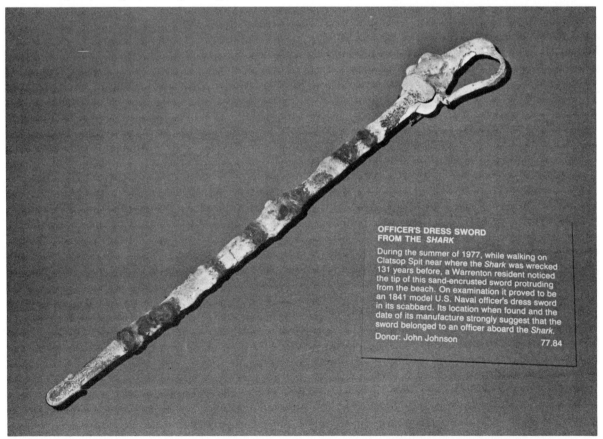

OFFICER'S DRESS SWORD FROM THE *SHARK*

During the summer of 1977, while walking on Clatsop Spit near where the *Shark* was wrecked 131 years before, a Warrenton resident noticed the tip of this sand-encrusted sword protruding from the beach. On examination it proved to be an 1841 model U.S. Naval officer's dress sword in its scabbard. Its location when found and the date of its manufacture strongly suggest that the sword belonged to an officer aboard the *Shark*.

Donor: John Johnson   77.84

A beachcomber's dream. This encrusted sword probably comes from the 1846 wreck of the Shark. (Columbia River Maritime Museum)

Numerous old hulls, wrecked, weather beaten and camouflaged by nature, dot the mud flats, rivers and beach dunes of the great Northwest.
(Marshall collection)

Unidentified wreck on the Oregon shore.   *(Oregon Historical Society)*

8

Columbia River, Tributaries, Idaho, Montana

AN INCIDENT AT THANKSGIVING ISLAND

Twenty-five year old Sam Gill stood wide-stanced upon the deck of the sternwheeler *Almota* and mopped rivers of sweat from his work-flushed face. The English-born American heaved a sigh of relief as a quickened river breeze eddied around his sweltering body; his tired muscles relaxed. He smiled at the thought of an odious job well done, for he had just spent hours scalding out the freight room to free it from the rancid stench of a raw wool shipment from Oregon's interior to Portland's mills. A broad grin broke across his damp face as he walked quickly down the gangplank on his way to report as engineer aboard the excursion boat *Idaho*, scheduled to transport The Dalles' children on a Fourth of July shipboard picnic.

Sam, excited at the prospect of showing off his engineering talents to a festive group of bright-eyed children, received a warm welcome from Captain Fred Wilson; the *Idaho*'s master was elated with having the services of Oregon Steam Navigation Company's popular young engineer. As the *Idaho* pulled out into the stream on that Fourth of July, 1878, little did the men realize they embarked upon a ten-day voyage bathed in the guilty and innocent blood of Indians and white settlers throughout the great state of Oregon.

The *Idaho*,[1] gaily draped with red, white and blue bunting and loaded to the gunnels with frolicking children, paddled her way through sparkling water to the village of Hood River, where the juvenile passengers enjoyed lemonade, sandwiches, swings and teeter-totters.

Although Oregon Steam Navigation Company donated their steamer's services for this patriotic celebration, they maintained a wary, mercenary eye; five paying passengers, scheduled to disembark upon the *Idaho*'s return trip, joined the merry group.

A few minor mishaps befell the *Idaho* as she steamed along the river. Captain Wilson, unfamiliar with the little stations of Mosier and Husbands, attempted to land his paying passengers from a too sharp approach angle. The ship bumped and ground to a dead stop at both ports. Fortunately she suffered no damage, but many hours were lost in setting up a deadman on shore, connecting a stout hawser to the forward steam winch and easing off the paddlewheeler. Midnight found sleepy but happy children clamoring for the honor of yanking the steam whistle cord as the *Idaho* approached The Dalles' landing. Captain Wilson and his deckhands anticipated a warm welcome from the parents on shore, but found themselves rudely pushed aside by a rush of hysterical mothers searching, calling

---

[1] A sidewheeler built at the Cascades, Washington. The 278 ton, 147' veteran of 1869 transferred to Puget Sound in 1881 where, following years of faithful service, was sold to Dr. Alexander DeSoto who ordered her tied up at the foot of Marion Street, Seattle, and converted into a mission hospital for the poor.

out, crying and finally clutching youngsters to their breasts while smothering them with kisses.

"Captain Wilson! Gill! My God, are we glad to see the two of you!" exclaimed Oregon Steam Navigation Company foreman James Smith as he shoved his way through the mad scramble of women. "We thought sure the Indians got you; the whole town's been scared half to death."

"Indians? What Indians?"

"You haven't heard? It's the Bannocks... they're on the warpath all along the river. The Army's asked for a steamer to transport their troops. Gill, get yourself up to Celilo and put the *Spokane* into running condition as soon as possible." The excited foreman paused only long enough to catch his breath, then continued, "Never mind the *Idaho*; we'll take care of her. Hurry, the train is waiting for you to grab your gear and get on her."

Gill's apprehension over the Indian uprising overshadowed the hypnotic, sleep-inducing rhythm of the train's wheels and swaying coach. The wheezing train arrived at 3:00 a.m. Gill leaped from the platform and raced for Celilo's dock and the idly floating, wool-laden dismantled steamer. Gill, along with a new hand named Stockman who knew nothing whatsover of mechanics, labored by kerosene lamp through the remainder of the morning and on into late afternoon of the 5th, allowing themselves only one short break for a quick breakfast. Finally, when finished, Gill ran to the train and shouted orders to Conductor Neal McFarland, "Bring me back an experienced engine room crew when you return with the army."

The train stood wooded and ready to make its run at 9:30 p.m. Word arrived that Indians now infiltrated the area between Celilo and The Dalles. Locomotive engineer John Carey shoved the throttle home; the train picked up speed as it wound along the tracks. It proceeded only a few miles before the frightened engineer threw the engine into reverse and steamed it back to the Celilo station.

"Indians!" Carey yelled as he jumped from the cab. "I seen several, fifty...no, at least a hundred of them squatting behind bushes along the track. They're getting ready to attack. I ain't taking this train nowhere 'til you put some armed men aboard her."

Volunteers met the engineer's demand and, once again, the train steamed toward The Dalles.

With the sun's rising came the realization that Celilo's seriously depleted ranks stood little chance of successfully thwarting an Indian attack. Company agent J. S. Schenck ordered the townfolk to board the *Spokane* for evacuation downriver and across to the Washington side. This included the Murphy family with their three small children, John Anderson with his wife and baby, mess hall hand George Erskine and wife and the fifty or so company employees engaged in building the 846-ton, 200' *Harvest Queen*. Evacuation of these souls proved risky at best, for not only did the *Spokane* lack an engine room crew, she lacked a competent captain as well. Agent Schenck appointed company watchman Dave Clapp to this task since he knew the river well and could also act as navigator.

Gill accepted Agent Schenck's command of the situation and thus, amid the wailing of frightened women and children, the cluster of carpenters and engineers, few of whom bore arms but almost all wielded axes, heavy crowbars or other items suitable to the complete and utter annihilation of savage boarders, the *Spokane* cast off her moorings at Celilo and slowly floated to mid-stream to begin her unpowered, down-river journey.

Company watchman-captain-navigator Dave Clapp whistled through the voice tube to the engine room. In the approved authoritarian-type voice he ordered, "Attention, Mr. Gill...you may proceed ahead."

No response came from the engine room.

"Ahem, Mr. Gill. You may proceed...Mr. Gill?"

Still no response.

"Oh, Mr. Gill...?" inquired "Captain" Clapp in an alarm-triggered falsetto.

"What the hell do you want, Clapp?" a sweating Gill growled.

"I want you to proceed, Mr. Gill," responded Captain Clapp.

"What will happen if I don't, Mr. Clapp?"

Gill snapped back, irritated at the lack of competent help in the engine room, at the helm and on the deck.

"We shall go over the falls if you don't, Mr. Gill," Captain Clapp managed to relate without the slightest quaver, although the falsetto reappeared.

"Do you mean . . . you cast off before I built up *steam*, you damn fool?"

"I'm afraid I did, Mr. Gill. I assumed . . . ," the Captain answered with an unmistakable quaver.

"Good God!" Gill strangled out as he leaped for the door of the firebox and hurled in as much kindling as the orifice would hold, followed by a kerosene-filled lamp and at the same time shouted to the new hand Stockham to race topside amongst the passengers and find a slab of bacon. One family, thus provisioned against hunger, suddenly found their precious fatty chunk confiscated and crammed into the ship's fiery maw. With that added fuel, steam built up quickly and in the proverbial "nick of time" saved the *Spokane* from the sharp rocky teeth of the rumbling falls and rapids.

During this period of the *Spokane*'s travail, the train returned to Celilo carrying Governors Perry and S. F. Chadwick of Washington and Oregon, Major John A. Kress, U.S. Army and some twenty soldiers, a few army musicians and one steamboat captain . . . the only men who could be rounded up on such short notice.

The *Spokane* chugged in from her near fatal accident. The much put upon engineer, ignoring protocol, pushed through the group of men and collared train conductor McFarland. "Where's my engine room crew?"

"Sorry, Gill," McFarland sheepishly replied, "I got so tied up with these Indian attacks, I plumb forgot to ask."

The 25 year old engineer exploded; he informed all within earshot, including the two

surprised governors, where they could go and what they could do with the 673-ton *Spokane*. The startled solons, aware of this young man's indispensable services, pleaded with impassioned political rhetoric that his inhumanity would result in innocent women's and children's scalps swinging from the lodge poles of rampaging savages. Surely he would not desert his mission at this critical time. They promised him his pick of crew from the men clustered around him and added that they did, indeed, have aboard the train a real honest-to-goodness *bona fide* steamer captain, Mr. W. P. Gray.

All was settled in good time and the *Spokane* pulled away from the dock on her errand of mercy. She carried a sparse crew of four, Captain Gray, inexperienced Mate-Navigator Clapp, Engineer Gill, Fireman Stockham and seventeen-year-old Lamp Trimmer-Watchman Tom Monohan. Twenty army men, the musicians and a Gatling gun[2] stood ready to protect the ship at every bend of the river.

The short-handed *Spokane* lacked the luxuries of a steward, cook and most importantly, supplies. The efficient Sgt. Connors, as good as any top-kick in the army, immediately set his boys to cooking breakfast for the crew. As the steamer plowed upriver, Gill, for the first time in three days, relaxed with a cup of hot coffee.

In the meantime, all eyes of the neophyte Indian slayers screened each blade of grass, each rock along the shore regardless of how slender or how small, for it was well known that the wily redskin could utilize the most innocent of objects to conceal himself, his horse and most likely his teepee as well.

Twilight approached and Major Kress invited all who were interested forward to watch a demonstration of their newest weapon, the formidable Gatling gun. Resembling a multi-barreled cannon, the easily ma-

---

[2] Dr. Richard J. Gatling, in addition to the gun for which he is famous, invented a number of machines including a seed sower, a steam plow and perfected a practical screw propeller for steamboats in 1839. His application for patent of the propeller was denied due to the granting of a patent of a similar item to John Ericsson a few months prior. The Gatling gun was designed for Civil War use; it fired 350 shots per minute in 1862. Two later models fired up to 600 spm. The weapon was not accepted until the end of the war and received limited use in the United States. Many European nations adopted it immediately. England used the weapon extensively against the Ashanti, Zulu and Sudanese in 1874, 1879 and 1883 with great effectiveness.

neuverable two-wheeled gun sat in all its majesty on the freight deck with its menacing mouths directed toward shore. Gill leaned against the doorway of his engineroom, lit his pipe and somewhat amusedly watched the proceedings.

On Sgt. Connors' command, a blue-coated private clattered a drum hopper into place atop the device and, as the ship pulled abreast of Long Island, took careful aim at the most menacing target yet encountered on this dangerous mission and began cranking six hundred one-inch caliber slugs per minute into the sandy beach where three little bunnies, in juvenile innocence, had picked this particular evening to frolic.

Loud raucous whoops, punctuated with "Get 'em" and "Look at 'em run, dang me I never seed anything like that," echoed across the cooling river. Minutes later another more ominous sound interrupted the deadly cough of the Gatling, that of rending, splintering lumber as the sternwheel jammed to a straining stop. Once again the inept Clapp, engrossed in the army's pyrotechnic attack upon Long Island's rabbit population, forgot to take stock of his navigational duties. The stern of the ship slewed, caught a shorebound stump and jammed it into the eighteen-foot diameter wheel, which in turn smashed numerous wheel buckets into matchwood and threw the splintered chunks into the starboard engine's eccentric rods. The force of impact carried away the rods, rendering the *Spokane* helpless.

All hands scrambled for the anchor while the *Spokane* drifted aimlessly in the river's swirling eddies. Frantic fingers wrenched the cover off the forward hatch and hoisted the rusty iron savior onto the wooden deck. The men pushed and pulled it toward the ship's side in a superhuman effort to pitch it overboard. . . only at the last second did someone realize that the instrument lacked an item vital to its proper function, a hawser. The men quickly attached a stout rope and heaved the anchor over the side. The wildly drifting *Spokane* came to a halt.

Gill and a small party of army men rowed ashore. They gathered rocks and driftwood to

fashion a small but adequate forge. Gill managed to straighten the bent eccentric rods and repair the cracked wheel flange. These temporary repairs enabled the steamer to limp, jackrabbit fashion, into Umatilla at 3:00 a.m. where Company Agent J. H. Kunzie anxiously awaited her arrival. He directed Gill to an old blacksmith's shop out in the sagebrush about a mile from town. Fortunately it was supplied with coal, blacksmith's tools and a rusty forge. Again, with the aid of the soldiers, Gill repaired the bent wheel rings, forged bolts and other iron work for the wheel; his fine craftsmanship restored the ship's equipment to almost new condition. Meanwhile the army boys busied themselves with carving driftwood into spare paddle boards.

A scout brought news that, during the night the Indians had successfully forded the river at the site of the *Spokane*'s last mishap, Long Island. Resignedly the paddlewheeler was turned around and ploddingly retraced her course in hopes of finding the elusive enemy. At Long Island the boat put ashore a wood cutting party and quite by accident they came upon an old man, a squaw with her papoose and a portion of goods cached in the brush; all left behind for later pick-up by the fast moving raiders. With an air of triumph the soldiers paraded their three prisoners and the loot back to the puffing *Spokane*; the vessel then steamed for the Washington shore with vague hopes of catching up to the marauders.

As the ship nosed toward shore a hail of bullets, fired from concealment atop a nearby cliff slapped into the sunburnt woodwork and spanged off the rusty hog-chains. No one was hurt, and after careful consideration and noting the swiftness of the water along the rock studded shore, Major Kress commanded the new course would now be for Wallula. Upon arrival they met the steamer *Northwest* which, on similar assignment from upriver, brought Captain M. C. Wilkenson (aide-de-camp to General O. O. Howard, friend and captor of the famous Chief Joseph), and a volunteer group of cowboys and farmers. The two forces joined, divided the experienced with the novices and formed two groups of approximately sixty men each.

Routine river patrol for the following five days lapsed into sheer boredom. By day the blazing July sun caromed off the sides of the steamer with much the same force as the earlier encountered hail of Indian bullets. At night, the ship anchored in the stream; the men slept fitfully, listening to the drone of mosquitoes, the incessant croak of bullfrogs and the cry of one loon to another. The men held their Springfields at the ready as they carefully noted each inflection in the suspect bird calls; every slight rustle and splash penetrated their erratic sleep. Day after long, hot day, heat radiated from the bare rocks draping the low, melted hills. Flies buzzed; the men wiped incessant sweat from their sunburnt brows. Spare rifles, stacked on deck, became too hot to touch. Farmers, cowboys and soldiers met on common ground; all wilted together on the hot, steaming ship.

The first few days of patrol revealed no hint as to the disposition of the Indians other than they carried Winchester rifles as they moved amongst the low hills. The soldiers barricaded the pilot house and engine room with bales of raw wool. The temperature in the engine room soared above 135° and the overpowering stench of raw wool seemed more of a threat to Gill's life than the now constant, but ineffectual, Indian sniping. He asked the men to remove the smelly barricade.

Meanwhile, general orders were issued that all redmen must return to their reservations or be considered renegades. With this, the river patrol investigated the mouth of Willow Creek on the morning of July 9th, then set a plodding course toward Umatilla. That afternoon, the *Spokane* neared Thanks-

giving Island; a lookout spotted a band of mounted Indians rounding a butte on the Washington side. "We sounded the steamer's whistle as a signal for the savages to gather at the water's edge." Unknown to the volunteers, the peaceful Umatillas were returning to their reservation.

Misunderstanding the whistling signal, the Indians hid in a small draw between two hills. The soldiers set up the Gatling gun and aimed their line of fire into the suspect area. Leaves flew from bushes as the bullets ripped home. Lead slugs ricocheted off rocks and peppered the ground with exploding dust pockets. As was later reported:

...the Indians, did not regard this as a very friendly action and instead of coming to shore for a consultation they hid back of the rocks and tried to get away. The boat was landed and some of our men sent ashore to get the Indians, Several of the horses had been wounded and several others, while not wounded, had blood on their backs, showing that their riders had been either killed or wounded.

About seventy horses, which they drove on board the boat, were recovered. The poor Indians

...did not realize that we were simply *trying out*[3] the Gatling gun and resenting the fact that several of their band had been killed stopped at the home of the Perkins family on The Dalles-Yakima road and killed the entire family, the same number of persons that had been killed out of their band.[4]

The patrol of the *Spokane* continued for eight more days, then blundered back to her starting point where everyone disembarked.

The Bannock War continued with varying success, but in the end, of course, the Indians were vanquished.

---

[3] Author's italics.

[4] Gill was mistaken in this portion of his account: Lorenzo Perkins and his pregnant wife were en route to Yakima seeking the services of a doctor. Always on friendly terms with the Indians the two invited the band to share their lunch unaware of the recent injustice that still burned bitterly in the minds of the survivors. Mr. and Mrs. Perkins were brutally murdered and after the discovery of their bodies a long chase ensued ending in the capture of seven Umatilla braves, six of whom were brought to trial and although sentenced to hang, not all did.

Of the seven, six attempted an escape before execution and were captured. One, Chuckchuck, rather than suffer the indignity of the noose, committed suicide. Another escape attempt resulted in the shooting death of Winecat and the wounding of Tewonne who also escaped the noose by dying the day before his scheduled execution. Saluskin and Kype were hung November 23, 1879, while Tomehoptowne eluded capture for almost three years; he was finally taken and swung January 24, 1882. The seventh, Moostonic, notably absent from the above incidents had turned state's evidence and escaped prosecution—he was so pleased he paid his court appointed attorneys J. W. Hamilton and Edward Whitson, 30 horses for their services.

Major Kress became a general for services rendered, it is said, and received the Distinguished Service Cross for heroism in military operations against an armed enemy of the United States near Umatilla, Oregon, July 8, 1878.

Captain Charles Painter and his forty-two volunteers from Walla Walla received praise for good conduct and bravery, as did the officers and crew of the steamer *Spokane*.

UP RIVER NAVIGATION!!

Is the Willamette river navigable above the mouth of the Yam Hill? The new keel boat *SALEM CLIPPER* !! will answer that question by informing the public, that she has successfully navigated this "Frightful" river during the summer as far as Salem, and will continue to carry freight to Salem or any other landing on the Willamette river, where there is sufficient business to justify it.

This boat will continue to run from the falls to any accessible point in the country above — terms reasonable.

Leonard White
Willamette River, Oct. 31, 1850

N.B. All freight will be delivered as dry and in as good order as when placed on board.

L.W.

Spectator classified ad of 1850

IMNAHA

The Lewiston Southern Company, a subsidiary of the Eureka Mining Company, which owned and sold, for phenomenal prices, stock in their company and property at Eureka, Oregon, built the beautiful sternwheeler *Imnaha*.

It appears the companies fronted a monstrous mining fraud and foisted it upon eastern investors. The true story remains shadowed; however, all clues lead to a well thought-out scheme that began in June, 1899 with the claims of two shady figures who, if they ever existed probably used aliases, recorded fabulous copper strikes just north of the mouth of the Imnaha on the Snake River.

The ensuing and inevitable rush of miners caused an overnight boom-town of 2,000 inhabitants. The two mystery men, Barton and Hibbs, immediately sold their interest in a small excavation high on the side of the west bank of the gorge for $100,000 and disappeared forever.

By 1903 Eureka had established a post office and, in spite of no profitable ore discoveries, flourished as a mining town until the loss of the *Imnaha* and her cargo of a huge ore stamp-mill on the ship's 14th supply trip to the small town.

The sternwheeler had been built at approximately 50% less strength than any boat on the entire western river system, but yet she navigated some of the roughest runs of water and rapids in the entire canyon. Whether her construction resulted from shoddy workmanship, frugality or a ploy to thwart salvage in the event of an accident and thus successfully close Eureka, whose life depended upon the supply ship, will never be known.

The mines never paid off and soon after the steamer's loss miners trickled out of the area in search of greener pastures.

A second steamer, the *Mountain Gem*, half-heartedly serviced the route, but in a short time gave it up. Eureka officially closed her post office in 1906. Today, the skeleton of the town basks in the hot canyon sun while the rotten bones of the *Imnaha* and her supposed cargo of mining equipment lie under the rushing waters of Mountain Sheep Rapids.

THE KOOTENAI BARGE

The story of the *Kootenai* barge is an incident of interest to scuba enthusiasts diving in the beautiful area of Coeur d'Alene, Idaho. The following report was printed in the Golden Anniversary Edition of the *Coeur d'Alene Press*, authored by Fred Wilson who worked many years on the lake's steamers primarily as engineer, occasionally a boat builder and, in this instance, a disappointed salvor:

One afternoon while at the Old Mission Captain Nesbit received orders to bring two barges loaded with three hundred tons of ore in sacks to Coeur d'Alene, as the river was beginning to freeze. Everything went fine until we got to the present site of Springston. The Kootenai was about thirty feet wide, and the two barges were of about the same beam, making a broad front to push through the ice. Captain Nesbit decided to leave one barge at that spot with a watchman to guard it. The steamer went on with the other barge, towing it behind.

After getting over the bar at the mouth of the Coeur d'Alene River and into ice-free water in the lake, the mate took a lantern and went into the hold for inspection to see if the barge was taking any water. He reported everything all right. As it was near midnight everyone not on duty went to bed.

I was about to turn in when the engineer, Captain Waters, asked me to take his place at the engine as he was tired from answering bells all day. My whole duty was to oil the cylinders and answer the bells if there were any. After an hour of quiet I looked out the port window and saw that the barge was riding way over on its side. I rushed to the speaking tube and reported to the captain, I got the bell to stop the engines and waited for him to come down. Again I got the bell. Half speed ahead. The captain started for the shore about a quarter of a mile above McDonald's Point.

The ore was in three long tiers, running the length of the barge and piled about four feet high. When we were about three hundred feet from shore, the port pile toppled over and splashed into the lake, and of course in a minute the starboard pile went overboard, and then almost all of the center pile lurched into the lake. A few seconds later when the captain drove her into the shore, we rushed onto the barge to see only fifteen tons of the ore remaining scattered all over the deck.

The barge was safe now so we left her and went on to Coeur d'Alene, arriving about 5 o'clock in the morning. Reporting to Charles Griswold, later captain of the Georgie Oaks, he asked if I could locate the spot where the ore went down. I assured him I could. With a wide grin he suggested I quit the boat and try to salvage the ore that was in the lake. It seemed like a good idea.

We had a hazy idea that all we had to do was to go up and get that ore, and presto, it was ours. The ore was worth about $15,000 on the market. During the following summer the Northern Pacific brought a diver over from the coast and he told them it would cost more than the ore was worth to recover it, as the water varied from sixty to one hundred feet in depth.

But we both quit our jobs, got a big grubstake, some lumber, one hundred fifty feet of half-inch rope, some peaveys, a grappling hook, some nails

and spikes, loaded it into a 32-foot dugout canoe, got George Ford to go along with us, and paddled for McDonald's Point.

After a good night's sleep we started to build a raft of logs, covering the logs with the lumber we had brought. When it was finished we towed it up to where the barge had been and started to fish. The ore was in canvas sacks, mildewed and worn out, and each sack contained one hundred twenty-five pounds of ore. We worked faithful three or four days, brought up an ore truck and a locomotive headlight. We would pull up heavy objects but when we got them near the surface they would drop back to the bottom. Whether we ever got hold of any ore we do not know, although we did bring up bits of canvas. Anyway, we quit.

THE WRECK OF THE HAWTHORNE TROLLEY

It's difficult to imagine a sternwheeler's involvement in the sinking of a trolley car, but the steamer *Elwood*, a 510-ton, 154 foot packet managed to cause such an incident as she plied her course through the brownish waters of the cold Willamette River. She blew her whistle to signal the Madison Street bridge[5] she was coming through on that frosty, misty morning of November 1st, 1893.

A Portland-bound trolleycar, loaded with early morning commuters, winged its way on a 90° tack toward the same bridge. The bridge gate went down and the lip of the bridge slowly separated from its shore-bound mate. At the top of the east river grade the streetcar motorman espied the barrier through the cold, gray mist. He routinely turned his control lever to "Off" while his other hand cranked the brake.

The *Elwood* throttled down and eased toward the open span; Pilot James Lee noted his ship drifted a mite closer than usual to pilings along shore. Suddenly, the screeching of metal wheels straining against steel track knifed the coldly silent mist. Pilot Lee and the *Elwood*'s crew shouted warnings as they watched the shadowy figure of the motorman fighting at the controls to halt the sliding car. Their voices were drowned out by a splinter-

---

[5] Known today as the Hawthorne Bridge.

ing crash as the trolley burst through the flimsy wooden barrier.

The car shot from the end of the track and momentarily hung suspended upon the river's mist. Then, with deadly finality, it plunged and was swallowed by the Willamette.

There was no stopping the steamer's forward motion as she cruelly cut through the gasps and bubbles of those unfortunate souls trapped on the river's bottom. Men and women clawed their way to the surface from the crammed interior of the silt-blackened trolley.

The *Elwood*'s crew raced aftward, knowing if their ship reversed, the giant paddlewheel would chew through those flailing souls as they rose from the boiling water. Slowly the ponderous steamer circled to retrace her course; the pilot continuously pulled the whistle lanyard. Its piercing intermittent scream alerted those on shore of the disaster.

Longshoremen, manning skiffs and boats pulled from hidden recesses, oared to the rescue. They pulled some twenty souls from the chilled, swirling water. Seven remained trapped in the wreck of the Hawthorne Trolley.

SHOSHONE SLEIGH RIDE

Oregon Steam Navigation Company controlled a major portion of waterways connecting to the mighty Columbia River in 1866. Although the company charged high fees for steamboat transportation, they maintained outstanding service by providing Portland to Cascades passengers a choice of daily round trips aboard the *Wilson G. Hunt, New World* and *Cascades*, fast steamers that elegantly rivaled the Mississippi's famed boats. The big sidewheelers *Oneonta* and *Idaho* catered to travelers along the middle river. The *Julia*, under Captain William Smith, moved stock and freight along the lower river while the *Iris* and Master Fred Wilson served above the Cascades. Passengers traveling beyond The Dalles boarded the *Yakima*, Captain E. F. Coe; the *Webfoot*, J. H. D. Gray, and the *Tenino*, Captain C. C. Felton. The *Owyhee*, *Nez Perce Chief* and the *Okanogan* rounded

out the OSNC's versatile combination of ships and captains.

The company jealously guarded their possession of the river system by ruthlessly driving off or buying out all serious competitors. Expansion became the company's theme song and the 1866 Idaho and eastern Oregon mining boom heralded an opportunity for the company to monopolize freight and passenger service into the interior on the upper Snake River between Fort Boise and Old's Ferry.

OSNC ordered the construction of a steamer at Fort Boise, Idaho, safe in the knowledge that no competitor enjoyed the financial reserves to challenge their new venture. Probably no other steamboat was built under more trying or adverse circumstances. Its cost proved astronomical; one ship was built for the price of three. Mules packed in each piece of iron; trees, cut in the mountains, were transported to and whipsawed on the scene; a forge, fired by coal or charcoal dug from or manufactured in the mountains, provided the ship's ironwork. Fittings and other specialty items ordered from Portland and other far-away cities caused constant expensive delays. When completed, the elegant utility sternwheeler *Shoshone* registered three hundred tons, 136′L × 27′W × 4′6″D.

The stout craft, with her 6′ × 48″ engine, eventually traveled more continuous miles than any boat then in service even though by the time her keel tasted water, the mining boom slowed and other, shorter routes to the towns were established. For three years she ran in the red, moving occasionally on small hauling jobs, but never earning her owners a dime's worth of profit. She became the jinx of the fleet by thwarting her company's policy of earning more than their original investment on each completed trip.

The *Shoshone* sat idle until 1869. Her deplorable condition of planks shrunken by the burning sun and decks and roofs rotted under damp winter snow forced the OSNC to issue an ultimatum via Captain Cy Smith...bring her downriver to Lewiston, Idaho or wreck her in the attempt.

Experienced mariners well knew the impossibility of steamboating *up* the Snake River, or Seven Devil's Canyon as it was then called, but none knew if it were possible to get the boat *down*. Meriwether Lewis, Donald McKenzie, Wilson Price Hunt and the U.S. Army's Ben Bonneville visited the Snake, but imparted little information regarding navigation of its waterways. Lewis' journal, dated June 2, 1806, described the amount of food available, "... the indians inform us there are plenty of Moos to the S. E...." and three paragraphs later, "The other horses which we castrated are nearly all recovered..." The deepest gorge in the world, the boundary between Oregon and Idaho, the bleak, brown, black-starved cliffs boasting two hundred archaeological sites, the muddy river below roaring through a narrow canyon rim 7,900 feet above the high water mark (deeper than the Grand Canyon of the Colorado), a canyon which averages a depth of more than six thousand feet from Hell's Canyon's Hat Point to Saulsberry Saddle, rated little more notice than a castrated horse and a mis-spelled moose.

Captain Smith, with little preparation and less fortitude, brought the *Shoshone* past Huntington and Oxbow through a twenty foot drop in two miles. He navigated through Kerr and Cattle Rapids to a short distance below Lime Point where he tied her to the shore and abandoned the mission.

J. A. Ainsworth, OSNC president, felt inclined to let her rot on the spot, but changed his mind after talking to Captain Sebastion Miller, former *Elk* explosion survivor and engineer of Astoria's mail boat, and Chief Engineer D. E. Buchanan.[6] The two men convinced President Ainsworth they could do the job; he ordered them upriver March 21, 1870. They steamboated to Umatilla, then changed to buckboard. By sled, wagon, horseback and foot they reached Union. They departed April

1st and progressed another one hundred and thirty miles to Lime Point. A two-day canoe trip brought the men and their guide to the waiting *Shoshone* and her two guards, Mate Livingston and Fireman Smith. Guide W. F. Hedges was hired on the spot as a deckhand.

The group overhauled the ship's machinery as first order of business since the gears had not been turned for six months. With the aid of the repaired deck pump, they poured continual water upon the deck and planks to swell the shrunken wood and close all gaps... caulking was impossible due to lack of proper materials.

A traditional April run-off brought a rise in the river. Captain Smith had originally reported to his superiors the falls were impassable but by the 20th, the men deemed the water deep enough to attempt navigating Copper Falls which lay a mere two hundred yards downstream from their present position.

The crew situated candles in the hold for illumination in order to discover and instantly patch any leaks during the ship's descent. Captain Miller studiously scanned the rushing current. Although unfamiliar with the ship and her reaction to the river's currents, he decided to run the huge paddlewheel in reverse as a means of gaining steerage for the rudders. Taking his position at the helm of the three-hundred-ton steamer, Captain Miller signaled Buchanan to bring the ship 'round to midstream. Although approaching with extreme caution, the two hundred yards to the rapids proved too short a distance for the ship to be correctly positioned. The first eddy caught the *Shoshone* in a vicious whirlpool and spun her end-for-end three complete turns before spitting her out of the vortex and toward a declivity in the rocky water-covered barrier. The ship's bow poked into pure air as she teetered precariously upon the lip of the falls. Water built up under her stern; with a

[6] Born 1858 in Ohio and orphaned at a very early age, he was a blacksmith and locomotive engineer apprentice for 6 years... a man anxious to educate himself whenever possible. He arrived in Oregon in 1869 and worked various branches of steamboating. Eventually he entered government service and quickly rose to the position of superintendent over the building of all scows, tugs, and snagboats used to clear the Columbia River channel. He invented and operated a successful dredge for deepening the Columbia Bar and the infamous "Hogback" located just above Astoria... a navigational hazard that had resisted all prior attempts to correct.

whooshing sigh, the steamer bowed to the inevitable. She slowly dipped her forepeak, lifted her stern and, with her paddlewheel beating futilely against the blue sky, roller-coastered a fifteen foot drop as she raced through two hundred feet of raging torrent. The five-man crew clutched for the nearest rail, stanchion or supporting projection in a white-knuckled effort to hang on. The pile-driving vessel threw chairs, tables, charts and coffee cups forward, then aft, then forward again. The *Shoshone* slammed into the water at the base of the falls, smashing over half of her dried, sun-rotted wooden wheel buckets. Against this cacophony of interior noise and the roar of the river, a rending, barely-heard crash signalled the loss of over eight feet of her bow, ripped cleanly away above the water-line by a projecting ledge of rock.

Another sudden wrench of the hull threw open the boiler's safety valve; the escaping steam sent forth a high-pitched scream that ended in a wailing gurgle. Each man threw a here's-another-fine-mess-you've-gotten-me-into look to his wild-eyed partner and held on tighter. Cork-like, the battered hulk bobbed into a comparatively quiet stretch of the mad river. With the languorous touch of a drifting leaf, she gently nuzzled the shore with her broken bow. Men and ship had successfully passed their first hurdle.

The bruised crew secured the vessel, then set about installing new buckets and attending to the damaged bow. The well-constructed craft's first bulkhead blocked the tons of water scooped up by the now spoon-shaped bow, leaving the remainder of the hull dry.

By 9:00 a.m. the next day, the men had patched the tough *Shoshone*. She stood ready to once again challenge the raging river's unexplored waters. Captain Miller placed two men in the ship's boat and sent them ahead in search of dangerous rocks. The slow-moving *Shoshone* poked here, then there, like the cautious prodding of an old lady's cane. She encountered several more whirlpools and rapids, but the previous day's dousing kept her planking tight. The men converted trees along the bank and dried driftwood into fuel which they stacked on the main deck forward within easy reach of the fire room.[7] They estimated two and a half cords per hour for their downhill run. The steam was up and the helm handled easily. Deckhand Hedges, doubling as cook, served hot coffee to his exhausted skipper in the texas[8] and the main deck crew. Spirits rose as the men sipped the stimulating brew.

Suddenly, without warning, the *Shoshone* plunged pell-mell into another whirlpool. A crashing wall of water, armed with hundreds of cordwood chunks, blasted through the double fireroom doors. The crew dropped their mugs, grabbed for the overhead and just barely pulled their legs out of the swirling, boiling cauldron of water and wood. As the ship spun, the water whipped out dry-cycle fashion, leaving the dampened cordwood rolling around the floor. Stumbling, bruising shins, the men scrambled to the deck. Steam billowed from the engine room as hissing water recoiled from the furnace's massive, closed iron doors. The men again clutched frantically to the nearest support as the vortex hurled the *Shoshone* into a chute-like passage way...the furious, funneled Mountain Sheep section of the Seven Devil's Canyon. The steamer careened through high, solid rock cliffs that allowed only a few inches leeway between her port and starboard rails.

It was almost 5:00 p.m. before the tired crew, their throats raw and voices hoarse from answering orders over the incessant roar of raging water now behind them, tied up at one of the few encountered calm spots. They dined, then began working on damaged paddlewheel buckets. Precariously short of staging, the men searched the ship for extra overlooked planks.

The steamer set out again in the teeth of a booming gale on the 23rd. The *Shoshone*'s high wheelhouse acted as an unwanted sail that shoved the vessel from one side of the rocky river to the other. Captain Miller con-

---

[7] Firerooms were opened to the front of the steamers on the main deck to take advantage of the incoming breezes to feed the fires.
[8] Steamboaters designated certain cabins in honor of the States; the captain's was always the largest, hence texas. It could also mean, depending upon the type of steamer, a structure on the awning deck containing the officers' cabins with a pilothouse in front or on top.

tinually spun the wheel port and starboard in hopes the main and slave rudders would stabilize the ship's erratic course.

Engineer Buchanan raced about the engine room in response to chaotic clanging of bell signals ordering ahead, reverse, full, then half and, occasionally, all at once. Buchanan excused his captain's idiocy upon discovering the wheelhouse had been jarred loose and, as it rocked, alternately tightened and released the signal line from the texas to the engine room.

The river leveled out enough on the 24th for the ship to proceed with her cautious poking here and there for hidden dangers while the ship's boat sounded the waters ahead. The steamer covered only ten miles that day.

Tragedy struck on the 25th. Captain Miller, while gathering cordwood, crossed the path of a rolling log. It knocked him down and ran over him, causing severe injuries that laid him up for nearly the remainder of the trip.[9]

The next day started well and by 9:30 a.m. the ship arrived at the mouth of the Salmon River. Following a short respite and early lunch, the men continued their journey with only minor difficulties. They reached the mouth of the Grande Ronde and the final lap of their remarkable adventure.

At 7:00 a.m. the excited argonauts battened down all equipment aboard the strained and battered steamer. With good-luck handshakes all around, they cast off into the fearsome Wild Goose Rapids. The *Shoshone* passed through without a hitch and arrived at Lewiston two hours later, heralding their victory over the Snake River with deep-throated, unmelodic blasts of their one-note brass whistle.

Shore hands eagerly grasped the lines. Flabbergasted dock workers, miners and citizens swarmed aboard. With unbelieving eyes they surveyed the extensive damage. The *Shoshone* and her crew enjoyed a welcome as if having returned from the dead, as indeed

the townsfolk believed. The damaged portion of the ship's bow, ripped off her first day out, floated with its shattered jackstaff the length of the river to Umatilla; the little community assumed the *Shoshone* and her stalwart crew were no more.

"I say, Buck," the bone-weary Captain Miller proudly proclaimed from his wheelhouse to his engineer surveying damage on the deck below, "I expect if this company wanted a couple of men to sail a steamboat through hell, they'd send for you and me!"

Upon this triumphant note, the tale of the *Shoshone's* sleigh ride ends. The battered ship eventually sailed the Willamette and realized a profit for her owners. She came to grief in 1874 on a rock opposite Salem. Despite herculean efforts, she refused to be raised. Salvors removed her machinery and left her to the unkind elements.

Down, but not yet counted out, the *Shoshone* dared to challenge the river once more. In January, she floated free and rode the currents as far as Lincoln. Too tired to venture further, she grounded and, for her pains, suffered the ignominious fate of becoming a land-locked chicken house.

HOLD THE PRESSES!

The importance of maritime shipping in the early days of Oregon goes beyond measure; surely any form of commerce would have been held up for days, even months, were it not for the immense waterways that crisscrossed much of the state. Mariners utilized canoes, bateaux, keelboats and even rafts to their fullest potential.

Inevitably power, in the form of steam, would be put to use and, in 1850, a group of determined men built a magnificent steamer at Milwaukie, Oregon. Her official name, by act of the Territorial Legislature in honor of her builder, was the *Lot Whitcomb of Oregon.* She was formally launched on Christmas

---

[9] Seven years later, at the same location, a famous Oregon Indian chief named Joseph led his people across the river in a courageous retreat that ended in Montana, a heart-breaking five miles short of the Canadian border and their salvation. Chief Joseph eloquently surrendered, "...from where the sun now stands, I will fight no more forever." Exiled forever from his homeland and people, Joseph died of a broken heart shortly thereafter.

day, an appropriate date for such an auspicious occasion. Territorial dignitaries[10] delivered speeches extolling the vessel's virtues and officially declared her the second Oregon-built steamer. Booming cannon punctuated Fort Vancouver Army Band's lively music. Indeed, local excitement ran so high that an over-zealous Captain F. Morse, master aboard the schooner *Merchantman* which lay anchored in the stream, overcharged his ship's cannon. The device exploded, killing him instantly. The next edition of the *Spectator* reported the incident, but to avoid dampening the spirit of the occasion piously mentioned, "...thus it ever is with us mortals, truly in the midst of life we are in death," then blithely continued, "...but, this being a day for launching, with everything ready, she slid into the water like a meteor from the heavens, safely and without straining the boat or any other damage or accident." And so the attitude of hardy pioneer stock prevailed; Oregonians stoically accepted the fact that while one life had gone out, another was launched...thus, the elegant 600 ton *Lot Whitcomb* became an accepted member of the family.

Captain J. C. Ainsworth, determined to prove the amazing capabilities of the *Lot Whitcomb*'s powerful eighteen foot diameter side wheels, pushed a 160 foot riverboat from Astoria on the lower Columbia to the Willamette's Oregon City...a distance of 114 miles in a record-breaking time of just ten hours. This magnificent feat assured Oregonians they would soon match, ship for ship, the maritime trade of the Hudson and Mississippi rivers.

The town of Astoria spearheaded the drive for river commerce with the assembling of the steamer *Columbia* and placed her under the tutelage of Captain Frost. Being strictly a utilitarian vessel, she offered none of the refinements of the beloved *Whitcomb* but even so, she was, so to speak, home grown and that's all that mattered. Soon, the *Willamette*, an iron-hulled propeller owned by the Pacific Mail Steamship Co., the *Hoosier*, *Eagle* and *Blackhawk* joined the ranks of numerous commercial ships which plied up and down the mighty Columbia River. But of all the vessels, the *Lot Whitcomb* remained a favorite in the hearts of pioneer Oregonians.

One catastrophic day, shattering news spread like wildfire up and down the watercourses; Oregon's favorite ship lay damaged and grounded on a bar below Oregon City, whose entire populace went into immediate mourning.

"No, not the *Lot*; it just can't be..."

"Who's the danged fool what run her on that bar?" were only a few quotes from incredulous, angry citizens.

Others voiced a bit more faith and redeemed the actions of neophyte steamboaters with, "Ain't nobody's fault. It were an *uncharted* bar what she hit."

Five long days passed while Oregon City's waterfront habitués waited in vain for the polished brass whistle's deep-throated blast of escaping steam to herald the approach of their adored sidewheeler. Except for keel boat traffic and a few canoes, the waterfront closed down. Hang-dog citizens paced the deserted port with their fists shoved deep into pockets and viciously kicked out at every innocent pebble that dared lie in their path.

Renewed hope arrived to the cadence of clopping hooves and the breathless shouting of a rider atop a racing, sweating horse. "She's free! She's free! She's acoming in...." The messenger saw no need to identify *she*.

David J. Schnebly, editor of the Oregon *Spectator*[11] sprang to his feet from behind his desk at this welcome revelation. He shouted across the open barn-like room to his apron-clad, ink-stained printer, "Hold the presses, Sam. This is *news*," then, amidst scattering paper, bolted out the door and raced down the street to Sam Markham's General Store.

"Elizabeth," gasped the shirt-sleeved editor as he sped through the door to the counter where Edwin Markham's mother[12] stood. "The *Lot Whitcomb*'s off the bar and headed

---

[10] Governor Gaines, Milwaukie's Mayor Kilborn and Mr. Lot Whitcomb, owner of Milwaukie's local newspaper *Western Star*.

[11] Oregon's first newspaper

[12] In later years Edwin Markham would become Poet Laureate of Oregon.

this way, and..." he pleaded, "the *Spectator* is ready to go to press. I want you to write a poem in honor of this day. I'll hold up the paper for half an hour. Can you do it? I'll wait."

The diminutive Mrs. Markham, a veteran of an 1847 wagon trek from the east, smiled, nodded agreement and perched herself upon a stool behind the wooden counter. With a quill pen, she wrote:

> Lot Whitcomb is coming!
> Her banners are flying—
> She walks up the rapids with speed;
> She ploughs through the water,
> Her steps never falter—
> Oh! that's independence indeed.
> Old and young rush to meet her,
> Male and Female to greet her
> And waves lash the shore as they pass.

> Oh! she's welcome, thrice welcome
> to Oregon City;
> Lot Whitcomb is with us at last.
> Success to the Steamer,
> Her Captain and crew,
> She has our best wishes attained.
> Oh! that she may never
> while running the river
> Fall back on that sand bar again.

When the passengers aboard the refloated steamer stepped onto the wharf at Oregon City, they were surprised and delighted to be greeted by wildly cheering citizens and a laughing managing editor of the *Spectator* skipping up and down the waterfront as he hawked ink-wet newspapers sporting headline and front page tribute to their beloved river steamer.

SHIP DISASTERS
Columbia River, tributaries, Idaho, Montana

A. A. McCully 5/22/1886 Sternwheel, 498 tons, 148' × 30' × 4.1'. Launched at Oregon City on 7/3/1877. Under Captain Z. J. Hatch and while waiting high water at the lower Cascades for a lift to the middle river, she caught fire and burned. Insured for $12,000.

Albany 1/6/1875 Sternwheel, 328 tons, 126' × 27' × 3.6'. A total loss at the mouth of the Long Tom at Willamette. The ship was built at Canemah in 1868. Her captain, Mr. Vickers, thoroughly soaked when his ship went down, died February 13th from the effects of exposure.

Alexander Griggs 1905 Sternwheeler, built at Wenatchee in 1903 by George Cotterell, owned by Columbia & Okanogan Steamboat Co. Wrecked at Entiat Rapids.

*Alliance 1886 Bark, British, rolled onto steamer *Ocklahama* at Portland.

Alliance 4/25/1889 Steamer sunk in collision with *Danube* at Post Office bar in the Willamette River.

Ann 4/1869 Sternwheeler, 83 tons, 78' long, built at Umatilla, Oregon in 1868. Ex-*Lewiston*, the first steamer on the Long Tom River. Wrecked between Harrisburg and Everly's Landing.

Annie Comings 12/30/1907 Sternwheeler, 452 tons, ex-*William M. Hoag*, built in 1887, rebuilt at Portland in 1903. Owned by the Western Transportation Co. The 150 foot vessel was rammed by the French bark *Europe*; she sank in three minutes in the Columbia River at St. Johns. The crew, including a woman, climbed to the deck of the surviving vessel via her anchor chains. All were saved.

Annie Faxon 8/14/1893 Sternwheeler, 514 tons, 165', rebuilt at Texas Ferry, Washington in 1887. Purser J. E. Tappan reluctantly left his new bride in their cabin in order to check the ship's lading as the steamer crossed Wade's bar at 7:30 a.m. for her regular landing at Lewiston, Idaho. A terrific explosion racked the ship from stem to stern, catapulting Captain Harry Baughman out of the bridge and onto the shore. Crewman William Kidd was blown to pieces and Thomas McIntosh was beheaded by a splintered board (he was standing next to Tappan, who escaped almost unhurt). Mrs. Tappan, John McIntosh, S. McComb, Paul Allen, A. E. Bush and George F. Thompson were killed.

Asotin 1915 Sternwheeler, built at Celilo for U.S. Army Corps of Engineers and crushed in the ice at Arlington, Oregon.

Aurora 2/1849 Ship, American, under Captain Kilbourn. Ship became a total loss when she went aground in 8' of water in the Tongue Point Channel; crew and passengers saved. The *Magnolia* grounded at the same spot.

---

* Refloated or partially salvaged.

Bateaux 1/13/1851 Keelboat, owned by Mr. Morris of Lafayette. Capsized with a load of wheat at the Narrows at Rock Island. The current tore the freighter apart as the passengers safely reached shore after walking down the rapids. S. M. Morris (owner), George Richey, Albert Duncan of Missouri (he left a wife and 5 children), James Browner, William Hupp of Tualatin Plains were drowned; no bodies were recovered.

Batteaux 7/3/1830 Peter Skene Ogden recorded that he lost, at The Dalles, this freighter along with 9 voyageurs, 11 pieces (packages of about 90 lbs each) and 500 beaver pelts when the vessel was trapped in a whirlpool in a place where none was expected. The large freight canoe went down by the stern and the French-Canadians panicked. Strangely enough, for all their ability with these huge canoes, very few voyageurs knew how to swim.

Bear 12/12/1950 Tug, owned by the Shaver Transportation Co. and skippered by Claude Burleson, built in 1947. While towing the *Falcon* she went under near the Hawthorne Bridge in 50' of water.

Beaver year unknown. Sternwheeler, aka *G. W. Shaver*, owned by Peoples Transportation Co., foundered at Canoe Rapids on the Columbia. Her remains were covered by the waters of the John Day Dam.

Bismark 1898 Sternwheeler, 104' × 20' × 4.4', engine 11" × 36", 191 tons, built in 1892 at Woodland, Washington and supposedly very poorly constructed. She went for a total loss on the Willamette for unknown reasons.

Bonanza 1888 Sternwheeler, 651 tons, 152' long, owned by Oregon Steam Navigation Co., built in 1875 at Oregon City to replace the *Albany*. She sank once at Rock Island where she stayed under three months before being raised. She then went down for the count after hitting a rock at Wallings on the Willamette, and was stripped and abandoned.

Boneta 1905 Sternwheeler, 96' × 16', built by Johnson for the White Star Navigation Co. of Coeur d'Alene, Idaho. Under Captain Reynolds, the ship was rammed by her rival *Idaho* just above the O. W. R. & N. bridge on the St. Joe. Nothing was proved at the trial held to determine the cause of her sinking.

Bonita 12/7/1892 Sternwheel, 527 tons, 155' long. She encountered a gale while en route Portland-Cascades and driven upon Fashion Reef. The 17 year old vessel under Captain Gus Pillsbury became a total loss.

Brandon 6/15/1889 Aground on St. Helens bar. NFI.

Camano 5/27/1902 Sternwheeler, 59 tons, 90' long, put into service in 1898 by Captain E. H. McMillan at Wenatchee, Washington. Under Captain Dwight Barrett, the ship and her 500 sacks of wheat stopped on her downriver run to take on wood at Entiat Landing. Upon leaving, she refused to answer the helm and listed heavily to port. Water entered the lower deck, which caused her to become even more unmanageable. She went on her side. The crew scrambled through doors and windows on the starboard side and 11 of them rode the ship in her undignified position for some distance through the swirling Columbia. One unfortunate soul slipped off and was drowned. At the same time, the life raft tore loose; four men, unable to climb the sides of the floundered vessel, grabbed the raft, but were not safe yet, for they became caught in the clutches of a whirlpool which sucked the raft down to the men's shoulders before it released its hold and allowed the raft to drift quietly into the shallows alongside the defunct steamer.

Canemah 8/8/1853 Sidewheeler, 135' × 19' × 4', built by Captain A. F. Hedges and Captain Charles Bennett at Canemah in 1851. She claimed several *firsts* to her credit: the first steamer to carry the grain crop as far upriver as Corvallis, the first Oregon Post Office (she served communities along the river under the direction of Nathaniel Coe), first Oregon steamboat to explode, which occured at Champoeg (first seat of Oregon government). Her explosion wasn't big, as explosions go, but it was enough for passenger Marion Holcroft...he was killed. A number of people besides Hedges and Bennett (killed by Indians in 1855) had a hand in her building. They were Alanson Beers, John McCloskey and Hamilton Campbell. The McCloskey family became prominent in Oregon history as steamboat men. Hamilton Campbell was the engraver of the now-famous and valuable Oregon Beaver money. After creating the dies, he took up photography at Corvallis and later, San Francisco. Somewhat of a nomad, Campbell left for Guaymas where he became a mine superintendent. Attacking bandits killed him at the mine on June 12, 1863.

Carrie Ladd 6/3/1862 Sternwheeler, 128 tons, 126' × 24.4' × 4.6', two decks, built at Oregon City in 1858, owned by OSNC. Sank 18 miles below the Cascades.

Cascades 1943 Sternwheel, built at Portland in 1912, 407 tons, 160' long. Explosion and fire took its toll at Swan Island.

Charles R. Spencer 7/12/1904 Sternwheel, sank fifteen miles above Hood River on the Columbia. NFI.

Chelan 7/8/1915 Sternwheel, 244 tons, 125' long, built at Wenatchee, Washington in 1902. Went under at the foot of 5th Street at Wenatchee, a total loss by fire.

City of Anacortes 5/8/1933 Gas boat. Lost in the Portland Canal. NFI.

Claire 1948 Sternwheel, struck a submerged object and sank three miles below Camas and later raised.

Clan MacKenzie 12/28/1889 Ship, British. The *Oregon's* bow, when she struck the ship at Kalama, penetrated some 30' between the Clan MacKenzie's stem and cathead. Although two of her crew were reported killed, their bodies were never recovered and it is believed they deserted. The vessel was raised January 27, 1890.

Clatsop Chief 2/28/1881 Sternwheel built at Skipanon in 1875. The steamer *Oregon* (which seemed to resent the presence of other ships on the river) rammed and cut the *Clatsop Chief* in half at the Willow bar, sending the vessel and the ship she towed immediately to the bottom. Four drowned. Engineer W. S. Holmes went down with his ship, but felt his way along the engine room steampipes to the gangway, then along the carlings to a door and managed to come to the surface. W. E. Mitchell captained the ship at the time of the accident.

Columbia 11/14/1898 Bark. While under tow by the *Wallowa* she suffered some undisclosed mishap and became a total loss in the Portland Canal.

Columbia 1894 Sternwheeler built at Little Dalles in 1891. The 529 ton, 153′ long ship burned at an undisclosed location.

Columbia 7/8/1915 Steamer, 341 tons, built in 1905. She burned to a total loss at the foot of 5th Street, Wenatchee.

Corvallis 1896 Sternwheel, built in Portland in 1877. The 100 footer was lost on the Columbia. NFI.

Cowlitz 9/1931 Sternwheel, 99 tons, 109′ long, built at Portland in 1917. She was bound downstream from The Dalles with a full cargo of wheat under a severe buffeting by a 25 mph upstream gale that poured tons of water over her bow, which raced across the deck and managed to find access into her engine room. The fires hissed out and the totally helpless ship went under. Fortunately, her superstructure wrenched free; the crew scrambled aboard and rode it for more than an hour before rescue.

Cricket 3/12/1914 Steam schooner, caught fire while berthed at Portland. Her 4,000 barrel asphalt cargo prompted the pier's owners to cut the *Cricket* loose in order to save their pier, which they did, but saved only their own. The vessel, now a mobile torch, touched at the next pier, set it afire, broke loose and touched at the next. After that one was burning nicely, the *Cricket* moved on to another and another, driving the fire department in circles trying to keep up with the marine incendiary before she finally beached in an unoccupied area and burned out, smugly satisfied with the havoc she had created.

Daisy Ainsworth 11/22/1876 An OSNC owned sternwheeler launched 4/23/1873 at Dalles. The beautiful ship registered 673 tons, 204′ × 28′ × 7.8′ with a 21′ diameter wheel. Under Captain John McNulty and with pilot Martin Spelling, she headed downriver for the wharf at Cascade Locks. Spelling mistook a dim light in the soupy, foggy distance for one which lay on his opposite quarter; he spun the wheel over, but the *Daisy* managed to find an offending rock. Engineer Bill Doran engaged the pumps immediately, but it proved too late. Two hundred and two cattle, all Astoria-bound, drowned in the accident. Although many of the beasts arrived at

their destination, they did so as floaters. Her engines were removed and the lightened hull bobbed away in the spring freshets. She was picked up and towed to Vancouver.

Dalles City 9/14/1912 Sternwheel. Those acquainted with the Columbia River Gorge will appreciate that a steamboat can be wrecked by a *sandstorm*, and that is exactly what happened to the *Dalles City*. Totally blinded by stinging sand and opaque-etched pilothouse windows, her skipper ran the steamer ashore at Stevenson, on the Washington side.

Diamond O. 4/25/1934 Sternwheel, owned by Drake, Henry and Richard O'Reilly, built in 1891. Captain William Maki. While towing an empty oil barge, she struck a bridge at Vancouver, rolled and sank upside down on a sand bar. Ship was valued at $35,000.

Duc de Lorges 1848 Brig, French. Divers of the Pacific Bridge Co. discovered the old wreck in July of 1928 and tentatively identified her as the *Duc de Lorges*. This is a new one on me, but it is supposed to be located in the Willamette River at the foot of Davis Street. NFI.

Elk 11/1857-60 Sternwheel built in 1857 by Captain Chris Sweitzer, who died on the wreck of the *Northerner* (see *California Shipwrecks*). The *Elk*, servicing the Dayton-Yamhill run, exploded just below the Yamhill at Davidson's Landing. Her entire upperworks went, along with her Captain Jerome. Years later, he still regaled the local citizens with his tale of how, while in the air with a number of other objects, he looked through the smokestack and observed his pilot, Sebastian Miller, sitting on the bank where he had been thrown. Fortunately, no one lost their life.

E. N. Cooke 1890 Sternwheeler, 416 tons, 150′ × 25′ × 6′ with an engine 16 ″ × 60 ″, built at Oregon City in 1871. Captain W. H. Patterson lost her on the Clackamas Rapids.

Enterprise 7/12/1915 Sternwheeler, 129 tons, 86′ long, built at Wenatchee in 1903. Captain McDermott. Ship foundered at Brewsters Ferry. See fire of *Columbia*, *North Star*, *Okanogan* and *Chelan*.

Europe 12/30/1907 Bark, French. See *Annie Comings*.

Fannie Troup 1874 Sternwheeler, 229 tons, 124′ long, built at Portland in 1864 by James Clinton and W. H. Troup, owned by OSNC. Captained by John W. Babbidge, she wrecked on the Cowlitz.

F. B. Jones 1907 Sternwheel, 303 tons, 143′ long, built at Portland in 1901. Rammed and sunk by tanker *Asuncion* on lower Columbia River; abandoned at Portland in 1937.

Fearless 8/10/1949 Oil screw, 68 tons, built in 1912. Burned on the Columbia below Longview.

Feltrie 2/17/1937 Italian motorship. Captain Mario Ranieri sailed on the Columbia near Prescott, Oregon, when the *Edward Luckenbach* rammed and sunk his ship. There seemed to have occurred a misinterpretation of whistle signals. The $185,000 cargo of silver was recovered almost before the ship settled in the mud. After repairs at a cost of $300,000, she sold to Pacific Fisheries for a mere $55,000. Re-named the *Clevedon*, the U.S. Army put her to work as a transport. At Yakatat, Alaska on January 13, 1942, she caught fire while carrying a cargo of munitions. The SS *Taku* towed her from the dock and shoved her ashore at a safe distance. The ship exploded, a total loss.

Flatboat 2/2/1851 The old keelboats and *bateaux* never enjoyed the honors due them as makers of Oregon history. Using sweeps, sails or paddles, these workhorses of the rivers carried immense loads hundreds of miles and, although hailed in eastern waters from Canada to Louisiana, they are seldom mentioned here. This particular vessel was owned and operated by McClure and Lemmons of Salem. The ship, caught in the narrows at Rock Islands, became a total loss. Her cargo consisted of 100 bushels of wheat, 1,000 bushels of potatoes, 100 bushels of oats, 400 lbs. of butter, 50 dozen eggs and 18 hogs, all bound for California. Undaunted by the wreck, Captain Lemmons later that day brought through two *bateaux*, each carried 250 bushels of wheat . . . c'mon, you Mike Fink fans, top that!

Flyer 1938 Steamer, Coeur d'Alene Lake, by fire. NFI.

Frederick K. Billings 7/1900 Sternwheeler, 749 tons, 200′ × 37′ × 6′, built at Celilo in 1880 and rebuilt several times. She finally foundered in the Columbia. NFI.

Gazelle 4/8/1854 Sidewheeler, 145′ long, owned by the Wallamette Falls Co. Captain Robert Hereford pulled the *Gazelle* into Canemah alongside the *Wallamet*. She had no sooner tied up before her engineer, Moses Turner, raced down the deck, climbed over the rail and hightailed it for parts unknown. Within moments, the *Gazelle* disintegrated and many an Oregonian suffered the loss of an ancestor. Moses Turner never returned to collect his wages. See Appendix "C" for casualty list. The ship's owners rebuilt her as the *Senorita* and used her for the Astoria run. In later years, a gale at the Cascades tore off and smashed her entire hurricane deck.

Gazelle 3/12/1885 Steamer. Captain Hiram Olney's ship burned for a total loss on the Stillaquamish River. NFI.

General Hubbard 2/16/1914 Steamship collided with the SS *Portland* and was repaired.

General Sherman 1899 Steam propeller, built at Coeur d'Alene in 1884. She sank near the Northern Pacific dock in 1893; Sanborn, McCarty and Shallis raised her and put her into service on the St. Joe run until 1899. Retired, she was eventually put to rest in Lake Coeur d'Alene. Her obituary appeared in the press, "Steamer General Sherman, in the Crystal Waters of Coeur d'Alene Lake you were Christened and to her waters we consign you."

George Burton 1948 Sternwheel. Hit a reef at the lower end of the Celilo Canal. The vessel was designated as a floating museum, but washed off in flood waters to sail over the canal wall and become a total loss.

George W. Elder 1/21/1905 Steamship, freighter, another fiasco built by Roach & Son at Chester, Pennsylvania. Launched in 1874, she measured 204′ × 38′ × 21′, 1710 gross tons. Under Captain Randall and pilot Snow, the nicknamed *George W. Roller* rammed a rock one-half mile south of Goble as she sailed en route to Portland. The vessel, with a spar and hurricane deck, was insured for $150,000, her 1100 tons of miscellaneous cargo for $50,000; ship and cargo declared a total loss. She was raised 16 months later.

Gerome 1905 Sternwheeler, aka *Gerone*, built at Wenatchee in 1902. She wrecked on the rapids of the upper river.

Gwendoline 1897 Sternwheel, 98′ long, built by Captain Armstrong in 1893. The *Gwendoline* followed the *Ruth* into Jennings Canyon; a log became caught in the *Ruth*'s sternwheel, jammed it and threw her into the path of the *Gwendoline*. Both ships collided and sank. The *Gwendoline* was refloated.

Gypsy 1900 Sternwheel, built at Portland in 1895, 101′ long, 213 tons. NFI.

Harrison no date Sternwheel, reported to be almost the same size as the *Georgie Oakes*. Burned at Brautigan's Dock, Coeur d'Alene.

Harvest Queen 11/19/1896 Sternwheeler, 846 tons, 200′ long, built at Celilo for OSNC. She sank when she hit the piling of a fishtrap at Oak Point, 60 miles south of Portland. She was raised and worked until 1899, at which time her machinery was removed and placed in *Harvest Queen II*, the first Columbia River sternwheeler to be equipped with a radio (1924).

Helen Hale 1913 Sternwheel, 52 tons, 100′ long, built at Kennewick in 1912. Lost by fire on the upper Columbia.

Henderson 12/11/1950 Sternwheel, towboat, built in 1912. While towing the decommissioned *Pierre Victory* to storage at Tongue Point, she struck a submerged object near the jetty at the lower end of Cottonwood Island.

Hercules 1933 Sternwheel. Wrecked at Three Mile Rapids at a spot known as Big Eddy where she tore out her bottom and sank in 170′ (???) of water.

Hercules 1/5/1934 Sternwheel, 560 tons, built in 1899. She foundered at Three Mile Rapids (probably same as previous listing).

Hermina 8/23/1888 Propeller, steamer, built in 1884. Lost by fire at Willow bar.

Hoosier 1853 Sternwheeler of a mere five tons at her birth and constructed, or assembled, from a lengthened ship's longboat and equipped with a piledriver's engine. On one occasion when the shaft broke, the engineer and a deckhand carried the pieces four miles into Salem for welding. The *Hoosier* was re-built innumerable times; each time she was cut in half for lengthening. Local jokers advised the carpenters to throw *both* ends away. At the time of her loss, her 6 ″ × 20 ″ engine was geared to 3 × 1. Captain Swain and pilot George Pease suffered much ridicule with their mechanical arrangement of a 3 × 1 which moved a spur wheel that (after an almost indefinite distribution of power) finally moved 2 or 3 sets of cogs connected to the drive shaft. She was heard buzzing long after she passed. Lost at an unknown location, if anyone cared.

Idaho 1915 Sidewheel, 800 hp, 147′ × 23′ with 22′ wheels, a dynamo capable of powering 125 lights and a capacity for 1,000 passengers. Launched 2/20/1903 with a price-tag cost of $45,000. The Joe Transportation Co. ship rammed and sank the *Boneta* in 1903. The *Idaho* burned and sank in Blackrock Bay in 1915 in Lake Coeur d'Alene.

Illitch 6/24/1944 Russian freighter, 2407 tons, 390′ × 45′, built in 1895 at Dumbarton as the *Emperor Nicholas II*, a gift from Germany to Russia and used as a yacht by Czar Nicholas. The communists converted the ship to a freighter and named her *Illitch*. The beautiful steel ship with a clipper bow and long bowsprit could not keep up with the ravages of hard use and time. While docked at Portland, she simply gave up; crewmen claimed they heard a "pop" and she began swallowing water. Down in 30 minutes with the loss of one female crew member, she was declared not worth the expense of raising. She was torched and blasted into the mud.

Imnaha 1903 Sternwheeler, built at Lewiston in 1903, 330 tons, 124′ long. Total loss. See story, "*Imnaha*."

Invader 4/1949 Steel towboat, 141 tons, 75′ × 24′ × 7.5′, 1200 hp. Caught fire in the middle of John Day Rapids and was totalled; her hull was saved.

Ione 2/4/1937 Sternwheel, 389 tons, 148′ long, built at Vancouver in 1911, owned by Western Transportation Co. at a cost of $50,000. The vessel struck Copleys Rock, Clackamas Rapids, near Starkweather Chute in the Willamette. The collision tore some thirty feet of planking from her starboard hull. The crew lashed a barge to her wounded side in an attempt to keep her afloat and upright, but their efforts failed. She rolled while the men were transferring 400 tons of rolled paper products.

Isabel 1/22/1890 Steamer, 201 tons, 120′ × 21′ × 5′, built at Salem in 1885. Ship and her cargo of bricks went under at Sellwood.

James Clinton 4/23/1861 Sternwheel. Sparks from a midnight fire in the warehouse and flour mills on the Linn side at Oregon City set this little gal on fire; she burned to the water's edge. She was the first steamboat in Oregon to be lost by such a cause. Her engines went into the *Union*. Built in 1856 at Canemah, she was the first steamer to ascend the Willamette as far

as Eugene. She arrived amid much fanfare on 3/12/1857, having dodged snags for three days above Corvallis. On her return voyage, she was loaded with wheat, the sale of which nearly paid for her construction. John Gibson Cochran, Leo White and James Miller captained her at various times.

J. D. Farrell 6/1898 Sternwheel, 359 tons, 130′ × 26′ × 4.5′, built at Jennings, Montana in 1897. The very plush river steamer sported electricity and bathrooms. Captain McCormack lost his ship to a hurricane in Jennings Canyon.

J. N. Teal 10/22/1907 Sternwheel, 513 tons, 160′. She was the first lower-river steamer to reach Lewiston, Idaho. Captain Arthur Riggs, in the employ of the Regulator Co., attempted to control docking at Hood River in 1915 by renting space at the dock, tying up the largest barge he could find and thus effectively limit tie-up space for other ships. Open River Line tied the *J. N. Teal* to the offending barge, pulled the throttle wide and yanked the barge, along with several bitts and pilings, out to the river. A dock fight started, the sheriff arrived and the docks were once again opened to regular traffic. The *J. N. Teal* burned at Portland.

John Day Queen Sternwheel, 40′ × 10′ × 1′, built in 1895 by Charles Clarno. As the only steamer on the John Day at Clarno, she served as a ferry until the bridge was built. Clarno attempted in 1897 to bring his ship downriver, but failed at the first set of rapids. The wreck occurred 109 miles south of the Columbia at an elevation of 1,290 feet, the highest steamboat wreck in Oregon.

J. Ordway 1/8/1890 Steamer lost by fire at Weidler's Mills, Portland. NFI.

Kiyus 1866 Sternwheeler, 140′, built at Celilo in 1863. NFI.

Kootenai 1898 Sternwheeler, abandoned and sunk at Three Mile Point. See story, "Kootenai Barge."

Leona 1912 Sternwheel, 179 tons, built at Portland in 1901, 105′, ex-*McMinnville*. Lost by fire on the Willamette.

Lewiston 7/12/1922 Sternwheeler, 513 tons, 165′, built in 1894 and re-built in 1905, both times at Riparia, Wash. She sank once in the Snake River Rapids and was raised. While tied alongside the *Spokane*, she and her neighbor burned at Lewiston.

Logger 1938 Sternwheel, 156′, 750 hp. Sank at Shaver mooring, Portland. Dismantled.

Lot Whitcomb 2/1853 See story, "Hold the Presses."

Lucia Mason 1891 Sternwheeler, 140 tons, 109′ × 20′ × 4.2′, built at St. Helens, Oregon in 1883. The old gal worked the Lewis River for eight years, sinking now and then, but still making money until her final loss.

Lurline 11/21/1906 Sternwheel. Rammed and sunk by the *Cascade* at Rainier.

Madeline 3/23/1925 Sternwheel. Snagged and sunk on the Cowlitz near Rainier with the Oregon Agriculture College Band aboard; they barely escaped with their lives.

Magnolia 3/7/1851 Sailship grounded in Tongue Point Channel at same spot as the *Aurora*. NFI.

Marion 5/20/1891 Steamer broke up over the rapids on the upper Columbia. NFI.

Mascot 1911 Sternwheel, 299 tons, 140′ long, built at Portland in 1908. Lost by fire in unknown location.

*May 2/10/1943 Tug, 50′ long, used as a shipyard ferry to Vancouver. Capsized when leaving the dock with 19 aboard; nine died. The vessel was built in 1910 at Randolph, Oregon and owned by Russell Towboat and Moorage Co. Captain C. Harvey was in charge at the time of the accident. An indictment for failure to maintain a vessel in seaworthy condition was placed against the owner.

Messenger 1879 Sternwheel, 136 tons, 91′ long, built at Empire City, Oregon in 1872. Lost by fire at unknown location.

*M. F. Henderson 1911 Sternwheeler, 534 tons, 159′ long, built at Portland in 1901 and owned by the Shaver Transportation Co. En route Astoria-Portland with a Standard Oil barge in tow when rammed by the *Daniel Kern*, a tug towing rock barges to the Columbia jetty. She capsized to her side in shallow water and was dismantled.

Multnomah 6/1929 Steam schooner, wood, 969 tons, built by McCormick at the St. Helens yard in October 1912...the first of 42 vessels to be constructed there during the next 15 years. The ship sent a distress call when she ran into difficulty on the Columbia bar on June 16, 1929. The Coast Guard had their hands full with the wreck of the *Laurel*, but managed to aid both vessels and removed fifteen passengers from the foundering *Multnomah*. Quick repairs kept the ship afloat while she was escorted over the bar to relative safety. The damage left her unfit for sea duty and she was moved upriver to St. Helens where she burned, whether by accident or design remains unknown. A wreck erroneously identified as the *Multnomah* reportedly lies at Lat. 46°53′00″, Long. 124°20′00″ in 180 feet of water. I have no idea as to the true identity of the wreck.

Norma 1910 Sternwheeler, built at Huntington, Oregon in 1891 by J. D. Miller and Jacob Kamm. Captain W. P. Gray crammed the *Norma* full of staging lumber to ward off the blows of sharp rocks. He traversed down the Snake River in much the same fashion as the *Shoshone* and wrecked at the mouth of the Deschutes.

*North Star 4/1898 Sternwheeler, 250 tons, 130′ × 26′ × 4′, built at Jennings, Montana in 1897. Wrecked in Jennings Canyon.

North Star 7/8/1915 Sternwheeler, 199 tons, 100′ long, built at Wenatchee in 1907, owned by the Columbia & Okanogan Steamboat Co. She lay tied up and for sale at the foot of 5th Street at Wenatchee.

Captain McDermott was interested in purchasing the ship, but had not yet closed the deal with her owners, who planned on paying the insurance premium on the rest of their fleet with monies received from the sale of the *North Star*. To their misfortune, a fire broke out on the *North Star* and quickly spread to their *Chelan* moored along side. A hot, July wind fanned the sparks and they soon devoured the next ship in line, the *Columbia*. By the time the fire department extinguished all the flaming ships, the *Okanogan* lay in ashes alongside her sisters. The distressed company hopelessly foundered when the *Enterprise* went to the bottom at Brewsters Ferry a few days later. Their last steamer, the *St. Paul*, went up in smoke later in the year.

North Star 1929 A popular name for river steamers. This one was owned by J. C. White and later by Fred Herrick of Idaho. In the employ of Potlatch Forests Co., the ship tied up along side the *Boneta* at St. Joe, Idaho. Her crew, anxious to see the new vaudeville act in town, called it a day and ran for the theater. Apparently no one banked her fires and both she and the *Boneta* went up in flames.

*N. S. Bently 12/25/1886 Sternwheel, 150′ × 32′ × 4½′, engines of 16″ × 60″. Captain J. L. Smith in command when she sank at Salem with 3,800 bushels of wheat. She was raised.

Oakland 10/6/1912 A small passenger steamer on the upper Klamath Lake. She capsized in a gale; Captain Reed and others were fortunate to be rescued by the steamer *White Pelican*.

*Ocklahama 1886 Sternwheel towboat, 152′ × 31′ × 8′, engines 21″ × 72″, owned by the Willamette Transportation Co., a subsidiary of the powerful OSNC. This hard worker had towed more ships than any other boat on the river. She sustained damage by the capsizing of the British bark *Alliance* at Portland.

Okanogan 7/8/1915 Sternwheeler, 432 tons, 137′ long, built at Wenatchee in 1907. See *North Star* of 1915.

Olympion 1906 Sidewheel, iron steamer, sister to *Alaskan*, built at Wilmington, Delaware in 1883. NFI.

Oregon 1854 Sidewheeler, 100′, built at Fairfield, Oregon in 1852. Snagged and sank below Salem in eight feet of water. The *Gazelle* quickly moved alongside to salvage her freight; while doing so, she bumped the *Oregon* hard enough to dislodge her from her perch. She drifted downstream, hit another rock and broke in two.

*Oregona 12/10/1909 Steamer, owned by Oregon Transportation Co. Struck a snag on the Willamette and beached 3 miles above the Weston landing.

Oregona 12/26/1913 Steamer en route from Corvallis on her last run of the season. Under the command of Captain Bluhm, she rammed the government dredge *Champoeg*, which lay at anchor. The *Oregona* received a three-foot gash below her waterline and headed for shore. She struck the Meldrums bar and settled a short distance below Clackamas Rapids.

Orient 1894 Sternwheeler, 587 tons, 154' long, built at Portland in 1875. She struck the Morrison Street bridge in 1893, sank and was raised. The following year she hung up on a rock in the Cowlitz and was left high and much too dry when the water fell. The crew attempted to get her off, but somehow managed instead to ignite her, a total loss by fire.

Oswego 2/11/1902 Screw steamer, built in 1883. Sank at Oak Point on the Columbia. NFI.

Pacific 7/1861 Steamer. Struck Coffin Rock and run ashore to prevent her sinking. NFI.

Portland 3/17/1857 Sidewheel steamer, 90' long, built at Portland in 1853. She was swept over the falls at Oregon City and into the basin of the Clackamas. Captain Archibald Jamieson and two others died. Jamieson belonged to a real steamboat family; of his three brothers, only one managed to die in bed. One brother went up in the explosion of the *Cariboo* at Victoria, British Columbia and the other was killed in the explosion of the *Yale* on the Frasier River.

Portland 9/3/1922 Steam dredge. Rammed by the steamer *Santa Clara*, went to the bottom of the Willamette. Three dead.

Pronto 11/28/1918 Towboat owned by Port of Portland. Rammed by the 8,800 ton *West View*; she sank in 5 minutes at Municipal Terminal, Dock #1. Three saved.

Ranger 11/4/1869 Steamer, 199-ton sternwheeler, 113' × 20' × 4' with 2 decks, built at Portland in 1865. Captain J. N. Fisher sailed her en route to Rainier from Portland; she caught fire and was totalled at Sauvie Island.

R. C. Young 7/22/1892 Sternwheeler, 108 tons, 83' long, built at Salem in 1892. Burned at Dove's Landing.

Regulator 1/24/1906 Sternwheeler, 508 tons. After being hauled out and placed on the ways at St. Johns, she caught fire and exploded, killing two.

Relief date unknown Steamer of 84 tons, 77' long, ex-*Columbia*, built at Blalock, Oregon in 1906 for the Open River Transportation Co. She settled quietly through the ice there and was never raised.

Rescue 1867 Sternwheeler, 113' × 20' × 4'. Lost by fire while on the Cowlitz, en route Rainier-Portland.

Resolute 4/12/1872 Tug, steam, 57' × 12' × 3', built at Portland in 1870. Her boiler exploded, blew downward like a torpedo and instantly sank the vessel at Portland.

Robarts 6/15/1948 Oil screw of 58 tons, built in 1887. Ship foundered in a slough at Portland. NFI.

Robert Young 1934 Sternwheel, foundered on the Willamette. NFI.

Rosetta 2/2/1883 Steamer. Struck a sinker on the Willamette while en route Knappton-St. Johns; her smoke stack was visible above water for many years.

Rustler 1892 Sidewheeler, 90 tons, 79' long, built at Portland in 1882. Engineer John E. Nelson died when the ship went down at Goble.

Ruth 1897 Sternwheel, 100 tons, 131' long, built at Jennings in 1896 by Louis Pacquet. She collided with the *Gwendoline*.

Saint Paul 1915 Sternwheeler, 208 tons, 116' long, built at Trinidad, Washington in 1906. Lost by fire on the Columbia.

Sally 1796 Brig. Supposedly the first casualty in the Columbia River. An ancient wooden block identified as having come from the wreck of the *Sally* is displayed at Astoria's Clatsop County Historical Museum; however, my search for any records of this wreck proved fruitless.

Santa Catalina 10/18/1914 Freighter, oil, 420' × 53.9' × 29', 6309 gross tons, built in 1913 for W. R. Grace Co. at Philadelphia. The ship, en route New York-Portland, was one of the first through the Panama Canal and, at that time, one of the largest ships to navigate the Columbia. She suffered a fire and explosion in her engine room when twenty miles from Portland; fireman Gus Johnson was trapped and killed in the engine room. Captain J. F. Rose beached his stricken ship, but the cases of ammunition which formed a portion of her 2000 tons of mixed cargo exploded. The $700,000 vessel was repaired at Portland for a cost of $300,000.

Sarah Dixon 1/18/1912 Sternwheel, built in 1892, rated at 368 tons, 161' long, owned by Shaver Transportation Co. and named for Shaver's wife. After her explosion at Kalama which killed Captain Fred Stinson, 1st mate Arthur Monical and fireman Silas Knowles, she was rebuilt as a towboat and machine ship. The *Sarah Dixon* went up in smoke in 1926 at Portland.

Sedalia 7/1/1874 Steam tug, built at Astoria in 1873 by E. C. Spedden, 2 masts, rated approximately 44 tons. Burned at Kalama.

Selkirk 5/15/1906 Sternwheeler, 223 tons, 111' long, built at Wenatchee in 1899, owned by Columbia & Okanogan Steamboat Co. Wrecked at Rock Island Rapids.

Senator 5/6/1875 Sternwheel, 298 tons, 132' long, built in 1863 by John Thomas at Milwaukie for the Peoples Transportation Co. The *Senator* sat quietly chuffing away waiting her departure from the foot of Alder Street, Portland, while Captain Dan McGill stood on the deck conversing with Clackamas County Legislator Joseph Locey. Fireman George Warner carefully checked his water gauges and crewmen Cosgrove and Crowley took in decklines as passenger Klaus Beckman watched the men going about their business. Suddenly the pilothouse to the king-post, including McGill, Locey, Warner, Cosgrove, Crowley and Beckman, was swept clean in one gut-ripping explosion. The *Vancouver* raced to the *Senator*'s side and removed the survivors before the out-of-control vessel drifted into the current and beached at Albina.

Sesnon #3 11/14/1924 Barge, foundered in the Snake River at Columbia.

Shoalwater 5/1853 Sidewheeler, 93 tons, built at Canemah in 1853, owned by Captain Leonard White. She remained afloat after her explosion at Rock Island in which no one was injured. Rebuilt and renamed *Fenix*.

Shoshone 11/1874 Sternwheeler, 300 tons, 136' × 27' × 4.6', 6" × 48" engine. See story "Shoshone Sleigh Ride."

Sidi 3/1/1874 Bark, French, 276 tons, owned by George Warren and William Koerner. Captain Cometoux's ship went down somewhere in the Columbia, refloated by Captain William Koerner, placed under American registry and renamed *Sea Waif*.

Skookum 11/17/1927 Tug owned by St. Helens Towing Co. Sank at St. Helens dock in 40' of water.

Sol Thomas 1/4/1885 Tug, steam. Captain James Hill stood aft as he prepared to depart Luse Wharf at Empire City with a schooner in tow. The *Sol Thomas* suddenly exploded, raining bits of wreckage and portions of seven bodies over a goodly portion of the waterfront. Captain Hill, although injured when the blast hurled him into a pile of hawser, survived.

Spokane 5/1895 Sternwheeler, 400 tons, 125' long, built in 1891 at Bonners Ferry, Idaho, owned by Columbia-Kootenai Navigation Co. Both cargo and vessel destroyed by fire at either Kalso, British Columbia or Kelso, Washington. Most likely it occured at the British Columbia location.

Spokane 4/5/1887 This popularly named ship was built on the Snake River by A. H. Butler in 1882 and put to work on the Snake, Flathead, Pend Oreille and Kootenai lakes. Her pilot discovered the mistake of taking his passenger's advice during the *Spokane's* maiden trip up and then down the Coeur d'Alene River; she struck a snag and capsized, drowning City Clerk of Spokane Mr. J. C. Hanna, Col. N. J. Higgins of Bangor, Maine, L. Pike from Portland, Edward Jerome of Lewiston and one unknown. Raised and re-named *Irene*.

Spokane 1938 Steamer on Coeur d'Alene Lake capsized. Five drowned. Possibly the previously listed vessel.

State of Washington 6/23/1919 Sternwheeler, built at Puget Sound in 1889, owned by Shaver Transportation Co., 605 tons, 170' long. Captain Harry (Casey) L. Chase, with *Barge #93* in tow, sailed en route Astoria-Portland when his vessel exploded just north and slightly upriver from Tongue Point. The ship went down; pilot Perly Crawford sailed up, over the barge's mast to land in the water on her opposite side and the airborne boiler sallied forth on a 1000' trajectory. The fireman died. Six persons sustained injuries.

S. T. Church 12/1/1878 Steamer reported as breaking up at Government Island at Gervais Slough on the Willamette. NFI.

Swan 3/29/1930 Barge, doubled-decked party boat propelled upriver by the tug *Dix*, under command of Captain Jack Mitchell. The *Swan*, owned and operated by Captain Dick Billand, ran without lights as she returned 286 party-goers from the much-publicized grand-opening celebration of the Longview-Rainier bridge. A sudden ramming of the darkened *Swan* by the schooner *Davenport* opposite Warrior Rock, St. Helens, resulted in eight deaths. Captain Mitchell of the tug *Dix* was held responsible for the tragic accident and lost his license for one year. The *Dix* and *Swan* were salvaged.

Telephone 1/5/1892 Sternwheeler, 386 tons, 172' long, built at Portland in 1885. She burned in 1887 and was rebuilt to 500 tons, 200' in length. She sank after striking a revetment in the fog at the mouth of the Willamette. Her passengers were taken to Coon Island. The vessel eventually sold in San Francisco.

Three Mile Point This is not the name of a ship or steamer, but is a location said to be the gravesite of several old Coeur d'Alene Lake steamers. Known as the "Steamboat Graveyard," the area is believed to hold the bones of:

Bonanza, NFI.

Colfax, propeller steamer. NFI.

Harrison, sternwheeler. NFI.

Samson, tug. NFI.

Saint Maries, tug, 85'. NFI.

All were scuttled.

Toledo 1896 Sternwheel, 226 tons, 128' long, built in 1878 at Portland. Lost somewhere on the Willamette.

Traveler 12/3/1878 Steamer. While descending the fog-shrouded Willamette en route from Oregon City, she was hit amidship by the *McMinnville* and beached near Milwaukie.

Umatilla 1941 Sternwheeler, built at Celilo in 1928, 551 tons, 160' long. Lost at an unknown location.

Venture 1859 Steamer, built at upper Cascades by R. R. Thompson and Laurence Coe. The vessel sailed out and over the upper Cascades; raised and re-named a more prosaic *Umatilla*.

Veto #1 9/9/1887 Steam ferryboat, sidewheel, built at Portland in 1879. Burned at Sellwood, Oregon.

Victoria 4/8/1846 Fort Vancouver Britishers reported the *Victoria's* demise for publication in the *Spectator*: "The beautiful and elegantly fitted yacht Victoria capsized and sank at Vancouver on the Columbia. Cargo wheat most of which was saved. There was no loss of life H. B. S. Modeste sent boats to the rescue..." A bit of rivalry seems to have existed between the Americans and the British, for the editor chose to further comment, "...the Victoria was anything but 'beautiful and elegant.'"

Wallamet 4/8/1854 Steamer, heavily damaged by explosion. See *Gazelle*.

Welsh Prince 5/28/1922 Steam freighter, 2322 tons, screw, built at Bristol, England in 1871 by the Sotherland Co., owned by Furness-Prince Line. Pilot Sullivan guided the *Welsh Prince* through the stream about 10 miles upriver from Astoria when he collided with pilot Pearson and the American-Hawaiian *Iowan*. The *Welsh Prince*, ignited by a boiler explosion, went to the bottom in 30 minutes. Seven died. The ship, with her cargo of lumber and steel, proved too difficult to raise and was dynamited.

W. E. Mahoney 9/4/1947 Tug, owned by Diesel Towing Co. of Portland and named in honor of Bill Mahoney, Marine Editor of the *Oregonian*. Captain Robert Osborne found his 1926 vessel rammed and sunk in the Columbia River, just off shore south of St. Helens, by the *SS Anna Shaw*, a liberty ship en route Seattle-Vancouver.

Wenatchee 1901 Sternwheeler, 77 tons, 79' long, built at Wenatchee in 1899. Burned on the upper river.

Westport 12/18/1886 Sidewheeler, 201 tons, 118' × 22' × 5.6', engines 10″ × 16″, built at Westport, Oregon in 1878. Burned at Westport.

*W. H. Pringle 10/9/1906 Sternwheel, 575 tons, 166' long, built at Pasco, Washington in 1901. Ship foundered on the Entiat Rapids.

Willamette Chief 11/1894 Sternwheel, 693 tons, 163' × 31' × 6', engine 20″ × 60″, built at Willamette, Oregon in 1874. Lost by fire at unreported location.

Wilmington 2/5/1893 Steamer, owned by the notorious smuggler Merchants Steamship Co. Captain Peter H. Grim saw his vessel and cargo of lime go up in flames, then sink near Linnton on the Columbia, a total loss.

*Woodland 3/27/1926 Sternwheeler. Captain George M. Walker's command rolled 1½ miles below Wilsonville and sank in 20' of water.

Yakima 1875 Sternwheeler, 455 tons, 150' × 29' × 5', built at Celilo in 1864, a very elegant river steamer with 3 decks and 26 staterooms. Captain Coe steamed her from Celilo to Lewiston in 41 hours and 35 minutes in June, 1867, an amazing time in spite of running against the current and through many rapids. The *Yakima*, while heading downstream at John Day Rapids, hit a rock so forcibly that her bottom tore from bow to aft boiler and gave engineer Peter DeHuff the fright of his life. The ship was turned toward the Oregon shore, but sank. When raised, she proved too badly damaged to be of any further value.

Yaquina 5/25/1882 Steamship, a new vessel owned by Z. J. Hatch & S. Tuthill. While berthed at Pacific Dock in Portland, her 3,600 barrels of lime ignited. She was cut loose and left to drift. Captain Denny and most of his crew fought a losing battle against the blazing inferno. They eventually towed her to shore and scuttled the $36,000, uninsured vessel.

The result of too little ballast and no camels (t'gall'nt masts or spars lashed, floating to the waist of the ship) to steady her. The British Alliance *rolled onto the steamer* Ocklahama *at Portland.*

(*Oregon Historical Society*)

Asotin *crushed in ice near Arlington, Oregon.* (*Oregon Historical Society*)

With her wheel completely out of water, the Frederick Billings *finally came to the end of her line at Blalock.*
(Oregon Historical Society)

It was planned to make the George Burton *into a floating museum. Disaster cancelled all hopes in spring flood of 1948.*
(Oregon Historical Society)

George W. Elder *on the rocks near Goble, Oregon. Steamer* Ocklahama *standing by. Freighter went down in 1905 and was raised 16 months later. Due to poor sailing qualities, she was also known as the "George W. Roller."*　　　　　　　　　　　　　　　　　　　　　　　　　　　　*(Oregon Historical Society)*

Steamer Gypsy wrecked at Independence, Oregon.　　　　　　　*(Oregon Historical Society)*

Twin sisters, twin cities, the Lewiston *and* Spokane *lived, worked and died together.*

(Oregon Historical Society)

Lewistonites saw two of their favorite steamers go up in smoke July 12, 1922.

(Oregon Historical Society)

Evenly settled, the Lurline *receives an assist from unknown steamer in background.*
(Columbia River Maritime Museum)

Norma *made it safely down the Snake River but ran into trouble at the mouth of the Deschutes.*
(Oregon Historical Society)

N. S. Bently *resting quietly at Albany.* *(Oregon Historical Society)*

Down for good at Blalock, Oregon. *(Oregon Historical Society)*

The Sarah Dixon, *destroyed by fire while undergoing renovation.* (Oregon Historical Society)

July 23, 1920. Astorians were rocked by concussion of boiler explosion, then the State of Washington *disappeared beneath the Columbia.* (Oregon Historical Society)

Heavy fog, a grinding crash and seven men's lives ended in the wreck of the Welsh Prince.
(Columbia River Maritime Museum)

In spite of a cautious captain, the Welsh Prince *was rammed by the steamer* Iowan.
(Columbia River Maritime Museum)

Graveyard on the Coquille. Practically nothing remains of the once beautiful steamers Myrtle, Telegraph *and the* Dora. *(Oregon Historical Society)*

Many fine ships like the Levi G. Burgess *were driven onto sandbars in the Columbia River and burned for their metal.* *(Oregon Historical Society)*

Faithful to the end, the old Klamath, *waiting for a cargo that will never come. The location is near Pelican Bay Lumber Co.*
(Oregon Historical Society)

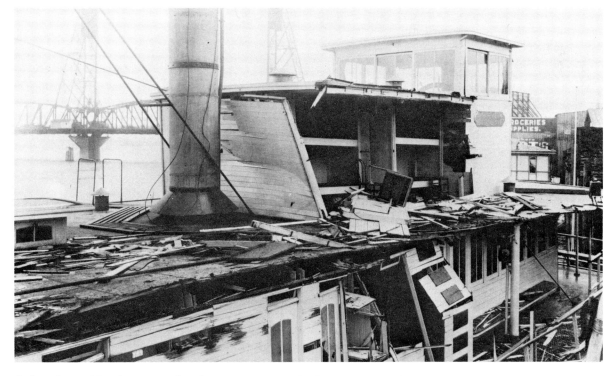

"That danged bridge jumped right in front of me." The steamer Grahamona.

(Oregon Historical Society)

Appendix A

Passengers and Crew of the Brother Jonathan

B. Mathewson — body recovered at Chetco, Oregon
Mrs. Luckey, two children
Major E. W. Eddy, USA
G. Canel
Moses Beitier
Joseph Orseli
H. Definnie
George W. Annis
J. Strong, body recovered
S. P. Craig
Mary A. Tweedale (Altree) — saved
Patrick Dwyer
John Adams
2 unknown Indians
R. S. Manly
Henry Abrams
Thomas Gullan
C. Bisner
Isaac Weil, body recovered
Ed DeRutte
Mrs. Mina Bernhardt and child, saved
Mrs. Martha Stott and son, saved
Mrs. Martha E. Wilder, saved
Mr. Leach, orderly to Gen. Wright, body recovered
E. J. Lount (Lonate), body recovered
D. Parrish, body recovered
Joseph Lord (Wells Fargo agent)
J. Anchoine, body recovered
William Perkins, body recovered
Robert M. Frazer
John R. Craig
William Bilinsky (Billmitsky)
J. S. Bonn
Mrs. Woodlock
Conrad Adams
Fred A. Pound
Gilman Cilndruaid
James Lynch
A. Ingraham, M.D., USA
James P. Richards, body recovered
Victor Smith
Miss E. P. Snow
James Connell
J. G. Gar and wife
Miss Shiser, nurse, body recovered
M. L. Hefron
George Pollock (survivor of *Washoe* explosion in California), body recovered
Charles C. Northrop

J. C. Hunsaker
Mrs. A. C. Brooks
Miss Hensley
William Logan and wife
Mrs. C. Fountani, daughter and small child
D. C. Rowell, wife and four children — Mr. and Mrs. bodies recovered
A. A. Stone, wife and infant — Mrs. body recovered
Mrs. J. Stanford
Mrs. James Church
Mrs. Wendell and child
P. Leffer
Gen. G. H. Wright and wife, bodies recovered
Lt. E. D. Waite, USA
Miss Mary Berry, body recovered at Eureka
S. Meyer
David McHendle
A. L. Styles and wife
W. M. Logan and servant
James Nesbit, body recovered seven miles at sea
James Trites (Frietes), body recovered
M. Crawford
T. Dawson
Miss Mary Place
Mrs. Stackpole, infant and young child
J. Wheil
Anna Craig
Mrs. Lee and infant, saved
A. C. Henry, Surveyor of Washington Territory
L. G. Tuttle
B. H. Stone, wife and infant, Mr. and Mrs. bodies recovered
Capt. Chaddock, USRS
Joe Lane
Mrs. Jno. C. Kennan and seven ladies
S. B. Morgan
S. N. Luckey, wife and child
Miss Forbes
Charles M. Belden
Albert Micklett
George Wedekind
Joseph Berton
Thomas Moyle and wife
J. S. Geddes

Approximately 25 passengers came aboard without signing the register prior to departure. Tickets were purchased aboard the ship while en route, a common practice in those days.

222

Crew of the *Brother Jonathan*

Samuel J. DeWolf, Captain
W. H. Allen, 1st Officer
J. D. Cambell, 2nd Officer
James Patterson, 3rd Officer, saved
John S. Benton, purser
Albert Dyer, freight clerk, body recovered
Elijah Mott, chief engineer
J. Francis, 2nd engineer
G. White, 1st engineer
William Anderson, oiler
G. W. Hill (Hall), 3rd engineer, saved
Patrick Lynn (Linn), fireman, saved
A. Collenburg, fireman
Frederick Malers, fireman
Arthur Harvey, fireman
J. Thompson, fireman
William Lowery, fireman, saved
John Hensley, fireman
John Gorman, coal passer
John Clinton, coal passer
John Hilton, coal passer
James Perkins, seaman
Jacob Yates, seaman, saved
Henry Walker, seaman
A. Gonsels (Gonzalas), seaman
William Penn, seaman
L. Domingo, seaman

J. Silva, seaman
William Foster, seaman
Federick Douglas, seaman
James Fowler, seaman
D. Deas, pantryman
Thomas Tierney, porter
Henry Miller, baker, saved
Ed Shields, waiter, saved
Charles Rice, waiter
Manuel Herrlia, waiter
C. F. Laurend, watchman
Richard Daulton, steward
H. G. Brown, steward
David Farrell, steerage steward, saved
John Miller, pantryman
Charles Law, cook, body recovered
James Law, cook
Henry Lee, cook
C. Stevenson, stewardess
John Hutton, cabin boy
Armand Lee, cabin boy
Edward Franklin, cabin boy
Lewis Johnson, cabin boy
John Foster, cabin boy
Mateo Salinas, cabin boy
Steven Moran, cabin boy, saved
John Welch, cabin boy

Crew of the Alaskan

Lost

Seymour T. Weeks, 2nd Officer
Walter Swain, Chief engineer
A. G. Mitchell, 1st Asst. Eng.
Albert Rahles, Steward
James Stevenson, Watchman
W. Emerson
James McGeary, Watertender
T. Wallace, Oiler
Wm. Hunter
J. N. Graham
J. N. O. Brown, Quartermaster
Tom Gilligan
Patrick Manning
Patrick Conner
P. E. Wheelman
John Carrington
J. Ahern
Wm. Collins
Henry Mahon
Patrick Sullivan
John Welch, Coal passer
Charles Albert, Coal passer
William Johnson, Porter
James Keweley, Cook
J. Monaghan, Waiter
Fred Norman, Baker
B. Bernhardt
Walfred Johnson
Andy Venson
R. Jewell
W. Denny
J. Roscoe
W. Norris
Theodore Froid
3 unknown stowaways

Saved

R. E. Howes, Captain
G. W. Wood, 1st Officer
M. McLean, Water tender
M. Kellerher, Fireman
Edward Sharpless
G. H. Ross
E. Ward, Pantryman
James McKinley
Emile Wenzle
E. A. Carlson, Messboy
H. Johnson
J. Murray, Coal passer
Edward Barnes, Coal passer
George Shielderup, Died shortly after rescue

Passengers and Crew of the Gazelle

Dead

Rev. J. P. Miller of Albany
Judge Burch of Luckiamute
Mr. Morgan
Mr. Hill
James White
Dan Lowe
David Fuller
C. Wadsworth
David Page
John Clemens, pilot of the *Gazelle*
J. M. Fudge, pilot of the *Wallamet*
Jacob Bloomer
Mr. Hatch
J. K. Miller
Mike McGee
Henry Traul, steward of the *Gazelle*
Mr. Plant, engineer of the *Gazelle*
three unknowns

Injured

Mrs. J. P. Miller
Charles Garchuer
Robert Pentland
Miss Pell
C. Dobbins
R. Shortess
B. F. Newby
Robert Hereford, Capt. of the *Gazelle*
John Boyd, mate of the *Gazelle*
James Partlow, pilot
John Dailey, cabin boy of the *Gazelle*
16 unidentified

Passengers and Crew of the General Warren

Passengers

R. J. Provin
Thomas Mickle
Alanson Pomeroy
John F. Duncan
A. Cook
D. O. Buck
A. Stanly
John Dellon
W. H. Hart
Benson
Randolph
Montgomery
Miller
Fuller
Luther
Schloss
and 17 others, unknown

Crew

Charles Thompson, Captain
Johnson, Purser
O'Neil, Engineer
George Hatch, Porter
Nelson, Steward
Jamieson, Steward
T. Harvey, Cook
R. E. Hutchinson, Cook
W. Bruen, Seaman
P. Turen, Seaman
G. Williams, Seaman
H. T. York, Seaman

Left in ship's boat and saved

George Flavel, Pilot
J. G. Wall, Passenger
E. L. Finch, Passenger
Henry Marsh, Passenger
Matt Nolan, Passenger
James Nolan, Passenger
Edward Beverly, 1st Mate
William Irons, 2nd Mate
James Murray, Seaman
Isaac Sparrow, Seaman

Bibliography

Ashworth, William. *Hell's Canyon — the deepest gorge on earth.* New York: Hawthorne Books, Inc., 1977.

———. *Daily Astorian Newspaper.* Astoria, Oregon.

Baarslag, Karl. *Coast Guard to the Rescue.* New York: Farrar and Rinehart, Inc., 1937.

Beckham, Stephen D. *Coos Bay Pioneer Period 1851-1890.* Coos Bay, Oregon: Arago Books.

Blacker, Irwin. *Hakluyt's Voyages.* Reprint. New York: Viking Press, 1965.

Botsworth, J. B. *English Society in the Eighteenth Century.* New York: 1924.

Cook, Warren L. *Flood Tide of Empire.* New Haven, Connecticut: Yale University Press, 1973.

Cooney, D. M. *A Chronology of United States Navy 1775-1865.* F. Watts, 1965.

Eisenchiml, Otto and Ralph Newman. *Civil War — American Iliad.* Bobbs and Merril, 1947.

———. *Espinosa y Tello, a Spanish Voyage to Vancouver.* Translation by Cecil Jane. Condon, Oregon: Argonaut Press, 1930.

Falk, Edwin A. *Perry to Pearl Harbor.* New York: Doubleday-Doran, 1943.

Fischer, Anton Otto. *Foc'sle Days.* Charles Scribner and Sons, 1947.

Franchere, Gabriel. *Adventure of Astoria.* Oklahoma: University of Oklahoma Press, 1967.

Gerhard, Peter. *Pirates on the West Coast of New Spain.* A. H. Clark Company, 1960.

Gibbs, James. *Pacific Graveyard.* Portland, Oregon: Binford and Mort, 1964.

Hanson, Inez Stafford. *Life on Clatsop.*

Holt, Ruby El. *Steamboats in Timber.* Portland, Oregon: Binford and Mort, 1952.

Irving, Washington. *Astoria.* Portland, Oregon: Binford and Mort.

———. *Lincoln County Lore.* Lincoln City, Oregon: Lincoln City Historical Society.

Maraini, Fosco. *Meeting with Japan.* New York: Viking Press, 1959.

McKee, Alexander. *Mary Rose.* New York: Stein and Day, 1974.

Mills, Randall A. *Stern Wheelers up Columbia.* California: Pacific Book, 1947.

Morton, Harry. *The Wind Commands.* British Columbia: University of British Columbia, 1975.

Napier, William. *Pacific Voyages.* New York: Doubleday, 1973.

Newell, Gordon and Joe Williamson. *Pacific Lumber Ships.* Seattle, Washington: Superior, 1960.

Newell, Gordon and Joe Williamson. *Pacific Tugboats.* Seattle, Washington: Superior, 1958.

Newell, Gordon. *Lewis and Dryden History of Pacific Northwest,* vol. II. Seattle, Washington: Superior, 1966.

O'Mera, Walter. *The Savage Country.* Cambridge, Massachusetts: Houghton Mifflin, 1960.

———. *Oregon Historical Quarterly,* vols. I through LXXXIII. Portland, Oregon: Oregon Historical Society.

———. *Oregon Statesman Newspaper.* July, August, November, December, 1865.

Orita, Senji and Joseph Harrington. *I-Boat Captain.* Canoga Park, California: Major Books (paperback), 1976.

Peterson, E. and A. Powers. *A Century of Coos and Curry.* Portland, Oregon: Binford and Mort, 1952.

Rasky, Frank. *The Polar Voyages.* McGraw-Hill-Reyerson, Ltd., 1976.

Shrader, Graham F. *Phantom War in the Northwest.* Oregon: Oregon State University Press, 1969.

Shurz, William L. *Manila Galleon.* E. P. Dutton, 1939.

———. *State Journal of Eugene.* Eugene, Oregon: July-December, 1865

Timmen, Fritz. *Blow for the Landing.* Idaho: Caxton Printers, 1973.

Verrilly, A. Hyatt. *The Real Story of the Whaler.* New York-London: D. Appleton, 1916.

Webber, Bert. *Retaliation.* Oregon: Oregon State University Press, 1975.

White, John R. *A Chronology of Upper Willamette Valley Prehistory,* vol. 44, #3. American Antiquity, 1979.

Williams, L. R. *Our Pacific County.* Washington: Raymond Herald, 1930.

Winther, Oscar O. *The Old Oregon Country.* Lincoln, Indiana: University Press, 1950.

———. *Wreck Charts,* WC-1101, WC-1244, WC-1364 and WC-1468. Fairport, New York & Maitland, Florida: Wreck Chart Company.

Wright, E. W. *Lewis and Dryden History of Pacific Northwest,* vol. I. Seattle, Washington: Superior, 1967.

Index

A A McCully 203
Abe Lincoln 163
Aberystwith Castle 132
Acadia 10
Acme 42, 45
A Companion of Felons 119
Active 45
Adel 42
Admiral 113, 127
Admiral Benson 127, 135
Admiral Nicholson 72
Admiral Peary 45
Admiral Wainwright 42
Advent 42
Alaska 42
Alaskan 55, 72, 208
Albany 203, 204
Alexander Griggs 203
Algonquin 120
Alice H 26
Alice Kimball 72
Alice McDonald 127
Allegiance 163
Alliance 1886 203, 208
Alliance 1889 203
Almira 72
Almota 191
Alpha 72
Alsternixe 127
Alta 1904 183
Alta 1923 183
Alvarado 42
Amak 127
Americana 127, 183
Amethyst 61 (footnote), 132
Ancient Ship Timbers 183
Ancon 75
Andrada 183
Andrew Jackson 27
Angel Dolly 27
Anita 27

Ann 203
Anna 184
Anna C Anderson 184
Anna Shaw 211
Annie Comings 203, 205
Annie Faxon 203
Annie G Doyle 65, 73
Annie Gee 74
Antelope 96
Anvil 73
Arago 43, 44
Architect 107, 127
Argo #1 84, 86, 96
Argo #2 84
Ariel 1866 128
Ariel 1886 128
Arrow #2 163
Arthur I 184
Asotin 203, 212
Asuncion 205
Atalanta 73
Aurelia 163
Aurora 203-204, 208

Baltimore 43
Bandon 43
Bandorille 67, 73
Barcore 185
Barge #93 210
Barges 1947 128
Barkanteen 134
Baroda 43
Baracouta 6 (footnote)
Barracouta 168
B-A-R Spells Danger 90
Bateaux 204
Batteaux 204
Battle Abbey 128
Bawnmore 43
Bear 204

Beaver 74, 129, 158 (footnote), 204
Beeswax Flotsam 179, 180
Beeswax Ship 168, 178, 182
Beeswax Symbols 182
Beda 73
Bella 73
Belle Savage 61 (footnote)
Berwick 73
Bessi K 184
Bismark 204
Blackhawk 202
Blanco 73
Bobolink 73
Bonanza 204, 210
Boneta 204, 207, 208
Bonita 204
Bordeaux 128
Bostonian 21 (footnote), 31, 61 (footnote), 73
Brandon 204
Brant 96
Bristol 26
Broderick Castle 128
Brother Jonathan 1, 27, 66 (footnote), 185
Brother Jonathan, Oregon Mystery 1
Brother Jonathan, Comments on, 8
Brush 43, 47
Bully Washington 73
Bulwark 184
Bunkalation 27
Buster 128
Butcher 184

Cadzow Forest 184
Cairnsmore 128, 135, 136
C A Klose 128, 136

California 116
Calmar 128
Camano 204
Cambridge 5, 9
Camden & Larry Doheny 11
Canemah 204
Caoba 119, 128
Cape Wrath 184
Captain Lincoln 43
*Captain Lincoln & The Great
     Government Surplus
     Sale* 29
Captain Ludvig 73
Carib 185
Cariboo 209
Carmathan Castle 96
Caroline Medeau 73
Carrie Ladd 204
Cascade 207
Cascades 198, 204
C A Smith 43
Cavadonga 174 (footnote)
Cavour 128
Champion 66, 128
Champoeg 208
Chansey 43
Charles Devans 43
Charles Hare 10
Charles H Merchant 96
Charles Nelson 73
Charles R Spencer 204
Chatham 128
Chelan 108, 204, 205, 208
Cherub 148, 158 (footnote)
Childar 107, 128
China Ship 168
Chinook 43
City of Anacortes 204
City of Dublin 128
City of Rio de Janeiro 184
City of San Francisco 67
Claire 204
Clan MacKenzie 204
Clarmeont 43
Clatsop Chief 205
Clevedon 206
Coastal Descriptions:
     Alsea Bay to Salmon River 69
     Blacklock Point to Tenmile
          Creek 39
     California-Oregon border to
          Blacklock Point 21
     Cape Falcon to Cape

Disappointment 123
Cascade Head to Nehalem
     River 93
Umpqua River to Yachats
     River 67
Cohansa 43
Colfax 210
Colgate 132
Columbia (tug) 43
Columbia 158, 202
Columbia 1892 164
Columbia 1894 205
Columbia 1898 205
Columbia 1915 205, 208
Columbia 1924 43, 47
*Columbia River Lightship
     #50* 88, 128
Commodore 3, 43
Condor 73
Confederate Chicanery 37
Congress 43, 48
Coos Bay 14
Coquille 10
Cordelia 184
Cornelia Terry 65, 73
Cornelius 184
Corsica 128
Corvallis 205
Cottoneva 27
Courser 184
Cowlitz 1893 184
Cowlitz 1931 205
Cricket 205
C T Hill 96
Curacao 128
C W Wetmore 43
Cyclone 27
Cyclops 44
Cynthia Olson 44, 45
Czarina 44, 49, 50, 51

Daisy 44
Daisy Ainsworth 205
Daisy Freeman 128
Dalles City 205
Daniel Kern 208
Danube 203
Dauntless 184
Davenport 210
David Evans 134
Dawn 44
Delharrie 128

Della 97
Del Norte 44
Demerest 184
Denbigh 38
Derby 61 (footnote)
Desdemona 164
Detroit 96
Devonshire 128
Diamond O 205
Dilharree 164
Discovery 184
Dix 210
D M Hall 44
Dolphin 128
Dolly 77, 149
Dora 220
Dorothy Joan 73
Douglas Dearborn 184
Dreadnaught 128
Drexel Victory 128
Drumcraig 128
Duc de Lorges 205

Eagle 202
Eagle figurehead 188
Eco 38 (Blockade Runner)
Echo 44
Ecola 75
Edith 162
Edith Lorne 129
Edward Luckenback 205
E Iona O Kanaloa 112
Electra 129
Elfin 164
Elida 184
Elihu Thompson 129
Elk 199, 205
Ella Laurena 44
Elnorah (Elinorah) 66, 184
E L Smith 44
Elwood 197
Emily 44
Emily G Reed 84, 85, 97
Emily Stephens 129
Emma Claudine 129
Emma Utter 73
Emperor Nicolas II 207
Empire 5, 44, 184
Encarnacion 171 (footnote),
     174 (footnote)

E N Cooke 205
Energy 44
Engine #4 115
Enterprise 1873 74
Enterprise 1915 205, 208
Epervier 109
Erria 164, 166
Escort 44, 75, 186
Espiritu Santo 172, 176
Essex 148 (footnote), 158
    (footnote)
Esther Colos 27
Etta Kay 74
Eureka 44
Europe 203, 205
Ewing 36
Express 44

Falcon 204
Fannie Troup 205
Fanny 65
Fawn 31, 74
F B Jones 205
Fearless 128, 186
Fearless 1873 74
Fearless 1883 75
Fearless 1889 74
Fearless 1949 205
Feltrie 205
Fenix 210
Fern Glen 129
Fifield 44, 51
Firefly 164
First Columbia Pilot 106
Flatboat 206
Flora 129
Florence 184
Flyer 206
Flying Fish 185
Forest King 120
Forest Queen 184
Fort Bragg 44, 52
Foss #2 129
Francis H Leggett 129
Frank Buck 129
Frank W. Howe 129, 137
Frederick 74
Frederick K Billings 206, 213
Fred Gower 184
Fremont 5
Friendly Enemies 82
Friendship 14, 27

Fulton 27

Galena 129
Galleon of Nehalem 170
Gamecock 129
Garcia 97
Gazelle 1854 206, 208
Gazelle 1885 206
G C Lindauer 72, 74
Gem 97
General Butler 44
General Canby 44, 162
General Custer 165
General Hubbard 206
General Sherman 206
General Warren 44, 116, 129,
    185
General Wright 7
George And Martha 117
George Burton 206, 213
George L Olson 45, 53
George R Vosberg 97
George W Elder 206, 214
George W Prescott 129
Georgie Oakes 206
Gerald C 97
Gerome 206
Gertrude 37, 45
Gillnetters 161
Glasgow 132
Gleaner 164
Glenbreck 184
Glenesslin 129, 137, 138, 139,
    140, 141
Glenmorag 129, 142
Gold Beach 34 (footnote)
Golden Bear 45
Golden Gate 88
Golden Rule 4, 9
Golden West 45
Governor Moody 129
Grace Darling 184
Grace Dollar 42
Grace Roberts 129
Granhamona 221
Graywood 74
Great Admiral 184
Great Republic 164, 166
Grecian 134
Grecian lady 187
Guatimizin 61 (footnote)
Gussie Telfair 38, 39, 45

Gwendoline 206, 209
Gypsy 206, 214

Harriet Rose 27
Harrison 206, 210
Hartford 74
Harvest Queen 192, 206
Harvest Queen II 206
Hazard 129, 133
Headstone of Donald McTavish
    159
Helen E 45
Helen Hale 206
Helori 74
Henderson 206
Henriette 164, 167
Herald of the Morning 131
Hercules 1933 133, 206
Hercules 1934 206
Hermina 206
Hill 97
Hold the Presses 201
Homer 28, 43
Hossier 202, 206
Hornet 109
Hugh Hogan 27, 46, 74

Ida D Rogers 45
Idaho 191, 198, 204, 207
Ida M 45
Ida McKay 185
Ida Schnauer 97, 99
Idzumi 129
If I Live, I will Return...After
    Breakfast 116
Illitch 207
I Merrithew 130
Imnaha 196, 207
Incident at Thanksgiving Island
    191
Incredible Drift 84
Industry 107, 130
International Distress Signals 91
Intrepid 130
Invader 207
Inveravon 130
Ione 207
Iowa 130, 142, 143
Iowan 211
Irene 210
Iris 198

Isaac Todd 148, 153
Isabel 207
Isabella 164
It Just Never Happened 161
Ivanhoe 185

J A Chanslor 27
Jackson 45
James Clinton 207
James Monroe 14
Jane 77, 155
Jane A Falkenburg 1865 8
Jane A Falkenburg 1872 130
Jane A Falkenburg 1899 185
Japanese Submarines:
   I-7, I-8, I-9, I-10, I-15, I-17,
    I-19, I-21, I-23, I-25, I-26.
    88, 89
   I-25 11, 13
Javas Road 159
J C Champion 182
J C Cousins 130
J D Farrell 207
Jennie Ford 130
Jennie Thelin 45
Jenny Jones 130
J Marhoffer 74, 76
J N Teal 207
Joan of Arc 27, 28
Joe Lane 164
Joel Munson, Business Lifesaving
   107
Johannah M Brock 185
John Aspin 70, 74
John Cudahy 119
John Day Queen 207
John Hunter 74
John McDonald 185
Jordan Hill 184
J Ordway 207
Joseph and Henry 185
Josephine 130
Joseph Hume 162
Joseph Warren 74
Julia 198
Julia H Ray 45
Juliet 74
Juliet in Oregon 64

Kate Heath 36
Kate L Heron 97, 178
Kenai 12

Keoka 185
Kiyus 207
Klamath 221
Known Only to God 168
Kootenai Barge 196
Kootenai 207

L 16, Russian Submarine 14
Laguna 97, 98
Larry Doheny 13, 27
Launch of the *Peacock* 111
Laura May 45
Laurel 127, 131, 144, 208
Laurel Bank 185
Lausanne 110
Leipzig 129
Leona 207
Leonese 165
L'Etoile du Matin 165
Lewiston 207, 215
Levi G. Burgess 220
L H Coolidge 74
Lifeline 97
Lifesaving crew 99
Lila and Mattie 97
Lizzie 67, 74
Logger 207
Lottie 185
Lot Whitcomb 201, 207
L Roscoe 74
Lucia Mason 207
Lupatia 131
Lurline 207, 216

Madeline 207
Magallanes 170
Maggie Ross 74
Magnet 107, 165
Magnolia 204, 208
Maid of Oregon 185
Maine 131
Makah 131
Manchester 185
Manila Galleon 177
Marconi 45, 52
Maria E Smith 185
Marie 131
Marion 208
Mary Ann 10
Mary E Moore 45
Mary Gilbert 74, 76
Mary Hanlon 97

Mary Schowner 45
Mary Taylor 106, 130
Mascot 208
Massachusetts 165
Mauna Ala 131
May 208
McMinnville 207, 210
Melancthon 184
Melanope 27
Meldon 74
Merchantman 202
Mercury 61 (footnote)
Merrithew 185
Messenger 1876 45
Messenger 1879 208
Methven Castle 118
M F Henderson 208
Michigone 185
Mighty Columbia, River of the
   West 147
Milla Bond 178
Millie Bond 97
Mimi 80, 81, 82, 97
Mindora 165
Minnie E Caine 129
Minnie E Kelton 61, 165
Mississippi 75
Mizpah 131
Modeste 82, 152 (footnote)
Monitor 131
Monterey 45
Morning Star 79
Moro 45
Mose 27
Mountain Gem 196
Multnomah 208
Murphy's Law 36
Myrtle 220
Mysterious Wreck of 1808 57
Mystery of Flores Lake 169

Nabob 185
Name of names 91
Nassau 32, 74
Natoma 165
Nautilus 109
Naval sword 188
Neahkahnie Mountain Ancient
   Ship Timbers 182
Nehalem 97
Nehalem Beach Beeswax
   Symbols 181
Nelly 34 (footnote)

Neptune 131
Nettie Sundberg 74
New World 45, 198
Nez Perce Chief 198
Nightingale 131
Nimbus 131
Nisqually 132
Nokomis 129
Nomad 185
Norma 208, 216
North Bend 1928 132 145
North Bend 1940 74
Northerner 205
North Star 1887 185
North Star 1898 208
North Star 1912 45
North Star 1915 205, 208
North Star 1929 208
Northwest 194
Northwester 27
Nothing To It 38
Novelty 45, 54
Noyo 45
N S Bently 208, 217
Nuestra Senora de la Vida 171

Oakland 1912 208
Oakland 1916 97, 100
Occident 1870 45
Occident 1897 97
Ocean Bird 185
Ocean King 27
Ocean Pearl 185
Ocean Spray 75
Ocklahama 164, 203, 208, 212
Oh, That Wild, Wild West 32
Oh, Yeah! 90
Okanogan 198, 205, 208
Oleum 132
Olivia Schultze 75
Oliver Olson 45, 54
Olympion 208
Ona 75
Onandaga 130
Oneonta 198
Only Fools Rush In 15
Ontario 152
Onward 5, 45
Orbit 165
Ordeal of *Minnie E Kelton* 61
Oregon 130, 204, 205, 208
Oregona 1909 208
Oregona 1913 208

Oregonian 45
Orient 209
Oriole 77, 132
Orion 132
Ork 75
Orpheus 66 (footnote)
Oshkosh 87, 121, 132
Osmo 27
Osprey 46
Oswego 209
Otter 58
Owhyhee 164
Owyhee 198
Ozmo 46

Pacific 5, 66
Pacific 1861 209
Parker Barge #1 165
Parker Barge #2 75
Parkersburg 46
Peacock 109, 132, 152 (footnote)
Pearl 61 (footnote)
Perpetua 46
Peru 132
Pescawah 119, 132
Peter Iredale 101, 103, 105, 129, 131, 132
Phil Sheridan 75
Phoebe 148, 158 (footnote)
Phoebe Fay 75
Phoenix 97
Phyllis 27
Pierre Victory 206
Pilgrim 75
Pilar 176
Pilots Bride 97
Pinmore 132
Pioneer 97
Portland 1857 209
Portland 1914 206
Portland 1922 209
Port of Pasco #510 46
Potomac 15, 132
Potrimpos 132, 144
Primrose 132
Pronto 209
Protection 132
P T & B Co. #1684 & #1685 132

Quadratus 46
Queen 132
Queen of The Bay 97

Queen of The Pacific 128, 132
Quickstep 75, 162

Raccoon 133, 147, 152 (footnote) 154
Railroad to The Rescue 113
Rambler 133
Randolph 46
Ranger 209
Rathdown 186
R C Young 209
Reading The Barometer 91
Red Rover 186
Redwing 107, 133
Refuge 165
Regulator 209
Reliance 186
Relief 209, 217
Republic 33, 133
Rescue 209
Resolute 209
Ricky 133
Rio de Janeiro 12
Rip Van Winkle 162
Rival 133
Roanoke 1853 75
Roanoke 1911 133
Robarts 209
Robert Bruce 67
Robert Young 209
Rochelle 62, 165
Rogue River 27
Romp 186
Roosevelt 108
Rosalind 27
Rose Ann 133
Rosecrans 118, 133
Rosetta 209
Ruby 58
Rules of The Road 90
Rustler 1892 209,
Rustler 1919 27
Ruth 206, 209

Sacramento 46
Sagamore 97
Salem Clipper 196
Sally 209
Salvage Chief 44, 74
Samaria 186
Samson 210
Samuel Roberts 35, 75

San Agustin 176
San Antonio 176
San Buenaventura 27
San Cristo de Burgas 174
San Francisco Xavier 175
    (footnote), 176
San Geronimo 171 (footnote)
San Jose 171 (footnote)
San Juan 176
San Juanillo 176
San Lucas 170 (footnote)
San Nicolas 171 (footnote)
San Pablo 170
San Sabiniano 173
Santa Ana 174
Santa Catalina 209
Santa Clara 46, 209
Santisima Trinidad 173, 174
    (footnote)
Sarah Dixon 1912 209
Sarah Dixon 1926 209, 218
S D Lewis 133
Sea Adler 132
Sea Eagle 75
Sea Foam 44
Sea Gull 17
Sea Island 98
Sea Otter 57, 58, 75
Sea Thrush 133, 146
Sea Waif 210
Sedalia 209
Selkirk 209
Senator 209
Senorita 206
Sequin 106
Sesnon #3 210
Shark 82, 133, 152 (footnote),
    153 (footnote)
Shark+Oriole=Morning Star 77
Shenandoah 5, 6 (footnote), 8
Shoalwater 210
Shoshone 210
Shoshone Sleigh Ride 198
Sidi 210
Siege of Battle Rock 16
Sierra Nevada 10
Sinaloa 46
Skookum 210
Sol Thomas 75, 210
Sonny Boy 186
South Coast 186
South Portland 27
Sparrow 75
Spokane 192

Spokane 1887 210
Spokane 1895 210
Spokane 1922 207, 215
Spokane 1938 210
Staghound 129, 133, 145
Star of China 74
Star King 186
Starling 152 (footnote)
State of Washington 210, 218
St. Charles 75
S T Church 210
St. Maries 210
St. Mary 109
St. Nickolas 19 (footnote)
St Paul 208, 209
Strathblane 133
Struan 62, 63, 75
Success 73
Sujamico 46
Sulphur 133, 152 (footnote)
Sunken Submarine Myths 88
Sunshine 168, 186
Surprise 186
Susan 133
Susan Olson 28
Sutil 176
Swan 210
Sylvia de Grasse 160, 165

Tacoma 75
Taku 206
Tatoosh 134
Tecla 84
Tejon 186
Telegraph 220
Telephone 55
Telephone 1887 165
Telephone 1892 210
Tenino 198
Teton 128
Thielbek 166
Thode Fagelund 166
Thomas Corwin 132
Thomas P Beal 120
Three Mile Point 210
Tillamook 133
Tokuyo Maru 133
Toledo 210
Tonquin 106, 112, 133, 149, 155
    (footnote)
Tough Breed, Those Oystermen
    65
Traveler 210

Trouble With Jane 153
Truckee 75
Truxillo 186
T W Lucas 28
Tyee 1933 98
Tyee 1940 98

Umatilla 210
Uncle Sam 186
Union 207
Unknown Sloop 133
Unknown Spanish vessel 186
Unknown steamer 48
Unknown wreck 24, 189, 190
Up River Navigation 196
Urania 186
U.S. Grant 133

Vancouver 106, 133, 209
Vandalia 134
Vanderbuilt 38
Vazlav Vorovsky 134, 146
Venture 210
Venus 98
Veto #1 210
Victoria 1846 210
Victoria 1883 28
Vida 98, 100
Vigilant (tug) 57
Virginia 134
Volante 75

Wachusett 186
Wallacut 46
Wallamet 206, 210
Wallowa 205
Wallula 116, 134
Warrior 38
Washcalore 28
Washington 62, 134
Washtucna 75
W B Scranton 107, 134
Webfoot 134, 162, 198
Welcome 46
Welsh Prince 211, 219
W E Mahoney 211
Wenatchee 211
Western Belle 186
Western Home 46
Westport 211
Westview 209

Whistler 134
White Pelican 208
Whitney Olson 134
W H Pringle 211
Wilhelmina 75
Wilkes Report 107
Willamette 202
Willamette Chief 211
Willapa #2 28
William and Ann 106, 134
William H. Bessie 134
William Nottingham 134
Wilmington 211

Wilson G Hunt 198
Windward 166
Winkleman 129
W L Hackstaff 15, 28, 36
Woodland 211
Woodpecker 134
Wreck of the Hawthorne Trolley 197
W S Porter 113

Yakima 198, 211
Yale 209

Yaquina 1882 211
Yaquina 1935 75
Yaquina Bay 75
Yaquina City 75
Yarora 186
YMS #133 46
Yrazu 164

Zambesi 44

29C8221 134
29P859 134

"God works in mysterious ways
His wonders to perform
He puts his footsteps in the sea
And rides upon the storm."
                    William Cowper
                    1731–1800

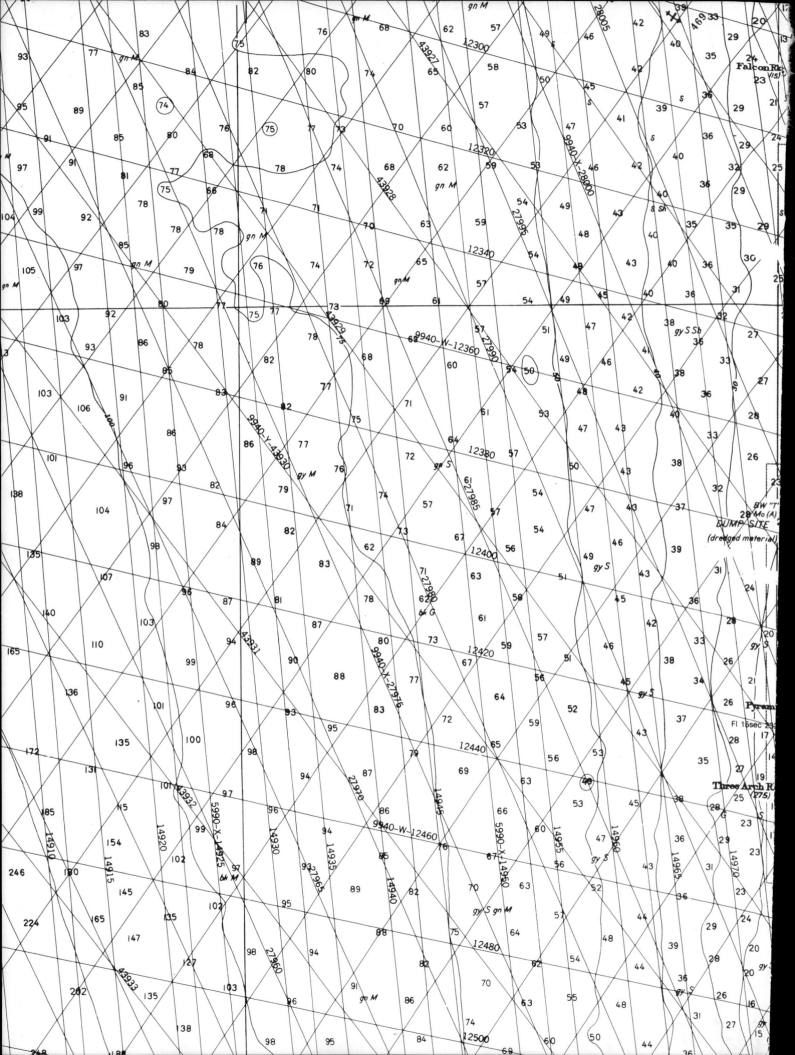